CULTURE, SOCIETY, AND DRUGS

The Social Science Approach to Drug Use

ED KNIPE

Virginia Commonwealth University

WAVELAND
PRESS, INC.
Prospect Heights, Illinois

For information about this book, write or call:
Waveland Press, Inc.
P.O. Box 400
Prospect Heights, Illinois 60070
(708) 634-0081

Cover illustration: "Audience" by Diana Ong. Credit: Superstock, Inc.

To my children,
Mary, Mark, John, Amy, and Katie

Contents

11 Drug Use: The Social Science Approach   425

Foreword

Why do people care so much about drugs—whether in favor of them or in opposition? Part of the answer lies in a profound liking that most people (and, for that matter, other animals) have for changing moods and perceptions. And, just as some individuals seek out and embrace such experiences, there are those who avoid them and abhor their use by others.

And why should we care about the social sciences? A simple part of the answer lies in the fact that they help us to understand—and some would say, to change—the important human component of the world around us. Or, for that matter, to deal with a complex question like the one about drugs, even when people who use them live in different terrain with very different climates, hold diverse religious beliefs, and make a living in ways with which we are unfamiliar.

Here is a pioneering volume that deals with both of these subjects, with about equal weight, in a fascinating way that sheds light on both of them without presupposing specialized knowledge about either.

This is an unusual book—not only timely and timeless, but also immediately relevant in practical terms and full of theoretic and conceptual significance. It is timely and practically relevant in providing a clear picture of the many roles that drugs play in contemporary societies and cultures, and in showing how a social science perspective can help us to understand better those roles, together with how and why they affect our lives, even if we ourselves choose not to use drugs. It is timeless and theoretical in using the interesting and sometimes dramatic evidence about drugs in social and cultural context to illustrate a broad range of concepts from the social sciences and to show how they help us better discern the meanings of attitudes and behavior in general—not just concerning drugs.

Knipe gives us a window on the age-old question, "Why do some people use drugs—and why do some react so strongly against such use?"—not just in the United States today but, in dramatically different ways, cross-culturally around the world and throughout our own history. At the same time he shows how drugs can be a window on the key question, "How does a sociocultural system work?"—not just helping us to understand the many and complex ways in which the parts of a society fit together, but also illustrating how they function to maintain social order as well as valued patterns of belief and behavior. And he goes on to show that social institutions are not monolithic, but that they have enough flexibility to allow variation among individuals and adaptation in the face of changing circumstances.

The drugs that are discussed range from the commonplace to the exotic, from tobacco and alcohol to kava, qat, and pituri. They include some that are close to nature and have limited distribution (traditional snuffs and coca) and others that are highly refined by processing and are widespread (heroin and cocaine). Each of the drugs is described in some detail, showing how historical, aesthetic, normative, and ideological factors distinctive of a given time and place make for drug use that is both distinctive and, in some respects, meaningfully comparable with others. Especially interesting in this connection are instances where the same drug plays very different—sometimes diametrically contrasting—roles in different sociocultural systems. One is peyote—religious for some and aesthetic for others; another is marihuana—an energizer for Costa Rican stevedores and Jamaican sugarcane-cutters, but a "drop-out" drug for European college students or North American yuppies. And there are others.

It should come as no surprise that drugs are employed not just for medication and recreation; some readers may be fascinated to learn about the variety and complexity of their links to religion, economics, politics, and other aspects of culture. Similarly, it soon becomes evident that whatever problems may be associated with drugs—whether they be social, psychological, economic, or other— they tend usually to be determined more by the mores of a group than by the pharmacology of a substance or the biochemistry of the human body.

The richly contextualized vignettes in which different drugs are featured throughout this book also serve to highlight a broad range of basic descriptive and analytic concepts from the social sciences.

In this way, the reader can learn in a concrete and meaningful sense such distinctions as between prediction and explanation; correlation and causality; dependent, independent, and intervening variables; invention and diffusion; structure and function; formal and substantive economics; and legal and informal social controls, among others. This is not sugar-coated social science by any means, but it is sure to engage most students, for whom the unifying topic of drugs appears to have unending interest; and the social science perspectives add important dimensions to our understanding, not just about drugs but about the world we live in.

An imaginative reader—or instructor—may even want to go beyond the excellent and well-chosen cases that the author has selected, to explore different ways in which dynamic processes operate in different cultures, or at different times, or with respect to different drugs. In doing so, they can best express the spirit of this book, which is fundamentally to explore the social science enterprise by focusing on a topic about which, for one reason or another, rightly or wrongly, many people care deeply.

This is truly an unusual book, and it will offer rich rewards to anyone who invests the time and effort to read it closely. It fills an important gap in the literature about drugs, which looms large between the highly technical and narrowly specialized works that scientists write for each other in academic books and journals on the one hand, and the largely simplistic, journalistic, or confessional pieces that are addressed to lay readers, on the other. It is a solid and informative book about drugs, just as it is a solid and informative book about the social science perspective. Where else could one find a modern evolutionary theory about the adaptation of systems that is seamlessly interwoven with an engaging overview of humankind's long-term fascination with ways of altering our moods and perceptions?

Dwight B. Heath
Brown University

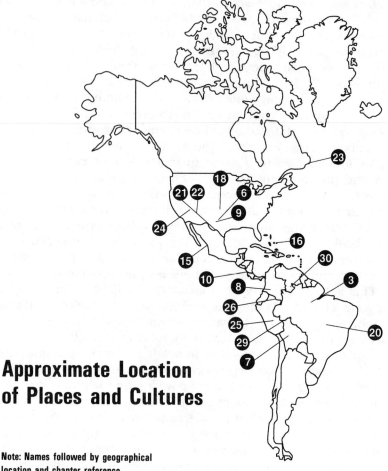

Approximate Location
of Places and Cultures

Note: Names followed by geographical
location and chapter reference.

1. Alice Springs (Northern Territory, Australia), ch. 6
2. Ban Lum, The Lisu (Northern Thailand), ch. 8
3. Batuque (Northern Brazil), ch. 7
4. Becedas (Spain), ch. 9
5. Bulawayo (Zimbabwe, Africa), ch. 6
6. Caddo (American East Plains), ch. 4
7. Camba (Eastern Bolivia), ch. 3
8. Colombia (South America), ch. 9
9. Comanche (American Southwest), ch. 4
10. Costa Rica (Central America), ch. 3
11. Crawley (England), ch. 4
12. Fang (Gabon, Africa), ch. 5
13. Fiji (Melanesia), ch. 6
14. Hmong (Northern Thailand), ch. 8
15. Huichol (Mexico), ch. 7
16. Jamaica (Caribbean), ch. 3, 5

Preface

When I was asked to consider teaching a course in "drugs," my first reaction was to respond "no." I did not have any academic interest in drugs, and the idea of preparing a new course did not appeal to me. There was far too much to do—and yet, the idea was intriguing. Knowing little about the topic, I could not make an informed decision either way. I owed it to myself to do a preliminary investigation. After all, there might be something there.

Between my colleagues and the library I was able to amass a small collection of books with the word "drugs" in their titles. This sample was discouraging. Many of the "texts" on drugs read like books on pharmacology or neuroanatomy, or they contained prescriptions on how to "help" people with drug "problems." Neither by training nor by inclination was I prepared to teach a course with these themes. In addition, the few texts written by sociologists focused on the American drug scene. My perspective is cross-cultural and comparative, and there were no texts written from this perspective. I knew from my own readings that anthropologists had written about drugs in various cultures, but none had assembled the various bits and pieces of research into a comprehensive volume. This finding placed more ballast on a negative decision but also piqued my interest. If nobody had written a cross-cultural, comparative text on drugs, might one be needed? One way to find out was to offer the course. If the difficulties proved insurmountable, I had only invested one semester, and the whole venture could be written off as another academic folly.

The students in the first class must have thought me daft. I hardly knew where to begin because I had no well-defined model or plan. It was, to paraphrase Robert Lowie's comment on civilization, "a course of shreds and patches." The only decision I made was that this course could not be organized in the same way as the texts I had read. Without exception, they all contained chapters or sections on specific drugs or categories of drugs. It struck me as somewhat inconsistent to present social science according to a model developed in pharmacology. Instead, if I were to continue this project, the course must be grounded in social science issues and employ the kinds of questions that social scientists ask. Clearly the chemistry of drugs was outside my realm of expertise and well under the control of others. What I wanted to know, and what I wanted students to know, is how drugs fit into social and cultural worlds. It took a few semesters to refine the outline I had in mind, but eventually an outline that could serve as a guide to the social science approach to drugs emerged. What follows in this book is a refinement of that guide.

This book could not have been written without the aid of the students who listened to lectures, argued and asked questions, and wrote research papers or critiques of articles in social science journals. Much of the material in the following pages was informed from their labor. My first impression that little had been written on drugs turned out to be incorrect. Quite the opposite, there is too much. Without the help of students searching through this vast body of literature, I would have missed many gems that they uncovered.

In preparing this manuscript I am indebted to several people. One is Pamela H. Colbe, who took the drug course and read early rough drafts with the keen eye of a student. Another is my colleague, John McGrath. His background in the area of drugs and youth was an invaluable resource. Both his and Pam's comments forced me to tighten up loose syntax and reasoning. I would also like to thank J. Sherwood Williams. As a colleague, he spent many hours with me discussing various topics in this book. As a friend, he assisted in the preparation of all the tables that used NORC data. In addition, I relied on Melvin Mednick's bibliographic memory for materials I surely would have never uncovered. Lastly, I would like to thank an unknown reviewer—designated only as "B"—from a publisher who rejected this manuscript. Comments from "B" provided a useful guide for revisions of the pre-published version of this book. To each of these people I am sincerely indebted. I would, of course, like to blame them for any errors in judgment or fact that readers may discover, but alas, they are mine alone.

In publishing a manuscript many hands are involved. Professor Dwight B. Heath at Brown University encouraged Waveland Press to publish this book. His critical comments and suggestions—and his willingness to write the Foreword—I humbly acknowledge. As important as Professor Heath's confidence in this project is Tom Curtin's vision that this publishing effort was worthwhile. Tom's continuous enthusiasm will not be forgotten. Several people at Waveland made the process of publication as seamless as possible. Steve Dungan cleared the way for permissions to use original source materials. Jan Weissman scoured sources and made contacts for permission to use photos. Carol Rowe and Gayle Zawilla labored diligently at copy editing and checking reference materials. Without their contributions the process of producing this volume would have been torturous.

Finally, I would like to thank Joe Marolla, Chairman of the Department of Sociology and Anthropology and David Hiley, Dean of the School of Humanities and Sciences, for enabling me to be on leave for the 1994–95 academic year. Their efforts made it possible for me to finish this project.

chapter 1

The Social Science Perspective

I n 1911, the American American writer Ambrose Bierce (1842–1914) defined rum as "generically, fiery liquors that produce madness in total abstainers" (1911). Although his definition applies to alcohol, were Bierce living today he might give a similar definition for "drugs." A cursory review of twentieth-century history of the United States reveals a series of what Stanley Cohen (1980) and Nachman Ben-Yehuda (1986) have called "moral panics." These are shared feelings that there is something wrong with our society because of a moral failure on the part of specific individuals. This moral failure is linked to the use of various substances called drugs. Alcohol has been a perennial symbol of moral weakness, but it is not the only substance held responsible for societal ills. At the turn of the century it was opium smoking by Chinese immigrants, followed by cocaine use by "Negroes" and marihuana smoking by Mexicans. More recently, a variety of substances, including PCP,

Angel Dust, LSD, heroin, cocaine, crack, and ice, have been viewed alternatively as either the cause or the result of those social "problems." Thus, poverty, crime, violence, promiscuity, homicide, illegitimate births, accidents, AIDS, divorce, and child abuse have all been "explained" by drugs. Viewers, listeners, and readers of the popular media in the 1990s were witness to psychiatrists, psychologists, physicians, social workers, school teachers, politicians, police, religious leaders, ex-drug users, athletes, talk show hosts, and pollsters all reporting the catastrophic results of drug "abuse" in America. While these "explanations" score high on moral indignation and public interest, they fail, in most cases, to be rooted in any systematic research. If research is cited, it is often of dubious merit and chosen to confirm conclusions already made. Bierce might have responded to all this by defining drugs as "any illegal substance which results in a moral madness among non-users."

The search for single causes of perceived problems is by no means an American phenomenon. In all cultures there are beliefs in malevolent forces, forces responsible for unwanted events. What differs from one society to another is the specific form these malevolent forces take. It might be evil spirits, witches, capitalism, industrialism, communism, or comic books—depending on that society's specific history. What was a malevolent force at one time might be a benevolent force at another period, and vice versa. All this adds up to a great deal of confusion on the part of the public, or perhaps it simplifies a confusing issue to a public unaware of a rather complicated body of research. Either way, what is missing from the rather strident cries of self-appointed "experts" is any sense of dispassionate understanding of one dimension of humanity, namely, the use of drugs.

The purpose of this book is to offer an explanation of drug use from the social science perspective. To accomplish this, it is first necessary to explain the perspective and then to report some of its findings. In this chapter, we will review some elementary concepts used in the social sciences. The remaining chapters examine issues, questions, and arguments which have intrigued and fascinated social scientists.

In one sense, this book is a pedagogical exercise. Pedagogue is a Greek word, one meaning of which is the name given to a slave or servant who escorted children to school. My task is to be the reader's pedagogue. I shall escort you to the work of social scientists, but do not assume that I can "teach" you everything about the social science approach to drug use. The materials presented in this book are but a sampling of what is known about drug use from the social science perspective. I shall give you some tools of the social scientists. Perhaps you will be able to fill in some of the gaps in this book by your own "research."

Understanding Human Behavior: The Social Science Perspective

The sciences are distinguished from each other, in general, according to what they study. Thus, chemistry studies the chemical characteristics of life and non-life forms; biology focuses on living matter in its manifold varieties, and physics is concerned with the nature of matter, from subatomic particles to the formation of the universe. Ideally, each of these sciences maintains proprietary rights over distinct domains, but in practice one finds chemists "doing" physics or biology and biologists working on the chemical basis of life forms. The same may be said of the "social" sciences. Disciplines such as anthropology, sociology, economics, political science, and history are all concerned with human activities. Some, like political science and economics, focus on one particular facet of the human condition. The remainder have broader and more diffuse concerns. Representatives of these disciplines often disregard these academic boundaries. For example, the economist might analyze marriage and family using an economic model, or an anthropologist will study the U.S. Congress as a tribal community.

What happens when members of the social science disciplines take to the media with pronouncements on various issues? The question we must address is whether those public appearances are reporting science or something else. Sometimes it is not clear. There is one way to unravel the scientific from the personal—that is to define what is "social" and what is "science." In so doing, readers can better understand the kinds of questions that social scientists ask and how they go about answering these questions.

The Individual, Society, and Culture

Science is the study of categories of things. It is *not* the study of *a* thing. The goal of the scientific endeavor is to increase certainty in prediction and explanation. **Prediction** is when one can antici-pate some future outcome from information one has at the present. **Explanation** informs us why something did or will occur. Ideally, science strives both to predict and to explain some phenomena but does not always accomplish that goal. Thus, one might predict the hemlines of skirts from knowing the Dow Jones average on the stock market but not be able to explain why this prediction is possible. Conversely, one might explain why the Aztec Empire fell but be incapable of predicting when Western civilization will fall. In the social sciences there are three possible candidates for the twin goals of prediction and explanation—the individual, society, and culture. Before we can understand social "science" it is necessary to discuss each of these phenomena as objects of social science research and thought.

The Individual

One view of the social world is that it is made up of a number of individuals, all of whom are in some way different from each other. Those who hold this view use the individual as the unit of analysis. Historians who take this perspective, for example, see history as a succession of individuals. The so-called "Great Man" perspective of history focuses on the biographies of notable individuals who, it is assumed, are the determinants of history itself. Much of clinical psychology is concerned with understanding individual thoughts, feelings, and behaviors. The important consideration for our purposes here is that the individual view of the world must, if it is science, develop ways of both predicting and explaining individuals and individual behavior. This would be a monumental task, considering all the individuals in the world, and ultimately could never lead to general propositions about human behavior. Therefore, both prediction and explanation of an individual is beyond the realm of social science.

Society

It is clear from even a cursory examination of humans that people who share similar occupations, histories, incomes, and age categories behave in strikingly similar ways. Without such predictability, orderly social life would not be possible, and there could be no social science. This is not to insist that all the behaviors of all individuals within a particular category are identical, but only that the very thing that determines a social category is shared behaviors. When viewed from the societal perspective, individuals as distinct units do not exist. What exists are social units. The noun "society" and the adjective "social" refer to sets of practices and behaviors. For example, in every society where alcohol is found, the proportion of males who drink is higher than the proportion of females who drink. Thus, if the social scientist is asked to predict who drinks (behavior) in a society with alcohol, the answer would be males. The who, in this case, is not which individual drinks but rather which sex consumes more. Of the social sciences, sociological research tends to focus on the question of predicting differences in behavior. From this research we learn, among other things, that college freshmen drink more than seniors, Episcopalians drink more than Baptists, marihuana is smoked more by Euro-Americans than by African Americans, and hard-core heroin users are overrepresented in lower-income categories. While these findings go a long way in improving our predications, they do not necessarily explain why these variations are noted. For answers to the question "why" these connections are observed, one needs to consider culture.

Culture

If academic disciplines are distinguished by what they study then it would be safe to say that anthropology is separated from sociology by its focus on culture. While anthropologists debate what culture is, there is some consensus that culture, in its broadest sense, is a system of rules, expectations, and patterns that serves as a guide for behavior and define how the world is ordered. It is not the behavior itself. Unlike behavior, which can be observed, culture is cognitive, a mental map, and hence unobservable. Culture exists only in humans because only they are capable of symbolic communication. The most striking manifestation of this ability is language. No two individuals speak in the same manner. Yet we can understand what is said (behavior) if we share the same language rules. For example, one can predict that the utterance (behavior), "passionate marihuana dances alphabetically," will be understood as grammatically correct by English speakers because the word sequence follows a grammatical rule (culture) in English— adjective:noun::verb:adverb. What, if anything, this statement means might be debated by speakers; that it is grammatically correct is not arguable. The understanding and use of culture as an analytic tool permits us to explain many different observed behaviors by a limited set of rules. Thus, speakers of English may make an infinite number of differently worded utterances, all of which can be understood by a finite number of grammatical rules.

In contrast to sociologists, anthropologists are concerned with uncovering shared cognitive meanings and rules that explain variations in behavior. Studies of cultures often contain descriptions of practices that reflect the variety of rules by which humans define meaning and impose order on the world. In this sense, culture is always an abstraction, but an abstraction that enables us to explain our observations of behavior.

Obviously, this contrast between sociology and anthropology, between society and culture, is a simplification. In fact, sociologists use culture as an explanation, and anthropologists report variations in behavior. In addition, the distinction that we have made between "society" and "culture" is not always maintained systematically. This inconsistency has led to a recent effort to examine the linkage between these two concepts.

Society and Culture Compared

Central to understanding future discussions in this book is the distinction between culture and society. Readers of the social science literature may be baffled by the oft-used term "socio-cultural" to describe various practices and beliefs. This confusion has led to a movement which insists that society and culture refer to two distinct, but related, phenomena. Morris Freilich, Douglas Raybeck, and Joel Savishinsky (1991) are recent contributors to this movement. Their use of the terms "proper" norms in contrast to "smart" norms highlights the distinction between cultural and social phenomena. Culture (proper norms) refers to expectations that serve as guidelines for behavior. Viewed this way, culture is a shared charter or framework which serves as a template for behavior. Society (smart norms), in contrast, refers to behaviors which represent a set of adaptive strategies that take into account environmental resources and constraints. Competitive team games illustrate this difference. The game is governed by a set of general rules understood by the players. This is culture. In the actual playing of the game, however, players are confronted with a multitude of situations to which they must respond behaviorally. These adaptive strategies are the social aspects of the game. In acknowledging the distinction between cultural and social phenomena, we note that behaviors do not always appear to be consistent with cultural expectations. This perceived "deviance" is what intrigued Freilich. He concluded that even though observed behaviors might appear to differ from expectations, they nonetheless were directed toward meeting those expectations through the resources available to participants. Thus, we should not always expect all social behaviors to be in direct compliance with cultural expectations. Freilich's observation is especially important if one wishes to understand drug use in Western culture. Drug users are often viewed as "deviants" or representatives of some drug "subculture." Freilich's discussion of the relationship between cultural rules and social behaviors sensitizes us to view drug use as both an adaptive behavioral strategy and an acknowledgement of broader shared cultural expectations. If we extend Freilich's discussion further, his analysis points to the importance of embracing both the traditional anthropological and sociological perspectives into a comprehensive understanding of the human condition.

"Free Will" and Units of Explanation

One of the more influential contributors to the social science approach was Émile Durkheim (1858–1917). If he is remembered for any single contribution, it would be his insistence that social science is the study of what he calls "social facts." For Durkheim a **social fact** is:

> . . . every way of acting, fixed or not, capable of exercising on the individual an external constraint; or again, every way of acting which is general throughout a given society, while at the same time existing in its own right independent of its individual manifestations. (1938, 13)

Durkheim argues that people are born into societies which have preexisting practices. The language one speaks, the beliefs one has, the money one uses, and the system of laws to which one conforms, all exist prior to the individual and therefore cannot be said to be part of any individual consciousness or cause. Even if one recognizes the existence of these social facts and attempts to avoid them, either social forces are brought to bear which punish the violator, or one must acknowledge the very mandate one is avoiding. Either way, these facts exist outside the individual. As a class of phenomena, social facts should not be confused with biological facts or psychological facts, nor can one explain a social fact by appealing to either of the other two. Social facts can only be explained by other social facts.

Durkheim thus dismisses the idea of "free will" as the subject matter of social science. If social facts are external to the individual and exert constraints on behavior, then individuals are not "free" but rather are bound to a deterministic world which is not of their own making. Readers may find this rather disquieting, especially those who have lived through or are presently living in the "just say no" generation, a slogan that assumes "free will." It would be folly for Durkheim, and for social science, to assume that the universe is based on the principle of free will. Taken to its logical conclusion, a world filled with free-willed individuals would be a world of total chaos and randomness. Even the most ardent defender of the "free will" idea would have to admit that the human condition is exceptionally orderly. When we drive down the highway, attend a class, have a drink in a restaurant, sit down with family members for Thanksgiving dinner, or have sexual intercourse, we are constrained to follow sets of rules along with the other participants in these social situations. That an individual "chooses" *not* to drive, take a class, drink in a restaurant, eat a Thanksgiving meal, or have sexual intercourse does not make those activities and the rules governing them disappear. An understanding of the rules that govern the lives of people is based on the same set of assumptions as is the understanding of rules that govern atomic structures, the inheritance of biological characteristics, or the weather. Neither the principles of nature nor social life are capricious. If they were, neither could persist. The issue of social science is not that the world is orderly but rather how to capture that order with a limited number of general propositions or "laws."

Levels of Social Science Prediction and Explanation

The vocabulary of science, like vocabularies of any language, consists of a set of words. In science these words are called concepts. The difference between language vocabularies and scientific concepts is that the latter are assigned meanings with reference to larger entities called models. In this sense, the meanings of concepts are relative to the kind of model used to organize how we predict and explain some phenomena. These models need not be "real" in the sense that what they portray is part of the physical world. Thus, in physics the atom existed as a concept prior to our identifying it as a "thing," and genetics worked with the concept of the "gene" long before it was identified as a sequence of chemical bases. Models are judged by how efficiently they improve our ability to predict and explain, not by whether there is a direct relationship between our model and the "real" world. The concept "culture," for example, describes a shared mental construct of the world that neither I nor anyone else can see. It does not occupy physical space. The concept "society," in contrast, describes the observable activities of corporeal beings. It can be seen. However, without the concept "culture," the behaviors of humans are not different from the behaviors of non-human animals. The dances of bees and the activities of ants are behaviors we can observe and describe, but we are at a loss to attribute meanings to those behaviors because both ants and bees do not have culture. Human behaviors may be observably different, but in reference to a common shared culture; or human behaviors may be the same, but in reference to different cultures. Either way, what gives meaning to those behaviors is the cultural context within which they occur. What is obvious when one reviews the social science literature is that authors acknowledge both culture and society as concepts, although this distinction may not always be clearly stated and often leads to some confusion.

Returning to our separation of culture and society, there are other useful terms associated with those analytical concepts. Each of these terms signals whether the social scientist is addressing cultural or social phenomena *and* the level of inclusiveness at which the researcher wishes to predict or explain. Culture and society are the most inclusive level. Statuses and roles are the least inclusive, and institutions and associations are at an intermediate level. These levels can be visualized in table 1.1.

Table 1.1. **Levels of Social Science Analysis**

BEHAVIORS	EXPECTATIONS
Society	Culture
Associations	Institutions
Roles	Statuses

Roles refer to the behaviors associated with statuses. **Statuses** are expectations for behaviors. For example, the status "physician" consists of a cluster of expectations (rules) which, let us say, distinguish it from the status "mother." If one behaves in a way that is consistent with these rules, one is acknowledged as having that status. The same is true for the mother status. An individual may be both a physician and mother, but only if complying with the rules of each status. If one focuses on the consequences of multiple occupancy of different statuses, it is easy to understand that in a culture where there are many statuses, the cluster of statuses held by any particular individual may be different from the cluster of any other individual. In cultures with many different statuses—"complex" cultures—one might conclude that "people are different," "everyone is a unique individual," and other verbal manifestations of "individuality." This individuality is often assumed to be some reflection of "personality." This conclusion disregards the fact that statuses are not individual isolated units but rather are lumped together with other statuses. Thus, the status "physician" exists only if there is the complementary status "patient." The status "mother" is bundled with the status "child." Within these bundles there are usually differences in authority or power. It is the physician who exercises authority over the patient, just as it is the mother who has power over the child. When these differences are vested in the status itself, the status has **prestige**. When linked statuses are characterized by differences in prestige they are described as **ranked**. Differences in ranked prestige of statuses should not be confused with differences in role behaviors. Differences in role behaviors are a recognition of different levels of behavioral competency. Thus, there are physicians who perform better than other physicians, just as there are some mothers who might be considered better than others. Those behavioral distinctions are always measured against the status expectations. Behaviors closer to the expectations are recognized through according **esteem** to an individual status holder. Thus, prestige describes ranked differences between status; esteem is a measure of variations in performances by status incumbents.

The smallest unit of social analysis is the **group**. The minimal definition of a group is "two or more people who interact with each other." The critical word in this definition is interact. Without interaction, there is no group. As with many concepts in the social sciences, the word group is used by non-social scientists in a way that is inconsistent with this definition. For example, in medical research several individuals are selected for research purposes. One-half of the individuals are given one drug. The other half are given another drug. Depending on the research question, those individuals given one drug may be called the experimental "group," while those given another drug are called the control "group." Because these individuals do not interact with each other, they would not be a group in the social science sense. Another misuse of the term "group" is in reference to a **social category**. A social category is a distinction made by either members of a society or a researcher. Examples include females, the middle class, students, professionals, and criminals. There may be a group of women, or students, or criminals, but women and students and criminals are not a group unless one can demonstrate interaction. One further misuse of "group" is as a descriptor of a **statistical aggregate**. Statistical aggregates are used by researchers to describe some segment of a population by a shared measurable characteristic. Males sixteen to twenty-four years of age, females fourteen to forty-four years of age, or people whose yearly income is below $10,000 are all statistical aggregates. To describe sixteen- to twenty-four-year-old males as a group, one must be able to show that the members interact with each other.

The interaction among group members and among groups may be described differently, but what goes on among members of a group is determined by the behavioral expectations of the statuses each participant occupies. There are three basic interaction patterns, sometimes called **social processes**, which can be used to describe this interaction. One is **cooperation** and involves agreement on the part of all parties to behave in accordance with the expectations of the statuses they occupy. Another is **competition**. In competition, the parties attempt to gain some scarce resource by means of a set of agreed-upon rules (expectations) for how this is done. We see these processes exemplified in sports. Members of a football team (group) cooperate with each other even though what they do may be different from what other members of the team do. At the same time, they compete with the opposing team in order to obtain a higher score. The third type of interaction is **conflict**. Although this concept has been used to describe interaction in pursuit of scarce resources where people are hurt or killed, I do not think this emphasis on violence is adequate to make it different from cooperation. As I shall use this term, conflict refers to interaction without shared rules. Thus, when interaction occurs without statuses or any other set of expectations, the interaction is one of conflict. This concept of conflict becomes very important when considering change. Change is, by definition, a transition state from one set of statuses and corresponding roles to another. It does not imply violence or death, as some social scientists would insist. For example, the traditional status of females in our culture as full-time mothers may be in conflict with the full-time status as physicians because the expectations of these different statuses may be impossible to fulfill simultaneously. Changes in the expectations of women as full-time mothers or changes in the expectation of physicians as full-time healers can lead to the disappearance of conflict between these two statuses. The important thing to remember is that none of these processes is determined by individuals who occupy the statuses in a culture. It is the pattern of relationships between statuses, the **structure** of statuses, that determines whether cooperation, competition, or conflict will dominate interaction.

The interlocking and interdependent bundling of statuses into larger units form **institutions**. Mothers and children are part of that institution we identify as kinship. Patients and physicians are part of the institution we might call health care. Institutions are distinguished from each other in their focus on some specific dimension of human activity. Thus, in our culture, there are economic institutions that are concerned with the production and distribution of goods and services; political institutions with rules regulating how power and authority are distributed; religious institutions which are concerned with achieving salvation; educational institutions which focus on the distribution of knowledge, and so forth. Corresponding to each of these institutions and their associated statuses are **associations** made up of people (groups) whose behaviors both comply with their status expectations and behaviors which represent specific adaptations to shifting environmental demands. There are work groups, political parties, different churches, and different schools, colleges, and universities. At the most inclusive level, society reflects all the associations and their interrelationships, while culture is the totality of all the institutions.

What we note from this discussion is that there are different levels of social science prediction and explanation. Some social science research efforts focus on roles and status. Other research endeavors to understand society and culture. Whatever the particular level of analysis, what makes it social *science* is the way in which one goes about collecting and analyzing information.

Morality and Social Science

Social science, as science, differs from moral philosophy. The goal of moral philosophy is to determine the morality—goodness or badness—of an idea and to set about developing a set of rules to achieve the "best" life for all. Such is the stuff that bothered the utopians. From Thomas More (1474–1535) to followers of B. F. Skinner (1904–1990), the question is the same: "How does one develop a just and fair social order?" The failure of these movements, in spite of their good intentions, speaks to the inability of humans to construct a perfect moral order. Social systems develop in response to histories, geographies, population sizes and densities, as well as ideas. In that sense, social worlds are as "natural" as the physical and biological worlds that are the focus of the natural sciences. The social sciences are the youngest of the sciences, but they have adopted a perspective and strategy that differs little from their older cousins. What distinguishes the social sciences—sociology and anthropology—from the physical and biological sciences is not method but subject matter. Sociology is concerned with understanding the principles that govern society. The goal of anthropology is to discover the rules that determine culture.

A basic premise of sciences is that there are rules or laws which govern their subject matter, and these rules or laws are not subject to alterations by people. Hence, like it or not, it is not possible to change Boyle's Law, or the Second Law of Thermodynamics, or the principle of dominance or recessiveness in genetic transmission. If these could be changed, they would not be laws. What distinguishes the social from the other sciences is that they have yet to develop any statements equivalent to laws in the physical sciences. This has led many, even social scientists themselves, to conclude that there cannot be a social science. Leaving aside the fact that most of the biological, physical, and chemical world is not explained by "laws," how can we assume that a social science can exist? The answer is simple. Science is a method, a strategy, an approach. It is a way of looking at phenomena. As a method, it assumes that greater understanding can be gained if we follow specified procedures which reduce the possible influence of our wishes, desires, and morality. For this reason, we will be examining the relationships between "drugs" and society and drugs and culture as a scientific problem, not as a question of morality—at least not our morality. Why drugs are defined as evil or good by social groupings can be analyzed scientifically; that drugs are evil or good cannot. Therefore, it is necessary to review the assumptions of the social sciences as well as the strategies they employ to meet these assumptions.

The Holistic Approach

In anthropology a basic assumption is that no practice can be understood outside the cultural matrix within which it is found. Further, no aspect of culture makes "sense" outside of this broader framework. This is a systems approach. A **system** is any unit made up of parts that are interrelated and form an integrated whole. Thus, a **social system** is a set of interdependent behaviors, and a **cultural system** is a set of interrelated expectations. The parts of a system may not all contribute equally to the maintenance of the whole system; some may be more important than others, but each is necessary if the system is to exist as it does. For example, the peyote cactus (*Lophophora willamsii*)[1] is a prominent plant in the religious system of the Huichol Indians of Mexico. Peyote, along with the deer and maize, are important symbols of Huichol culture. If removed, one might predict that their religious system would change dramatically. In contrast, wine is one part of the Eucharist for Catholics, but wine is not central to Catholicism as a belief system. Grape juice could be substituted for wine and the belief system would not be significantly altered. In this case, the use of peyote is more important to the Huichol way of life than wine is to the beliefs and practices of Catholics.

Sociology, in contrast to anthropology, takes a somewhat more restricted systems approach. Sociologists are more likely to focus their attentions on particular behaviors within an institutional framework. For example, the sociologist might analyze the function of drinking at art gallery openings (one dimension of expressive culture), the use of marihuana among college students (the institution of education), or the use of cigarettes among inmates in a prison (legal or jural institution). Conversely, anthropologists would be more interested in how the use of drugs fits into the whole culture. This different approach in asking and answering questions is, to a large degree, a function of the units studied by these two disciplines. The work of sociologists is carried out in large, densely populated Western urban cultures. Anthropologists usually work in small non-Western communities where it is possible to know more about the whole "society." This kind of intimate knowledge about the United States might not be possible. The variations in behaviors and cultural practices are simply too large. Because of this, the sociologist usually samples small pieces of the whole society for analytic purposes. The results of these studies are then extrapolated to larger units through the use of statistical techniques. Anthropological research relies more on detailed descriptions— **ethnographies**—of whole communities. As a result, anthropological analysis is capable of determining how a particular practice fits into the totality of practices for that community.

Throughout this book I shall present examples of both of these approaches. One should not assume that one is better than the other—only that the kinds of information, and hence the kinds of analyses each provides, will be different. Each approach, in its own way, contributes to a more complete understanding of the human condition.

Cultural Relativism

A corresponding assumption to the holistic approach is cultural relativism. Relativism is concerned with the interpretation and meaning of behaviors. Two identical social behaviors may have two totally different cultural meanings. For example, the practice of smoking marihuana (*Cannabis sativa*) by members of the Rastafari, a political-religious cult which originated in Jamaica, is interpreted by them as an integral part of their religious experience. To most American users, marihuana smoking is part of a recreational experience. To make sense of marihuana smoking behavior, the social scientist interprets it relative to the cultural context in which it is found. The assumption of the social science approach is that behaviors have no intrinsic meanings but rather are given meaning relative to the broader cultural context within which they are observed.

In addition to expectations for behavior, culture provides a meaning system that determines a people's view of the world. Social scientists often refer to these views as norms or values. At the social level, **norms** are shared behaviors. For example, regardless of whether one occupies the status of doctor, mother, or garbage collector in American society, one is not supposed to appear in public with certain parts of the body uncovered. In other societies those same body parts may be uncovered. Thus, what is defined as nudity varies from one culture to another.

Values are shared beliefs about what is valuable. In American culture there is a value placed on self-reliance and individuality. People are expected to take care of themselves and be different from others. In other cultures self-reliance and individuality are not valued, and persons displaying behaviors that express these values are viewed as deviant, odd, strange, or perhaps crazy. For example, among the Hopi Indians, the world is viewed as beneficent and predictable. If one behaves according to the Great Scheme, the world will continue to be beneficent and predictable, but if one behaves differently—individualistically—that orderly world will change for the worse. Persons who attempt to change conditions by behaving differently are most likely to accused of witchcraft and, if found guilty, killed. If our task as social scientists is to understand the human condition, then it is imperative that we understand it in its different manifestations. The principle of cultural relativity suggests there are no universal standards by which to judge specific human practices.[2] In other words, there is no universal "right" or "wrong."

The concept of cultural relativism has applications beyond comparing distinct cultures to each other at one time. Cultures are constantly changing, which means that the norms and values that characterize a culture at one time may be replaced by other norms and values. For example, during the eighteenth century in the United States, opium was lauded as the wonder drug of medicine. It, along with cocaine and marihuana, was found in many widely distributed patent medicines and was freely prescribed by physicians. As part of the medical system, the opiates were defined as acceptable treatment for a wide variety of illnesses. These same substances were redefined beginning in the early part of the twentieth century as non-acceptable for any use, including medical purposes. Those who continued to use opiates were then defined as addicts and were subject to prison or commitment. In this example, an understanding of opiate use does not rest on knowledge about opium as a substance. Those who used opiates at one time conformed to normative standards; at a later time, the same behavior was a violation of normative standards. What had changed were the normative standards, not opium. To understand opiate use it is necessary to interpret it relative to a social context, which in this case changed.

Ethical Neutrality

If the goal of social science is to understand human behavior in an objective manner, it is necessary to suspend value judgements about that behavior. This consideration is reflected in the difference between a "social problem" and a "social scientific problem." A **social problem** is "a condition which is defined by a considerable number of persons as a deviation from some social norm which they cherish" (Fuller and Myers 1941). This definition infers the idea that something should be done to correct this deviation. A social problem, then, is a social condition that some segment of a society *feels* strongly about. It does not have to be an objective condition— that is, a social problem may be a belief about some condition. One can usually identify a social problem by the words that are used to describe it. Aside from the word "problem" itself, one notes other words such as environmental "pollution," juvenile "delinquency," "underworld" activities, AIDS "epidemic," and "abuse" when applied to spouses, children, and drugs. These are all words in American culture which convey strong negative feelings about a "problem." These are not the words one is likely to find in social "science" research.

A **social scientific problem** is a question that can be answered using methods and techniques which do not assume a moral judgement. The sociologist Robert Merton (1959) suggests that the formulation of a social scientific problem involves several steps. The first step is to ask questions that are rooted in "facts." In the example above, we noted that in the United States the definition of opiate use changed. This fact was reflected in the passage of city and town ordinances which specifically prohibited the use of opiates and the subsequent punishment of those who used them. From this observation one might ask several questions. The most obvious is, "Why was there a change in the definition of opiates?" On closer examination, one notes that the first place in which local ordinances against the use of opium were enacted was the West Coast. The next question one might ask is, "Why the West Coast?" What was different about the West Coast that might explain this change? One possible difference between the West Coast and the rest of the United States was the composition of the population. On the West Coast there were many Chinese who had migrated into the United States during the middle 1800s. Could the new legislation prohibiting the use of opium have something to do with the presence of Chinese workers? Keep in mind that we are simply speculating about possible contributions to our understanding of why these changes occurred when they did. We have not yet begun to "do" science.

Continuing our speculative questions, we note that the Chinese population brought cultural practices with them from China that were different from American cultural practices. One of these practices was the smoking of opium. Now a possible connection begins to emerge between anti-opium ordinances and Chinese practices. Note that none of these questions assumes any moral position. We have not maintained that opium smoking is a good or a bad practice. Further, we have not taken a position on these changes in ordinances. That ordinances changed is a fact; that some Chinese immigrants smoked opium is a fact. What we wish to explore with these questions is the possible relationship between these facts. To say that opium smoking was a social problem or that the Chinese abused opium does not help us answer this question.

However, we do not yet have a social scientific problem. The next step is to determine what, if any, contribution can be made to social science by answering this question. What is it we wish to know? Do we only want to know something about the Chinese, or only about changes in the California opium smoking laws? If the answer to this last question is affirmative, then social science is not needed. Science is concerned with the development of explanatory schemas that are more general. The ultimate goal of social scientific problems is to ask questions about the human condition. In our example, a more general issue is the relationship between proscriptive rules and population characteristics. The anti-opium ordinances and the Chinese are then just one example of this broader concern.

Having asked these questions, as Merton suggests we do, does not mean that we are doing social science. The scientific enterprise really begins when we employ methods that are ethically neutral. We will discuss these methods in the next chapter, but now we must turn our attention to the issue of whether ethical neutrality is possible in the social sciences.

The position of ethical neutrality in social science is not without its critics. Robin Room (1984), a sociologist, suggests that anthropological research has tended to deflate the "social problems" associated with alcohol in New Guinea. In contrast, he suggests that the works of epidemiologists, psychiatrists, and governmental officials are characterized by problem amplification. This under-reporting of alcohol "problems" can, according to Room, be explained by three factors which are related to the attributes of anthropology and anthropologists themselves. First, anthropology has traditionally taken a "functional" view of society. This perspective holds that any persistent activity, including alcohol consumption, must contribute to the maintenance of the whole society or a part thereof. If one begins with this assumption then one is likely, in Room's view, to disregard the disruptive, "dysfunctional" aspects of drinking.

The second factor leading to deflation and/or amplification is methodological. Anthropological research focuses on the everyday; epidemiology and psychiatry study rare events. The goal of the former is to understand the "normal" workings of a society; the latter focus on specific diseases or behaviors which *they* view as pathological. The goal of epidemiology and psychiatry is usually to formulate some policy that is designed to reduce whatever has been defined as the problem. To make a case for such policy, the condition is often overreported. Conversely, anthropological research sees the so-called pathology as one small part of a large number of behaviors.

The third factor, which Room suggests accounts for deflation of alcohol "problems," is generational. Anthropologists writing about alcohol are representatives of the "wet" generation, a generation of American intellectuals who grew up in the 1930s when drinking was not only acceptable but a mandatory reaction to the conservative temperance atmosphere at the turn of the century. The mandate that anthropologists collect data directly from peoples in various parts of the world brought them in contact with missionaries who often stressed the "evil" effects of drinking on native peoples. To dissociate themselves from missionaries with their anti-alcohol zeal, anthropologists internalized the "wet" perspective in reporting drinking "problems" among native peoples.

In addition to the three factors cited above, Room suggests that most anthropologists are unfamiliar with the literature on alcohol. As evidence for this, he states that studies which report on alcohol use among native peoples fail to include any discussion of the physiological hazards associated with drinking. Rather, coupled with the functional perspective, drinking has been viewed as just another social activity having integrative rather than disruptive consequences.

In response to these "charges," Michael Agar (1984) makes the point that Room's use of "problem inflation" and "problem deflation" assumes the privileged position of knowing the "true" extent of the "problem." In Agar's view:

> There are probably few communities in which the "problem" due to drugs or alcohol are the "norm." When you isolate the "problem" and focus on it, you get one picture; when you look at broader patterns of community life, you get another. Arguing that one is privileged and the other is inflated or deflated does not seem productive. (179)

Dwight Heath's (1984) response to Room is directed at both his assumptions and his goals. The charge that anthropologists deflate problems associated with heavy drinking or drunkenness is based on the assumption that drinking and drunkenness always lead to trouble. This may be true for the United States, but it is not a relationship found in all societies. For example, Jacek Moskalewicz (1984) reports that the absence of extremely *unsober* males at a Polish peasant wedding would be an embarrassment to the host. To say that insobriety is a "problem" for Polish peasants is to make an **ethnocentric** evaluation of Polish drinking habits. Ethnocentrism is the moral position that uses the standards in one's own culture to judge practices in other cultures. Moskalewicz suggests that if there is a "problem," it must be defined by those being studied, not by the culture of those doing the study. Heath's final point is that there is a difference between the goals of the policy-oriented researcher and those not concerned with policy. He states:

> Perhaps most ethnographers *do* differ in outlook from some more policy-oriented sociologists. We don't feel obligated to teach people how miserable they ought to be feeling, and therefore, with respect to drinking problems (as with respect to anything else), we don't deflate what sometimes isn't there. (181)

The discussion above illustrates that social scientists are not themselves in agreement about ethical neutrality. This should not, however, be viewed as a weakness. The history of science is filled with debates and arguments about a variety of issues. The obligation that scientists engage in this give and take, or push and shove, is beneficial to the scientific enterprise. These confrontations test the usefulness of ideas, the productivity of concepts, and the value of theories—and ultimately lead to a more efficient and more comprehensive understanding of the world in which we live.

Definitions: Toward a Social Science of Drugs

If one thinks of science as "an intellectual method for reducing error" (Kaplan and Manners 1986, 28), then certainly one of the first obligations in "sciencing" is to define the words one uses. Words are symbols, the meanings of which are arbitrary. As long as writer and reader, or speaker and listener, share the same definitions, communication will be facilitated. When the same word means something different to speakers, meaningful discourse is impossible. In scientific writing one notes a great deal of attention given to definitions. This is not just an academic exercise but a crucial step in the process of accumulating knowledge and making comparisons.

Suppose, for example, that one researcher used the word "social class" in describing differential drug use and found that the higher the class, the greater the drug use. Another researcher found that the lower the class, the higher the drug use. With only this information, one might conclude that these results are in conflict. This might not be, however. If our first fictional researcher defined class as the amount of income earned, and the second researcher defined class as the amount of education obtained, then the findings are not directly comparable. The same word was defined differently. That is, "social class" meant something different to each of our researchers. By knowing what each meant by the word "social class," this apparent conflict can at least be understood. The same holds true for "drugs." What one researcher perceives as a drug may be different from the perception of another researcher. It is this type of confusion in definitions that we wish to avoid. We can do this by observing a few rules for definitions. According to Eric Goode (1972), definitions should (1) group together all the things that share a given relevant trait and (2) set apart those things that do not share that trait.

A trait is an **attribute**, a characteristic of something—size, weight, social ranking, for example. In reference to drugs, we must ask the questions, "What is the defining trait that all things called drugs share?" and "What separates a drug from something that we do not call a drug?" (Goode, 17)

Many writers on the subject of drugs simply define them as any substance that modifies biological, psychological, or social behavior. The problem with this definition is that it does not distinguish a drug from a non-drug. A final examination or a loaded gun pressed to your head might modify your heartbeat, but we would not consider exams and guns in the same category as cocaine and caffeine. Rain on a tin roof or the sight of a coffin might alter one's emotional state, but we might be hesitant to lump this experience together with LSD and marihuana. Red and green traffic lights alter social behavior, but they are not the same as alcohol or heroin. The failure to differentiate between a wide variety of substances that are capable of modifying biological, emotional, and social behaviors only creates ambiguity.

Another way to define drugs is pharmacologically. In this field a drug is any chemical substance that affects living protoplasm. This is simple enough, but is there any common effect that drugs have? As Goode notes:

> There is no effect that is common to all "drugs" that at the same time distinguishes it from "non-drugs." Some drugs are powerful psychoactive agents—they influence how the mind works; others have little if any effect on mental processes. Some drugs have medicinal properties; others no medicinal value at all. Some drugs are toxic—they require very small amounts to kill living beings; the toxicity of others is extremely low. Some drugs build tolerance very rapidly . . . ; others do so slowly or not at all. Some drugs are "addicting"—they produced a physical dependence; others are not. There is no conceivable characteristic that applies to all substances considered drugs. (18)

Like the words "nice" and "very" in English, this definition of drugs can include a wide variety of substances that are quite different. Therefore, it must also be rejected.

An alternative to the pharmacological approach is to define drugs from a social or cultural perspective. Here a drug is simply "something that has been arbitrarily defined by certain segments of society as a drug." According to this definition there is a shared meaning of what is and is not a drug. The thing called a drug need not have a specific pharmacological effect. Whatever substance people "think" or "believe" is a drug will be labeled a drug. As with any other cultural definitions, this definition is "real" if there are social consequences. If the use of "drugs" is defined as immoral or illegal, the consequences of using a drug may include a variety of punishments—banishment, jail, therapy, or any other action that those in positions of power are capable of exerting. Conversely, if substances defined as drugs are believed to have positive effects—enlightenment, happiness and so forth, people who use them will respond accordingly.

The one possible limitation of this social definition of drug is that it assumes the existence of a lexical category, a word reference in every vocabulary. In American culture, the word "drug" refers to a limited number of pharmacological substances. A person who *takes* insulin is not a drug user; a person who *uses* heroin is. A person who *takes* penicillin would not be defined as a drug user; a person who *uses* marihuana is. We do not define bars as drug stores, yet alcohol is pharmacologically a psychoactive drug. Beyond American culture, one finds that no lexical category "drug" exists as part of many vocabularies. The Huichol Indians have several words that refer to peyote (*hicouri, hikuli, hìkuli*), but no word for "drug." To understand the linguistic categories in one culture does not automatically mean that one can apply these categories to another culture. Bernard Barber (1967) makes this point:

> . . . almost anything can be called a "drug." There is nothing intrinsic to any physical or biological substance that makes it a drug or does not. The same substance can be called a "drug" in one social context and called something else in another. For example, the ink that is used in a fountain pen is not a drug when used in that way, but it may legally be defined as a drug when it is used as a diagnostic agent in connection with anti-fungal material which are also defined as drugs. When we look at drugs in a generalized comprehensive way, what we see is that it is not so much the substance of the material that makes it a drug but rather some particular social definition.

Given the limitations of the definitions suggested above, I would propose the following as a first approximation of a comprehensive social science definition of drugs:

Any non-food substance, external to the body, whose shared definition by a people includes the belief in the ability to alter "normal" body functions when ingested.

I would suggest that this definition enables one to include a wide range of substances, both in the United States and in other cultures. It does not demand the existence of a specific word in a language that could be translated as drug, nor does it assume that what is defined in one culture as a drug will be a drug in another. The criteria for a substance being a drug are **behavioral** and are defined through the believed consequences of ingesting the substance. It does, however, demand that the scientist view this substance relative to the cultural definition of "normal." I will discuss this topic in the next section, but for now the definition of "normal" reflects how this state of being is defined by the culture being studied.

An assumption of this definition is that we adopt what is called an **emic** perspective. The concept "emic" is borrowed from structural linguistics. One category of language studied by linguists is the phoneme. A phoneme is a sound or sounds in a language that distinguish one sound from other sounds and result in different meanings. Thus in English, the words c/ar and f/ar do not have the same meaning. Since the sound /ar/ is the same in both words, then what distinguishes these two words with their different meanings, are the sounds /c/ and /f/. The linguist discovers the phonemes in a language by accepting the native speaker's definition of car and far as being different words with different meanings. The emic approach to understanding cultural phenomena incorporates the native's distinctions and definitions; it analyzes elements from *within* the system.

This perspective is different from the **etic** approach, which is also a concept of linguistic origin. In the etic approach, the researcher uses criteria for labeling and classifying cultural phenomena that may not be recognized by the native—that is, the analysis takes place in isolation from the system. For example, the researcher who uses "years of formal education" to classify people is employing etic criteria if those to whom he applies this distinction do not make distinctions among themselves based on education. If they use age as a basis for distinction, then age would be an emic category. Throughout the rest of this book the emic-etic distinction will be used. Therefore it is important that you understand the difference, not only for this book, but also in your reading of other social science materials.

In applying the above definition of drugs to American culture, substances such as diuretics, penicillin, insulin, or any other substance believed to **restore** or **maintain** "normal" body function would be excluded as a drug. On the other hand, it would include coffee, cigarettes, and even placebos, if they are taken with the intention of changing "normal" body function. These functions may be physical or psychological. Thus, any substance believed to increase metabolism—coffee and cocaine—would be included, along with substances believed to extend or expand "normal" consciousness, such as LSD and psilocybin, peyote, mescaline, and heroin. Also included as drugs would be substances believed to decrease metabolism such as alcohol and marihuana. Other substances believed to extend normal physiological body functions, such as physical strength or sexual prowess, would be incorporated under this definition of a drug.

This definition has several social scientific merits. It does not reduce drugs to chemistry. It does not make any difference if the substance does or does not actually change the chemistry of the body. Rather, it is the **belief** that the substance will. For example, if one eats mandrake root with the belief that it will increase sexuality, then mandrake root is a drug. This definition avoids any moral or legal assumptions. The use of peyote by the Huichol of Mexico to communicate with the supernatural is neither right nor wrong, and within that cultural setting it is not illegal. The consumption of alcohol in one culture may be mandatory. In another culture it may be prohibited and harshly punished. The intention of this definition is not to exclude pharmacological or legal considerations in understanding drug use. To do so would be shortsighted, because legal and pharmacological reasoning may be part of emic explanations. Rather, we wish to overcome the strict limiting effects that these perspectives might impose on our understanding of drug use in humankind.

The Normal and the Pathological

There are alternative ways that social scientists view the world and hence the object of their study. These variations can be charted along a continuum ranging from normal to pathological. The assumption of the normal model is that the world is an orderly place governed by rules and principles, and it is the job of the scientist to uncover these rules. In contrast to the normal, the pathological approach focuses on phenomena at variance with the normal. Western medicine, for example, assumes a pathological or disease model, as does much of psychology and sociology. Studies of "normal" behavior are rare in clinical psychology, and sociology devotes much attention to the analysis of crime, deviance, and social problems. Many modern sociologists seem to have forgotten their "normal" history. Émile Durkheim (1951) argued that even those behaviors that are publicly defined as pathological may be normal. If suicide rates remain constant within a society over time, then suicide is normal behavior. If a set of behaviors socially defined as crime continues, in spite of efforts to alter those behaviors, Durkheim would conclude that crime is normal. The task of social science, according to Durkheim, is to uncover the rules that explain why behaviors such as suicide or crime are part of the normal workings of society.

One might think that the concept "disease" would be immune from these definitional problems. No so, maintains Charles Hughes (1968). His analysis suggests that theories of disease imply normality but that normality is not easy to define on a universal basis. Normal is culturally defined. Afflictions common enough in a group to be endemic, though they be clinical deformities, may often be accepted simply as part of man's natural condition. Erwin Ackerknect (1946), for example, noted that the Thonga in Africa believe that intestinal worms, which pervasively afflict them, are necessary for digestion. The Mono, also of Africa, feel that primary and secondary yaws are so common that they say, "That is no sickness; everybody has that." North Amazonian Indians, among whom dyschronic spirochetosis is prevalent, accept its endemicity to such an extent that its victims are thought to be normal, and individuals who have not had the disfiguring disease are said to be looked on as pathological and consequently unable to contract marriage. It is obvious, even from this brief review, that culture, not nature, defines disease.

Unlike the physicist who studies one universe, the relativistic social scientist must look for the normal within the context of each culture being studied. The particular behaviors that are normal in one culture may be quite different from another culture. Ultimately the goal of the social scientist is to produce an explanation, or limited number of explanations, that makes sense of these observed differences. This is what science is all about. Science is the search for universal principles. This is the intent of the definition of drugs offered above. A drug is no more a particular thing than a disease is a particular biological condition. A drug is defined within a larger cultural context. Approaching the concept of drug from this perspective permits us to carry out research that is driven by scientific logic and has universal applications.

Theory: The Driving Force in Science

One of the most confusing weapons in the scientific arsenal is the concept of theory. Often it is easier to define what theory is not, rather than what it is. The often heard statements, "It's just a theory" and "That's just your theory," best describe a belief, an attitude, or an ideology. The critical distinction is that beliefs, attitudes, or ideologies are ideas that are not subject to independent verification, nor are they capable of generating statements that can be verified—that is, they are not subject to testing that might prove them false. Beliefs, attitudes, and ideologies are "proved" by carefully selecting data that support them or, more simply, recruiting more adherents who accept them. In this latter sense, beliefs, attitudes, and ideologies are democratic. Their continuation depends on counting those who accept them. The larger the number of disciples, the "truer" they are. In contrast, scientific theories are judged by their ability to either explain or predict some category of phenomena. The more inclusive the category, the more valuable the theory. At the same time, theories must be able to produce statements that can be disproved. The scientific theorist has a responsibility that lawyers, politicians, and religionists do not—to present theories that are falsifiable. The level of confidence at which one accepts a scientific theory is not just how much it explains or predicts but also its ability to resist being disproved. The more a scientific theory resists being disproved, the more acceptable it is.

Theories are not **empirical generalizations**. Empirical generalizations are statements which report observable and measurable regularities. "Tobacco is used in all societies" is an example of an empirical generalization. Such a statement is possible only after we have observed tobacco use in all societies. In other words, we make the generalized statement from individual observations. This process is called **induction**. Such statements may be useful as a basis for a theory, but they are not theories. Theoretical statements explain *why* tobacco is used in all societies. If the theoretical statement only explains why tobacco is found in all societies, it is called a **middle-range** theory. Middle-range theories are restricted to a narrow range of phenomena, in this example tobacco, and may be helpful in the construction of **unified** or **grand** theories. For example, Gregor Mendel did experiments with the garden pea. He observed certain regularities (empirical generalizations) in how their characteristics are inherited from one generation to the next. He then constructed a theory to explain why one found these regularities in the garden pea, a middle-range theory. He then went on to construct a theory which explained how all living matter, plants and animals, pass on characteristics from one generation to the next—a grand theory. Mendel's theory was the result of induction. The beauty of Mendel's theory is that it not only can be applied to all living matter, but it can be disproved. It combines two characteristics of "good" theory—comprehensiveness and falsifiability.

Thus far I have suggested that theories are constructed from the bottom up or, to be more formal, "post factum," after the fact or facts. However, another consideration in evaluating theory is the ability to predict outcomes. This is the process of **deduction**. The principles Mendel developed to explain how the garden pea passed on physical characteristics can be used to predict the future distribution of any one characteristic of any life form by knowing what the distribution of that characteristic is at the present. We can now add to our list of criteria for a "good" theory the ability to predict future outcomes.

Many predictions in social science are based on empirical generalizations. Starting with the observation, "In almost all societies where alcohol is used, more males consume alcohol than females," we could then predict, with only the knowledge that a particular society used alcohol, that more drinkers would likely be male. Of course this empirical generalization does not permit us to predict the drinking behavior of any particular person, male or female, in that society, nor could one conclude that all males drank and all females did not. It also does not explain why such a relationship was observed. What it does enable us to do is to make "probabilistic" predictions. This type of prediction is usually phrased as an "if/then" statement. Rephrasing the above statement to reflect probability, one might say, "*If* a society has alcohol, *then* it is more likely that more males will drink than females." If one could predict that in societies where alcohol is used, all males drank and all females abstained, we would then have a **law**. Alas, the number of laws in the scientific world are small in number; in the social sciences there are none. There are, however, many probabilistic statements that can be made on the subject of drugs, as we shall see.

Thus far we have noted three criteria for judging a theory—falsifiability, comprehensiveness, and prediction. It is now time to give an example of how these criteria might be applied to a theory of alcohol consumption. We have already reported the empirical generalization that in all cultures more men than women consume alcohol. How does one explain this observation? The reader might conjure up several "explanations." To ideological feminists, the reason might be the exploitation of women. To the biopharma-cologist, the explanation might lie in physiological differences in the way males and females metabolize alcohol. Neither one of these "theories" is very comprehensive. They only attempt to explain gender (cultural) or sex (biological) differences in drinking patterns. Good theory, on the other hand, would explain a larger number of different empirical generalizations. Just what are those generalizations about alcohol consumption? David Mandelbaum (1965) notes that drinking is a social, not a solitary, activity and therefore is an appropriate topic for social science. It is more likely to occur in **groups** made up of persons with similarly ranked **statuses**. Drinking is usually less appropriate for those whose status has the expectation that they perpetuate the rules of society—a priest or judge, for example. Conversely, drinking is not only appropriate but may be mandatory for those whose status requires one to deal with forces outside the society, such as warriors or shamans.[3] Using just this last generalization, how might we construct a general theory of drugs and a specific theory of drinking?

One way to construct a theory is by starting with an **axiom**, a self-evident truth or principle. The idea here is that the axiom is proved if what one derives from that axiom is supported by research efforts. We might, for example, posit the axiom, "The primary function of cultural practices is to perpetuate cultural practices." We assume that all cultures are segmented into institutions, which are composed of statuses that have responsibility for perpetuating the "normal" (current practices) and passing on this "normal" from one generation to the next. If cultural rules did not make provisions for this function, society would consist of atomistic individuals whose behaviors did not follow any norms. Everybody would be "doing their own thing," and eventually both the society and the culture would become extinct. Staying with our axiom, we observe that cultures are not themselves isolated but rather must contend with forces outside themselves. Those forces might be natural, supernatural, or social. Thus, not only are all cultures segmented into statuses which maintain internal continuity (the "normal"), but there must be statuses which are concerned with external forces. Given this axiomatic assumption, we are now faced with explaining drug use. Drugs are defined as "any non-food substance, external to the body, whose shared definition by a people includes the belief in the ability to alter 'normal' body functions when ingested." "Normal" is the key word here. What is normal is what is generally shared, whether what is shared is an expectation (cultural) or its behavioral manifestation (social). If alcohol as a substance is defined as altering the "normal" (and therefore according to our definition is a drug), then we can derive the proposition that "Statuses that require interaction with forces outside society (away from the normal) are more likely to consume alcohol." The **corollary** (opposite) to this statement is, "Statuses that require one to perpetuate the rules of culture (the normal) are less likely to consume alcohol." Just which specific statuses have the responsibility for perpetuating the "normal" can vary from one culture to another. In cultures where the status "mother" carries with it the expectation that one is responsible for socializing children, then "mothers" would be expected to drink less than non-mothers, or not at all. Note that "mother" is in quotes. The reader might have assumed that only females can be mothers. However, in social science, "mother" is the name of a status, not necessarily a reference to a sex. Obviously males cannot give birth to a child, but a male can be a "mother," just as a female can be a "father." This is the distinction between sex and gender. Sex is a biological fact. Gender is a cultural fact. Males and females (sex) learn to be boys and girls, women and men (cultural). Our theory is a cultural theory; therefore, what we must explain is the relationship between drinking and gender. Thus, if there were a culture where males where expected to socialize children, then we should expect that they would drink less. It is not a male-female thing, but rather a matter of what is expected of statuses within a culture. In this sense, this explanation is more comprehensive than single-focus feminist or biopharmacological explanations. It is also attractive in its ability to predict outcomes. In American culture, for example, one could predict that females in military statuses should drink more than females in the mother status; or males in military statuses should drink more than males in priest statuses or mother statuses. The third criteria for good theory—falsifiability—is also built into this theory. We can actually measure drinking behavior for mothers, warriors, and priests! If our measurement shows differences in drinking, regardless of sex, our axiom is supported. If our measurement does not show differences, then our axiom is not supported.

I entitled this section "Theory: The Driving Force in Science" for a reason. One may get the impression that science is a body of knowledge, a collection of "facts." Indeed, knowledge and facts are found in science, but they are not exclusive to science. It is the existence of theory, with the characteristics outlined above, that distinguishes science from non-science. Facts are not self-explanatory. In and of themselves they mean nothing. Collecting facts in science is ultimately for constructing and testing theories, and the purpose of theory is to give meaning to those facts. Whether stated or not, any scientific inquiry begins with some kind of theory. Scientists observe, examine, and experiment under the guidance of the seen or unseen hand of theoretical considerations. Just how they conduct their inquires and the kinds of "facts" one gets from these inquires is discussed in the next chapter.

Summary

The basic premise of the conceptual model for the social science approach to drug use is that social and cultural phenomena are different and that an examination of each is necessary if one is to understand drug use from the social science perspective. This introduction to the social science perspective provides a format for an inspection of the contributions of social scientists toward our understanding of drug use. The following chapters apply this model to the vast body of research and theory that has focused on drug use in many social and cultural settings. In doing so, it will be necessary to translate the vocabulary of different social scientists into the proposed model. Where researchers have confused social and cultural phenomena, we will try to make their usage consistent with the model. Thus, what follows is as much a test of the efficacy of the model as it is a review of the literature.

In addition to the model, the chapter reviewed several parameters of social science. Included was the observation that social science is concerned with uncovering the systemic rules which regulate human activities, and that those rules should not be restricted to a specific time or place. We noted that social science is relativistic, objective, and ethically neutral. Just how social scientists go about acknowledging and implementing these attributes is reflected in scientific methods. In the next chapter we examine the strategies employed by social scientists to achieve these goals.

Endnotes

[1] Throughout this book the botanical species name will be indicated by italicized binomials following the popular or common name used by various human populations.

[2] The concept of cultural relativity, like many other concepts in social science, has been vulgarized by some writers. Allen Bloom, in his popular diatribe, *The Closing of the American Mind* (1987), selects anthropology in general and cultural relativism in particular as one of the main academic contributors to a loss of "good"

(his definition) normative standards among college students. As a not-so-astute observer of American culture, he has confused a change of norms in American culture away from moral elitism and toward equality with the methodological principle of cultural relativism. It is not cultural relativism that has taught American college students to equate their cultural practices with those of other cultures any more than the study of the distribution of physical characteristics "teaches" racial superiority. While Bloom, and other intellectual "flat-earthers," may extol the virtues of a Newtonian universe, failure to understand that changes have taken place in the way that universe is perceived is no excuse for moral outrage.

[3] A shaman is a religious specialist who is believed to deal directly with the supernatural. In contrast, a priest is a religious functionary who orchestrates preexisting rituals.

chapter 2

Social Science as Behavior
Methods and Techniques

The last chapter discussed what is meant by "good" social science. Good social science is an ideal against which social scientists measure what has been done. In this sense, "good" social science exists only in the heads of social scientists. As an ideal, social science is a set of expectations and, therefore, properly belongs under the category of culture. The way in which social scientists go about implementing those ideals is through a set of behaviors. Hence, what scientists do is part of the social domain. There is, in the science world, a constant interplay between these ideals and how the scientist translates these ideals into behavior. To meet the goals of good social science, several behavioral procedures have emerged which help guide the actual work of social scientists. These procedures are called methods and techniques.

The methods and techniques employed by social scientists are the ways social scientists have of gathering information from the social and cultural worlds that they wish to understand. We can think of this as a continuum: one end is the lofty world of theory, and the other end is people going about their everyday lives. Such a continuum might look like this:

THEORY ◄————————► HUMANKIND

This continuum is the ideal representation of how we understand humankind in general. Grand theory or unified theory ultimately attempts to achieve knowledge about that elusive concept, "human nature," or Culture spelled with a capital "C." Remember that good theory must be capable of generating testable statements about real people. This is illustrated by a second continuum.

HYPOTHESES→METHODS → TECHNIQUES→SAMPLES OF HUMAN POPULATIONS

Theory is the basis for specific relational questions (hypotheses) that can be tested on some small part of humankind (samples of human populations). Between the hypotheses and the samples are the methods and techniques that are used by social scientists. In this chapter, we will review the standard ways social scientists go about actually studying human populations.

Methods and Techniques

Information used to construct empirical generalizations and to test theories may be gathered through the use of different methods and techniques. Method refers to the logic of inquiry. Technique is the actual step-by-step procedures used to implement the method. Methods and their corresponding techniques determine the kinds of information that are collected. In this section, three methods are discussed—experimental, survey, and ethnographic.

The Experimental Method

The word "experiment" enjoys rather wide popular usage. For example, one might read, "Prohibition was an experiment that failed," or "There are a lot of people experimenting with drugs." These examples are not, strictly speaking, experiments in the scientific sense. Most simply an experiment is, ". . . a comparison between two sets of circumstances, which exactly match each other in all respects except one" (Madge 1965, 291). The purpose of an experiment is to determine the effect of some treatment free from any contaminating influences. To do this, one selects some people—**subjects**—who share characteristics in common. They may be the same age, sex, weight, height, religion, or any other characteristic the experimenter thinks might influence the outcome of the treatment. These people are then divided in half. One half is the **control "group"**;[1] the other half is the **experimental "group."**[2] The experimental subjects are given the treatment; the control subjects are not. The response by the experimental subjects, if different from the control subjects, is then said to be the effect of the treatment. Under these conditions, the experimenter can only measure the influence of a limited number of treatments. In most instances only one treatment can be measured. In addition, the experimental situation is artificial or contrived; that is, not part of the "normal" patterns of behavior which characterize the subjects. Subjects may share little in common other than being subjects.

The Survey Method

Like the experimental method, the survey method is concerned with controlling factors that affect outcomes; but the similarities end there. The survey method obtains information from samples of a larger number of people. Instead of prematching the units, the survey method matches units after the information has been collected. The primary tool of the survey method is the questionnaire. The questionnaire contains questions that **respondents** (individuals selected by the researcher) are expected to answer. The questions may be asked by an interviewer or read by the respondents. Like the experiment, the questions are those of interest to the researcher, not necessarily to the respondent. The same may be true of the responses to the questions. Both the questions and the range of answers in the questionnaire are for the convenience of the researcher. Such standard fixed responses as: "yes/no," "strongly agree/agree/no opinion," "agree/disagree," all insure that answers are uniform and, when translated into numbers, can be statistically analyzed.

Although most surveys have more respondents than experiments have subjects, it should be kept in mind that in both of these methods information is collected from individuals, not interacting groups. Once information is collected using this method, it is controlled by statistical manipulation. For example, we might wish to know if gender influences responses to certain questions. By comparing responses from males and females it is possible to answer this question. In contrast to the experimental methods where one would select males and females prior to the experiment, in the survey method this is done after both males and females have been surveyed. If one does find differences in responses, then one might conclude that gender influenced how people responded. Depending on how many people were surveyed, it would be possible to "control" for several different influences, such as age, education, religion, occupation, and so forth. Thus, instead of focusing on a single or limited number of differences, the survey method can look at multiple "treatments" and at numerous effects.

The use of experimental or survey methods tends to divide along discipline distinctions. Surveys are most likely to be used by sociologists, while experiments are the norm within psychology. Both survey and experimental methods are etic approaches to collecting information. Both can be used to test theory through deduction, but neither is very helpful in gathering emic data. The method best suited for this task is ethnography.

Ethnography

As used in anthropology, **ethnography** refers to the description of cultural practices. An underlying goal of this approach is to gather information that best describes the way(s) people view their world(s). The primary technique of the ethnographic method is participant-observation. This technique requires the ethnographer to spend extended time with **informants**. Through various degrees of participation with and observations of informants in their natural settings, the ethnographer discovers the rules and principles which govern both the behaviors and beliefs of a people.

Participant-observation refers to a role played by the ethnographer. In that role the ethnographer continually alternates between standing back and observing what others do and fully participating in ongoing activities. Observation permits the ethnographer to see a wide variety of activities, while participation allows one to experience the activity itself. In addition, the ethnographer interviews informants to get their interpretations. The outcome of this process is "thick" description, a great deal of detailed information about many aspects of social life. This is the kind of information that makes possible a holistic analysis. Unlike the experiment or the survey, which can only tap into very select aspects of people's lives, the ethnography gives us a picture of the whole way of life of a people—their culture.

What the ethnographer does is called **field work**. The field is anyplace the ethnographer is studying. It may be a street corner in a large metropolitan area or a remote part of a forest in South America. It is not where one gathers data, but how one gathers data that defines ethnography. The data that one collects through participation or observation is recorded as **field notes** in the **field diary**. The diary contains everything that is observed and said—no matter how unimportant it may appear at the time. Some information may turn out to be unimportant; other information may become very important. The reason such detailed records are maintained is that ethnography is largely an inductive process. Before going into the field, one might have a general set of questions one wishes to answer. However, questions that were never anticipated will inevitably arise during field work. Because of this, ethnography permits a greater amount of flexibility in the formulation of social science problems than either experiments or surveys. It should be emphasized that it does require more time than either the experiment or the survey, and the number of people who can be observed in an ethnography is usually smaller than in the survey method.

Ethnography is not the exclusive domain of anthropology. There is a history of field work in sociology going back to the 1920s in the United States. The practice of studying people "up close" has been part of the anthropological tradition since the turn of the century. It has only been within the last few decades, however, that anthropologists have directed their attention to the urban setting. This has given rise to what is called "street ethnography" (Weppner 1977). These ethnographies provide us with data about drug use and drug users that would not have been possible using either experimental or survey methods. In addition, they are responsible for providing those using survey methods with response categories that consider emic variations and hence are more meaningful to respondents.

Other Data Sources

Although experiments, surveys, and field work are major sources of data in the social sciences, they are not the only sources. Documents, both official and unofficial, can and do provide information that is valuable. Government documents, such as census materials, can inform us about characteristics of populations, past and present. Court records, such as trial transcripts, contain verbatim transcriptions of conversations that can be analyzed. Legislation documents, business records, and personal diaries can be used to reconstruct and interpret the past. Data sources are only limited by the imagination of the researcher. The type of data one uses will depend on the questions asked. Just what those questions are, and in what form they are asked, is the subject of the next section.

Hypotheses and Hypothesis Testing

Thus far, the general concerns in social science with definitions, theory, and methods of data collection have been discussed. In this section the format used by social scientists in asking researchable questions is examined.

Theory is a formal statement of relationship between attributes. **Attributes** are characteristics of a category of phenomena. Going back to our example of Chinese opium smoking and legislation, the attribute we might use to understand the relationship between smoking and anti-opium ordinances is power. **Power** is one way of describing the ability of one social unit, such as a group or a society, to mobilize the actions of other social units. Keep in mind that you cannot see power. It is not a physical or corporeal thing, but it can be illustrated by specific social practices. The status "instructor" (more powerful) can assign a term paper or give an examination to the status "student" (less powerful). Because of the differences in power assigned to statuses within the institution of education, students will do the term paper and take the exam. Note that the same instructor cannot assign a term paper or give an exam to the traffic policeman who cites him or her for speeding. Within the legal institution, the status "policeman" has power over the status "driver." Remember, it is not the person who has power but rather the status that the person occupies. In the Chinese example, American society is made up of different social categories that can be ranked by power. These distinctions in power may be the consequence of different sized populations, of history, or of control over technological or natural resources. Just how these differences evolved is unimportant for the theoretical question at hand. More important is the question, "How is this power demonstrated?" One way, but not the only way, is through formal prohibitions of practices associated with the less powerful. It is not the behavior itself that is important but rather the prohibition of the behavior that is a measure of power differences. Our theory is concerned with the attribute "power" and its relationship to legislation. To test that theory, it is necessary to convert the attributes into variables and to restate the relationship as a hypothesis.

A **hypothesis** is a stated relationship between two or more variables. A **variable** is an attribute with a distribution. Continuing with our Chinese example, we could say that being Chinese and engaging in Chinese practices, which includes smoking opium, are attributes. The percentage of Chinese in a population is a variable. This percentage could vary from 0, no Chinese, to 100, all Chinese. Anti-opium legislation would be another attribute. One simple way of measuring this attribute is "yes" or "no." Either there is legislation prohibiting opium smoking or there is not. This could be further specified by measuring the intensity of punishment. It is a misdemeanor or a felony? How large are the fines, or how long are the sentences? How many people are arrested, and what proportion are Chinese? These are the kinds of measurements that transform our attributes into variables. This is what we actually test.

Remember that theory is a statement of relationship between attributes. Therefore, a hypothesis must also be relational. The usual format for a hypothesis is an equation: the greater the A the greater the B, for example. The A in this example is the **independent** variable; the B is the **dependent** variable. Which variable is independent or dependent will be determined by theoretical considerations. Basically, we want to know how one variable influences another. If power is measured by anti-opium legislation, then in a population with no Chinese one would hypothesize that there would be no anti-opium smoking ordinances. Therefore, our hypothesis would read, "The greater the proportion of Chinese in a population, the greater the likelihood for passage of anti-opium smoking legislation." In this case, the proportion of Chinese is the independent variable; legislation prohibiting opium smoking is the dependent variable.

Which variable is independent or dependent may be determined by time frame. What, for example, is the relationship between childhood socialization and adult alcohol use? Obviously, child socialization precedes adult use of alcohol. Therefore childhood socialization is the independent variable. In some hypotheses the determination of which variable is the independent and which is the dependent may be logically clear. For example, if one were interested in the relationship between drinking and age or gender, it would be difficult to argue that drinking determines age or gender.

For other research questions, the determination of independent and dependent variables is not clear. In fact, the research is an attempt to determine which variable is which. Consider, for example, the two variables, prostitution and drug use. Is prostitution or drug use the independent variable? Does drug use precede prostitution, or does prostitution precede drug use?

In hypothesis testing, we "control" the independent variable and see what happens to the dependent variable. That is, we organize our findings by the independent variable. In determining if prostitution precedes drug use, we might ask prostitutes if they used drugs before becoming prostitutes. If, on the other hand, drug use was the independent variable, we would ask drug users if they were prostitutes. In reading social science research it is important to keep this distinction between independent and dependent variables in mind. The declaration that one or another variable is independent is often a clue exposing the assumptions or "theory" of the researcher.

The simplest hypothesis is a statement of a single relationship. As a matter of convention, the independent variable appears to the left in the statement; the dependent variable appear to its right. Visually, it looks like this:

INDEPENDENT VARIABLE ⟶ DEPENDENT VARIABLE

Now that we understand the difference between independent and dependent variables, we can refine our understanding of the hypothesis somewhat further by introducing another variable, the control variable. The control variable is found in one of two places in the hypothesis statement, either before the independent variable or between the independent and the dependent variable. When the control variable is located before the independent variable, it is called an **antecedent** variable. When it appears between the independent and the dependent variable, it is called an **intervening** variable. We can visualize these variables:

ANTECEDENT—INDEPENDENT—INTERVENING—DEPENDENT

Control variables are used to test the strength of the relationship between the independent and the dependent variables. By strength I mean the ability of the independent variable to predict the dependent variable. Let us suppose that we have a theory from which the following hypothesis was suggested: "The more advanced the class standing of college students (independent variable), the lower the consumption of alcohol (dependent variable)." We collect data and indeed find that freshmen drink more than seniors. We would like to know what might explain these changes in drinking from the freshman to the senior year. We decide to control for gender. Now we have two hypotheses, one for males and one for females. We go back, control for gender, and find that male drinking does *not* change over the four years of college, but female drinking decreases. Thus, while overall drinking does decrease over the college years, that decrease is explained by gender and class standing, not class standing alone. By adding gender as the control variable, we have increased the strength of our ability to predict drinking from class standing.

The use of control variables helps to refine our hypotheses. But more importantly, the greater number of control variables we use, while still finding a relationship between the independent and the dependent variable, the greater confidence we have in the theory from which the hypothesis was derived. To our example we might have added membership in fraternal organizations, ethnicity, age, religion, or any number of other social variables. If the original relationship still holds, in spite of our attempts to disprove the hypothesis, we have done a good job of "sciencing." If, on the other hand, the original relationship disappears when we introduce controls, the original relationship is said to be **spurious**.

In the discussion thus far I have given examples of hypotheses that reflect probabilistic theories in the social sciences. Probabilistic theories, as you may remember from chapter 1, are statements that predict relationships in the "if/then" format. These are statements that link variables together in likely outcomes. For example, the statements, "If the number of males in a population between the ages of fifteen to twenty-four increased, then crime rates will increase" and "If life expectancy in a population increases, then divorce rates will increase," are both probabilistic statements. A word of caution is necessary here. Probabilistic theories are *not* causal theories. We cannot say that class standing in college "causes" drinking. We cannot say that drug use "causes" prostitution or vice versa. Were one to make such a statement, two conditions must be met. The "cause" must be both a **necessary** and a **sufficient condition** for the effect. In this case we would have to demonstrate that it is necessary to have college class standing for drinking to occur and that class standing is a sufficient condition for drinking. If one stated that drug use "causes" prostitution, it would be obligatory to demonstrate that all prostitutes used drugs *and* that all female drug users are or will become prostitutes. Since cause implies a law, and there are no laws in the social sciences, the use of the word "cause" in social science literature is misleading.

Linkages

Hypotheses are formal statements of relationships between variables. They are most likely to be used when data are collected using the experimental or survey method. A somewhat different way to present relationships is found in ethnography (Otterbein 1972). Ethnography often describes a culture by its **traits**. A trait can be a practice, a belief, or a tool. In describing a culture, or some part thereof, the ethnographer will construct a trait inventory, a listing of all the traits that characterize that culture. One use of the trait inventory is to make cross-cultural comparisons. Another use is to describe linkages between traits within a culture. This latter use is a description of how the parts of culture are integrated.

Linkages, like hypotheses, are not actual data. Rather, they are inferences about the relationship between data. Otterbein suggests there are three forms of linkages (205). The first is a functional relationship between traits. In this linkage two traits are defined as mutually dependent. A change in one trait will result in a change in another trait. This is very similar to a hypothesis. A second linkage is non-functional. When one trait changes, the other does not. Unlike the functional linkage, which may be said to be valid, the non-functional linkage is not. Here again this resembles a hypothesis. The difference between a hypothesis and a linkage is the method of determining validity; a linkage is valid if one observes the connection between two or more traits. A hypothesis is a statement of relationship that must be tested to determine its validity. A third type of linkage is a **tautological** relationship. A tautology is a relationship between two traits that results from overlapping definitions—for example, "As heroin use increases, there is a corresponding increase in crime rates." If using heroin is itself a crime, then this statement is a tautology. It is the overlapping definitions that create the relationship.

Linkages are not tested directly. They must be rephrased in the form of a hypothesis. Having translated theory or linkages into hypotheses that can be tested, it is now necessary to turn to techniques for determining if our hypotheses are supported by our data. One way of doing this is through the use of statistics.

Statistics

To test hypotheses, many social scientists use statistics. Although statistics often present a confusing image to many observers, an understanding of the basic assumptions and uses of this tool is necessary if one is to make informed judgements about the importance of some social science research.

Statistics is the study of **samples**. Samples are numerical units smaller than a **population**. For example, we may want to know if the social characteristics of marihuana smokers are different from non-smokers on the Caribbean island of Jamaica. In this case, everybody living in Jamaica is our population. We could, of course, carry out a population census of Jamaica, but this would be both costly and time consuming. An alternative to a complete census is to select a sample of the population. If every Jamaican had an equal chance of being selected as part of our sample (a **random sample**), then it should represent the whole Jamaican population. However, we might have been interested only in Jamaicans living in urban areas. In that case, our population would be people living in areas defined as urban. If every Jamaican living in urban areas had an equal chance of being included in our sample, then our sample should have the same distribution of characteristics as all urban Jamaicans. The important principle to remember is that samples are estimations of populations. It then follows that the larger the size of the sample, the more accurately we can estimate the population.

The way we sample populations is usually based on knowledge about the variables we wish to study. We might know that marihuana smokers are likely to be persons over the age of eighteen. Therefore, our population would be urban Jamaicans over the age of eighteen. How do we find these people? One way is to sample households. If we know there are 1000 houses in the city and decide that a 10-percent sample would be large enough to represent all these households, then we would randomly select 100 houses.[3] Having made a selection of 100 specific house addresses, we would then conduct a survey. We go to each of the houses and administer a questionnaire to all members of the household over the age of eighteen. The questions included in the questionnaire will reflect the variables in our hypothesis(es). Aside from the standard questions about age, sex, ethnicity, education, and occupation, we might have questions on the frequency of marihuana use, the use of other substances such as tobacco and/or alcohol, and so forth. Once this information is collected we can use statistical techniques.

It is possible to report the answers to every question for each respondent. Aside from making one's report extremely boring, the resultant long reports on paper would soon lead to deforestation of the earth. One way around this is to use descriptive statistics. **Descriptive statistics** summarize the characteristics of our sample (and, if random, the population). There are two general types of description—central tendencies and dispersion. **Central tendencies** are measures of "averages." These are: mean, median, and mode. The **mean** is determined by adding up one measure of our sample, let us say age, and dividing by the number in the sample. Using this calculation we might have found that the mean age of marihuana smokers in our sample was 21, while the mean age of non-smokers was 23. The **median** is the midpoint in the distribution of a variable. A median number describes that point which lies in the middle of the distribution of a variable. If our median for smokers was 23, this would mean that 50 percent of our sample was above the age of 23, and 50 percent was below 23. **Mode** describes the largest category in our distribution. A mode of 20 for smokers would indicate there were more 20-year-old smokers in our sample than any other age category.

   Dispersion of a sample is described by several terms. The **range** of a distribution indicates the lowest and highest values. For example, we might have found that the age range for non-smokers is between 18 and 67 years of age. The other measure is one with which college students are familiar. "Grading on the curve" is an emic concept that approximates what in statistics is called standard deviation. The calculation of the standard deviation involves some mathematical computations that we need not go into here. For our purposes, **standard deviation** is the measure of dispersion of a distribution in standard units from the mean. Those standard units are, for all practical purposes, 1, 2, and 3, and they range from − 3 to + 3 with 0 as the mean (table 2.1.). In the student lexicon, scores on exams from − 1 to + 1 translate to the grade of C. Those scores above + 1 to + 2 are a B, and those above + 2 are an A.[4] Because these are standardized, the percent of the sample between the standard units are the same for any sample, even though the actual

Table 2.1. **Standard Deviation Units from the Mean**

− 3	− 2	− 1	0	+ 1	+ 2	+ 3
			68%			
		96%				
	99%					
	Percent of Sample					

numbers may be different. For example, 68 percent of any total sample lies between ± 1 standard deviations. Thus, if our mean sample age for marihuana smokers was 21 and our standard deviation was 1.2 years, then 68 percent of our sample was between the ages of 18.8 and 22.2 years old.

A mean and standard deviation could be calculated for other variables, such as income per year or number of people per household. But for other variables, one cannot calculate a mean. Thus, there can be no mean sex or mean religion, but we could describe occupational prestige from low to high in numbers and then calculate a mean score. There can be no mean calculated for smoking marihuana, but for smokers one could report the mean number of cigarettes smoked over some standard time interval. Statistical descriptions of central tendencies are therefore applicable to some measurements and not to others.

Another function of statistics is to help us make decisions concerning hypotheses. This is inductive statistics. The two types of statistical tools that do this are measures of **association** and measures of **significance**. Association measures how well one can predict one variable from knowledge about the other variable or variables. Significance measures whether or not the association was due to chance. To illustrate these two functions we can ask the research question, "What is the relationship between smoking and drinking in the United States?" The two variables are smoking and drinking, and what we wish to know is which of these variables is the independent variable and which is the dependent variable. To answer this question, I selected two questions from the National Opinion Research Center's (NORC) survey of the U.S. population (Davis and Smith 1991). The two questions are, "Do you smoke?" and "Do you ever have occasion to use any alcoholic beverage such as liquor, wine, or beer, or are you a total abstainer?" These questions were asked of respondents in four samples from 1972 to 1988. Table 2.2 shows the cross-tabulated responses to these questions.

The drinking responses are found in the columns of this table; the smoking responses are reported in the rows. The figures off to the far right and at the very bottom are called marginals. The **marginals** display how many of our respondents gave which response to the questions about smoking and drinking. Thus, we note that 8,438 (or 72 percent) of the respondents answered that they drink, while 3,369 (or 28 percent) said they were abstainers. For the smoking question, 4,380 said they smoked, and 7,472 said they did not smoke, or there were 37 percent smokers and 63 percent non-smokers. Describing the distribution of answers does

Table 2.2. **Relationship between Smoking and Drinking**

DRINKING

		Use	Abstinence	Total
SMOKE	Yes	3,591	789	4,380
	No	4,892	2,580	7,472
	Total	8,483	3,369	11,852

$r = 41; \ p < .000$

not tell us anything about relationships. We want to know the strength of the association between smoking and drinking. We want to test the original research question.

One way to look at the strength of the relationship between smoking and drinking is by inspection. We might ask ourselves[5] the questions, "How well can we predict smoking behavior by knowing drinking behavior?" and "How well can we predict drinking behavior from knowing smoking behavior?" In our first question, drinking is the independent variable; in the second question, smoking is the independent variable. Let's start with drinking as the independent variable. We know that 8,483 respondents drank. Of those, 3,591 (or 42 percent) also smoked, but 4,892 (or 58 percent) did not smoke. Thus, our chances of predicting non-smoking from our knowledge of drinking are somewhat better than predicting smoking. If we use abstinence from drinking as our predictor, we find that 77 percent (2,850 of the 3,369 total abstainers) also do not smoke. If we use smoking behavior as our independent variable, we find something different. Of the 4,380 smokers, 3,591 (or 82 percent) also drank. However, 66 percent (4,892 of 7,472) of the non-smokers also drank! What should be obvious from this exercise is that there are a number of different predictions one can make from these data. In testing hypotheses, however, we wish to know how, in general, these two variables are related. For this purpose one calculates a **correlation coefficient**.

A correlation coefficient is a summary of all the predictions. It is usually expressed as some number between +1.00 and −1.00. If you want to know how that number is calculated, consult a statistician. In this illustration, if you found that every smoker drank and every non-smoker abstained, the correlation would be a perfect 1.00 and you would become famous—but it never works out that way. For this relationship, the correlation coefficient (r) is .18. This number, in and of itself, tells us little, but if you want to use that number to say something about prediction, just square it. This will give you the **coefficient of determination**. This coefficient tells you the percent of variation in one variable that is explained by variation in the other variable. By "explained," one means that by knowing something about smoking (yes or no) one can predict drinking (yes or no) better than if one did not know anything about smoking behavior. If we square the r of .18², we get .0324, or 3.24 percent. This means that you could predict drinking from smoking and smoking from drinking a little over 3 percent of the time. The reverse of this is that you would be wrong in your prediction 97 percent of the time. There is more error in your prediction than non-error. You would be wrong most of the time! I know this may be somewhat confusing, but it is, nonetheless, important if one wishes to interpret statistical findings. In general, the higher the r value (or its equivalent with other statistical measures of association) the stronger the association between the variables.

In the discussion of theory I mentioned that one of the criteria for evaluating a theory was its ability to generate hypotheses that can be falsified. One way to reject a hypothesis is by inspection. The correlation between smoking and drinking was admittedly low. We might, therefore, reject the hypothesis because it does not enable us to predict much about the association between our two variables. Another way to reject a hypothesis is addressed in the issue of **significance**. When using statistical tools to test hypotheses, we assume that what is being tested is what is called the **null hypothesis**. The null hypothesis is a restatement of the test hypothesis. We might expect that drinking predicts smoking for theoretical reasons. What we statistically test is that drinking and smoking are *not* related. This is the null hypothesis. Our decision is whether to accept or reject the null hypothesis. If we accept the null hypothesis this means that our test hypothesis is not supported, and we go back to our theory to see what went wrong. If we reject the null hypothesis, we have accepted the test hypothesis. How does all this work? First of all, I cannot emphasize enough that the word "significant" does *not* mean that what we found was important, although it seems to be interpreted that way in some of the social science literature. In statistical lingo, significance measures whether or not what we found was due to **chance**. In other words, how confident are we that our correlation was not random?

The clue to this question of confidence or significance is found in some curious numbers. Sometimes you will see P < .05, or P > .05, or P < .001, or .05 > P > .04. The P stands for the **probability** that what we found in these samples *does not* accurately represent the smoking-drinking correlation in this population. What is .05? That is a probability figure. It means that what we found could be sheer chance 5 percent of the time; that is, for every 20 samples that are drawn, one might not be representative of the correlation between smoking and drinking in this population. Most social scientists accept the .05 or less level of significance,[6] for example, .02, .01, .001. In our example, the p value was <.0000, or less than one in ten thousand. We would therefore reject the null hypothesis and conclude that correlation between smoking and drinking was not due to chance. This does not mean that we accept the test hypothesis that smoking and drinking are related; it only means that we reject the statement that they are not related by chance. In this way, scientific "truths" remain tentative and probabilistic. The more a hypothesis resists being disproved, the more confidence we have in it.

Once you have some basic understanding of how to interpret statistical figures, it is then necessary to make some decisions. In the example of the relationship between smoking and drinking we found that the correlation was significant; it was not due to chance. However, our ability to predict one variable from knowledge of the other was very low. We could have reported that the relationship between smoking and drinking was significant and left it at that. A naive reader might conclude that this finding was somehow scientifically important. The media would be alerted; news releases would be written and distributed, and soon everyone would know that "Scientists at Babel University find link between smoking and drinking." To the informed, this kind of statement should result in questions, not unequivocal acceptance. We would want to know something about the sampling procedures. Who and how many were asked what questions? We would want to know the strength of association and the level of significance found by what statistical procedure. Scientists are skeptical and cautious. Before admitting theories and findings into science, tough questions must be asked and answered.

What is important in this discussion is that you become aware of what statistics help us do. First, they describe relationships; second, they enable us to predict outcomes. What statistics cannot do is explain those relationships. To make sense out of the figures, it is necessary to go back to theory, the very theory that generated the hypotheses that were accepted or rejected through the use of statistical procedures.

At this point in the discussion of science, it is hoped that the reader might say, "Now I know what social science is, or at least

I have a better idea of what social scientists do." In the next two sections some of these concepts will be put to work by reviewing examples of the social science endeavor. The first section explores the use of induction; the second, the process of deduction.

Marihuana: An Explanation of Use

Beginning in the 1960s and continuing through the 1970s, there was an "epidemic" of articles and studies of marihuana use in the United States. With the "normalization"[7] of marihuana use (Johnson, O'Malley, and Backman 1986, 1987; Pope et al. 1981), the curiosity about its use diminished and research efforts shifted to other drugs, such as heroin and cocaine. As a result of this intense scrutiny, we have been left with a legacy of empirical generalizations about the social characteristics of marihuana users for that era. In this section we will first review these generalizations and then attempt, through induction, to develop a theory which explains them.

In Erich Goode's (1972, 1989) review of his own research, and that of others, several variables were consistently found to distinguish marihuana users from non-users. In general, high frequency users tended to be males between the ages of eighteen and twenty-five. High school marihuana users were likely to have parents who smoked cigarettes, drank, and consumed prescription drugs. These same marihuana users were themselves more likely to smoke and drink. Goode (1972) also found that university students who smoked cigarettes were twice as likely to try illegal drugs.

Other factors consistently found to be related to marihuana use by students were variables used to measure "social class." The higher the education, income, and occupational prestige of one's parents, the greater the likelihood of trying and using marihuana. This relationship also applied to those who were not in school. Persons with a college education were more likely to be users than those who only graduated from high school. The more financially successful the younger out-of-school users were, the more likely they were to use marihuana.

Use of marihuana was also associated with political preferences. "Liberals" were more likely to use marihuana than "conservatives." A similar relationship was found with religion. Those who attended church more frequently were the least likely to use marihuana. Those who never attended church were among the highest users.

Given these empirical generalizations, is it scientifically sound to conclude that being male, young, a cigarette smoker, a drinker, non-religious, and liberal "causes" marihuana use? How can these findings be explained? Our best explanation is probably to be found in the strongest predictor of marihuana use. In every study that measured this variable, having friends who smoked marihuana was the best predictor of the respondent's use of marihuana. Aside from discounting the popular notion that young people are "turned on" to marihuana by malevolent dope peddlers (they get it from their friends!), this finding suggests a general principle about the formation of human groupings. Whether in reference to marihuana use or to any other behavior, groups are made up of people who share characteristics and experiences in common. In other words, informal groups are composed of people who are similar to each other. What those commonalities are will differ from one society to another and, over time, within a society. That is, the specific social characteristics (age, gender, ethnicity, occupation, and so forth) or experiences (education, military service, citings of UFOs, and so forth) need not be the same in all societies. Even when some visible characteristic, such as gender, is shared by all members of a group, the characteristic is never the only criterion for membership. Something else must be added, and that something is not visible. Thus one might find a group of women who share the experience of being mothers, or a group of men who share the experience of having been in the military. If the similarity criteria (motherhood, military service) are invisible, then how are these groupings distinguished from each other? How are boundaries maintained between these groupings? How is the invisible experience made visible? Here again, any number of physical "things" may perform the symbolic function of distinguishing between groups and groupings. It could be a uniform, a tatoo, a vocabulary, a clothing style, a roach clip,[8] or a behavior such as smoking or not smoking marihuana. The item itself is unimportant as a thing; its importance is what it symbolically represents or what people believe it means. In this case, the items are visual manifestations of boundaries between groupings of people.

The value of this "theory" is that it is not just an explanation of marihuana use; rather, it is a general explanation for informal group formation and the maintenance of boundaries between informal groups. In explaining marihuana use, we might say that people who share characteristics in common are more likely to be attracted to each other and thus more likely to interact and form groups with each other. The general likeness in this case was age. The specific likenesses were social class, religion, educational attainment, and political ideology. The boundary between groups formed out of these similarities was marihuana use or non-use. It could just as well have been clothing or hair styles.

This general theory of attraction and group formation is appealing in three ways. First, it is comprehensive. It can be used to explain both marihuana user and non-user informal groups. Second, it is falsifiable. From this theory one can deduce empirically testable hypotheses. Third, it does not assume any motives for membership in informal groupings. It is not necessary to appeal to psychological drives such as frustration, rebellion, or escapism to "explain" marihuana use. We simply note that membership in informal groups is based on shared similar social characteristics and that marihuana use is one of any number of symbols which function to establish and maintain boundaries between different informal groupings. This is a social science theory.

Not all studies of drug use avoid motivational assumptions. Whether stated or silent, much of the research on drugs is based on the belief that drug use is the result of some social or psychological disturbance. This is the pathological approach. The classic study which used this deductive approach is our next example of research.

Insobriety: A Psychocultural Theory

Several "theories" have been offered to explain why people get drunk. The most frequently cited research among non-social scientists is the work of Donald Horton (1943). His study followed in the tradition of the psychologist C. L. Hull and his associates in their attempts to integrate behavioral theory with psychoanalysis (Field 1962). The classic study (Hovland and Sears 1940) from this perspective found that as the price of cotton fell in the American Deep South, the number of lynchings increased. This was explained by the "frustration → aggression" hypothesis. In this case, the falling prices of cotton led to individual frustration (a psychological state), which in turn was behaviorally reduced by lynchings. Horton's study adopted this same "theory" and tested it using cross-cultural data obtained from the Human Relations Area Files (HRAF). Because this data source is used throughout this book, it is imperative that readers have an understanding of what it contains, as well as its merits and limitations.

The Human Relations Area Files (HRAF)

In 1937, the Cross-Cultural Survey was founded by the Institute of Human Relations at Yale University. It was an ambitious attempt to codify what was known about human societies at that time. In 1941 George Peter Murdock used that survey to generate empirical generalizations about kinship in his classic book, *Social Structure* (1949). At the same time, Murdock designed what was to become the Human Relations Area Files (HRAF). Since then there have been over 300 studies which used these data (Levinson and Malone 1980).

The files contain original ethnographic data that have been sorted by cultural categories. The categories, which have been numbered, enable a researcher to examine what an ethnographer wrote on a particular topic for a specific culture. For example, suppose you wanted to know about the use of tobacco by the Yanomamö Indians in South America. All you would need to do is locate the file on the Yanomamö, and then turn to category 276, "Tobacco." There you would find the original ethnographic descriptions reported by the ethnographer(s) who studied the Yanomamö. Or you would find nothing because tobacco was not mentioned in any of the ethnographies. As one might expect, not every topic included in the HRAF is discussed in every ethnography.

Table 2.3 shows a copy of one page from HRAF. On the top of the page there is a source code. The ethnographer was Hans Becher (1960). The file number is SQ18 and the name for the file is Yanoama. This spelling is used because Becher's ethnography was the first to be included in the files. The handwritten words under Yanoama—Surára and Pakidái—are the names of two Yanoama groups studied by Becher. Along the left margin, one finds numbers. Each of these numbers identifies a specific cultural category. The number we are interested in is 276, tobacco. On this page, and on the following pages, this number will appear with a ● next to it. We can read these pages to see how the Yanoama use tobacco. After reading the material on tobacco for several of different cultures, we should begin to get a sense of the different uses of tobacco. It is then possible to code tobacco use. Our code might be a simple dichotomy coded as 1 or 2, with 1 = no tobacco, and 2 = tobacco. We then sample[9] different cultures and code them for tobacco use or non-use. This of course is a time-consuming and meaningless exercise unless we relate tobacco use to some other cultural practice. Depending on our theory, and the derived hypotheses, we would also code for other variables. Then we would construct a table

Table 2.3. **Sample Page from HRAF**

2: Becher--144 E-5   (1955-1956) 1960   SQ18 Yanoama SQ18
Sura'ra,
Paki dq'i

884 /67 cont./

86 poisonous snake of South America, which is over three meters

[302] long. The painting is supposed to help banish the dangers that
emanate from this and other poisonous snakes. As daily nourish-

[825] ment the two candidates may take only a ripe banana and half a

[262] liter of water. After two months they are very thin and appear to be
nothing but skin and bones. In order to suppress their feeling

● [276] of hunger and thirst, they constantly have the roll of tobacco
mixed with water and ashes between their lower or upper lip and

[782] teeth (see p.190). Moreover, they must blow large pinches of
the snuff-powder into each other's noses several time a day in

[276] order to make contact with the gigantic animal and plant spirits--
hekura'. Thus, they pass their training period in a regular trance-
state.

884 It is worth noting that the initiation rites of the male members

756 of the tribe take place comparatively late, and that in this way

776 all men are gradually trained as medicine-man helpers.
Through this, the Surara chief Hewemão explained to me, they
are able to protect themselves and their families against sickness
and accidents in an emergency. If, for example, a man is
threatened along the way by a poisonous snake or a jaguar, he is
now in a position to banish the danger by calling upon the tutelary
spirits. He must never fail to thank the hekura' after a successful
hunting expedition or a good harvest, however, for otherwise he

795 would incur their anger. Even when his wife, one of his children,

[753] or a relative falls ill, he himself must first try, by means of song
and dance in which he addresses the hekura', to hurl the sickness
back to the hostile tribe from which it was sent. Only if his efforts
remain unsuccessful may he appeal for the aid of the chief, who
is always willing and, with help of 8-9 assistants, carries out a
great rekura' (cure). Thus, during the day /68/ or at night among
the Surara and Pakidai one frequently sees one man, or often even
several men, praying or attempting to cure a member of the

[276] family. Before that, however, they must take snuff-powder because
contact with the hekura' can be made only in a state of intoxica-

[533] tion. The songs are somewhat monotonous and are combined with
animal sounds, animal movements, such as the beating of wings,

hopping, etc.

showing the code for tobacco matched with the code for the other characteristic(s). The next step is to calculate the appropriate correlation and significance figures to determine the correlation between tobacco use and the other variables.

If we used the files to examine the linkages between various practices of the Yanomamö, we would be "doing" cultural relativism. **Cultural relativism** assumes that each culture must be considered in its entirety and that each culture is different from all other cultures. If we compared bits of information from different cultures, we would be doing a **cross-cultural** or a **holocultural** study. The comparative approach should not be confused with cultural relativism. Comparativists suggest that it is possible to compare specific practices out of their cultural context to test hypotheses on the relationships between variables. The goal of this approach is to be able to make relational statements that apply to all cultures, not just one or two.

Horton's Theory of Drunkenness

Research which confirms cultural expectations are often cited as "proof" for such beliefs. A classic example of this is Donald Horton's (1943) study of drinking. Frequently referenced by those outside social science and equally assumed by many within (Heath 1987, 39), this study illustrates the tentative nature of social science findings and a procedure used in the scientific enterprise. Horton's explanation for drunkenness, or what he calls **insobriety**, was the first to use HRAF. Horton observed that insobriety varied cross-culturally. The question he asked was, "What accounts for this variation?" He suggests that drunkenness is a specific application of a more general psychological theory which states that frustration leads to aggression. His translation of the general theory required two assumptions, or **axioms**. The first of these was that "the primary function of drinking alcohol in all societies is to produce drunkenness." This is followed by the assumption, "The primary function of drunkenness in all societies is the reduction of anxiety" (223). Thus, for Horton the frustration ➔ aggression theory is restated as the anxiety ➔ insobriety theory. He argues that if these axioms are correct, cross-cultural data should support the hypothesis: The higher the level of anxiety in a culture, the higher the level of insobriety.

To test this hypothesis, Horton had to measure both anxiety and insobriety. Although there are no direct measures of anxiety in the HRAF, Horton suggested that it could be measured indirectly by combining descriptions that are found in the files. These included subsistence type, availability of food, warfare frequency, sorcery, and premarital sexual freedom. His review of ethnographies that contained information on these characteristics resulted in the variable **subsistence insecurity**, which he dichotomized into "high" or "low." From the ethnographic descriptions, Horton developed a three-point scale for insobriety. Phrases such as "excessive drinking," "drinking to unconsciousness," "great drunken orgies," and "complete drunkenness" were coded as **strong insobriety**. **Moderate insobriety** was drunkenness that did not continue for days or that did not end in unconsciousness. **Slight insobriety** is where the ethnographer stated that alcohol was rarely consumed or intoxication was rare.

At the time that Horton did this research, there were only 125 cultures in the Cross-Cultural Survey. From this number, Horton found 56 societies in the files that had information on insobriety and his measure of anxiety. Twelve of the societies were located in Asia; 13 were in Africa; 6 were in Oceania. Of the remaining 25, 14 were in South America, and 11 were in North America. The first step in testing his theory was to read the ethnographies in the files and code each for his variables. The results for cultures in Horton's sample are shown in table 2.4.

Reading from left to right, we note that the Toda had a medium rating on insobriety coupled with a low rating on subsistence insecurity. The Mongol and the Chukchee tied on strong insobriety and high subsistence insecurity. The Kazak were graded slight for insobriety and low for subsistence insecurity. We could, of course, describe each tribe separately, but these individual observations would only tell us the linkage between insobriety and subsistence insecurity for that particular tribe. We are more interested in the

Table 2.4.

Tribe	Degree of Insobriety			Subsistence Insecurity	
	SL	M	S	L	H
Toda		X		X	
Mongol			X		X
Kazak	X			X	
Chukchee			X		X
Yakut		X			X

general relationship between these two variables. Thus, we must summarize the individual tribal data. This is done by constructing another table (table 2.5). We are now at the point where we can convert the names of the tribes into frequencies for each of the variables. This yields another table (table 2.6).

Table 2.5. **Insobriety/Subsistence Insecurity Rating, by Tribe**

		Subsistence Insecurity	
		Low	**High**
Insobriety	Slight	Kazak	
	Moderate	Toda	Yakut
	Strong		Mongol Chukchee

Table 2.6.
Numerical Frequencies for Insobriety/Subsistence

		Subsistence Insecurity		
		Low	**High**	**Total**
Insobriety	Slight	1	0	1
	Moderate	1	1	2
	Strong	0	2	2
	Total	2	3	5

Using this table with numerical frequencies, it is now possible to apply various statistical procedures to determine the strength of the correlation between our variables. But more importantly, the relationships we find (or do not find) can be extended from specific cultures to a more general statement on the relationship between variables. This is an important consideration that should not be overlooked. Often in the social science literature we note specific limitations on research findings. For example, results may apply only to a particular high school or college campus. They may be further limited to a specific educational aggregate, or ethnic category, or to males and females. From this, the reader might conclude that the goal of social science is to make statements about specific populations or samples. I would insist that this conclusion is wrong. The goal of social science research, like all science research, is to test relationships between variables, regardless of the specific samples that are studied. Horton is not interested in the Toda or the Chukchee, or any of the other cultures in his sample. His concern is with testing hypotheses derived from a theory. What he wants to know is the relationship between anxiety and drinking, and it is only through larger samples of cultures that he is able determine what that relationship is.

Horton initially thought that anxiety could be measured by subsistence alone. He suggested that some systems produced more anxiety than others. In his sample there were five different subsistence types. Three of these (hunting, herding, and lower agriculture) he ranked "high" in subsistence insecurity. The other two (intermediate and higher agriculture) he ranked "low." The number of distinctions in his initial measurement of insobriety had to be reduced because his sample was not large enough to include cultures that represented all the possible relationships between drunkenness and anxiety. He therefore combined slight and moderate into one category and left strong as another category. Using these measures, he constructed table 2.7.

Table 2.7. **Association Between Type of Subsistence and Sobriety**

Type of Subsistence	Insobriety		Total
	Strong	Moderate to Slight	
Hunting, Herding, and Lower Agriculture	25	10	35
Intermediate and Higher Agriculture	10	11	21
Total	35	21	56

Gamma = .46   .10 < P < .05

To test the relationship between these variables, Horton used the statistical tool available to him at the time. I have reanalyzed his data with a measure that can be interpreted the same as r^2. Although a rather strong association was found between subsistence and insobriety (46 percent), the level of significance was more than .05. Although the correlation is not statistically significant, Horton argued that the hypothesis was supported if one considered only the extremes in subsistence. At the lowest levels of subsistence one found the highest level of insobriety. Conversely, in the higher agriculture category one found the lowest level of insobriety. This observation led to further refinement of the original subsistence variable. He suggested that the highest anxiety would be found if one controlled for occasional famines due to drought, insect plagues, famine due to cattle plagues, or seasonal periods of starvation or food scarcity. This new variable he called subsistence insecurity. Data on subsistence insecurity were available for 43 of the original 56 societies. Using subsistence insecurity as his new independent variable, he constructed table 2.8.

Table 2.8. Association Between Subsistence Insecurity and Insobriety

Subsistence Insecurity	Insobriety		Total
	Strong	Moderate to Slight	
High	9	2	11
Moderate or Low	13	19	32
Total	22	21	43

Gamma = .73   .02 < P < .01

Horton's controls not only increased the Gamma coefficient, but the significance was a much more acceptable .02 < P < .01. On the basis of this finding, Horton concluded that subsistence insecurity is the specific type of anxiety that resulted in high insobriety.

What we note here is the interplay between theory and research. By altering the specific measurements for each variable, correlations could be maximized. Further, by tinkering with these measurements he was able to restate the original theory in more specific terms. None of this, of course, "proves" that anxiety determines drunkenness, and several researchers have challenged Horton's conclusions.

Peter Field (1962) added six additional societies to Horton's sample and included updated scales for drunkenness and other variables. He argued that drinking is not the only means by which anxiety is reduced. For example, a society faced with food shortages might respond to this condition through a system of ritual magic which seeks to coerce a reluctant god to supply food (50). His re-analysis of the data suggested that the organization of society is the basis of drunkenness, not anxiety. Hunters and gatherers do have higher rates of insobriety than other types of societies, but not because of insecurity or anxiety. His correlations demonstrate that insobriety is related to the informal, friendly, personal interaction that is characteristic of egalitarian hunting and gathering societies.

Conversely, sobriety is correlated with formal, hierarchical social structure such as those found in state-level societies.

Others (Bacon, Child and Berry 1965) rejected both Horton's and Field's interpretations of drunkenness. They contend that patterns of drinking were linked to anxiety and conflict over "dependency needs," and suggested that:

> . . . amounts and patterns of alcohol consumption by adults have their antecedents partly in the degree and pattern of nurturance in infancy, the extent of demands for self-reliance and achievement in childhood, and the extent to which the expression of dependent needs is permitted in adult life. (31)

To test this hypothesis they sampled 139 societies. This sample represented the world, except Europe. Each society was coded for drinking behavior and indulgence of dependency. They concluded that: "indulgence of dependence is negatively related to frequency of drinking," and "societies which indulge dependency needs in infancy and childhood tend to show less alcohol consumption than those which are less indulgent" (35). The first finding suggests that when a society discourages expression of dependency and weakness (emotional displays), drunkenness will be more frequent. This may, of course, vary by sex or other social variables. For example, if men are discouraged and women are encouraged to display dependency, then men will engage in drunken deportment and women will not.

The most recent analysis of the statistical relationship between drinking and other variables was done by James Schafer (1976). He sampled 57 independent tribal societies. His two measurements of drinking were drunken brawling (yes/no) and extreme male insobriety (yes/no). These were correlated with 12 other variables taken from the literature on drinking. Drunken brawling was more strongly correlated with "simple political system," a system with little if any central authority, than it was with extreme male insobriety. The highest correlate of extreme male insobriety was low social complexity followed by social class distinctions absent. Other variables such as malicious, capricious spirits; residency; and kinship showed a very weak correlation to insobriety.

So what "causes" insobriety? This abbreviated review does not cover all the studies using the HRAF on this topic, nor does it provide us with an unequivocal answer to our question. The search for correlations between isolated or limited variables plucked from cultural wholes can, at best, only offer partial answers to this question. The sometimes contradictory correlations with different samples serve to illustrate a limitation of correlational studies. At the same time, the numerical measurement of variables complies with the social science goal of being "objective." If there is a lesson from this review, it is that no single bit of research constitutes a "final" word on theory. Redefinitions of variables and their measurement goes on constantly in science and our ability to understand research findings rests on an ability to "read" results, not as words, but as measurements.

Whatever the limitations or benefits of statistical analysis, it is clear that social scientists will continue to use this tool. Readers of social science studies should therefore be prepared to wade through tables of findings and statistical summaries. What has been presented here does not pretend to cover the vast area of statistical analysis and interpretation. It is hoped only that the reader has a heightened appreciation for how statistics are used in the social sciences.

Summary: The Question of Objectivity

In chapter one we noted that the research strategies of social science were objective rather than subjective. The issue of whether social science is or can be objective has stirred much debate. One view holds that because both the subject matter and the observers are human, objectivity is impossible. In part this perspective assumes that humans are capable of changing both their minds and their behavior when they will. Therefore any attempt to predict or explain humans is doomed to be inaccurate. I would question both of these assumptions. First, the object of social science is not to understand people. Rather, the object is to uncover the rules which govern human behavior. Social science, with an emphasis on science, is not a humanistic adventure. As scientists we must be willing to accept the fundamental premise that human activities are determined by broader structures that are not subject to willful alterations. The search for the principles which underlie those structures must follow some methodological guidelines which, for lack of a better word, are objective. The measure of that objectivity is simple. Whatever the methodology—participant-observation, experiment, or survey—researchers must demonstrate attempts to falsify their questions or hypotheses. In ethnography this measure is found in the ethnographic veto, a counterobservation in another cultural setting. In the experiment or the survey, the use of more controls serves this same purpose. In short, there is no one procedure to increase falsifiability; but the greater the effort to falsify, the greater our confidence in the objectivity of research.

What's Next?

Chapters 1 and 2 gave a brief guided tour of the rules which define the social science approach. In the following chapters we will illustrate how those rules have been used to research and therefore understand drug use as a social scientific issue or question. In these chapters the concepts and tools presented in the first two chapters will be used to review the linkages and correlations between drug use and several areas of social life. In chapter 3 the question is whether responses to drugs are learned or result from the physiological effects of the chemical ingredients in the drugs. This is followed by seven chapters in which specific social science issues and questions are reviewed. The question in chapter 4 is how drugs diffuse in time and space. Where do specific drugs come from, and how did they arrive where they are today? Chapter 5 examines the effects of social and cultural change on drug use. More specifically, we ask how changes in society and culture affect the acceptance or rejection of drugs. Chapter 6 explores the dominant theoretical assumption in the social sciences, namely functionalism. This approach assumes that social practices, if they are persistent, contribute in some way to the maintenance of social order. Using this perspective, we will review the function of drugs in several different societies. The next four chapters focus more narrowly on specific human activities and drugs. Chapter 7 reviews the relationship between drugs and "religion." Chapter 8 looks at drugs as part of larger economic structures. How drugs symbolically represent efforts to control behavior and hence insure predictability is examined in chapter 9. Finally, in chapter 10 the topic of drugs and political structures is reviewed. The final chapter attempts to pull the previous chapters together into a comprehensive statement on drugs and drug use from the social science perspective.

As readers go through the upcoming chapters they may question their pedagogue's qualifications to serve as escort! Some of the material they encounter may violate "conventional wisdom," "common sense," or cherished assumptions, or they may just be confusing. If this confusion occurs, return to these first two chapters and review the social science approach. In other words, "Take two chapters and reread the troublesome parts again."

Endnotes

[1] I placed quotes around the word "group" to indicate that the word is often used in experiments in a way that is different from how group was defined in chapter 1.

A group is a number of interacting people. In experiments there may be interaction among the subjects.

2 The experimental and the control "groups" need not be distinct units composed of different subjects. They could be the same subjects with and without the treatment. For example, one might be interested in the effects of a drug on eye-hand coordination. Subjects are asked to perform a series of tasks involving eye-hand coordination, and the results are noted. The same subjects are then given the drug, and the same set of tasks is repeated. Since the subjects are perfectly matched, any differences in the performance of the task are assumed to be the effect of the treatment, in this case the drug.

3 Although 100 households is the sample size we think is large enough to represent the total population, it is customary to increase the original sample goal. This is done to avoid the problem of people not being at home, or the possibility that the house no longer exists.

4 Having just written this, I realized that this is probably not an "emic" interpretation. When students say "grading on the curve," they usually mean some system of adding points to exam scores so that there are few "D's" and even fewer "F's." Using this emic understanding of the "normal" curve would result in the distribution being *skewed* toward the A-B end of the distribution.

5 We seem to be asking ourselves a lot of questions. Actually, I have dragged you into this process by using the collective "we." Scientists do talk to themselves all the time. The real issue is whether these internal conversations eventually lead to questions that can be answered scientifically. In other words, are these thoughts scientific? The first two chapters of this book are outlines to thinking (asking questions) in a social science manner. The rest of this book is an illustration of how social scientists think.

6 There is no statistical argument for accepting the .05 level of significance. Rather, it is an arbitrary norm within social science.

7 I use the term "normalization" here to describe the general findings that experience with marihuana was nationwide by the late 1970s. Users exceeded non-users among high school seniors, and the differences in social characteristics between users and non-users were, for all statistical purposes, nonexistent. See Johnson, O'Malley, and Bachman (1986, 1987) and Pope (1981).

8 A roach clip is a device that is used to hold a marihuana cigarette that has been smoked down to a size where it is difficult to hold in the fingers without being burned.

9 One does not randomly sample cultures from the HRAF. Depending upon the research question and the specific hypotheses, a sample consists of all the cultures that have information on the variables you wish to relate. Thus, if one were interested in the effects of altitude on cultural practices, one might sample cultures from high, middle, and low altitudes.

chapter 3

Human Behavior as Learned Behavior

T he question of the relative contributions of biology versus learning in understanding human behavior has a rather long history in the social sciences. Nowhere is this debate more evident than in the study of drugs. On one side of this polemic is the argument that the use of substances to alter the senses is one of the basic drives in all animals, sharing top billing with food, water, and sex (Siegel 1989; Weil 1973). Observations of animals from bees to primates suggest that, when given the opportunity, many species will ingest plants that alter consciousness before satisfying the need for food and water. In the hierarchy of needs, the quest for pleasure through consuming intoxicants takes precedence over even survival behaviors. Those who take this position argue that humans are biological beings; like bees and primates, they share the need to experience altered states of consciousness. Although the word "instinct" is not used by respectable scientists today, advocates of the biological explanation of drug use insist that drug use is an unlearned need or drive.

The other side of this debate suggests that the consumption of "drugs," like any other pattern of behavior, is learned. The culture into which one is born not only dictates what will be consumed but also defines the behavioral outcomes of that consumption. Proponents of this argument would eschew the position there is anything "natural" in the consumption of drugs. They would point out that if there were a "need" to become intoxicated, that need would be shared by all humans and therefore would not be helpful in explaining the wide variations both within and between cultures in the consumption of intoxicants.

The question addressed in this chapter is, "Does the taking of a drug *cause* a particular behavioral outcome, or must the behavior be learned?" In the following pages we shall present materials which directly or indirectly address this issue.

Alcohol and Culture

This is the title of an article by David Mandelbaum (1965) in which the author suggests some problems with those studies of drunkenness we presented in the last chapter. He points out that "drunkenness cannot be understood apart from drinking in general, and drinking cannot be understood apart from the characteristic features of social relations of which it is a part and which are reflected and expressed in the acts of drinking" (287). Thus, drunkenness should not be equated with "alcoholism," even though the behavioral outcome may be quite the same. In every society there are norms which prescribe "normal" times for drinking, and "normal" behaviors when "drunk." When these norms are violated, the violator is socially defined as pathological, alcoholic, criminal, or some other deviant status.

The practice of drinking alcoholic beverages is geographically widespread and extends back before recorded history. In reviewing this practice historically and cross-culturally, one notes a wide variety of meanings associated with this practice. The Kofyar of Africa (Netting 1962) believed that beer is an essential part of religious salvation and that those who drink it are blessed. The Hopi and Pueblo Indians believe that drinking was a threat to their way of life and banned it (Benedict 1959; Parsons 1939). The effects of drinking also vary. Among Japanese, small amounts are reported to result in a very relaxed convivial state. Aleut Indians become quite aggressive after consuming small amounts. The record for drinking probably goes to the Camba of eastern Bolivia. They frequently drink large amounts of a distillate of sugar cane which contains 89 percent ethyl alcohol (Heath 1962). The purpose of their drinking is to induce unconsciousness. In spite of this, the Camba never mention anything like the Western notion of a hangover, only irritation to the mouth and throat. Drinking patterns may also reflect changes in culture. In India, for example, during its period of egalitarianism, all men drank. With the development of the hierarchical caste system, drinking was permitted for only some of the castes. The recent shift back to egalitarianism ushered in more equal drinking patterns, or abstinence. So great are the variations in drinking consequences that Mandelbaum concludes that it is culture that determines the consequences of alcohol.

This short review by no means exhausts the variation in consumption patterns found throughout the world. It does question the position of absolutism that suggests that alcohol, in and of itself, *determines* behavior. This position may be visualized:

INDEPENDENT VARIABLE   DEPENDENT VARIABLE
Alcohol ————————————▶ Behavior
(variable)   (variable)

The argument for this model is that as the blood alcohol level in the body increases, there will be a corresponding change in behavior. The relationship is reproduced it in table 3.1 (Bogen 1932; modified from Ray 1972, 89).

There can be little doubt that the intake of alcohol affects such motor activities as eye-hand coordination and other motor

Table 3.1. **Behavioral Consequences of Blood Alcohol Level**

Blood Alcohol Level	Behavior
Less than .03%	dull and dignified
At .05%	dashing and debonair
At .10%	dangerous and devilish
At .20%	dizzy and disturbed
At .25%	disgusting and disheveled
At .30%	delirious and disoriented and surely drunk
At .35%	dead drunk
At .60%	probably dead

responses. There is also no question about how the body metabolizes alcohol. What about the other "behavioral" responses suggested by Bogen? What about all those "d" words like dull, devilish, disturbed, disgusting, and disoriented? Those who accept this model are in an awkward position when confronted with the variations in drinking behavior gleaned from the cross-cultural observations mentioned above. The response to these empirical variations may come in what Craig MacAndrew and Robert Edgerton (1969) call "conventional wisdom."

> The essential force of the conventional understanding has been both clear and consistent through the ages. When we are drunk we do sometimes do things that we would "never" do when we are sober. And whether we choose to explain this fact in terms of some neurological version of an alcohol-induced "cortical disinhibition" or, as the psychoanalysts do, in terms of an alcohol-induced paralysis, dissolution, or castration (take your pick) of the superego, we are simply selecting different words to express an essentially similar conception of how this assumedly self-evident loss of restraint comes about. The general thrust of the position is unvarying: *Just as changes in the efficiency with which we exercise our sensorimotor capabilities are consequent upon the action of alcohol on our innards, so too are changes in the manner in which we comport ourselves with our fellows.* (10–11, emphasis theirs)

Thus drunkenness has been used to explain such inversions of "normal" behavior as promiscuity, fighting, swearing, riots, theft, murder, lewdness, and any other behavior defined as "loss of control." This model might be visualized:

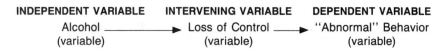

INDEPENDENT VARIABLE	INTERVENING VARIABLE	DEPENDENT VARIABLE
Alcohol ⟶	Loss of Control ⟶	"Abnormal" Behavior
(variable)	(variable)	(variable)

Note that in this model, the behavioral outcomes are always a violation of social norms, or at least in variance with them. Readers might want to consider if they have ever heard of alcohol being used to explain exemplary behaviors. For example, have you ever heard the following statements?

> He was a gentle man and never swore because he was a drunk.
>
> He was a good provider and never cheated on his wife because he drank.
>
> She never broke a law because of her drinking.

She was the best mother one could have because she drank.

She was an honor roll student because of her drinking.

To test this model we return to the work of MacAndrew and Edgerton. By examining drunken comportment ethnographically we can determine whether it differs from everyday behavior. The Abipone Indians of Paraguay have been described as a cheerful, gentle and kind people who avoid any verbal or behavioral discord. Conversely, when drunk they are hostile, aggressive, and murderous (Dobrizhoffer 1822). In contrast, the Yuruna Indians of South America are fierce and warlike, but when inebriated they withdraw and act as though no one else existed (Nimuendajú 1963). In William Mangin's (1957) account of the Indians of Vicos in the Peruvian Andes, there is yet another behavioral consequence of drunkenness. These Indians drink ceremonially, and there are many ceremonies. Drinking during these ceremonies usually results in sustained drunkenness by both males and females over several days. Mangin reports that crime is more frequent among the sober than the drunk, and the level of aggressiveness differs little from aggressive behavior in general. The only activity that seemed to increase during these drunken episodes was premarital sex, but not for the reasons one might expect. Some males purposely remained sober during the festivals so they could sneak off with a girl who had also remained sober. Extramarital sex, which was viewed as disruptive, was an activity of the sober. One could continue with further examples which refute the loss of inhibitions explanation for drunken comportment. What is clear is that alcohol, in and of itself, has no specific behavioral outcome, either directly or through lessening of cultural constraints. The determinant of behavior, drunk or sober, is culture—and culture is learned.

The model which suggests that culture, not alcohol in and of itself, is the best predictor of behavior associated with drinking might be visualized:

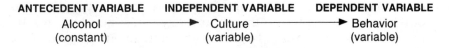

ANTECEDENT VARIABLE   INDEPENDENT VARIABLE   DEPENDENT VARIABLE
Alcohol ────────▶ Culture ────────▶ Behavior
(constant)   (variable)   (variable)

We have noted that the behavior of people who consume alcohol varies cross-culturally, yet alcohol as a chemical substance is the same, a constant. We are left with a logical dilemma. How can something that is the same explain something that is different? Can a constant explain a variable? The answer is that a constant cannot explain a variable. In this model, the variable is culture. As has been noted, the behavioral outcomes of consuming alcohol depend upon culture. It is true that we as biological beings have a metabolic system that processes alcohol in the same way, no matter where we live or what our culture is. This metabolic process is not learned; it is biologically determined and is constant to us as a biological species. The behavioral consequences of drinking alcohol are learned. We need go no further than any five-year-old child in any culture to learn what that behavior is. Without the benefit of consuming alcohol, that child will accurately act out appropriate drinking comportment.

If drinking behavior cannot be predicted without the benefit of understanding the characteristics of culture, perhaps other drugs will cooperate with the drug ⟶ behavior model. One such possibility is the explanation for why witches ride brooms.

Witches, Brooms and Altered States of Consciousness

The confessions of witches during the Renaissance that they flew through the air and engaged in orgies with demons have been dismissed by many modern scholars as mental aberrations of demented people. They insist that such behaviors are violations of the laws of physics, coupled with beliefs about the existence of supernatural beings. Julio Baroja (1964) and Michael Harner (1974) suggest there are a variety of plants of the potato family found in the New and Old World that possibly "explain" these reported experiences of witches and others. Included in this grouping of plants would be several species of the Datura genus which go by such popular names as Jimsonweed or Jamestown weed (*Datura stramonium*), loco weed, devil's weed, and so forth. Similar to the Datura in effect are mandrake (*Mandragora officinarum*), henbane (*Hyoscyamus niger*), and belladonna (*Atropa belladonna*). Each of these plants contain numerous alkaloids—colorless, complex and bitter bases containing nitrogen and oxygen. When ingested by humans and other animals, they produce hallucinogenic effects. These alkaloids include atropine, hyoscyamine, and scopolamine. One attribute of this category of alkaloids is that they are absorbable through intact skin. Thus, Harner argues that if the skin is rubbed with an ointment made of these plants, atropine would be absorbed into the system and the person would experience an altered state of consciousness, including the feeling that one flew through the air or danced with demons. Thus, accounts of witches' brew, ointments, salves, and other concoctions used to anoint the bodies of witches may be more than mystical fancy. What about the image that witches rode brooms? Harner suggests that:

> The use of a staff or broom was undoubtedly more than a symbolic Freudian act, serving as an applicator for the atropine-containing plant to the sensitive vaginal membranes as well as providing the suggestion of riding on a steed, a typical illusion of the witches' ride to the Sabbat. (131)

To the outsider observing a person using witches' brew, there were no changes in behavior. People did not fly about; they did not change into a wolf or other animal; and they were not involved in an orgy. The only behavior observed is that they would fall into a deep sleep from which they were unable to be awakened. Reports of the "trip" they experienced had to come from the users.

The potions that were mixed to achieve this altered mental state varied, but what Harner and others were trying to explain was the pharmacological basis of the experiences reported by so-called witches. What was critical to any mixture was one of the many hallucinogens that were available. What can be said of the experience itself? Is the drug itself responsible for specific images such as flying, meeting with the devil, or a transformation into an animal? On this point, Harner is clear. The differing results of these drugs is a function of the culture in which the person lives. In that historical period of Western culture where witches were believed to exist, the experiences of people reflected those beliefs. The drug or drugs do not "cause" the contents of the altered state; they only reify the existing beliefs.

LSD and "Psychotic" Behavior

The effects of LSD (d-lysergic acid diethylamide) on perceptions was discovered quite by accident in 1943. Albert Hoffman, a Swiss chemist, had been working on synthesizing the active ingredients in plants that were claimed to produce altered states of consciousness. On April 16 of that year he had fallen ill and had to be escorted home. After an initial feeling of dizziness, he began to experience quite vivid visual sensations. After two hours, the symptoms disappeared. Although animal experiments with LSD had not yielded anything noteworthy, Hoffman thought that his temporary illness might have been the result of inadvertently ingesting the drug. To test that hypothesis, he administered the drug to himself. His experiences this time were much more intense. He noted that:

> ... the following were the most outstanding symptoms: vertigo, visual disturbances, the faces of those around me appeared as grotesque, colored masks; marked motoric unrest, alternating with paralysis; an intermittent feeling in the head, limbs, and the entire body, as if they were filled with lead; dry, constricted sensation in the throat; feeling of choking; clear recognition of my condition, in which state I sometimes observed, in the manner of an independent, neutral observer, that I shouted half insanely or babbled incoherent words. Occasionally I felt as if I were out of my body. (Cashman 1966, 31)

During and after World War II, there was some interest by the military and the CIA in LSD. Psychiatrists, interpreting the response to LSD as similar to those they saw in psychotic patients, took the drug to gain insight into this condition. Like many other new drugs, it followed Abraham Kaplan's (1964) "Law of the Instrument." This law states: "Give a small boy a hammer, and he will soon find that things all about him need pounding." Psychiatrists had a new hammer in LSD and were soon administering it to a wide variety of patients with different symptoms, from paranoia to alcoholism to terminal cancer. The results of these "experiments" were inconclusive. The boy eventually became bored with his pounding, and experimentation with LSD stopped (Brecher 1972).

In the early 1960s LSD became part of the public consciousness in the United States and Europe. Timothy Leary and Richard Alpert, both researchers at Harvard University, were using LSD on "normal" subjects to explore "consciousness expansion." Their research soon became a media event, and reports of users becoming psychotic were commonplace. The claim was made that LSD would produce (cause) psychosis, and persons under the influence could and would engage in behaviors that were dangerous to themselves and others. As a result, LSD was defined as a dangerous drug and legislation was passed which criminalized its use.

There is little doubt that Hoffman and many others experienced something after taking LSD—but what did this experience mean? One of the earliest discussions of this question was by the sociologist Howard Becker (1967). Becker points out that our interpretations of experiences arise out of social interaction with others. Meanings are learned, and to be socially significant, they must be shared. Becker's own work on marihuana use found that becoming a "user" involved a series of steps, during which novices had to be told what they were experiencing (1953). Becker argues that the reports of psychosis by users of LSD come from "unexpected" responses to the drug coupled with social definitions of meaning. We know we are "normal" when the meanings we give to experiences or objects correspond to that of our fellows—but what if they do not?

> In any society whose culture contains notions of sanity and insanity, the person who finds his subjective state altered in the way described may think he has become insane. We learn at an early age that a person who "acts funny," "sees things," "hears things," "or has other bizarre and unusual experiences may have become "crazy," "nuts," "loony" or a host of other synonyms. (186)

What might lead users to the conclusion that they are "crazy" or have had a psychotic episode? Becker suggests that such a conclusion may come from the effects of LSD. The responses to this drug include a wide variety of visual, auditory, and motor experiences. Users hear things, see things, and do things that are outside the normal range of experience, and there is nothing to suggest that, like alcohol, one will get better in the morning. Readers might imagine their response if they felt they had had a few drinks—without the benefit of having consumed any alcohol. To have a certain feeling after a few drinks is perfectly "normal." To have that same feeling independent of drinking would probably result in some noticeable feelings of anxiety that needed immediate medical attention. With LSD, the uncertainty of the drug experience results in anxiety. It is an anxiety produced by how one interprets the drug experience, not the drug. In other words, one defines oneself as "crazy" or having a psychotic episode. Becker goes on to argue that this interpretation will disappear with repeated LSD experiences *along with* the development of a shared interpretation of those experiences. This is precisely what happened. The development of learned interpretations of the drug experience eliminated uncertainty. One no longer hears of "bad trips" and bizarre behaviors in association with LSD. The drug experience has been "normalized."

What we note with the example of both the witches and LSD users is the importance of culture in the interpretation of experience. In a culture where witches are "real," any translation of drug effect which includes references to witches would make sense to both the user and the non-user. In a culture where psychosis is "real," the definition of the experience with LSD as psychotic makes sense. The diagnosis of psychosis comes from verbal statements and behavioral clues. There is no physiological test for psychosis. If someone reports these out-of-body experiences to a psychiatrist, they will most likely be defined as psychotic and "treated" accordingly (Rosenhan 1973). Thus, the interpretation of the LSD user would be confirmed by others, such as police, health workers, friends, and so forth. With the development of a shared definition of the LSD experience by users that excludes any reference to psychosis, the drug becomes normalized.

Coca Leaf Chewing: Some Competing Explanations

Pharmacognosy is the descriptive branch of pharmacology that is concerned with crude drugs and medicinal plants. Those specializing in this area rely upon emic accounts from native populations about the non-food use of plants, herbs, and roots which form native systems of ethnopharmacology. Many of the so-called modern drugs that are an integral part of our pharmacopeia have been used for thousands of years by native populations around the world. For example, Hoffman's laboratory work on LSD was an attempt to synthesize the active ingredients in plants which had been reported by native users to bring about altered states of consciousness. In this section, we shall review a debate on the meanings and functions of coca leaf chewing by Indian groups in South America.

One result of the expansion of Western culture into previously unexplored areas of the world was exposure to the use of native plants to cure disease and illness. When the Spanish Conquistadors first contacted the Incas in the sixteenth century, they found them using the leaf of the coca plant as a chewable "money."[1] Although this practice of coca leaf chewing never found its way back to Europe, the coca plant did come to the attention of both European and American chemists. These early forerunners of modern pharmacology began including coca leaf extracts as an ingredient in many medicines and popular drinks, including Coca Cola. In spite of attempts by the Spanish to outlaw the practice of coca leaf chewing, it is still found today in South America, primarily among high altitude populations. The question we ask in this section is whether this practice can be considered a "natural" medicine, invented by these populations to "cure" physical responses to living in a high altitude environment—or is it something else?

The coca shrub (*Erythroxylon coca*) is widely cultivated in the warm moist valleys along the eastern slope of the Bolivian and Peruvian Andes between the altitudes of 300m and 1,800m (Rodriguez 1965). The plant, 1–4m high, is covered with small, dark-green leaves which are chewed throughout the Andean highlands, chiefly by Aymará and Quechua (ketch-wa) Indians. The leaves are known to contain no less than 14 alkaloids of potential pharmacological importance (Martin 1970), of which the best-known is cocaine. The Andean Indians chew coca leaves along with alkaline ashes of various edible plants. Lowland tribes use another species of the coca plant with a lower cocaine content. They prepare this in a powder form rather than mixing it with ashes. For a detailed discussion of the preparation, taking, and paraphernalia associated with the coca plant see Cooper (1949) and LaBarre (1948).

Written records of coca leaf chewing come from the earliest reports by Europeans. Columbus, Amerigo Vespucci and later travelers all report widespread use in Panama, Venezuela, Nicaragua, Chile, and Colombia. The archeological record contains both direct and inferential evidence dating as far back as 2,000 B.C. The direct evidence is carbon dating of coca plant leaves found in sites where people lived. The inferential evidence is in coca paraphernalia—lime containers, dippers, spoons, ceramic toasting pans, and pre-Hispanic clay figurines of coca chewers. The archeological record supports the conclusion that coca leaf chewing extended far beyond the formal boundaries of the Incan Empire.

A United Nations survey (1950) of South American Indian coca leaf chewers reported several emic explanations for chewing. Heading this list were references to reduction of pain associated with hunger, increased strength and energy which prevented fatigue, and reduction in dizziness and pain associated with high altitude. In spite of the fact that Western observers had reported similar effects, the United Nations dismissed the Indian responses as "superstitions" due to lack of education and suggested that the Indians were simply addicted. In contrast to the reasons for coca leaf chewing by Indians, studies of Western cocaine users report quite different effects. For example, a study of United States Army recruits (Nail, Gunderson, and Kolb 1974) found that users said they took cocaine primarily to enhance pleasurable activities, specifically sex. No similar reasons were given by Andean users. In addition, American users experienced behavioral changes after taking cocaine, while among Andeans, no behavioral changes were noted. Given the long-term and continued use by high altitude Andeans (with no measurable harmful effects such as those reported for American users), is it possible that their explanation for chewing is a physiological reality, linked to the reduction of physiological symptoms associated with high altitude living?

Andrew Fuchs (1978) put forth the hypothesis that coca leaf chewing is practiced to alleviate the discomforts of **hypoxia** (chronic oxygen deficiency), or "mountain sickness," associated with living in high altitudes. Fuchs presents data (Buck, Sasaki, and Anderson 1968, 99) which shows a positive correlation between altitude and coca leaf chewing. The higher the altitude of a village, the higher the percentage of coca leaf chewers. This finding, in general, confirms both the qualitative and quantitative observations of other researchers. Table 3.2 is an abbreviated display of this association.

Table 3.2.
Percent of Male and Female Coca Leaf Chewers 20 Years or Older in Four Peruvian Villages, by Altitude of Village

Village Name (Altitude)	Percent Male and Female Chewers	
	Males	**Females**
San Antonio (150m)	2.8	2.5
Cachicoto (720m)	35.7	21.8
Yacongo (1,945m)	45.4	10.4
Pusi (3,450m)	68.7	74.4

With no other evidence, these data do seem to indicate a "causal" relationship between chewing and altitude. We note that San Antonio, at an altitude of 150m, only had a small percentage of chewers. In contrast Pusi was 3,450m high and had a much higher percentage of chewers. However, as social scientists, we would like to have more information about the practice of coca leaf chewing. One thing we note is that there are differences in the preparation of coca leaves. Lowlanders roast and pound the leaves, mix the powder with ash and suck out the powder. In high altitude populations the leaves are consumed directly. We also note some differences in the social characteristics of chewers which distinguish them from non-chewers. *Mestizos* (persons of mixed Indian and European ancestry) and Europeans rarely chew, or at least they rarely report chewing. Coca leaf chewing appears to be a practice restricted to the Indian population. The one notable exception to this is that mestizo miners chew and will even refuse to work unless their employers provided them with coca. One last distinction is sex. Women tend to chew less than men, except at the highest altitudes. The question Fuchs asks is, "Why these variations in use by sex, occupation, and ethnic identity?" He answers this question by posing two possible explanations for differential coca use—cold stress and **polycythemia** (abnormal increase in red blood cells).

With reference to responses to cold stress, experiments on rats suggest that cocaine may decrease heat loss by acting as a peripheral vasoconstrictor (the constriction of circulation at the body extremities). However, studies of the skin temperature of Indian subjects showed only small differences between coca and non-coca users. Cold stress also does not explain coca use in warm weather or among miners who work in environments where temperatures are high. It does not explain the finding that more coca is consumed during the day than at night when it is colder nor why there is a difference between the sexes. The alternative answer to this question is polycythemia.

Polycythemia is a rather standard response to hypoxia. High altitude peoples have red blood cell counts much higher than sea level populations and higher blood viscosity (thicker blood). All this leads to increased physiological stress—the symptoms of which are headaches and fatigue. The sex differences in chewing are related to the way males and females produce hormones responsible for red cell production. Androgens (male hormones) increase the production of red blood cells while estrogens (female hormones) decrease their production. Coca leaf chewing by miners can be explained by the work environment. Aside from the reduced amounts of oxygen in the mine, miners suffer from silicosis (a condition of the lungs caused by the inhalation of sand dust which results in decreased functioning of the lungs) which affects blood oxygenation. The result is severe polycythemia.

Fuchs concludes:

> . . . the pattern of coca chewing is coincident not so much with either cold or high altitude per se, but with extreme polycythemic stress among individuals with no medical recourse. (280)

He then goes on to cite evidence that some ingredients in the coca leaf act upon critical areas of the posterior hypothalamus to depress erythropoiesis (red cell production). By doing so, they are antagonists to the hypoxia which stimulates excessive red blood cell production. The practice of leaf chewing is explained by differences in absorption rates. When chewed, the leaf contents are slowly and continuously absorbed by the user over an extended period; thus the effects are prolonged.

All of this sounds quite reasonable as an explanation. Fuchs presents his argument from emic explanations by natives, through behavioral differences in consumption patterns by altitude, to etic biochemical explanations. His model, in a simplified form, might be visualized:

High Altitude
silicosis ⟶ Polycythemia ⟶ Reduced by Coca Leaf Chewing
male/female   (headache/fatigue)

Not content with this explanation, Warwick Bray and Colin Dollery (1983) present a different interpretation of these data. They suggest that coca leaf chewing was widespread in all altitudes before European conquest. Citing ethnohistorical and archeological evidence, they suggest that coca is a general stimulant rather than a special purpose drug.

Given the early widespread distribution and use, the argument that coca leaf chewing is related to high altitude or any other stress is questioned by Bray and Dollery. They suggest that coca leaf chewing is related to "Indianness," or the degree to which a population is unacculturated, as measured by the perpetuation of traditional practices. They used language as their measure of "Indianness." Surely, it would be difficult to argue that language, a purely cultural phenomenon, is correlated with physical stress or altitude. Using language as a variable, they found that as altitude increased, there was a corresponding increase in Indianness. They argue that in the process of colonization, Europeans took the most productive lands from the native populations. The least productive lands, either in the high Andes or densely forested Amazonia, were left to the Quechua and Aymará speaking Indians. It is among these cultures that one finds the highest percent of coca leaf chewers. Given this evidence, Bray and Dollery conclude that Fuchs' "correlation" was spurious. It is not altitude that determines coca leaf chewing but the perpetuation of a widespread cultural practice from the past by the few remaining representatives of those cultural traditions. Table 3.3 illustrates how their argument might be visualized.

One criterion for judging any theory is comprehensiveness. Using this criterion alone, Bray and Dollery's interpretation explains high coca leaf consumption in both high altitude and low altitude populations. What about the claim that chewing relieves pain associated with hunger? Responses to a representative national sample of 3,513 Bolivians, over half of whom considered themselves chewers, revealed that 61 percent of the male respondents and 43 percent of the female respondents said they chewed coca leaves to

Table 3.3.
Association Between Coca Leaf Chewing and European Contact

Pre-contact Period	Post-contact Period	Present-Day
	Some natives incorported into European culture (Mestizos)	Disappearance of traditional practices, e.g., language and coca leaf chewing
Cocoa leaf chewing widespread throughout Bolvia, Ecuador, and Peru		
	Some natives remain isolated because lands not wanted by Europeans. (High altitude, lowland forest)	Perpetuation of traditional practices

assuage hunger (Carter et al. 1980). Could that many Bolivians be wrong? Undeniably, the diets of many Bolivians are below Western dietary standards. Could this be the reason why many persist in this practice? To test this hypothesis, Roderick Burchard (1992) compared the diets of 24 matched pairs of chewers and non-chewers from both high and low altitudes over a three-day period. Admittedly his sample was small, but his findings challenged the presumed diet-coca connection. He found no statistical differences between the diets of chewers and non-chewers, even though chewers ate more and had higher caloric and protein intakes than non-chewers. To the social scientist, this finding serves as a stimulus to search for non-biological explanations of variations in coca leaf chewing. One place to look is the actual day-to-day consumption pattern of chewers themselves.

The Coca Leaf Chewing Ritual among High Altitude Andeans

While scientists vigorously defend their interpretations of coca leaf chewing in academic journals, the Quechua perform the ritual practice of *hallpay* in accordance with well understood etiquette that clearly defines the appropriate place, time, and meaning of coca leaf chewing. This ritual is described by Catherine Allen (1981):

> To describe the etiquette I give an account of a coca-chewing session that took place in the house compound where I lived in

mid-May of 1975. Dona Juana stopped by to visit her sister Dona Maria, as she had agreed to pasture Maria's cow. The two sat down to visit for a while, and, because Juana was doing her a service, Maria offered her a small handful of coca saying, *Hallpakuy Mamay*, "Please chew, Mama." Juana accepted with both hands; accepting with one hand would have been rude. *Yusulpayki Urpillay*, "Thank you, dear," she answered. The two settled down to chew together, spreading their coca cloths on the ground in front of them and settling down for a good visit. . . . Reciprocity is the essence of the ceremony that surrounds coca chewing. Although Juana and Maria share with each other, first each of them shared with the Earth and Mountains, spiritual beings who surround them and are continually felt. They searched for their best leaves—dark, shiny green, sweet-tasting, unblemished by ragged edges, unspoiled by mold. Taking three or more leaves, Juana placed one on top of another, holding them between the thumb and the forefinger of her right hand. This small bundle is the *k'intu*. She waved the *k'intu* in front of her mouth, blowing on it and invoking the "powers that be," adding a prayer at the end. This act is *pukuy* (blowing the *k'intu*). She then put the *k'intu* into her mouth and chewed it.

The next step was to share with her companion. Once again she made a *k'intu*, extending it toward Maria, shiny side up. On a more formal occasion she might have extended it with both hands. *Hallpakusunchis*, "Let us chew together," she said. Maria answered with thanks and blew the *k'intu* before she chewed it. Meanwhile she had offered Juana a *k'intu*, with similar invitation and thanks; Juana blew on it for the spiritual beings and chewed it. Little by little each of them added leaves from their bundles to the wads in their mouths, pausing from time to time to offer each other *k'intu*.

At this point they were ready to add some *llipta*, a lump of compressed ash resembling a charcoal briquette, each taking a small bite and chewing it into her coca wad. This sweetened the leaves, and activated the stimulating alkaloids. With a fine quid of coca and *llipta* in her cheek, Juana was ready to work hard for another two or three hours.

Juana soon tied up her coca bundle; after a few minutes of quiet conversation she took the cow and left, calling out words of thanks and farewell. The *hallpay* lasted between 15 and 30 minutes. As experienced coca chewers, they swallowed the juices from the coca quid but almost nothing of the quid itself. When the quid was exhausted, about an hour later, it was taken carefully from the mouth and gently tossed away. Spitting coca is considered to be extremely bad manners. Coca is sacred (*santu*) and, chewed or unchewed, it must be treated respectfully. (159–160)

The hallpay ritual usually is performed five times a day—after breakfast, mid-morning, after the midday meal, mid-afternoon, and after dinner. Coca leaves are never chewed while working. In this sense, it is very much like the American coffee "break," literally a marker between activities. What one notices in the above description is that coca leaves are shared; however, there is a specified sequence in this sharing. K'intus are offered to men before women and to older people before younger people. In larger groups, one is not expected to share with anyone except those nearest, or any person who occupies a status with authority or power. Failure to reciprocate does not bring negative sanctions. Mental book-keeping will eventually settle accounts between people in the future.

Coca Leaf Chewing: Biology or Culture?

Considering the discussion above, what are we to conclude about the practice of coca leaf chewing? Here I think we have an example of a substance which is multi-functional. As a general-purpose stimulant, its function is recognized by native users to serve several anesthetic purposes. One cannot deny that the use of cocaine has specific pharmacological consequences. Unpleasantness from aches and pains, for whatever reason, will be lessened through its use. This does not explain the cultural use of coca leaves when there are no aches and pains or physical exhaustion. The daily enactment of the hallpay ritual serves as a powerful mechanism that both maintains boundaries between cultural categories (Quechua and non-Quechua), and reinforces distinctions between male and female, young and old, and equal and unequal. The ritual emphasis upon sharing equally, both visually and behaviorally, reinforces a dominant theme in Quechua life. To view coca leaf chewing as only a delivery method for cocaine is to deny that much human energy is devoted to maintaining cultural practices that have no immediate practical or biological consequences.

Marihuana and Ganja

Marihuana use was the subject of a moral panic in the United States in the 1930s. Early published reports suggested that users would not only experience unpleasant physical responses—nausea, vomiting, diarrhea, but that its use would reduce inhibitions—causing men to rape, murder, and become violent and women to become promiscuous. Like LSD, early reports cited psychotic episodes as a result of chronic use.

In the late 1960s and through the 1970s, marihuana use dramatically increased and social scientists became very busy collecting information from users on their subjective responses to this drug. Becker's (1953) classic statement on becoming a marihuana user suggested that not only does one have to learn the appropriate technique for smoking marihuana, but one also has to learn the effects of the drug. In other words, the experience from the drug is not an automatic effect of the interaction between the active ingredients in marihuana and human physiology. However, if we only listen to American users of marihuana, we note agreement on what smoking marihuana does. Most American users report feeling relaxed and peaceful. Many report an increase in sensory awareness, giddiness, mental insightfulness, and hunger. With rare exception, American users report the experience as pleasant and enjoyable. From these reports, one might conclude that marihuana "altered the senses" in a positive way. Food, sex, and music were all better when "high." Since there was consensus in the effect(s) of marihuana, might this be a biological response?

Marihuana is the name given to a variety of plants belonging to a single species, *Cannabis sativa*. The psychoactive agent in marihuana is THC (Delta-9 tetrahydrocannabinol), which is most concentrated in the upper flowering top of the plant. The proportion of THC found in street marihuana ranges from 1 to 5 percent. There are three physiological responses linked to THC: an increase in pulse rate, a decrease in saliva flow, and reddening of the eyes. The behavioral effects are a slight impairment of short-term memory which may account for overestimating the passage of time and a loss of the ability to maintain focused attention on a task (Ray 1983). Related to this last behavioral "effect" is the popular claim that marihuana use results in the "amotivational syndrome." This syndrome is defined by William McGlothlin and Louis West (1968) as:

> . . . apathy, loss of effectiveness, and diminished capacity or will-ingness to . . . endure frustration, concentrate for long periods, follow routines, or successfully master new material. . . . Such individuals . . . become totally involved with the present at the expense of future goals. . . . They report a greater subjective creativity but less objective productivity. (372)

The tendency to equate a weak physiological response to THC with social incompetency was common in the psychiatric literature during the 1960s and 1970s. The statement above tells us as much about those who made it as it does about users of drugs. The assumption is that one *ought* to endure frustration, concentrate, follow routines, be future oriented, and be productive; there is no explanation why these are positive virtues. To test the amotivational syndrome hypothesis, social scientists used both experimental and survey methods. The experimental data yielded mixed results (Hollister 1971). In task oriented experiments, seasoned marihuana users were unaffected in the performance of their tasks, while the performance of inexperienced users was impaired. One experimental study on simulated driving performance concluded that alcohol impaired performance, but marihuana did not (Crancer et al. 1969).

Surveys on the effects of marihuana on performance were largely confined to students. Bruce Johnson's (1973) sample of 3,500 college students in the New York metropolitan area investigated, among other variables, the relationship between marihuana use and respondents' performance in college. Johnson measured performance by grades, by whether respondents thought about or actually did drop out or transfer to another school, and by a scale which measured "deviance" from official rules (such as cutting classes, changing majors more than once, or getting in trouble with college officials for rule violations). He found that marihuana use, in and of itself, was an unimportant factor is explaining low grades, leaving college, and college deviance. Rather, he found that using and selling multiple drugs, his measure of a drug "subculture," was related to these variables. Thus, THC cannot by itself be demonstrated to result in a loss of motivation, at least for college students.[2]

The conclusions from experiments and surveys of college students have certain limitations in their applicability to the "real" world. Experiments are contrived social situations that last only a short time, and the behaviors of students in a university hardly represent behaviors outside the confines of the campus. For example, Lester Grinspoon's (1971) review of cannabis use in other cultures found it being used for ceremonial, medicinal, and other nonintoxicating purposes. The conclusion that marihuana use reduces motivation does not stand up against the findings that in other cultures it is used to relieve fatigue and increase productivity among manual laborers (Carter 1980; Chopra and Chopra 1957; Hamid 1980; Rubin and Comitas 1975). If one argues that biology is the determinant of behavior, and drugs alter biology, then one should expect to find the consequences of drug use to be the same the world over. One might alter this perspective somewhat when referring to the hallucinogens altering consciousness in general and culture providing the content of those altered states, but what about work? Work is not something one imagines or thinks about; it is actual behavior. If there is any example that should "prove" the biological argument, this is surely it. This is the critical test of the pharmacological theory; and it is to this test that we turn next.

There is one place in the world where marihuana use is, if you will excuse the word, high. This is Jamaica. Although it is illegal, it is estimated that somewhere between 60 and 70 percent of the working class in Jamaica smoke, drink, or eat "ganja," the local name for marihuana. Melanie Dreher (1982) carried out eighteen months of field work in four rural communities in Jamaica as part of a larger multidisciplinary study of the effects of chronic cannabis use. We will review one part of that study which focused on the amotivational syndrome (1983).

Unlike rum and other intoxicants, ganja is widely accepted by working-class Jamaicans as appropriate for the work situation. They claim that ganja has a calming effect and increases both wisdom and work productivity. This same view is not shared by the middle and upper classes. They hold that it has just the opposite effect. People who use ganja become lazy and irresponsible, and it leads to violence and mental confusion. To test these competing emic hypotheses, Dreher compared the work records of 151 cane cutters on three sugar farms which were part of one large sugar estate. Seventy-six of these cutters were marihuana users. Detailed records on days worked, productivity, and wages for all workers were kept by management. Dreher selected two different three-week periods as her measure of performance. During these two periods there was no inclement weather or labor disputes that might affect production. Who was, and who was not, a smoker was determined by interviews and observations of the men both in and out of the work setting. Dreher found that men were either non-smokers or heavy smokers. Smokers were those who smoked three or more "spliffs" (ganja cigars) per day, every day.

The statistical analysis of the data for the whole sample showed only one statistically significant difference between smokers and non-smokers. The average age of smokers was younger (42.9 years) than non-smokers (48.1). Although non-smokers tended to earn slightly higher incomes on all three farms, and smokers tended to produce slightly more tonnage on all three farms, the differences were not statistically significant. These findings do not lend support to either emic hypothesis. As a chemical substance, ganja neither contributes to nor detracts from the overall performance and earning of these cane cutters. Dreher did find statistically significant differences in wages and production between the three farms. These differences, she argues, are explained by variations in management policies which govern hiring practices, size of work gangs, compensation for reaping bad cane, and labor relations. Ganja smoking did not contribute to the differences between farms.

In another somewhat more controlled study of marihuana in San José, Costa Rica, the question of the amotivational syndrome was explored (Carter 1980). Using an experimental design, 41 male users were matched with non-users on several variables, including age, marital status, education, occupation, alcohol and tobacco consumption. This careful matching was done to control for any factors that might influence differences between smokers and non-smokers and thereby measure the direct effects of marihuana. When comparing the employment histories of users and non-users, it was found that non-users received more promotions and raises, were more upwardly mobile, and had full-time jobs that they changed less frequently. This finding appears to support the amotivational hypothesis. When the researchers examined the user sample, however, they found that those who smoked more marihuana cigarettes had the most stable employment histories. Users who had worked full-time as adolescents smoked an average of 10.7 cigarettes per day; those who worked occasionally as adolescents smoked 7.9 cigarettes per day. Users who, at the time of this study, were working at full-time jobs smoked 10 cigarettes per day, while those that did not work smoked 5.4 per day. Those who had experienced no unemployment consumed 12.4 cigarettes per day compared to 8.2 per day that were smoked by those who changed jobs several times a year. High daily consumers spent more money and had more material possessions. However, the high users were also more likely to be employed in illegal or extralegal activities most often associated with the marihuana trade itself.

A third study focused on middle-class "baby boomers" (those born in the late 1940s) in the United States (White, Aidala, and Zablocki 1988). This study suggests:

> Research has seldom focused on the relationship between drug use and the work-related behavior outside a clinical setting. We thus know little about how various levels of drug use affect occupational achievement and stability among adults. (455)

Several surveys found that the use of drugs was highest among the unemployed. These correlations have been interpreted to mean that drug use leads to unemployment. The problem with this interpretation is the same as it would be for clinical conclusions about the relationship between drugs and the kinds of problems people might have that would cause them to seek those in the "helping" professions. How do we know if drug use was the independent variable which led to these problems? To test the effects of drug use (marihuana and alcohol) on occupational achievement White, Aidala, and Zablocki selected a purposive sample of middle-class whites who were current users, former users and non-users of drugs. All 376 persons in this sample had been members of communes during the 1970s. Many in this sample had been involved in drug use for over 20 years. Nearly all the persons sampled had tried alcohol. Approximately 50 percent had, at some time, used marihuana daily for at least one year. Other than alcohol and marihuana, the drug used by the largest number of subjects during the previous year was cocaine (459). If the hypothesis that drug use decreased occupational success is correct, then this sample should substantiate this assumption. What did they find?

> Contrary to our expectations, we found no significant relationship between cumulative marijuana use and current level of income, previous financial problems, job mobility, or tenure in one's current job. Furthermore, the number of years in which subjects smoked marijuana at least monthly were not related to current work-related attitudes and behavior. (462)

These three studies cast doubt on the assumption that marihuana use, in and of itself, results in a reduction of motivation to work. In both Jamaica and Costa Rica, marihuana is perceived to have multiple effects, including the ability to improve sexual performance, sleep better, increase appetite, and work better. When taken with these different goals in mind, users will often achieve what they anticipated. That these goals differ according to age, gender, socioeconomic status, and group setting cannot be explained by THC levels. In the U.S. study, the crucial variables are the social characteristics of marihuana users. Being from middle- and upper-class families, the subjects of that study had already learned a type of work ethic that prepared them for white-collar jobs. Had the subjects been from blue-collar families, they would be most likely to enter those occupations where unstable and low paying employment was the norm, and the conclusion might have been that marihuana use negatively effected work patterns (Kandel 1980, O'Donnell et al. 1976).

Sex and Race: More Biological Considerations

In every society there are provisions made for training children. This process is called **enculturation** or **socialization** (chapter 9). It is through that process that one learns the rules of culture and also learns to defend those rules compulsively. Americans learn that monogamy is the "proper" system of marriage, that monotheism (one high god) is the order of heaven, that property is private, and that democracy is the "best" system of government. None of these beliefs requires any proof; all are accepted as absolute truths. There is no evidence that any of these "truths" are biological in origin. One may be "born again," but one is not born a Christian, a Jew, a Moslem, or a Buddhist. Humans are born male or female but learn to be masculine and feminine. Humans vary in their physical appearances, but it is culture that selects particular characteristics and gives them meaning. The failure to distinguish what nature determines from what culture determines is illustrated by the debate on the effects of alcohol on males and females and on "race."

In the last chapter, four studies of drunkenness were reviewed. In all of these studies, insobriety levels in a society were measured by the behavioral outcomes of drinking by males. The assumption of each of these studies was that insobriety was the result of anxiety brought on by scarcity of food, dependency, or social disorganization. The rather curious omission in these studies is that no mention was made of insobriety in females. The question we might ask is why those anxieties that supposedly drive men to drink do not have the same behavioral outcome on women. No clear answer to this question is found in that literature. One might speculate that women either do not experience anxiety, or if they do, it is not reduced by drinking. Another possibility is ethnographic bias by male anthropologists. Is it possible that male ethnographers underreport or de-emphasize female behavior? This last question has been systematically addressed by studies which reviewed male- and female-authored ethnographies found in the HRAF (Divale 1976; Martin 1978; Naroll, Naroll, and Howard 1961; Schlegel 1972; Whyte 1978). Interestingly, all of this research focused on male, not female, bias. The results of these studies indicate that when describing specific female behaviors, there was no difference between male and female ethnographers. In fact, male ethnographers tended to report more data on females than did female ethnographers. The only differences found were in "favorable" reporting of women's prestige and power. Females ethnographers tended to be more favorable.

With no consistent finding of male bias in ethnographies, the question of why women drink less alcohol and are less likely to be unsober is an intriguing one. One suggestion is that this difference might be explained by sex differences in the metabolism of alcohol. The most recent experiment, by Mario Frezza and his team, (1990) investigates sex differences in the oxidation of alcohol in gastric tissue. In their review of the literature, they cite several studies of male-female differences in the metabolism of alcohol. For example, females develop alcoholic[3] liver diseases more readily than males, and females have a higher blood ethanol concentration after equivalent oral doses than males. The subjects in their experiment were all Italian. There were 24 females and 20 males; six males and six females were "alcoholics." Each subject was given a standardized oral measure of alcohol and then tested to determine how much alcohol had been oxidized in the stomach after a fixed period. The results showed a difference between males and females. Females metabolized less alcohol in the stomach which resulted in higher blood-alcohol levels. Thus, it takes less alcohol for a female to get drunk.

How might the social scientist respond to this finding? Frezza and his team make mention of, but do not elaborate upon, the finding that gastric metabolism decreases with long-term ethanol consumption. This means that the longer the history of drinking alcohol, the less of it is metabolized in the stomach. The other point is that, while small in number, all the subjects of this experiment were Italian. If we compare yearly alcohol consumption cross-nationally we find that Italians consume 13.73 liters per person, compared to 8.57 liters for the United Kingdom (Efron et al. 1974). Although I do not have any data readily available on sex differences in alcohol consumption in Italy, this is certainly a variable we would consider using as a control.

Does knowing that males and females differ in the metabolism of alcohol explain variations in drinking behavior? As social scientists we are faced with cultural worlds that are variable. The empirical generalization that males drink more than females does not explain why males in one culture drink more than males in another culture. Nor does it explain why female consumption of alcohol varies cross-culturally. Male-female differences in ethanol metabolism, if true, would be specific to the biological species. While cultures may be different, there is no evidence to indicate that those variations are explained by different metabolisms. What is true is that culture may select specific physical variations. If strength is required for particular tasks, then males will generally perform those tasks. If infants and children must be breast fed, then women will perform that task. Biology does make distinctions between the sexes, but it is culture that sorts those differences into gender (cultural) differences.

The search for biological explanations for differences in drinking behavior has been extended to the subject of "race." Here, as with sex, the emphasis has been on "alcoholism." A. D. Fisher's (1987) analysis of both race and alcoholism points out some fundamental problems for social science analysis. First, alcoholism has several different definitions depending upon the variables used in the research and/or methods of "treatment." Thus, a medical definition might emphasize alcoholism as a disease, then search for the etiology (cause) of that disease. A social definition would stress the degree to which the consumption of alcohol interfered with personal, social, or occupational behavior. Still others have abandoned the concept "alcoholism," preferring to use the term "alcohol addiction," or "compulsive drinking," or simply alcohol "abuse." A brief review of the literature serves only to illustrate the muddle that emerges from these different definitions. What about race?

The concept of race has a rather curious history. One does not have to go back very far in time to find books entitled "Race Relations" in sociology. American anthropology also has a long history of the concept of race, primarily because one branch of that discipline is physical or biological anthropology. The demise of the concept "race" in much of the social science literature came about primarily because of social, not scientific, reasons. There was scarcely a whisper of dissent when the UNESCO *Statement On Race* was published in 1950. It was drafted by a panel of physical anthropologists and geneticists as a statement against the vulgarization of the term "race" as used by racists. It points out that racial classifications, as used by physical anthropologists, are based on physical characteristics which describe groupings that are highly variable. It goes on to declare the absence of scientific evidence to support beliefs that races differ in innate abilities or that race determines cultural practices or changes in those practices. Further, there was no evidence to substantiate the belief that "race mixture" has deleterious outcomes. Since this "statement," the word race has been replaced by the concepts **ethnic group** and **ethnicity**, which are used to describe variations in cultural practices.[4]

The concept of biological race is still used in physical anthropology to describe breeding populations whose distribution of inherited characteristics differs from other breeding populations. The term **cline** is used to describe the geographical distribution of specific physical characteristics, such as the genes responsible for blood types, skin color, hair form, and shovel-shaped incisors. The only other place that this concept is used is in clinical studies which attempt to establish relationships between emic taxonomies of race and one form or another of a medical or psychiatric pathology. Our concern is with alcoholism. If one assumes that alcoholism is genetically determined and "races" are groups defined by the different distribution of genes, then the question is, "Do different races have more or less of those genes which 'cause' alcoholism?"

Fisher reviews several clinical studies which address this question. Most of these studies draw their samples from alcohol treatment clinics or hospitals. The Fenna, et al. (1971) study, illustrative of these studies, begins with the observation that Amerindians (American Indians) have difficulty with alcohol "abuse." The study had 65 male subjects. Twenty-six were identified as Indian, 21 were identified as Inuit Eskimo, and 17 were identified as white. Alcohol was administered to each subject intravenously and blood alcohol levels were measured by a breathalyser. Individual rates of metabolism were recorded according to "racial" classification, and a mean for each "race" was calculated. The researchers concluded that while each "group" required the same amount of alcohol to achieve the same intoxication levels, the "natives" (Amerindians and Eskimos) metabolized alcohol at a slower rate than "whites."

Fisher points out several problems with this study. The most obvious is that people drink alcohol. In this study it was injected directly into the bloodstream. The other is that this small experimental "group" was individually identified as belonging to one of three "races." When used by physical anthropologists and population geneticists, the parameters of a breeding population (race) can only be determined when one randomly samples from within that population. The social scientists would be accused of malfeasance if, for example, they spoke only to Amerindians who were members of Baptist churches and concluded that Indians do not drink and are opposed to drinking. Another major problem was in the drinking histories of these "races." The Indian category had more "heavy drinkers" (more than twenty beers per week) than both the Eskimos and whites combined. Remember what we mentioned above about the effects of drinking on metabolism rates? In effect, this study compared heavy and light drinkers, not Amerindians, Eskimos, and whites. More formally, I would suggest that the relationship between Indianness and metabolism is probably spurious. When drinking histories are controlled, I would predict that the original correlation would disappear.

A curious contradiction to the hypothesis that "Indian" drinking and drinking "problems" are rooted in biology is found in the observation that far eastern populations drink very little and have few drinking "problems." This is explained by the **flushing response**, a biochemical reaction to alcohol that involves a flushing of the face and neck and an increased heart rate. This response is the consequence of a lack of a liver enzyme that breaks down acetaldehyde that is produced by alcohol metabolism. While almost all populations have some people who are deficient in this enzyme, the highest frequencies are found among Chinese, Japanese, and others from the Far East. The linkage between the flushing response and alcohol consumption is that the response is uncomfortable and will be avoided by those who experience it. Yuet Cheung (1993), in his review of these studies, suggests that this linkage is assumed rather than demonstrated. For example, Native Americans, who are Asian transplants, should have a similar response. Yet Native Americans have a higher rate of alcohol consumption and alcohol "problems" than Chinese. Further, this argument does not explain drinking variations within the North American Chinese population. Two studies (Sue et al. 1979, R. C. Johnson et al. 1987) found that those Chinese who were most assimilated into American culture consumed more alcohol than those who were less assimilated. Even among unassimilated Chinese, those who presented themselves in clinical settings for drinking "problems" were among the most poor (Chin et al. 1990–91). These findings point to something other than a genetically determined physiological aversion to alcohol.

Underlying almost all this research which attempts to link the physiological process of ethanol metabolism to some genetic predisposition is the somewhat imprecise assumption of "problem drinking" or "alcoholism." Both of these terms are labels that reflect a particular cultural perspective which are then applied to others. Whether the definitions include physiological criteria (such as cirrhosis of the liver) or normative criteria (such as family responsibility), they are based on a view of the world that is not necessarily shared by others (Waddell 1975). In contrast to the search for genetic markers of or "racial" predisposition toward alcohol use, the social scientist focuses on the social and cultural functions of drunkenness within cultural contexts. If Amerindians are said to have a drinking "problem," then whose problem is it? Hugh Brody (1977) addresses this issue in his analysis of Northern Canadian Amerindians. He found that although they exhibited a wide range of cultural differences, alcohol use is common to all of these cultures. Therefore, he sought another shared characteristic or condition that might explain alcohol use. He hypothesizes that alcohol use is related to a culture's means of production.

> More precisely, the Native people of the north live under very special economic and material conditions, and the relationship between these conditions and North American society as a whole is the guide to the alcohol problem. (40)

Unlike Horton and Fields, Brody concludes that Amerindians, in contrast to Europeans, enjoy drinking and drunkenness and do so without European feelings of guilt. The vocative celebratory drunkenness of Indian parties is done for pleasure, and members of these parties attempt to get drunk for as long as they can. If this results in late night quests for more to drink or another party, it may be disturbing to non-drinking Indians or whites. Drinking among those Indians is episodic. That is, Indians are spree drinkers. Brody argues that this is related to availability of alcohol. Because of the physical isolation of many Indian communities and historical legal prohibitions of drinking on reserves (the Canadian equivalent of the U.S. reservations), alcohol is not always accessible. Either liquor is brought in periodically, or one must drive to nearby towns, cities, or trading posts to obtain a supply. Using these two observations—heavy and episodic drinking—it is estimated that 70 percent of the Indian population is defined as alcoholic by U.S. clinical standards (Levy and Kunitz 1973). The difficulty with this conclusion is that at any one point in time these so-called alcoholics are not drinking. Does this mean that alcoholism only occurs at specific times and not at others? Is the disease part time? Are the genes "turned on" monthly or weekly? The use of the disease stencil to "explain" Indian drinking does not help us understand drinking among Indians any more than it explains non-drinking among Mormons and Muslims. The genetic characteristics of populations remain constant over time. Drunkenness or "alcoholism" does not. To understand this behavior it is necessary to employ social, cultural, economic, historical, and political variables. None of these are linked to biology.

Addiction: Social Science and the Opiates

Surely if there is one category of drugs that can be understood within the medical-pathological model it is the opiates—opium, morphine, and heroin. Conventional wisdom suggests that when these drugs are taken, the result is "addiction." James Coleman (1976) suggests that:

> Popular opinion and most authorities see addiction as a simple physiological process. An individual becomes addicted—i.e., has a continuing craving for opiates—when he or she consumes a sufficient quantity of opiates to cause a change in body chemistry. Once this change has occurred the individual automatically develops a craving for opiates, because he must have them to

avoid painful withdrawal distress. This craving for narcotic drugs is believed to have a very special quality, unlike the everyday cravings for ice cream, a new car, or an attractive sexual partner. The craving for drugs is seen as an overwhelming passion. The addict has a need for drugs which is so strong that it virtually overpowers his will. He or she may want to quit, but the power of the drugs is too great. Only a few addicts are believed to be able to overcome their habits, and then only with considerable assistance ... Another important theme ... concerns the corrosive effects of addiction on the drug user's life. The addict becomes a thief, liar, and hustler. There is virtually nothing he or she won't do to get a fix. (136)

Alfred Lindesmith, a social psychologist who began studying heroin users in 1935, proposed a social theory of addiction which illustrates how social scientists approach the question of addiction in general, and opiate addiction in particular (1938, 1963, 1968). Lindesmith sets forth three principles for a theory of addiction. First, the term addiction must be carefully defined and must clearly distinguish addicts from non-addicts. The second principle is that the theory not be restricted to a particular time or place (for instance, intravenous heroin users in twentieth-century America). The third principle is that the theory is testable; that is, it provides suggestions for evidence that could disprove it.

Lindesmith rejects those definitions of addiction that equate it with physical dependence and tolerance only. **Physical dependence** refers to changes in body chemistry as a result of prolonged drug use. **Tolerance** refers to a decline in effects with the same dosage over time so the user must increase the amount of the drug that is taken. Both tolerance and dependency are physiological, as is the third characteristic of opiates, the analgesic effect. A drug is said to be an **analgesic** if it increases the pain threshold. Persons who experience pain from organic causes will be indifferent to that pain after taking an opiate. If these three physiological responses to the opiates define an addict, then animals other than humans could also be addicted. Do newborns of addicts, rats, and primates exhibit addictive behavior? Can those who have used opiates but no longer do so be defined as addicts? What would they be called—ex-addicts, non-addicts, post-addicts? In other words, does the word addiction apply to any animal that takes opiates?

Lindesmith suggests that a definition of addiction must come from those "addicted" rather than those who have never used opiates, and that definition should reflect common experiences among this population. Unfortunately, addicts are often ignored because they are assumed to be liars, criminals, or otherwise unreliable. The result of this perception of addicts is that the "experts" on addiction are those who have never used heroin. Lindesmith noted that heroin users reported quite different effects of heroin depending on their experiences, the social contexts, and the methods of administration. Some addicts reported pleasurable responses to taking heroin; others reported just the opposite. Some reported long-term effects; others hardly any effects at all. This suggests that something other than pharmacology is at work in these responses. They all report, however, that continued use of heroin avoids the discomfort of withdrawal. This common response is the basis for a definition of addiction.

> . . . the addict's craving for opiates is born in his experience of relief of withdrawal distress which follows with[in] a matter of five to ten minutes after an injection . . . the craving develops in this situation only when the individual understands the withdrawal symptoms and attributes them to the proper cause. *A person who remains ignorant of the source of withdrawal symptoms and interprets them in some other way will not become addicted.* The only organism that can become addicted in the full human sense of that term . . . is one to which the withdrawal distress can be explained. (1963, 100; emphasis mine)

This definition illustrates the social science approach to definitions. It recognizes and reflects shared definitions by users as the basis for distinguishing addicts from non-addicts. Those who are unaware that they are consuming opiates through prescribed medication or patent medicines may be dependent upon their effects, but they are not addicts. Addicts not only know they are users of opiates, but they also know that failure to continue use will result in the unpleasantness of withdrawal. If this is found to be true of heroin addicts everywhere, then it is possible to construct a theory of addiction that makes sense to both users and non-users alike. Further, it does not imply a connection between addiction and other behavioral characteristics. Rather, it leaves that matter to future scientific inquiry.

Summary: Is Learning Enough?

This chapter reviewed several examples of the social science approach to the question of nature verses nurture, biology versus learning. It should be clear that the learning model used in the social sciences does not deny the importance of biology or the physiological effects of substances on the human body. What it denies is the insistence that biology alone determines human behavior. How cocaine users in Los Angeles behaviorally respond to the chemistry of that drug is quite different from the Quechua coca leaf chewer in high or low altitudes. Variations in the content and interpretation of "altered states" brought on by hallucinogens cannot be attributed to the effects of natural or manufactured substances on the human nervous system. The goal of social science is to understand the human condition in terms of practices and beliefs. This brief excursion demonstrates variation in that condition in spite of biological and chemical constants. Therefore, we can only conclude that responses to drugs are not natural but rather determined by factors that are extrasomatic, outside the body.

While social scientists agree that humans are creatures of learning, this does not mean that learning explains the human condition. For example, we learn to tie our shoes; but this does not explain the history of shoes or the meanings of different shoe styles and colors. Humans must eat; but that does not explain why one learns some specific form of eating etiquette or what is appropriate as a food. Humans learn to use drugs; but that does not explain what drugs are used, by whom, when, and where. Obviously, what is learned is part of a larger learned pattern or system, and it is only within these larger frameworks that drug use can be understood. In the following chapters we will explore those systems within which humans learn in order to better understand the human condition.

Endnotes

[1] Coca leaves were used as a medium of exchange by the Incas and were accepted by the Spanish as payment for taxes, hence the reference to "money."

[2] For a somewhat more updated review of the non-relationship between marihuana use and student performance and value orientation, see Miranne (1979).

[3] Consistent with the pathology perspective of medicine, most of the studies on sex differences in alcohol metabolism focus on subjects defined as "alcoholic."

[4] These concepts are not without their definitional problems. Heath (1990–91) argues that ethnicity has not been standardized. Although it has been used for census and medical reporting, the shifting categories of ethnicity for recording purposes would allow the same person to be counted in several different categories throughout his or her lifetime. One could be a "Jew" or a "Muslim" for one purpose, and a black or "other" for another. Even more confusing is when ethnicity is equated with "race." Is one's biological heritage the same as one's national or cultural heritage? The category "Native American," for example, includes a wide

diversity of cultures and languages. Where ethnicity is reflective of national origin, can one be justified in categorizing all members of a given category as being both behaviorally and culturally uniform? Adding to this confusion is the use of ethnicity as a description of church or religious affiliation. Catholics do not represent a homogeneous grouping any more than Jews or Baptists. The most recent application of ethnicity to women, gays, the elderly, the handicapped, and the poor shows even further disregard for scientific rigor. Although these categories may be "politically correct," there is nothing to warrant them being lumped together with biology, national heritage, religion, language, surname, and other categories.

The fundamental issue outlined by Heath is that when "ethnicity" is used to explain variations in drug use, it must, like all other scientific concepts, clearly delineate categories that are mutually exclusive if any meaningful comparisons are to be made. Unfortunately, much of the social science literature has not followed this basic principle.

chapter 4

How Do Drugs Get Where They Are?

I n the last chapter it was argued that the learning model of human behavior explained more about the human condition than models which emphasize genetic or biological determinants. Having made this argument, it must be stressed that the underlying explanation for why cultures persist or change is not rooted in the simple fact that humans learn, but that humans are able to pass on what they have learned to future generations. This ability to share learned experiences not only distinguishes humans from all other animals but is the basis for understanding both continuity and change in culture.

Why culture changes was one of the central issues of social science during its formative period in the nineteenth century. In this and the following chapter, we address the general question of culture change and how the theories and methods that emerged around this issue can be applied to understanding drugs and drug use.

In chapter 1 it was pointed out that social science is not restricted to a single geographical space or historical period. As science, its theories and principles should apply universally. It has also been stated that human behavior and thought is determined by the characteristics of culture. Why then did the formalization of social science models of change and evolution have to wait until the nineteenth century? Why indeed was the nineteenth century known for the development of the evolutionary sciences? A social science that proposes a deterministic model as I have done must be able to understand itself in the same way it explains other social phenomena. This was one of the early criticisms directed at Émile Durkheim in response to his insistence that the units of social science analysis are "social facts." If culture is the independent variable that determines the behaviors and beliefs of humans (dependent variable), then how is it possible to contemplate social facts free from the influence of those same facts?[1] This is the kind of "heady" question that philosophers of science will surely debate for years to come (Wagner 1975). I do not have a simple answer to this question other than to say that social science has an obligation to make social scientific sense of itself. One way that this can be done is to reconstruct the evolution of social science.

The historic foundations of what we have defined as the social sciences are rooted in nineteenth-century Europe and North America. In the eighteenth century an underlying assumption was catastrophism. **Catastrophism** views history as a series of creations, or dramatic changes over short periods of time. In geology, this idea was refuted by Charles Lyell (1797–1875), the founder of modern geology. Lyell's systematic observation of the earth's stratigraphy demonstrated that, rather than by dramatic changes, the earth had evolved slowly. This process he described as **uniformitarianism**. This concept, along with a revised history of the earth, contributed to the biological evolutionary theories of both Charles Darwin (1809–1882) and Alfred Wallace (1823–1913). Herbert Spencer (1820–1903) in sociology, and Lewis Henry Morgan (1818–1881) and Edward Burnett Tylor (1831–1917) in anthropology, were also indebted to Lyell for their models of cultural evolution (Harris 1968, 111–113). Why did this change in ideas about change have to wait until the nineteenth century? Was it the presence of Lyell, Darwin, Wallace, Spencer and the others that determined this "revolution" in thinking? The social science answer is "no." It is culture that determines the ideas of any time. When culture changes, so do the ideas of people.

For three hundred years, beginning in the 1600s, there were a series of rather dramatic changes in the organization of some

Western societies, notably France, England, and Colonial America. During the sixteenth and seventeenth centuries there was an increase in both eastern and western trade from Europe. The nineteenth century witnessed an ever increasing emphasis upon production. The industrialization of the West, coupled with expanding colonialism, resulted in the reorganization of Western culture. Monarchies fell and were replaced by the landed mercantile classes; peoples moved or were pushed away from an agricultural way of life into newly formed industrial communities and cities within nation states; and new sources of energy replaced the physiological limitations of human and animal muscle power. These changes were appropriately marked by political revolutions—some noisy, as in France and America, others somewhat less boisterous. It is no surprise that against this backdrop of change, thinkers in all the sciences began to abandon the view that the physical, biological, and social worlds were fixed by some great unseen powerful hand. Lyell, Darwin, Spencer and Tylor did not cause these changes in the reorganization of government and work; rather they reflected them in their own academic works.

Two other factors contributed to the emergence of the idea of cultural evolutionism. One was the uncovering of fossil remains of humans throughout Europe. The physical remains of these anatomically modern humans show an antiquity beyond the "great flood" story of the Old Testament or the then current date for a single creation. More important for the social sciences was the consistent finding that these early Europeans had different types of tools that could be arranged into a time sequence. The earliest of these tools were made from stone, hence the "stone age." These stone tools were followed in time by bronze implements and, more recently, by iron. Thus, the archeological past was not random but appeared to follow a lawlike evolution of tool materials and traditions. As more materials were uncovered in different locations, the same or similar sequences of tools were found. In science, which emphasizes unifying principles or laws, the findings of these nineteenth-century archaeologists held great promise toward achieving this goal.[2]

The other influence was the expansion of colonial empires which brought the Western world into increased contact with native peoples all over the world. Up until this time, most histories of the West traced their descent (more accurately, in their view, ascent) directly from empires in the Middle East. The "discovery" of native populations, such as the American Indian or African populations, introduced new questions about history itself. Where did these peoples come from, and what, if any, relationships existed between them and Western history? Where did "they," and correspondingly "we," fit into the grand scheme of history? Unlike the faceless material artifacts which were used by populations in the past, encounters with other living peoples were both disturbing and challenging. Most of all, their existence demanded explanation. To explain the connections between these societies and Western culture, the nineteenth-century social theorists developed grand theories of cultural evolution. In their search for origins of different cultural practices and the evolutionary sequence for the changes in these patterns, these theorists broadened their theoretical nets to include Culture with a capital "C."

If past cultures went through stages from stone to bronze to iron, then what of other cultural practices? Did they follow a single line of change in the same **unilineal** sequences as the material objects? Cultures were encountered whose people used stone implements. Were these people remnants from the "Stone Age," living representatives of a bygone time? No other animal considers its past. Humans do, and the intimacies of that past were being dug up from the ground and encountered above the ground in those areas of the world that held resources to fuel the engines of industrialization. What an intellectually stimulating period the nineteenth century must have been. There were new data in search of a theory.

One common theme that united the theories of the nineteenth century was that evolution, whether biological or cultural, began with simple forms that were replaced by complex forms. The actual stages in this process might have been debated, but Lyell's idea of uniformitarianism applied equally to geology and culture. In Spencer's view this theme was linked to the idea of "progress." As culture became more complex, it got "better." This idea reflected practices that were already in place. Both the colonial administrators and the religious missionaries viewed native peoples as childlike and less than fully human. For the administrators this was authorization for exploitation; for missionaries this was justification for conversion. Either way, the proof for being more "advanced" was in the success of the West in subjugating large numbers of "simple" peoples.

One advantage of small samples is that one can construct grand theories. As sample sizes increase, so do the number of exceptions to early ideas about evolutionary "laws." Not all past cultures "progressed" from stone to bronze to iron. Not all native peoples behaved in the same way. The harsh reality was that some peoples successfully resisted being colonized by even the "superior" military strength of the "progressive" West, and some natives rejected the "better" (more evolved) religious teachings and practices of those same powers. The outcome for social science theory was that the unilineal models fell out of favor—and have remained out of favor ever since.

This section began with a reference to the cumulative nature of human learning. Just as we are indebted to peoples 10,000 years ago in the Near East for the bread we eat, modern social science has a debt to these early evolutionists. Ralph L. Beals and Harry Hoijer (1971) remind us that it was the nineteenth-century evolutionists who first emphasized the comparative method in constructing their evolutionary models, although only one (Lewis Henry Morgan) had personally collected any ethnographic data on other cultures. They were also the first to separate culture from race. The prevailing idea had been that differences between cultures were explained by variations in physical characteristics. The nineteenth-century evolutionists argued that culture and biology are separate entities, quite independent of each other. They were the first to reject any "great man" idea of history and to suggest that culture was a system that could be understood through the use of rigorous scientific procedures.

Beginning at the end of the nineteenth century, there was a move away from the grand scope of these unilineal evolutionists. If grand times encourage grand theories, then less grand times call for moderation. The suggestion that scientific methods and data collection be used to investigate culture meant that it was necessary to form hypotheses which could be applied to specific cultures. The idea of evolution was not dead, but the focus of attention was directed at specific cultures and a narrow range of cultural practices. Anthropologists were moving from the armchair to the field, and the grand theories of the nineteenth century were replaced by the less grand models of those who studied particular cultures (written with a small "c"). Those who took to the field were the diffusionists.

The early diffusionists assumed that people were not very inventive. Practices began in one place and then moved from that place to other parts of the world. To test this idea, it was necessary to assemble different practices geographically in order to determine where they began and how they moved. To do this, it was necessary to collect ethnographies of different cultures. Since the information for these ethnographies had to come from observations of living peoples, it was necessary that they do field work.

In constructing an ethnography of a particular culture, it is customary to begin by assembling an inventory of cultural items. This is called a **trait inventory**. A **trait** is a particular practice or item which characterizes a culture. The traits on this list might include material items such as a drug, a tool, a house design, or a type of clothing. In addition, non-material items such as religious rituals, beliefs, rules of organization, or words in a language could be placed in an inventory. The reader is already familiar with this cataloging of traits in the HRAF, and the analysis of those traits by Horton, Fields, and others. The trait inventory includes traits that had been combined from an existing trait inventory, an **innovation**, as well as traits that had come from elsewhere through the process of **diffusion**. Diffusion occurs when cultures come into contact with each other, and traits from each culture are borrowed. As a result, cultures in geographical proximity to each other will be similar because of diffusion. Conversely, cultures that are separated by great distances will be different from each other. Cultures that share traits in common and are geographically close form what social scientists call a **culture area**. Thus, alcohol may be part of a culture's trait inventory as a result of **contact** with another culture that had alcohol as part of its trait inventory. Depending upon the traits used, what one observes is that traits are not equally distributed. In some areas certain traits are concentrated; in other areas there are few of the traits. The area where the frequency of traits are most concentrated is the **center** of a culture area.

In the early part of the twentieth century, American anthropologists, in particular archaeologists, added a relative time[3] variable to the culture area approach. They argued that it takes time for a trait to diffuse from its point of origin outward to other areas. It follows then that if a trait is widely distributed, it must be older than a trait that is not so widely distributed. The name that Clark Wissler (1923) and others gave to this method of estimating the relative age of a trait was the **age-area hypothesis**. The age-area hypothesis states that the more widely diffused a practice or artifact, the older it is. Traits found worldwide are presumed to be older than those we find only in limited geographical areas. Such worldwide traits are called **universals**.

Worldwide Distribution of Drugs

Joel Fort (1969) provides us with a rough sketch of the worldwide distribution of various drugs for a specific time. I have translated his narrative into table 4.1 and have taken the liberty of including tobacco. To this listing one could also add other substances (traits) such as coffee and tea, or compound drugs such as amphetamines and barbiturates.

Table 4.1.
Distribution of Selected Drugs by Major Continents

Drugs	Asia*	Africa	Australia Oceania	South & Central America **	Europe	North America
Alcohol	X	X	X	X	X	X
Tobacco	X	X	X	X	X	X
Cannabis	X	X		X	X	X
Opium Smoking	X					
Heroin	X				X	X
Kava			X			
Coca Leaf Chewing				X		
Qat or Khat	X	X				
Hallucinogens				X	X?	X
*Includes Middle East **Includes the Caribbean						

Obviously, this is a very crude listing. Continents are not cultures. For example, within Africa there are several quite distinct cultures. However, this listing does illustrate the culture-area approach. Each drug is considered a trait. Its presence or absence is then mapped for a specific time, in this case the late 1960s. What we note is that two drugs, tobacco and alcohol, are everywhere. They are universals. Marihuana is used everywhere except aboriginal Australia and Oceania. Other drugs, such as kava or coca leaf chewing, are found only in one geographical area. A strict application of the age-area hypothesis would suggest that alcohol and tobacco, because of their wide distribution, are older traits than kava or coca leaf chewing. We will explore this conclusion below.

To test the age-area hypothesis, it was necessary to demonstrate a single point of origin for a trait. Did tobacco and alcohol originate in one place and diffuse throughout the world, or are they examples of independent invention? **Independent invention** is the term used to describe the finding of identical or similar traits in geographically separated cultures who have not had previous contact and therefore cannot be explained by diffusion. Obviously, if a trait had a wide geographical distribution as a result of independent invention, it might not be as old as another trait that was not so widely distributed.

This question of whether a trait is the result of diffusion or independent invention was posed in 1889 by the British statistician, Sir Francis Galton (1822–1911) and is known as "Galton's Problem." His question was actually in response to E. B. Tylor's use of what he called "survivals." A survival is a belief, practice, or thing that is found in both simple and complex cultures in different parts of the world. To evolutionists like Tylor, the existence of survivals was proof not only of the antiquity of the practice but also of the cumulative nature of human learning. Culture evolves and changes, but some experiences or practices are perpetuated. Galton asked how one distinguishes between correlations (alcohol and subsistence type, for example) as a functional linkage from the diffusion of a particular item (alcohol). In other words, is the correlation between alcohol and subsistence type spurious because the societies in our sample are not independent? If so, then the conclusion that cultural traits belong together as a characteristic of Culture in general might be erroneously accepted. Several solutions have been suggested to solve this problem (Naroll 1961, 1964; Naroll and D'Andrade 1963; Pryor 1976; Schafer 1974), and readers are encouraged to review the alternative proposals for ways of overcoming Galton's rudeness in bursting the bubble of early evolutionists, the arch-diffusionists, and users of HRAF.

It might be helpful at this point to review what is known about the diffusion of the two most widely diffused drugs—tobacco and alcohol. An analysis of the diffusion process may focus on the movement of a single trait, several traits (a **trait complex**), or a process. A process is a method for doing something. For example, the process for domesticating an animal in one trait inventory may be borrowed and used to domesticate a different animal in another trait inventory. The animals are different, but the process is the same. The term used to describe the diffusion of a process is **stimulus diffusion**.

Chapter 2 outlined the major methodologies in the social sciences. In that same chapter we discussed data sources. One's data may come from living people—subjects, respondents, and informants. It is possible to use written historical documents as a source of data. What does one use to reconstruct "history" in the absence of live people and no written documents? In the area of drugs, alternative methods can be employed to recreate what might be called "inferential history." **Inference** is an analytical process that uses the presence of physical data to suggest practices for which no direct data are available. For instance, one might infer there had been a parade on a street by the presence of litter, animal droppings, and other materials that normally would not be there. We did not see the parade; we inferred that a parade had taken place. Inference has been used to reconstruct the origin and diffusion of drugs in the absence of "hard" physical data. Linguistic analysis is one possible data source. The emic names used to identify plant species (**ethnobotany**) are not the same from one language family to another. In the process of diffusion, the borrowing culture may adopt the name of the drug along with the drug. For example, "marihuana" is not an American English word. It is a Mexican-Spanish word. Just knowing this, we might infer that marihuana, the drug along with the name, diffused from Mexico. In India, the smoked form of marihuana is called "ganja." Because the word ganja is used in Jamaica to identify marihuana, one might infer diffusion from India. Another source for reconstructing history is through archeological analysis of **artifacts** that remain from past cultures. Artifacts are usually durable objects such as stone tools, pottery, and other items which may be used to infer something about activities in the past. Archaeologists also use pollen and seed analysis to infer what plant species existed in the past. If the pollen and the artifacts can be assigned dates, it is then possible to infer diffusion patterns. An additional data source is genetics. Many plants are hybrids of native species. By knowing the genetic characteristics of the hybrid and the genetics of the native species (if still living), one can infer both origin and diffusion of the plant.

Thus far the theoretical issues and problems related to the process of diffusion have been outlined. "How do things get where they are?" is not just a question of traits moving through space without any meaning, however. Objects, in and of themselves, have no intrinsic meaning. The meaning of anything is relative to the cultural contexts in which it is found. In the following sections we will explore the geographical and temporal movement of different drugs as a way of illustrating how social scientists go about using inference to extend understanding beyond limited time and space restrictions. At the same time, this exercise will serve as an introduction to the problem of dealing with the thorny issue of object meaning.

Single Trait Diffusion: Tobacco

Tobacco is native to the New World[4] and therefore did not come to the attention of the rest of the world until after contact in the late 1490s. By 1900 it had diffused to almost everywhere in the world. Tobacco use should not be equated with "smoking." Tobacco is a natural thing; smoking is a cultural process. Richard A. Blum (1969a) cites historical and archeological evidence to indicate that substances other than tobacco might have been smoked in parts of the world that did not have tobacco until recently. In the mountains of Central Asia, Farphu shamans have been observed inhaling smoke from mulberry leaves (Friedl 1965), and Blum personally observed other shamans from the same region using juniper leaves for this same purpose in 1967. But while smoking non-tobacco may predate smoking tobacco, it is the widespread diffusion of tobacco smoking that Blum suggests led to the smoking of opium, cannabis, and other substances.[5] If this is true, then reconstructing the diffusion of tobacco smoking is critical to an understanding of other substances.

Diffusion of Tobacco in the Old World

The word tobacco comes from the Spanish *tabaco*, which sounds like the Arawak Indian word for cigar. Columbus observed the Indians smoking tobacco, and other European travelers found tobacco being used almost everywhere in the New World except the Arctic, Subarctic, and parts of the Northwest Coast.

Students of diffusion can find no better example of rapid diffusion than tobacco smoking. There has been no other single trait that parallels the speed and widespread acceptance of this practice. Table 4.2 outlines the early historical diffusion of tobacco (Corti 1931; Driver 1969; Blum 1969a; Goodman 1993).

By the eighteenth century, European colonists reintroduced tobacco to those parts of the New World where it was not part of aboriginal trait inventories because it could not be grown. The Danes initiated the Greenlanders; the British and French brought it to most of the Subarctic; and the Russians transported it to Alaska.

The "history" of tobacco diffusion after contact with the New World is relatively simple to reconstruct using written documentation. The expanding world trade markets left records from ships' manifests, written accounts from travelers, and public records. This written legacy is an important data source for those doing history,

Table 4.2   **Diffusion of Tobacco**

1558:	From the Americas to Portugal
1560:	From Portugal to France
1560:	From France to Holland
1561:	From Portugal to Italy
1570:	Imported plants cultivated in Belgium, Spain, Italy, Switzerland and England
1571:	From Mexico (via Spanish traders) to Philippines
1590:	From Turkey to Poland
1595:	From Macao (via Portuguese traders) to India
1600:	From Macao (via Portuguese traders) to Java
1600:	From Macao (via Portuguese traders) to the Near East
1605:	From Macao (via Portuguese traders) to Japan
1607:	From Macao (via Portuguese traders) to West Africa
1610:	From Japan to Korea
1610:	From India to Ceylon
1630:	From China to Siberia, Mongolia, Turkestan and Tibet
1630:	Imported plants cultivated in West Africa

but how do we reconstruct "histories" without writing? How do we piece together the diffusion of tobacco in the New World before contact?

Evidence For Diffusion in the New World Prior to Contact

Without historical records, the reconstruction of the diffusion of tobacco in the New World must rely on inferential evidence. One bit of evidence can be obtained by an examination of the genetic characteristics of tobacco plants. That tobacco originated in the New World is well accepted. There are over a dozen native species of tobacco, most of which are found in the New World. At least two species are **cultigens**, plants that have been hybridized (a genetic combination of native species), and were cultivated in areas where no native species lived. The cultigens are *Nicotiana tabacum* and *Nicotiana rustica*. *Tabacum* was taken to Europe and spread by Europeans to other parts of the world. *N. tobacum* is a hybrid of two wild forms, *Nicotiana tomentosum* (found in Peru and Bolivia) and *Nicotiana sylvestris* (found in northern Argentina). After its origin in one of these localities, it spread by diffusion or migration to the West Indies, where it was discovered by Columbus. The other hybrid, *N. rustica*, is a genetic combination of two wild species growing on the west side of the Andes near the border of Ecuador and Peru. *Rustica* spread by diffusion and migration to a much larger territory than *tabacum*. It diffused south to Chiloé Island off the coast of Chile, and north to the limits of agriculture in New Brunswick. In North America its distribution followed that of maize domestication.

Another inferential data source comes from archeology. Archeology is concerned with reconstructing past cultures through the analysis of artifacts (physical traits) that remain long after the people who used them have disappeared. Of all the specializations in the social sciences, archeology has maintained the diffusion tradition. One artifact that has been used to infer the use of tobacco is the pipe. One must, however, exercise some caution with using this linkage. Pipes were not always used for smoking and may have been trade items. In isolation, the uncovering of pipes is not conclusive evidence for tobacco smoking. When pipes are found in association with maize agriculture (which parallels tobacco domestication), the inference that tobacco was used becomes stronger. Based on this evidence, the best guess is that *N. rustica* probably spread from south to north along with other cultivated plants.

What is clear is that the wild ancestors of *rustica* did not exist in North America, which would have made it impossible to have originated there. By the time Europeans settled in Virginia, *N. rustica* was being used by Native Americans. The Europeans adopted the plant and grew it commercially until it was replaced by *N. tabacum*, which was diffused by other Europeans from the West Indies.

Several tobacco species were either cultivated or harvested in the New World. In fact, tobacco was the most widely used plant in the New World. It was found both in those areas where maize was domesticated and elsewhere. It appears that Native Americans were as "hooked" on tobacco as the world is today. Harold Driver and William Massey (1957, 261) constructed a distribution map of different species of tobacco in North America.

Uses of Tobacco: North America

Driver's (1969, 105–109) review of ethnographic descriptions of tobacco use among North American Indians revealed that they often mixed tobacco with other plants. For example, in the eastern United States, sumac leaves and the inner bark of a species of dogwood

Species of Tobacco in North America

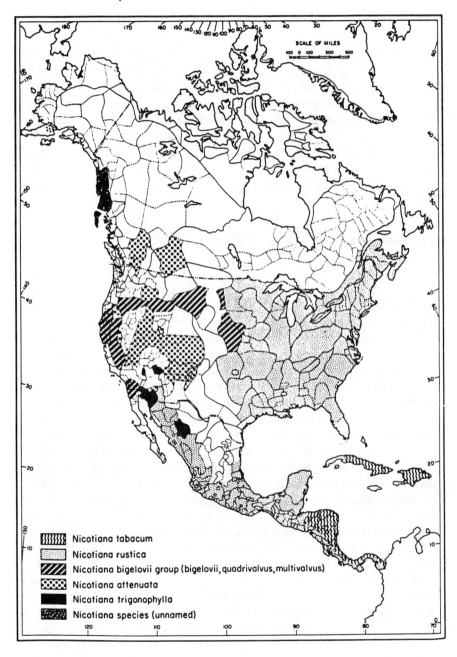

Source: Harold E. Driver and William C. Massey. 1957. *Comparative Studies of North American Indians*. Transactions of the American Philosophical Society, XLVII.

were used as additives. The reasons cited for this practice were: scarcity of tobacco, improvement of flavor, and dilution of strength. While it was smoked everywhere except the northern Northwest Coast, smoking was not the only method of ingestion. Among Northwest Coastal tribes it was chewed with lime. In California and Nevada it was ground with lime and water and licked off the pestle; sometimes it was mixed with *Datura* (Jimsonweed) and drunk. Among the Creek, it was an ingredient of the famous "black drink" (the primary ingredient was the leaves of the tree *Ilex cassine*). The Aztecs ate tobacco leaves straight and ground them into a powder that was snuffed. Since smoking did not occur in those areas of South America where *N. tabacum* and *N. rustica* originated by hybridization, this suggests that chewing or snuffing preceded smoking.

Tobacco as Cultural Artifact

The diffusion of tobacco as a thing can be reconstructed by using genetic, archeological, and linguistic data. But tobacco is not just a thing; rather it is an object that is attributed with meaning. What gives it meaning is the cultural context within which it is used. In North America it had both a religious and a secular meaning. Shamans used tobacco to alter consciousness in order to establish rapport with spirit beings and to cure disease. Tobacco played a role in almost all public rituals as well. It was not always smoked, chewed, or snuffed, however. Sometimes it was burned as incense, cast into the air, or buried. Among the Plains, Prairie, and Eastern Indians, medicine bundles usually contained tobacco and a pipe. Whenever the bundle was used for religious purposes, tobacco, along with other substances, was smoked. The popular image of the "peace pipe" is rooted in the practice of some American Indians sealing political contracts by each party smoking from the same pipe.

As tobacco diffused around the world, it took on different cultural meanings. Why was there such a worldwide acceptance of tobacco? One explanation for its universal appeal has been attributed to the "addictiveness" of nicotine (Brecher 1972). Nicotine use does conform to Lindesmith's definition of addiction. Tobacco is unique among drugs in another way. It has successfully resisted becoming illegal in spite of attempts by popes, kings, czars, and legislative bodies to prohibit its use, sometimes even by capital punishment (chapter 10). Not only did tobacco become a trait in all cultures, but it was a trait that was widely used by people within those cultures. Is the answer to the question of tobacco's appeal simply physiological? The answer is no! Heroin, cocaine, and other drugs may also be addictive. Yet in spite of their "addictiveness" they are not widely diffused, and in cultures having these in their trait inventories only a small percentage of the population actually uses them.[6] To explain diffusion of any trait, it is necessary to demonstrate the "why" of acceptance or rejection of the trait. That explanation ultimately comes from understanding how the trait fits into existing cultural practices.

Why Is Tobacco Found Everywhere?

One of the consistent findings of diffusion research is that cultural items move with greatest ease between cultures that are similar in their trait inventories. One can cite many examples of acceptance or rejection of traits based upon this general principle. For example, the Yanomamö blow a hallucinogenic powder up their nose which produces vomiting and some other interesting effects; throughout the South Pacific betel nut (*Areca cathecu*) is chewed, which turns the teeth and gums a bright red color. It is not likely that either one of the these practices would be adopted in the United States, because having green mucous running from your nose or bright red gums and teeth are inconsistent with American standards of public etiquette and beauty. Tobacco seems to violate the principle of diffusion between cultures similar in trait inventories. Tobacco, for all practical purposes, is found everywhere. One suggestion for this widespread diffusion comes from the only ethnography of tobacco use ever undertaken. In Peter Weston Black's (1984) ethnographic account of Tobi, he suggests that the acceptance of a cultural trait is linked to the characteristics of the trait itself and the trait inventory of the adopting unit. The concept he uses to explain diffusion is **symbolic specificity**. The diffusion of items from one culture to another depends upon whether the adopting culture has certain items or practices in its cultural inventory. For example, if books were to be adopted by a culture, literacy would be a necessary trait. To adopt an automobile, gasoline would have to be present. The more any particular trait necessitates the presence of other traits, the more symbolically specific it is.

Ethnohistory of Tobian Tobacco Use

Magellan and his crew introduced the cultivation of tobacco to Guam in 1521. It reached Tobi somewhere between 1833 and 1901.

The earlier date was determined by reference to a report made by a shipwrecked American seaman who stayed on the island for three years. His diary made no mention of tobacco use. The latter date marks a German expedition, which arrived to raise the flag for the *Sudsee* empire and noted that the Tobians were users of what was by then a valuable commodity.

The Tobian story is that the first person to own tobacco on Tobi was ignorant of its use. He decided that it was valuable because of the amount of the island's produce needed to obtain it in trade. When it proved inedible he hid it away. Some years later he learned from a returning Tobian who had been working for Europeans that it was a very fine thing and made people "happy" when they smoked it.

This story marks the end of isolation for Tobi. Beginning in the early part of the twentieth century, self-contained island communities such as Tobi became part of an exchange economy made possible by Europeans who traded metal, cloth, and tobacco for copra (dried coconut meat which is a source of coconut oil), and sennit. Metal replaced clam shell adze heads, metal wire was bent into fish hooks; and cloth was used for clothing and sails. It is easy to see that both iron and cloth "fit" into existing cultural practices. The adze, fish hooks, clothing and sails were already being used by Tobians prior to contact, but why was tobacco adopted? Black argues that not only do Tobians believe that tobacco makes one happy, but its possession marks one as a competent person familiar with (among other things) elements of alien cultures which have been adopted. Tobacco, like metal and cloth, must lack symbolic specificity. The form and function of the adze, the fish hook, clothing, and the sail remained the same after the adoption of metal and cloth. Tobacco, therefore, must have "fit" quite nicely into the existing cultural practices of the Tobians, or it would not have been adopted.

Tobian Tobacco Imports

Until recently, Tobians had to chase passing ships to get their tobacco supplies. Today the island is visited six to ten times a year by ships which stay anywhere from thirty minutes to one day. Tobians are very adept at getting tobacco from people on these ships.

Most tobacco comes from a U.S. Government vessel that visits from the administrative center of Koror in Palau, almost 400 miles north of Tobi. During its stay traders buy copra and sell supplies, including tobacco. Tobacco comes in two forms. One is the twist, a molasses saturated stick of rough cut tobacco, six and one-half inches long, one inch wide, and one quarter inch thick. The other form is American manufactured cigarettes. The actual amount of tobacco available during any one visit usually exceeds the amount purchased. Additional tobacco comes as gifts from relatives and friends, as well as through passengers who trade cigarettes for handicrafts or for services. However, the total amount is seldom enough to last until the arrival of the next ship. Thus, the supply of tobacco on Tobi varies by ship schedules. Soon after the departure of the supply ship there is a large amount of tobacco; before the arrival of the next ship the supply has dwindled.

Tobacco and Tobian Society

There are 58 people on Tobi. They are organized into several matrilineal exogamous clans.[7] Other organizational units are flexibly organized extended families, gender, age, and special interest groups. On the island there is a health aide and a school teacher who are employed through governmental administrative units in Koror. Leadership is the joint responsibility of a traditional chief and an elected magistrate. Black argues that tobacco plays an important role in each of these social units.

All able bodied persons engage in subsistence activities, and all adults are responsible for securing tobacco for themselves and their dependents. Some of the senior men are distinguished from others. These men are the heads of what Black calls the "in-charge system." This system is led by men between the ages of forty and seventy who are defined as competent. Behaviorally they control the kitchens which provide at least one culturally prescribed meal a day. That meal consists of male-produced fish and coconut, and female-produced taro or sweet potato. Tobians believe that this meal is necessary to maintain good health. Most of the people who attend the meal are members of the senior man's in-charge system, but others who may not have their own kitchen also attend. Each guest is expected to contribute something to the meal. After the meal, the senior man passes around tobacco.

Tobian Views of Competency

Tobians believe that only older males are competent. All others are antisocial and need the competent male to take charge of them. The social marker of competency is the possession of tobacco by the senior male, who is responsible for distributing it within his network. He does so through a series of interconnected **dyads** (two-person groups). Tobacco thus moves from the senior male to his directly subordinate dyad partner. This person, in turn, passes it down the chain until all members of the system have received tobacco.

Managing the distribution of tobacco requires much administrative skill and planning. As mentioned, tobacco supplies vary according to the supply ship visits. In times of plenty, the competent man can easily supply his network with tobacco and thus fulfill the value of sharing and cooperation. When supplies are low this expectation becomes more difficult to meet. This is the test of competency. When other less competent people are low or out of tobacco, the competent male must regulate the distribution of his own, sometimes meager, supply. Tobacco then is the physical object that measures the ability to manage. More importantly, it is the uneven distribution of this "thing" that tests the ability of competent adult males. It is not tobacco or the nicotine in tobacco that created the in-charge system; it is tobacco that objectifies that system.[8]

This example from Tobi illustrates how different meanings have been associated with tobacco. For American Indians tobacco was used to bind contracts, to converse with the supernatural, and as part of a health regime. Tobians, on the other hand, incorporated tobacco into their existing system of social relationships. Beyond this ethnographic example, the concept of symbolic specificity sensitizes us toward understanding acceptance or rejection of other drugs cross-culturally and over time.

The diffusion of tobacco can be measured by its presence or absence. As mentioned earlier, the process of diffusion may also account for the movement of a stimulus rather than a trait. A stimulus is a procedure, not a thing. For example, the process for domesticating plants and animals was first discovered about twelve thousand years ago. This process diffused and was applied to many species of plants and animals, some of which were successfully domesticated; others were not. One example of stimulus diffusion is the distillation of alcohol.

Stimulus Diffusion: Distillation of Alcohol

In general, the history and distribution of alcoholic beverages is linked to horticulture[9] in both the Old and New World. However, there are a number of exceptions. Beverages have been made from numerous natural plant species by peoples who were not horticulturalists. Various species of cacti, wild plums, honey, mesquite, pineapple, and sarsaparilla root have been used as bases for fermentation (LaBarre 1938; Driver 1969, 109–110). I would suggest that the presumed linkage between the beginnings of alcoholic beverages and settled horticulture may be a function of traits associated with settlement. In cultures that have domesticated plants, one is likely to find artifacts that permit the storage of water, grain, and other items. Nomadic hunters and gatherers, even if they have knowledge of fermentation, are not likely to have vessels for storage. Having containers means that fermented beverages can be produced on a continuous basis. Only when production is continuous is there a concern with control over the usage, and the subsequent development of rules which regulate by whom, when, and why alcoholic beverages are consumed. Thus, even with knowledge about the process of fermentation, peoples without the means to produce them will have few, if any, rules regulating their use.

The origin(s) of fermentation is lost, but it is obvious that the process was independently discovered in several different places. Historical reconstructions from written records indicate the production and use of alcoholic beverages in all the early civilizations (Blum 1969b). Fermentation as a process was not invented. It is a naturally occurring outcome. Fermentation will occur without human intervention. It would be more appropriate to classify fermentation, like fire, as a process of domestication. In domestication, a natural process is guided by humans. The same cannot be said of distillation. Distillation does not occur in nature. Rather, it is an innovation.

Berton Roueché (1963) suggests that the earliest reference to the process of distillation can be traced to the ninth-century Arabian alchemist, Jabbir ibn Hayyan, who was known in the West as Geber. The word alcohol comes from the Arabic, "alkuhl," which originally was the name of a powdered eye cosmetic. Its meaning later changed to refer to the essence of any thing. Geber's process for distillation was hidden in such obscure prose that it is not clear whether Geber saw any practical use for the product of his process.

It was not until the end of the thirteenth century that Arnaldus de Villanova, professor of medicine at the University of Montpellier, "popularized" alcohol as a medicine and gave it the name, "aqua vitae," the water of life. He and others hailed "aqua vitae" as a cure for several illnesses, an elixir for prolonging life, and even a cure for baldness. (Remember Kaplan's Law of the Instrument in chapter

3?) Aqua vitae was initially distilled from wine and therefore would now be considered a brandy, from the Dutch word *brandewijn* (burnt wine). The process of distillation was not confined to producing drinking alcohol. The same process was applied to the making of perfume and extracts of flowers and herbs that were used for medicinal purposes during the fourteenth century.

Apparently aqua vitae diffused rather rapidly throughout Western Europe. By the middle of the sixteenth century it had become commonplace in Germany and Holland. It reached England in 1585 and within a few years had almost replaced beer.

The discovery that other fermented beverages could be distilled is attributed to Franciscus Sylvius, a seventeenth-century professor of medicine at the University of Leyden. When grain beer was used as a base, this new distillate become known as *junever*, the Dutch word for juniper, a herb used to mask the distasteful raw alcohol. The French changed the word to *geniévre*; the British called it "geneva," which was latter shortened to "gin." In Russia it was known as "vodka," or "little water." The production and distribution of aqua vitae throughout Europe was encouraged by government. In 1690, the English government passed legislation favorable to the production of brandy and spirits from corn. By 1694 the annual production was nearly one million gallons. This increased to 11 million gallons in 1733 and 20 million gallons by 1742. The enthusiastic support by governments to increase production was not an act of altruism. The practice of increasing tax rates on imported and exported distilled beverages became an important source of income, and this practice has continued into the present.

Although the distillation of grain for much of Western Europe is traced to Holland, the practice had its beginnings earlier and quite independently in Ireland. Although enthusiastically attributed to St. Patrick who died in 461, the earliest evidence would place the practice's beginnings in the twelfth century. The Irish name for this distillate was *uisgebeatha*, which later became whiskey. It probably diffused to Scotland through migration (some Scots originally came from Ireland) and was well established there by the fifteenth century. The early Irish and Scottish whiskey was distilled from a mash, or cereal base, composed entirely of malted barley. It was not until the eighteenth century that Scotch, or Scottish whiskey, was manufactured. The difference between Scottish and Irish whiskey is that the Scots "malted"[10] their barley in peat-fired kilns. This produces a distinctive smoky flavor which found favor among the Scots but not the English, who had become accustomed to the taste of gin.

In 1826 Robert Stein, a Scottish distiller, invented a process for the rapid distillation of grain whiskey. Four years later, Aeneas Coffey, an Irish excise officer, patented a more efficient process which was to become the standard in distillery. This process produced a light grain spirit that tasted nothing like malted whiskey. In 1860, Andrew Usher, a distiller from Edinburgh, combined the grain alcohol produced by the new patent still with single malt whiskey to produce the first "blended" whiskey. The consequence of this "innovation" was the diffusion of "Scotch" whiskey to England and then to the rest of the world.

Around 1640, the first distillery in the United States was founded by the Dutch in New York City. Twenty-four years later it was taken over by the British. Originally it produced brandy and gin. The British distilled rum (or rumbullion or kill-devil) from molasses. Rum originally was distilled by early European settlers in the West Indies sometime in first half of the 1600s. By 1657, a rum distillery was operating in Boston which used molasses shipped in from the West Indies. Rum was a major source of wealth in New England, and New England distillers were active in the slave trade. Rum became an international currency.

> Slavers of all nations used New England rum as a means of filling their holds from the slave pens on the Guinea coast. The slavers then headed for the West Indies. There they sold their slaves . . . and took on a load of slave-produced molasses. The molasses was then brought to New England and traded for another cargo of rum. (Roueché, 179)

Eric Williams (1966) argues that:

> Rum was an essential part of the cargo of the slave ship, particularly the colonial American slave ship. No slave trader could afford to dispense with a cargo of rum. It was profitable to spread a taste for liquor on the coast. The Negro dealers were plied with it, were induced to drink till they lost their reason, and then the bargain was struck. (78)

The other drug which contributed to the slave trade was tobacco. Jerome E. Brooks (1952) suggests that the Portuguese developed exclusive purchase rights with some West African slave dealers because of the type of tobacco they used as currency.

> Prices for slaves became fairly standardized: a Negro trader in Guinea, for instance, would be paid six or seven rolls of Brazil tobacco (each weighing seventy-five pounds) for the delivery of another Negro into servitude. (105)

It is clear that the increased European markets for tobacco and rum, along with sugar and molasses (which was used to make rum) were in large part a justification for the practice of slavery in the New World. They, along with cotton, were responsible for the development of trade, manufacturing, and shipping cities in the United Kingdom such as Glasgow, Bristol, Newcastle, Manchester, and Liverpool. The cotton was transformed into cloth which was traded around the world, while rum filled the stomachs and tobacco the lungs of slaves and slave masters alike.

With the decline in the slave trade as a result of an 1807 act prohibiting the importing of new slaves, and a change in public taste for cheaper domestic whiskey, the New England rum industry fell into ruin. But rum or "demon rum" remained a generic name for any distilled spirit in the United States into the twentieth century. (Remember Ambrose Bierce in chapter 1?) The domestic whiskeys that replaced rum were bourbon and rye. Roueché suggests that the production of these two were the continuation of cultural practices brought to the United States by Scottish and Irish immigrants. Whatever the source, both became a frontier currency. In Virginia and Kentucky that currency was bourbon made from corn; in Maryland and Pennsylvania it was rye whiskey made from rye. By the end of the nineteenth century, the application of the process of distillation to plants and grains stopped. In the United States during the twentieth century there were further attempts to disguise the taste of alcohol as "mixed drinks" for the increasing proportion of the population that drank.[11]

This short history of the diffusion of distillation sheds some light on the movement of a cultural trait through time. However, it does not explain "why" it was adopted, nor do we have any better understanding of its function. Knowing the history of alcohol is not social science, but it does provide us with information that can be used for social sciencing.

The question of why fermented beverages were independently invented in different but non-contiguous areas may be due to opportunity. MacAndrew and Edgerton (1969, 170) suggest that the raw materials are available everywhere. Almost any organic material will ferment. Secondly, the technology is simple; almost anybody can learn the process. However, having the raw materials and knowing the process is only a "possiblism." Drinking, argue MacAndrew and Edgerton, especially drunkenness, is rooted in society itself (166–169). Beginning with the axiom that the majority in any society will, through socialization, behave in a manner that is consistent with cultural expectations, they suggest that this process is never complete. That is, not everybody will behave according to the ideal. The result is potential conflict. This potential may be handled in two possible ways. One is **ineligibility**.

Ineligibility may apply to mentally ill persons who are defined as incapable of learning cultural rules. Persons so defined are placed into a special category which grants them permanent immunity from the everyday rules. The other is what MacAndrew and Edgerton call **time out**. This is any behavior that is granted temporary immunity from cultural rules. Several behaviors may fall under this category depending upon the culture. One is the "altered state of consciousness" that is believed to result from the ingestion of numerous "drugs." Under the believed influence of the drug, people are "not themselves" and their behaviors are excused. Alcohol has a temporary effect in altering consciousness or behavior. Because alcohol is so available, it fits this universal societal "need" to explain deviation from cultural rules.

Another theory posits that the type of drug adopted or rejected by a society is related to the effects of the drug and how it fits into the existing system of expectations. This theory (which I call **cultural consistency**) suggests that where action and aggressiveness are dominant cultural themes, drugs such as marihuana will be rejected and alcohol, amphetamines, or some other similar drug will be accepted (Fort 1969; Murphy 1963; Carstairs 1969; Benbud 1957). Conversely, where passivity is a dominant cultural theme, alcohol will be rejected, and marihuana will be accepted. In other words, the believed effects of the drug must be consistent with the norms for behavior in general or the drug will be rejected and those who use them will be defined as deviant, crazy, or criminal. This argument is similar to Black's symbolic specificity but with the added benefit of including rejection of drugs.

It is not necessary to elaborate upon these explanations here except to note that the three "theories" presented thus far—symbolic specificity, time out, and cultural consistency—all focus on a single or limited number of drugs—tobacco, alcohol, or marihuana. Each of these theories assumes that culture is the independent variable. The adoption or rejection of any one of these substances will depend upon the characteristics of the existing cultural framework. Because each theory is drug specific, it may have limited application. By definition, these theories do not have to be quite so elaborate as an explanation for the diffusion of a trait complex. Most drug diffusion research focuses on some specific drug, but there is some research which focuses on the diffusion of a bundle of traits, one of which happens to be a drug. One example of this is the diffusion of the peyote cult among American Indians.

Diffusion of a Trait Complex: The Peyote Cult

Peyote (*Lophophora williamsii*) is a small, spineless, carrot-shaped cactus that grows wild in the Rio Grande Valley and southward in Mexico. In mature plants there are nine alkaloids with both strychnine- and morphine-like properties which are somewhat antagonistic[12] in action. Although the effects of peyote have been differently described, it is reported to produce an altered state of consciousness. This reaction probably reflects its antagonistic chemistry. The strychnine-like alkaloids produce exhilaration followed by depression and nausea. Under the influence of the morphine-like alkaloids, users report vivid color visions.

Richard Schultes (1938) suggests that peyote use in Mexico goes back over 2,000 years. Historical documents show that as early as 1591 the Spanish attempted to prohibit it in Mexico and interpreted its use as satanic or diabolic (Shultes 1972). By 1720, peyote was prohibited throughout Mexico, and rituals associated with its use had to be carried out secretly. Today it is still used by the Huichol Indians in Mexico (chapter 8) and is freely available in Mexican herb markets. Peyote diffused to American Indian tribes initially as a single trait and was included in the "medicine bundles" that were used in curing ceremonies. This diffusion was facilitated by the nomadic life-style of many American Indians of the Southwest, which brought them into contact with tribal groups in Mexico that used peyote. Regardless of when the first contact with users of peyote was made, there is no evidence of the peyote cult much before the middle of the nineteenth century.

The peyote cult refers to both a religious group and a set of practices. As a cult it was a minority practice. Thus, cultists were part of a larger tribal affiliation that included other cults as well as more generally practiced rituals in reference to the supernatural. In analyzing the diffusion of the peyote cult, the focus is not peyote but rather a complex of practices which includes rituals, songs and beliefs.

One of the earliest writers on the peyote cult, Morris Opler (1938), suggested that its initial diffusion was from the Carrizo in Mexico to the Lipan Apache in the Galveston-Houston area of Texas in the early nineteenth century. The evidence for this diffusion is that some present-day cult practices (including the acquisition of visions, the passing of the drum and rattle among the participants as they sang, and the ceremonial breakfast) were part of Carrizo rituals in the early nineteenth century. Remember the age-area argument that the more widely distributed a trait, the older it is. Other characteristics, more recently added to the ritual (the use of the mound for an altar, the whistle and the feathers, the appearance of the morning woman with water) were not associated with the early nineteenth-century ritual performance.

Opler's reconstruction of the early diffusion of the peyote cult suggests a methodology based upon the analysis of "survivals." If the same practices are found in the rituals of two societies, one can assume that one either adopted from the other, or they both adopted from a third source. If we can affix dates to when the practices began, then it is possible to test which of these two explanations is correct.

One of the most ambitious reconstructions of the spread of peyotism among American Indians was done by Weston LaBarre (1975). Field work for his doctoral dissertation on the Kiowa peyote cult began in 1935. The following year he observed peyote services in fifteen different tribes. Since that time, his published dissertation has gone through four revisions and enlargements to include all the published and unpublished accounts of the peyote cult. His lifetime work illustrates how this methodology can be used for reconstructing the diffusion of this trait complex.

The first step in this reconstruction is to deconstruct the ritual itself into component traits and then compare different tribal practices on this trait inventory. LaBarre selects several ritual attributes. Some of these include: time of the meeting, purpose of the meeting, place of the meeting, bathing, painting, visiting, clothing, officials, smoking, various paraphernalia (such as drums, whistle, feathers, fire and fire stick) shape of the altar, songs, and so forth. Once these have been identified through observation, the next step is to note how each attribute varies—in other words, construct a variable list for each attribute. The next step is to map these variables by tribal affiliation. An example of how this might be done is shown in table 4.3.

Unlike tables constructed from the Human Relations Area Files which are used to determine correlations between variables, the purpose of this exercise is to discover diffusion pathways. Agreements in ritual elements would suggest the possibility of diffusion. A further test of diffusion would be through mapping of tribal territories. If the ritual elements are similar and the tribes reside close to each other, this lends further support to the diffusion argument. The next step is to cull through ethnographies and histories of those tribes that appear to be linked together by similarities in ritual elements and spatial location. Using this research strategy, LaBarre was able to identify several ways that the peyote cult diffused. Within regions, some tribes were influential

Table 4.3.
Tribal Comparisons of Peyote Ritual Variables

TRIBES	Time of Ceremony	Place of Meeting	Face Painting	Drum	Doctoring as Purpose of Meeting	Women permitted as Participants	Christian Elements
Comanche	Sunday	tipi	yes	yes	no	yes	no
Seminole	Sunday	tipi?	no	yes	yes?	?	yes?
Mescalero	Saturday	tipi	no	yes	yes	yes	no
Omaha	Saturday	round house	no	yes	yes?	?	yes
Taos	Saturday	member's house	no	yes	yes	yes	yes
Winnebago	Saturday?	tipi	yes	yes	yes/no	yes	yes
Kickapoo	Saturday	?	no?	yes	no	yes	yes

in its diffusion. Through the use of oral histories, it was possible to reconstruct specific tribal or individual carriers of peyote cult practices. In some cases, peyotism was the result of multiple contacts with different peyote-using tribes or individuals. Peyotism was also diffused through intertribal marriage. A more recent source of rapid diffusion was through the United States government's attempts to detribalize Amerindians. This was done through forced education at either special Indian or white schools. Instead of discouraging tribal affiliations, friendships between boys had the effect of increasing intertribal awareness—and spreading many cultural practices, including peyotism.

By bringing together the distribution of cult characteristics and specific histories from oral, governmental, and ethnographic sources, the diffusion pattern of the peyote cult becomes more clear. LaBarre (1975, 122) used all these sources to reconstruct the diffusion of the peyote cult in table 4.4. He agreed with Opler that the initial diffusion occurred sometime in the middle of the nineteenth century, first with the Lipan, who passed the practice on to the Mescalero, who then passed it on to the Kiowa. At that time, the Comanche and the Kiowa became culture centers for several other tribes. From the Comanche, it diffused directly to five

Table 4.4.
Diffusion of the Peyote Cult

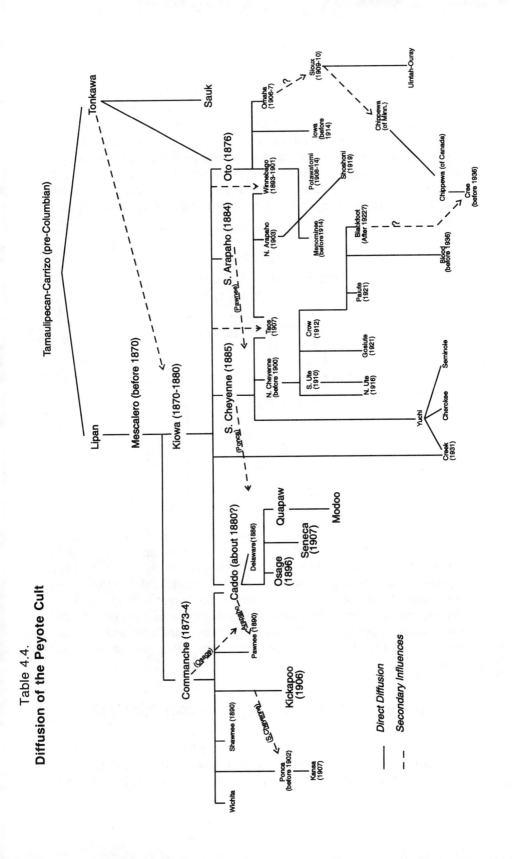

tribes from 1889 to 1890. The Caddo adopted it from both the Comanche and the Kiowa around 1890. The Kiowa were then responsible for diffusing it to three tribes directly, who in turn were responsible for further diffusion. By the mid-1930s, most of the Plains, Southwestern, and Middle Northern Canadian tribes had some members who were cult practitioners.

Using the dates provided by LaBarre, one can construct a table which indicates the number of tribes by year of adoption. This I have done in table 4.5.

Table 4.5.

Diffusion of Peyotism
Number of Tribes by Year

Years	Number
Before 1870	1
1871–1880	5
1881–1890	7
1891–1900	2
1901–1910	11
1911–1920	4
1921–1930	3
1931 +	3

Two "waves" of diffusion occur, one in the nineteen-year period from 1871 to 1890 followed by a nine-year lull from 1891 to 1900. From 1901 to 1920 there is another period of diffusion. While these figures mean nothing in and of themselves, they do suggest that one probe further to explain this particular pattern. Why are these two periods characterized by a high frequency of adoption of this innovation, whereas other time periods are not? We will discuss some possible reasons and theoretical explanations in the next chapter.

Diffusion: The Social Psychological Approach

The interest in diffusion never caught on with sociologists as it did with anthropologists, although Gabriel Tarde (1843–1904), one of the influential "fathers" of sociology, was interested in the topic.

Tarde was an opponent of the Durkheimian approach to sociology. He rejected the idea of social facts and emphasized the importance of psychological factors in explaining social behavior. Tarde's theory of "imitation" suggested that the continuity of social practices was an imitation of both our ancestors and our contemporaries. He used this concept of imitation to explain why the adoption of new ideas seemed to followed a normal, S-shape distribution. Diffusion begins with a few individuals, then spreads to a larger number, and finally levels off. This process of adopting an innovation is explained, according to Tarde, because the psychological characteristics of those who adopt early are different from the later imitators (Tarde 1903, 87–88). Within sociology, the social psychological, S-shaped curve tradition of diffusion has been continued primarily by rural sociologists, who have had a longtime interest in the process of adoption of innovations by farmers both in the United States and elsewhere.

Everett Rogers (1962), following the Tarde tradition, reviewed over 500 studies of diffusion to determine if there were any empirical generalizations that could be used to construct a general theory of the diffusion process. Starting with a definition that diffusion is characterized by the

> (1) acceptance, (2) over time, (3) of some specific item—an idea or practice, (4) by individuals, groups, or other adopting units, linked (5) to specific channels of communication, (6) to a social structure and (7) to a given system of values, or culture. (Katz et al. 1963, 240)

Rogers and his staff read and coded studies of the diffusion of practices, things, and ideas. From these studies they were able to present fifty-two empirical generalizations about the process. For Rogers the process involves five steps, beginning with awareness of an innovation and ending with the adoption of that innovation. Individuals vary in their degree of innovativeness depending upon their interaction framework (membership in groups). Thus, access to information provided by one's interaction framework may increase or decrease awareness of an innovation. Going back to the example of marihuana use among young people during the 1960s, one would assume that membership in a group that has information about the use of marihuana will increase one's awareness of the drug. The decision to use (adopt) marihuana (an innovation) would be related to one's position within that group. Those who adopt earlier ("early adopters" in Rogers' classification system) are more likely to have more information from a greater variety of sources. Because adoption requires information, and the acquisition of information takes time, some people will be "late adopters." This is Rogers' explanation for Tarde's S-shaped curve.

Rogers' review of the diffusion literature enabled him to speculate on what happens *after* individual adoption occurs. Here there are a limited number of probablistic outcomes. One is that adopters will continue to use the innovation. Another outcome is that they will discontinue use. The same outcomes are possible for non-adopters. They may continue to reject the innovation, or they may become late adopters. If the readers finds this unnecessarily complicated, they may be correct. The difficulty with this approach is that Rogers is attempting to understand variations in individuals' behaviors, a goal which has been rejected as outside the scope of social science. This does not mean that his "theory" and findings should be rejected. What Rogers unwittingly confirmed was the S-shaped curve. His attempt to find shared characteristics of early and late adopters was not as fruitful. The range of personal characteristics of early and late adopters were so wide as to be nonconclusive. This suggests that the explanation of the S-shaped curve is due to factors other than the characteristics of individuals.The study of heroin diffusion provides an alternative explanation.

Heroin Diffusion: The Epidemiological Model

Some researchers have studied the spread of heroin by using an epidemiology model. Epidemiology models have been borrowed from research on the spread of disease. The recent AIDS "epidemic" has brought this model into the consciousness of Americans and Europeans. Starting with a very few carriers, it has been transmitted within certain subgroups (homosexuals, intravenous drug users) at what appears to be an alarming rate. This rate is a geometric progression, from one to two to four to sixteen, and so forth, until it affects a sizeable proportion of those subgroups. The question asked by epidemiologists is, "When will it stop?" or "Will it continue at this geometric rate until the whole population is infected?" This same question may be asked about drug use. The media has often brought forth the disparaging news that this or that drug will soon take over. The marihuana "epidemic" was followed by the LSD "epidemic," which in turn was replaced by angel dust, cocaine, crack, and the most recent drug, ice. While public attention is focused on the latest "epidemic," the last "epidemic" fades from our collective memory. Obviously, something is happening to these so-called "epidemics." Just what is happening and why can be answered by a systematic review of the diffusion patterns of drugs.

Leon Hunt and Carl Chambers' (1976) review of heroin incidence studies contributes to our understanding of drug epidemics. **Incidence** refers to the rate of occurrence of new cases within a population during a specified period of time. This is not the same as **prevalence**—the number of cases per some unit of population. Unlike diseases such as measles, heroin use is a crime and has a social stigma associated with it. Incidence rates are therefore likely to overrepresent some segments of the population (such as those who use public health facilities) and underrepresent other users (such as higher income users who can afford private treatment and are less likely to be arrested). The usual measure in drug "abuse" studies—**relative incidence**—measures new cases by some unit of time (weeks, months, or years). Whatever the limitation of using relative incidence, the findings of heroin use studies are consistent. Heroin use, like many other practices, diffuses within groups of persons who know each other. Use follows a predictable diffusion pattern, very similar to the pattern found for the spread of contagious diseases.

Hunt and Chambers reviewed three studies of heroin use for their analysis. One of these studies took place in Crawley, England; the other two were Grosse Pointe, Michigan and Chicago, Illinois. Each of these studies found that heroin was introduced from outside the local social system, usually by a member of that system. Once introduced, it spread rather rapidly through existing networks of relationships. Hunt and Chambers found that the incidence interval between generations of users is about one year. This may be partially explained by the process of addiction to heroin, which normally occurs somewhere between six months to a year of continued use. After addiction, the life pattern of the addict changes, and the pre-addiction network to which he or she belonged is replaced by a new network made up of addicts. They conclude that ". . . it is the new user, and not the confirmed addict, who is contagious and who is responsible for the spread of new use (13)." It is the new non-addict user who is responsible for any contagion. The addict becomes part of an addict network.

The relative incidence curve for all three studies was similar. The curve for Grosse Point in table 4.6 illustrates this general pattern. The application of the "epidemic" label to heroin use depends upon where the observer is, relative to the time since the introduction of heroin. In these cases, the years one through three appear to have only a few users, hardly an "epidemic." Beginning in the third year

Table 4.6. **New Cases of Heroin Use: Grosse Pointe, Michigan**

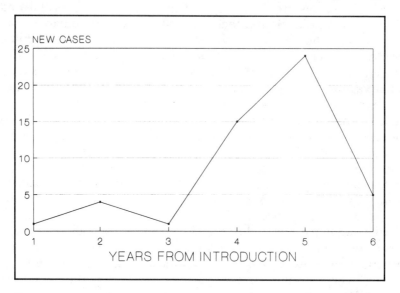

Source: Hunt, Leon Gibson and Carl D. Chambers. 1976. *The Heroin Epidemics. A Study of Heroin Use in the United States, 1965–75*, p. 9. New York: Spectrum Publications.

and continuing through the fifth, there appears to be an "epidemic." If this curve continued at this rate, almost everybody would be an addict. The curious thing is that in all of these cases there was a rapid drop in the incidence of new users soon after the fifth year. Is this decline due to overt action on the part of law enforcement or educational programs? I think not. If one examines the diffusion of heroin in the same manner as the diffusion of any other innovation, the adopting network soon becomes saturated with those who might adopt. Some people who adopt will do so for a short time and then stop. As those who have adopted drop out, some others may take their place, but eventually the limits of potential users in the existing social networks will be reached. The overall trend is then to decline. Heroin use appears to violate the observation of the "S-shaped" curve observed by Gabriel Tarde and the sociological diffusionists. If heroin use followed that curve, it would stabilize instead of decreasing.

Sociometry and Diffusion of Heroin

The epidemic curves for heroin use describe overall usage of heroin. They do not show the specific process of diffusion at the social structure level. For this it is necessary to reconstruct the linkages between specific individuals in this process. This method of reconstructing groups based upon interaction was first developed by J. L. Moreno (1934), the founder of sociometry. Although concerned with establishing groups that could work together with the least amount of conflict, Moreno nonetheless developed methods by which the structure of groups could be analyzed. Four types of methods have emerged from the original work of Moreno. These are graphic analysis, index analysis, statistical analysis, and matrix analysis (Proctor and Loomis 1951). Graphic analysis includes the sociogram. The **sociogram** visually portrays the structure of groups based upon choices of others made by members of that group. For example, one might ask students in a class with whom they would most like to study. On the basis of their responses, individuals (represented by circles) are connected by arrows showing whom they chose and who chose them. Usually in these cases, one or more persons show up as receiving more choices than others. They are the "stars." Others may receive no choices at all. They are the "isolates." Group structures which show no stars or isolates might be thought of as highly integrated, cooperative, and "democratic"; those with a high proportion of stars and isolates might be less integrated or hierarchical. What is important is that one can visualize the structure of the group and then make comparisons between groups. This same strategy has been used in the epidemiological approach to heroin use. Once users are identified, they are asked to name the person from whom they first received heroin and when it was first taken. In addition, they are asked the name or names of those they had introduced to heroin along with the dates of this introduction. From this information a sociogram is constructed. The sociogram for the Chicago study is reproduced in table 4.7.

This sociogram illustrates the limits of interaction networks. Although urban societies have large populations, individuals within those societies "know" or interact within a relatively small network of kinsmen, friends, neighbors, schoolmates and workmates. For example, one study of Tupperware® parties (Taylor 1978) found that most people who start in this business eventually fail. Once they have used friends and relatives within their interaction network, they run out of potential customers. Their sales curves show an early increase followed by a rapid decline. Those who survive in these business ventures must go outside personal networks and operate in the impersonal world of strangers. Initial heroin diffusion is not dissimilar to Tupperware parties. Those who

Table 4.7   Macroepidemic Sociogram for First Year of Heroin Use: 1964-1971

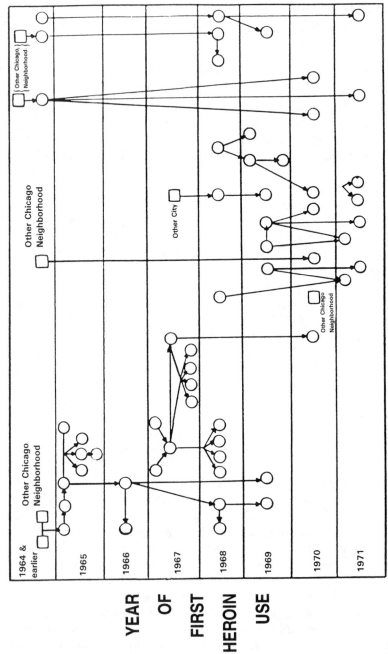

Symbols refer to relationship between users and successors.

Source: P. Hughes and G. Crawford. Cited in Hunt, Leon Gibson and Carl D. Chambers. 1976. *The Heroin Epidemics. A Study of Heroin Use in the United States. 1965-75*, p. 8. New York: Spectrum Publications.

survive (continue use), however, must do so in impersonal interactive systems made up of persons with similar drug-taking interests.

Going beyond the interpersonal network to the level of macrodiffusion, Hunt and Chambers found that heroin use diffused from large to smaller cities. Because of the time necessary for diffusion to take place, epidemics in small cities came after epidemics in large cities within the same region. In New Mexico, for example, Albuquerque, with its population of 224,000, experienced the beginnings of epidemic use in 1965; two years later Santa Fe's (population 41,000) epidemic began, and it was not until 1969 that Carlsbad (population 21,000) "caught" the heroin epidemic.

Migration and Diffusion

Diffusion may occur when a trait or process moves from one culture to another. This we have noted with tobacco and distillation of alcohol. However, cultural traits may also diffuse when people having these traits migrate. One example of this is opium smoking in the United States.

The opium poppy—*Papaver somniferum*—is similar to some other drug-producing plants in that it is a multipurpose species. Evidence for its non-drug use extends back to prehistoric times. Mark David Merlin (1984) suggests that not only are the leaves of the plant useful as a salad vegetable, but the oily seeds can be eaten raw, baked into poppy cakes, and ground into poppy flour (89). The oil from the seeds can be used as an edible oil or a fuel for lamps. As a plant which requires little tending (ecologically it is a weed), it grows without encouragement over a wide range of ecologies otherwise hostile to many early domesticates. This probably accounts for the conflicting accounts of its origins. The suggested locations for its origins are Southwest, Southeast, or Central Europe; the European Mediterranean Region; Western Asia; and Asia in general. The use of seed plants as food is not restricted to prehistoric populations but is found today in many parts of the world.

The first use of the opium poppy as a source of opium[13] is still subject to debate. The ancient Sumerians who lived in what is now Iraq, Iran, and Turkey may have been the first to recognize the effects of opium. Its use is inferred from the discovery of a clay tablet between 6,000 and 7,000 years old, on which was an ideogram for opium that translates as "joy" or "rejoicing." Wherever its specific origin, opium use spread to other parts of the Old World either through diffusion or the vigorous efforts of Arab traders who, it is claimed, introduced it to China (Lindesmith 1968; Merlin 1984).

In Arab cultures, opium was used primarily in the treatment of diarrhea. The Greeks also used it to treat a variety of medical complaints. Its sleep-inducing effects, as the name *somniferum* implies, were noted by both Greek and Roman writers such as Homer and Virgil. In addition to its medicinal use, its use as a food is evidenced by the existence of opium cakes and candies in Greece. Its use as a food, a medicine, or as a possible mind-altering substance spread throughout Europe during the sixteenth and seventeenth centuries.

In 1804, the German chemist Friedrich Wilhelm Adam Sertürner discovered the primary active alkaloid in opium and named it morphium. In 1898 heroin (diacetylmorphine) was isolated. Each of these alkaloids proved more powerful and as habit-forming as the previous ones. These alkaloids were used in a variety of patent medicines and were freely available to the public. The practice in the West was either to drink opiates (this practice was called opium "eating" after Thomas DeQuincey's popular 1821 book, *Confessions of an English Opium Eater*) or, after 1865, to inject it with the hypodermic needle. While the delivery systems for opium changed in the West, the Chinese, especially Chinese peasants, continued the practice of smoking opium.

In the United States, opium was not associated with any criminal activities in the nineteenth century. On the contrary, it was used primarily by upper-class, respectable members of society. Unlike present-day heroin users who tend to be males, the "typical" users of the nineteenth century were women. Because opiates were available freely and openly,[14] there were no "dope peddlers." This specialized occupational status would not be invented until after the passage of the Harrison Act in 1914 which prohibited the open sale of opiates. Those who were addicted—either by choice, through exposure during the Civil War or through the large variety of home remedies—were viewed as having a personal problem.

In contrast to the typical opium "eater" and intravenous user who was upper class, highly educated, and predominantly female, the public image of the opium smoker was quite different. Chinese peasants were coming into the country in considerable numbers during the 1850s. They were recruited to work on the transcontinental railroad, in mining camps, and in a host of other service occupations. With them they brought the practice of opium smoking. Pushed into the most unappealing sections of cities and parts of towns, their contacts were with an already established lower-class criminal population. It was to this population that this practice diffused. According to Lindesmith:

> The opium smoker of the nineteenth century belonged to an elite underworld group which despised and generally avoided all contact with the hypodermic user or "opium eater" of respectable society. Smokers usually regarded the hypodermic habit as more vicious and difficult to break than the smoking habit. They applied the term "dope fiend" to those who used the drug in some manner other than smoking, but did not apply it to themselves. (215)

In nineteenth-century America the use of opium was firmly established and acceptable. Also established was a ranked class system, in which membership was distinguished by different consumption patterns. The marker between upper and lower classes was not in opium use but rather in the method of using. The Chinese introduced a delivery system for opium that was different from the prevailing system that was identified with a system of stratification. Differences, not similarities, mark a society with a stratified class system. The Chinese practice was accepted by non-Chinese as both a confirmation of an existing widespread practice and a clear behavioral difference.

The use of different drugs to mark boundaries between social categories is not limited to the United States. One can cite many examples of this today. Males and females differ in the type of alcoholic beverages they consume; African Americans are more likely to smoke menthol cigarettes; and marihuana use tends to be highest in younger age categories. When cultures use sex, race and age as a basis for social differences, it should come as no surprise that these differences will be reflected in a variety of consumer patterns, including drugs. For example, in South Africa, Brian DuToit (1977) found that Africans used tobacco, beer, and cannabis; Indians used alcohol, tobacco, cannabis, and opium; Europeans used alcohol, tobacco, and cannabis. Gibson and Weinberg (1980), in their ethnographic analysis of drinking in a remote alpine village, suggest that the rather elaborate etiquette for what, where, and with whom one drinks is related to preserving two identities. One, the public identity, is displayed in one of two village cafes; the other, a private identity, is acted out at home. The public etiquette distinguished between villager and outsider; the private etiquette preserved the autonomy and independence of the household. Ann Pinson (1985) made a similar discovery in Iceland. She noted that drunkenness and drinking differed by setting and associates. Drunken comportment occurred most frequently in public settings while in the company of strangers. In contrast, kinsmen, friends, and working associates drank with each other. She suggested that in addition to marking the boundaries between public-intimate relationships, drunkenness provided a legitimate excuse for drinking outside the bounds of those relationships that were defined as most important to Icelanders.

Conclusion: Is Necessity the Mother of Invention?

Ultimately in reviewing diffusion studies one must face the question of "why" innovations of any kind are adopted. Conventional wisdom suggests that both the process of innovation and the adoption of innovation are driven by need. If people need something, they invent it or borrow it. Herbert Spencer, who was mentioned at the beginning of this chapter, was an intentionalist who embraced this view. The theory he suggested was that "need" was the independent variable which was responsible for the dependent variable, cultural evolution or, in his terms, progress. He assumed the existence of the free-willed human who was driven by the satisfaction of needs—"necessity is the mother of invention." In his view, but not his words, he might have argued that cultures experiencing stress invented or borrowed drunkenness. An alternative theory is based on modern Darwinian selection. The Darwinian model begins with the assumption that evolution is opportunistic and random. Traits are randomly distributed and are assumed to have no function initially. That they may eventually be "needed" is determined by the situation. In this sense, the trait exists first (independent variable) and the "need" (dependent variable) is the result. In modern society, for example, what "need" was met by the invention of the automobile, the airplane, the personal computer, or Nintendo? Innovations occur as the result of several human activities. They may be products of play, accident or ignorance. Once in existence, their fate depends upon their multiple uses (symbolic specificity). Most innovations disappear or, in Darwinian terms, "are selected out." Some traits persist and become widely distributed. The appeal of this latter approach is that we do not have to assume motive or intention for innovation. As the Greek dramatist Aeschylus (525–426 B.C.) reminds us, "Things are what they are, and will end as they must."

In researching the topic of drug diffusion one finds that the Spencerian model, while not stated, is most often followed. This same model characterizes most historiographies. The way we construct a story is not the same as the way we tell a story. Historical research and diffusion research are usually constructed from the present back to some point in the past. One begins with a trait, let us say heroin, and then looks for the most immediate antecedent drug—morphine. From morphine the story extends back to opium until one runs out of connections. When the story of heroin is told, one begins with opium, then proceeds to morphine, and then to heroin. Yet if we go back to any particular historical or prehistorical period we may find numerous substances which would qualify as a "drug" according to our definition. These drugs are conveniently ignored because they complicate the analysis or they interfere with "good" story telling. In the modern Darwinian model there is no assumption of goals. The object of biological evolution is *not* to produce humans, nor were humans inevitable. The object of cultural evolution is *not* to produce us; we are not inevitable. To assume so is to attribute intention to a process. The purpose of social science is to uncover the rules governing the process, whether that process is diffusion or evolution, not to infer goals or intentions.

The research on drugs which uses diffusion models gets us closer to addressing some dimensions of social science, namely the issues of space and time. The spread of tobacco from South America throughout the world has been traced and explained by looking at the item diffused and its ability to fit in every social structure. The analysis of the diffusion of heroin in different communities enables us to predict the numbers of users over time. We have not, however, explained just why these items have been adopted when they were. The psychological theory of positive reinforcement suggests that a pleasurable experience will be repeated, while an unpleasant experience will not. This explanation seems reasonable for cocaine which, by all accounts, is a pleasurable first-time experience. How does one explain the acceptance of tobacco, however? Early experiences with its use are usually accompanied by extreme physical discomfort, dizziness, vomiting, and general feelings of incapacity. This effect may fit into the repertoires of Amerindian shamans but would not be the desired or believed outcome of smoking for residents of Tobi or Toledo, Ohio. The explanation of why specific drugs are used is hinted at by the "time out" model of MacAndrew and Edgerton and the "cultural consistency" theory of Fort. What happens when culture and social networks change, resulting in culture and drugs both being variables? We shall now shift our attention to those broader changes in the structure of society itself.

Endnotes

[1] I would propose that we cannot think about our own culture's social facts independent of the influence of those facts if we only study our own culture. We can understand the social facts of other cultures because we are independent from their determination. This may give those who study other cultures some advantage, as social scientists, in understanding the rules of culture and ultimately in understanding our own culture.

[2] While the stone-bronze-iron sequence appeared to describe an evolutionary pattern for Europe, later archeological findings elsewhere in the world did not confirm this as a universal chronology. Thus, the hopes for a "law of evolution" were spoiled.

[3] Relative time should not be confused with absolute time. Relative time is comparative. A trait is old**er** than another trait if it is more widely distributed. **Absolute time** measures are capable of translating differences in time into years. Thus, a trait may be 4,800 years old while another trait is 2,600 years old.

[4] The New World is North and South America. The Old World is everywhere else.

[5] Blum also suggests that the invention of the hypodermic syringe led to the widespread injection of other non-legal drugs in the United States.

[6] The United States is no exception. In spite of the wide media attention devoted to heroin and cocaine, less than one percent of the total population are active users.

[7] Matrilineal refers to the rules and principles which determine descent. In a matrilineal system one is related to one's mother, her brothers and sisters, and the children of those sisters. **Exogamous** refers to the prohibition of marriage to a relative. In this case, one cannot marry a person who is related through matrilineal descent principles. A **clan** is a grouping of people formed through unilineal descent principles. In the Tobian case this would be a group who trace their descent using matrilineal principles. The clan is distinguished from the **lineage**. In a lineage, descent can be demonstrated. That is, one can actually "prove" that one person is related to another. In the clan relatedness is stipulated, and the common ancestor need not be proved. These common ancestors often take the form of a clan totem, usually but not always an animal.

[8] Smoking in the United States was often associated with adult status. Legislators wrestled with the question of age in reference to smoking with various outcomes. According to Brecher, et al. (1972) in 1921, fourteen states had prohibited tobacco smoking and twenty-eight others had anti-smoking legislation pending. By 1927 all of the tobacco prohibition laws were repealed. The only concession to the anti-smoking forces was the imposition of fines or convictions for sale or distribution of tobacco to minors. One might make the argument that in both the United States and Tobi, smoking and competency have been linked.

[9] Horticulture is the earliest technology for domestication of plants. Horticulturalists have gardens and generally two associated tools—the hoe and the digging stick. Agriculture, which is more recent, employs the plow and draft animals. In horticultural systems what is grown in the gardens is for local use: a subsistence economy. In agricultural systems there is usually a surplus, which is traded or sold in markets: a surplus economy.

[10] "Malting" is the early stage of fermentation when the grain is steeped in water and then heated over a low fire, which results in the grain beginning to sprout. When mixed with water, the malted grain will produce a mash which is then distilled.

[11] Dwight Heath (personal communication) reminded me that the change to home-produced grain alcohols was, in part, a nationalistic response to anything British,

including rum. In addition, the surplus in high volume grain production could be more efficiently and profitably transported in liquid form.

[12] Antagonistic, as opposed to synergistic, action refers to the effects of one chemical in the plant which cancels out the effects of another chemical. For example, Irish coffee is a drink that contains Irish whiskey and coffee. Coffee contains caffeine, a stimulant, and Irish whiskey contains alcohol which is a depressant. Thus, the effect of drinking Irish coffee is that the active substances tend to cancel each other out. Readers who have consumed large numbers of Irish coffee will testify that the effects of alcohol tend to win in this battle of ingredients.

[13] Opium is the thickened juice or sap that exudes from an excised capsule of the opium poppy.

[14] Opium literally poured into the country during the latter half of the nineteenth century. From 1860 until the turn of the century, the legal importation of opium increased almost fivefold, from 110,305 to 513,070 pounds.

chapter 5

Drugs and Social Movements

hroughout this book there has been an attempt to maintain a distinction between social and cultural phenomena. The issues and questions discussed thus far have emphasized both the analytical need to separate these two realms and the empirical necessity to demonstrate their interrelationship and interdependence. In a real sense, neither can exist without the other. In this chapter the issue is social and cultural change; that is, changes in behavior (social) and changes in expectations and rules (cultural). The specific question has to do with the influence of drugs on the change process.

In the last chapter the analysis of diffusion patterns of drugs focused on the movement of a few items—tobacco, alcohol, opium, peyote, and heroin. The acceptance or rejection of these traits depended on how well they fit into existing social and cultural patterns. The key word here is "existing." Tobacco, for example, fit into the existing organizational structure of Tobi. Opium smoking was adopted by the existing underclass in northern California. Heroin use was diffused through existing social networks. The peyote cult, on the other hand, was accepted by different tribal groups at different times. If one accepts the diffusion model without question one might conclude that the units which adopt or reject drugs are somewhat static or fixed. But this assumption defies what is known about societies and cultures. Regardless of the theoretical explanations (Applebaum 1970), societies and cultures are constantly changing, albeit at different rates. The implication of this observation is that for any given trait, including drugs, what may be acceptable at one time may not be acceptable when the society or culture changes. This means that drugs, as isolated traits, are not and cannot be the units of analyses. Rather, drug use can only be understood relative to changes in society and culture.

Most of the social science research on drugs takes place in a single time frame. If the question of change is addressed at all, it is often assumed that drugs are either the cause or the effect of the change process. In other words, drugs are either the independent or the dependent variable and are linked to some part of society or culture as a corresponding dependent or independent variable. The discussion of the diffusion process in the previous chapter demonstrated that this was not the case. In fact, what was demonstrated was that drugs are neutral and random as a trait. What gives them meaning, and influences whether they are accepted or rejected, rests entirely on the social and cultural frameworks in which they are found. This is not to say that any single trait, including drugs, cannot have or has not had far-reaching consequences for a culture or society. For example, some American Indian cultures were dramatically altered as a result of the introduction of the horse by the Spanish. Not only could those who adopted the horse travel farther and faster than they had on foot, but the horse made possible the accumulation of property that could be carried by nomads. In twentieth-century United States, the automobile altered many cultural practices including dating patterns, sexual behavior, migration, and residency. In both of these examples, the new trait altered **norms**. Norms are behavioral standards without regard to the purpose or goals of those behaviors. The behavior of American Indians changed from walking to riding from one place to another. Americans drove as individuals or in small groups from place to place. Norms should not be confused with **values**. Values are expressions of desirable goals. That riding or driving to some destination is considered valuable is part of a world of expectations.

The distinction between norms and values can be visualized in table 5.1.

Table 5.1.

**The Place of Norms and Values
in the Levels of Social Science**

Analysis

Behavior	Rules
Society	Culture
Associations	Institutions
Norms	*Values*

Norms properly belong to the social dimension of the social science model, while values are part of the cultural domain. All societies and cultures are bound together by both normative and valuative structures, within either associations or institutions. Within these structures, norms and values perform the function of maintaining orderly relationships. When innovations are absorbed from outside (the horse from the Spanish), or occur within (the automobile), both the normative and value structures change. In this way both society and culture change.

The question of what factor(s) "cause" change is beyond the scope of this chapter. One manifestation of change is the appearance of new social forms. In this chapter we examine the question of how large-scale changes in society and culture are manifested in the formation of new groupings of people. The subject here is social movements.

Social Movements

Social movements may be viewed as attempts to reformulate the structure of society. Note that I have said that they attempt to reformulate the structure of society—not that they are responsible for that change. Change occurs as a result of innovation (Barnett 1953), and innovation is the combination of two or more cultural traits. As new traits are adopted through the process of diffusion, they are potentials for innovation when combined with existing traits. The accumulation of these traits over time and the resulting innovations alter the structure of society. One consequence of this process is that the old values (culture) are no longer consistent with the new norms (social), but new structures have not yet developed that legitimate the new order. Durkheim (1951) describes this condition as **anomie**, or a situation of normlessness. Although, by definition, no society could be without norms, anomie can be a useful concept for describing various degrees of inconsistency between norms. The attempt to adjust to cultural inconsistencies, either through behavioral or cognitive means, is the purpose of social movements.

The sociologist Herbert Blumer (1969) has classified social movements into three categories, each with its own particular characteristics. The three types of social movements are general, specific, and expressive.

The general social movement is characterized by gradual and pervasive changes in society, a condition that Blumer calls **cultural drift**. During this stage, there are no clear ideas about what changes have occurred or the ultimate consequences of these changes. What is perceived is that things are not the same as they had been. Thus, there is a condition of anomie or conflict. This may be expressed in any number of vague general feelings of uneasiness. One notes that during cultural drift many possible solutions to the "problem" are suggested. Sometimes specific "others" are assumed to be responsible for this feeling of uneasiness. It might be witches, communists, liberals, environmentalists, ethnic groups, or drug sellers and/or users. The source might be things, such as comic books, pornography, or drugs. The specific emic expressions of the underlying causes of anomie will vary cross-culturally and over time within a culture. One signal that a society is experiencing the consequences of general change is the lack of any clear-cut consensus on what the problem is and how it can be solved.

Out of this stage there may develop more specific and focused remedies for anomie. These are found in the emergence of groups with more precise agendas. This is what Blumer calls specific social movements. They may take three forms: revolutionary, reform, and expressive. The revolutionary movement takes as its goal a major reorganization of a whole society; the reform movement focuses on some specific goal. In both the revolutionary and reform movements there are attempts to direct the activities of the movement to some issue outside the movement itself. For example, they may attempt to change behaviors of those not in the movement. This is precisely what makes this a *social* movement. What specific behaviors they desire to change will, of course, vary. For example, the movement may have the goal of stopping drunk driving, stopping the consumption of alcohol, getting drug dealers out of the neighborhood, or electing a public official.

In contrast, Blumer's third type of movement seeks to resolve the problem by total withdrawal from society. This is the expressive social movement. Usually a result of the perceived inability to alter the social order, this type of movement focuses inward on the members of the movement and emphasizes personal experiences as a goal. Such movements often accentuate ritual behavior. This sharing of ritual performances is accompanied by beliefs and values that are often inversions of the general norms of a society. If wealth is a general norm, then poverty might be the norm of the expressive movement. If science is the general norm, then tarot cards, crystals, astrology, and channeling might be the norms of the expressive movement. If sobriety and social distance are part of the general norms, then insobriety and intimacy might be the norms of this type of movement. Here, as with the other types of movements, we expect to find cross-cultural variations in the specifics of the movement.

Whether revolutionary, reform, or expressive, these movements seems to go through similar developmental stages. During the early stage (anomie), one notes that the typical "leader" is what Blumer calls the "agitator." The function of the agitator is to increase awareness of the problem. During this early stage, individuals may feel that they alone have this feeling of alienation brought about by the unstructured condition of society. The agitator plays the important role of making people aware that these same feelings are shared by others. This period is followed by one of popular excitement. During this stage there is a more focused effort to alleviate the conditions of unrest. Leaders during this stage are likely to be either "prophets" or "reformers." While the agitator may increase awareness, his or her fervor is usually short-lived. In contrast, the prophet or reformer symbolizes a basis for group identification through the development of a "we-feeling." This gives the members of the movement an identity that is shared with other members of the movement. Under the prophet or reformer, members can identify those who are "in" and distinguish them from those who are "out." This may manifest itself in a variety of ways such as parades, rallies, and demonstrations—complete with uniforms, banners, music, and other insignia of the grouping. As the organizational structure of the movement develops, one finds the prophet or reformer being replaced by the statesman or politician. During this stage there is an attempt to formalize statuses and to develop rules by which people can occupy those statuses. During this formalization stage there are more clearly defined goals along with the tactics for achieving those goals. Questions about who is and is not eligible for membership, formalization of rituals and symbols, and the development of a formal justification for the movement are of paramount concern during this phase.

The final stage of the social movement is institutionalization. At this stage the new organization has garnered enough power, influence, or people to legitimate itself within the fabric of the total society and culture. Once established, the bureaucrat, the administrator, or the priest are the recognized leaders. Their job is to perpetuate the organization, not change it. Of course, as society changes, the bureaucrat is replaced by the agitator, and the whole cycle begins again.

Not all social movements survive to the institutionalized stage. Witness the rather large number of utopian movements in the United States. The Shakers, the Amana Community, and most of the communes of the 1960s have disappeared. Each in its own way was an attempt to respond to changing conditions. It is not their success that is at issue but rather the fact that they existed when they did that bears witness to social movements as attempts to establish order out of chaos. In the randomness of human responses, most movements do not succeed. Others, either in whole or in part, have survived to become integral parts of a changed society. All of the world's religions began as social movements under conditions of anomie and value conflict. All of these religions have adjusted their norms and values to accommodate changes that have occurred in society since their founding. This same observation is true of governmental forms, educational systems, and all the other institutions that make up any culture. Humans live in systems that are constantly adjusting to environmental, technological, demographic, and other influences. Change is ubiquitous. We can visualize this process of change and conflict in table 5.2.

Culture and society move from one stable state to another. The question at hand is what, if any, contribution drugs make to this transition. This we will explore in the next few pages.

The Native American Church

The Native American Church is a religious group composed of Amerinds (American Indians). One of its practices has received a great deal of attention by scholars—the incorporation of peyote into its ritual. Its important place in the rituals of the Native American Church has its genesis in the late 1800s and the early 1900s. As

Table 5.2.
Change and Conflict in Society

(time I) Integrated Society	*CHANGE* *ANOMIE*	(time II) Integrated Society
Culture	*VALUE CONFLICT*	Culture

the name Church implies, its practices are institutionalized—the final stage in a social movement. In order to understand how this church came into being and why its membership is restricted to Amerinds, it is necessary to review the historical results of cultural contact (more properly, cultural conquest) between Europeans and Native Americans during the last century.

The early invasion of Europeans into the New World had little impact on Native Americans in the Plains. The French and English fought for control of the eastern part of North America. With British victory, attention was directed toward the Plains as a buffer against the intrusion of Spain and Mexico. The Gold Rush in 1849 attracted Europeans to the West Coast and led eventually to the demise of the California Indians. The native populations of middle America had adopted the horse from the Spanish and firearms from the French. As a result of increased efficiency of hunting by Native Americans and the growing demand for Buffalo hides by Europeans, the large herds of buffalo on whom the nomadic Indians depended began to vanish. When Indians were forced onto unproductive lands to engage in agriculture or cattle raising, their traditional cultural patterns rapidly disappeared. Unaccustomed to large-scale cooperation between different tribes, the Amerinds were no match for European military discipline and technology. With the notable exception of Custer's Last Stand at Little Bighorn in 1876, tribal societies were soon "pacified" and placed on government reservations.

The condition of anomie provided the fertile conditions for an expressionistic social movement. Unable to fight the Europeans, a movement emerged which emphasized the traditional Amerind way of life. This was the Ghost Dance (LaBarre 1970). The Ghost Dance first appeared among the Paiutes of Nevada in 1870 when their society was experiencing devastating changes. A Paiute named Wovoka claimed to have a vision that directed him to teach a new way of life. The basic message was that if one engaged in a particular dance, the dead ancestors would return, the Europeans would leave, and their land would be restored. The Ghost Dance diffused west to California where it met with indifferent acceptance. The central theme of the Ghost Dance that the dead ancestors would return was not compatible with the fear of the dead that dominated the belief systems of certain northern California tribes. It did not move east at that time because the Plains Indians were still militarily strong enough to resist the Europeans. Twenty years later in 1890 the Plains Indians' position had deteriorated to a level similar to the California Indians'. A descendent of Wovoka had kept the movement alive, and it was adopted by the Plains Indians who added the return of the buffalo to the belief. Indians laid down their arms and danced the slow hypnotic dance in the hope that the good old days would return. Unfortunately, the American troops were not sympathetic, compassionate observers of this behavior. Remembering George Custer's humiliation at Little Big Horn, they did not believe that the Indians had given up. On December 22, 1890 a group of Sioux were camped under guard at Wounded Knee, South Dakota. They began to dance and refused to stop when ordered by the troops. Interpreting this as an act of hostility, the troops opened fire and 200 Indians, along with 60 soldiers, were killed. This effectively put an end to the Ghost Dance, but it did not stop the emergence of a new expressive movement, the peyote cult.

Well before the peyote cult, drugs were part of herbal remedies and religious systems. Among the Plains Indians, for example, there were mescalbean (*Sophora secundiflora*) societies with their own dances, medicine bundles, and paraphernalia. In addition, Jimsonweed, tobacco, alcoholic beverages, and peyote itself were not unknown. The Comanche and Shawnee included peyote in their war bundles, and individuals used it to alter consciousness. As mentioned previously, the existence of peyote as part of the trait inventories of Amerinds should not be taken as evidence for a set of rituals and beliefs that are associated with the peyote cult. The cult is a social and cultural phenomenon.

A ceremony similar to that of the later Plains Indians was practiced by the Mescalero Apache from 1870 to about 1910. Prior to adding Christian elements, peyote was used to confer power. For the Apache, power was acquired through dreams. Peyote use, however, never turned into a cult or sect with regular members and officers. It was simply incorporated into the existing repertoires of shamans.

The Kiowa and the Comanche were two of the first Plains tribes to take up the cult (1875). The Kiowa had participated in the Ghost Dance in 1882 and again in 1887. A group within these movements, Sons of the Son, was strongly opposed to peyote. After the failure of the Ghost Dance, members of this group became practitioners of the peyote cult. The Comanche adopted the peyote cult after Quannah Parker, the popular Comanche chief, claimed that it had cured him of an illness. From Oklahoma, where these tribes were settled at that time, it spread to other tribes in the Plains.

By the early twentieth century there were several variants of the peyote cult, each with its own leader and set of practices and beliefs. The cult did not, however, avoid the attention of authorities. In Oklahoma, legislation against peyotism was passed as early as 1888. After failed attempts to have cult practices recognized by Protestants, the Oklahoma peyotists incorporated the First Born Church of Christ in 1914. Three years later The Native American Church was granted a charter in Oklahoma. Similar difficulties were encountered in other states when practitioners attempted to obtain charters as a religion. By 1955, a national organization was established with the name, Native American Church of North America. Some of the state churches remained independent; others became affiliated with the national organization. By the mid-1960s, peyotism was practiced by more than fifty tribes from California to Michigan (Witt 1965).

This brief history of the Native American Church suggests several questions. One is the question of the "cause" of this movement. David F. Aberle (1962) suggests that **relative deprivation** is a condition which leads to the formation of religious movements. Relative deprivation is "a negative discrepancy between legitimate expectation and actuality" (209). It is clear that American Indians had faced major disruptions in traditional practices as a result of subjugation by Europeans. What had been legitimate expectations prior to the invasion of Europeans no longer were an actuality after the establishment of military control. The diffusion of the short-lived Ghost Dance seems to follow this pattern. The first movement west was to tribes that had experienced relative deprivation. The later movement east into the Plains occurred after those tribes fell prey to European domination. As pointed out in chapter 1, the term "cause" can only be used when the causal factor is both a necessary *and* a sufficient condition. Aberle's suggestion that relative deprivation is the cause of religious movements may be half right. Relative deprivation may be a necessary condition to bring about a religious or any other type of movement, but it is not a sufficient condition. Other factors, such as those related to symbolic specificity, have to be entered into the equation to explain both the emergence and continuation of any movement.

Another question is whether peyotism has reached Blumer's final stage, institutionalization. Is the Native American Church a *church*? A church is a social unit, distinct from religion which is cultural and includes beliefs, values, and perceptions of the world. Churches are social units that are bureaucratized. They have officers (bureaucrats, priests) whose function is to carry out prescribed rituals and functions. One way to determine whether the Native American Church is a church is by reviewing the peyote ritual.

Bryan Wilson (1973) describes the "typical" present-day meeting:

> While there are some variations, the peyote rituals are all fundamentally similar. The basic ritual is an all night meeting in a tipi around a crescent shaped earthen mound (the moon) and a ceremonially built fire. A special drum, gourd rattle, and carved staff were passed around in accompaniment to ritual singing. The occasion for a meeting was usually to produce a healing, to allay troubles, to ensure warfare, or to show hospitality and goodwill to friends. Special meetings might celebrate the first four birthdays of a child, and in more recent times, public holidays have been occasions for the practice. Meetings were sponsored. Sponsors paid for them and also supplied the peyote. Sponsors chose the road chief, or leader, who would supply the paraphernalia to be used. Other officers were the Fire Chief, who tended the fires and lit the pipes, the Drummer, and sometimes a Cedar Chief. Ceremonial dress was usual, and some older participants painted their faces. Meetings were once confined to old men and warriors. Later women were permitted to attend. More recently they became active participants. The meeting usually began and ended with set songs. In between there was additional singing, prayer, and the consumption of peyote. Silent prayers, which might be directed to the Earth-creator, or to a more christianized conception of God, and just smiling were followed by an intense blessing ceremony. All participants were expected to eat (usually four) peyote buttons, although they might consume more during the night.
>
> As soon as the peyote was consumed, the staff and drum were passed from person to person in strict order. Each person would sing four songs as the staff came to him and a friend would drum for him. At midnight cedar wood would be put on the fire for a blessing to be obtained from its smoke, accompanied by a midnight song. Water was brought at this time and a number of ritual acts were performed, before the meeting resumed. The pattern of singing continued until dawn, when water is again brought, this time by a woman. The leader then sang four

Figure 5.1. **The Basic Plan of the Plains Peyote Ceremony**

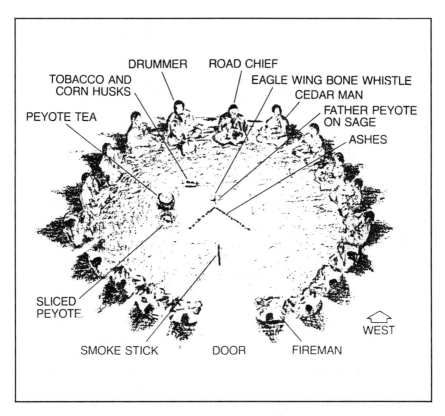

Source: Anderson, Edward F. 1980. *Peyote, The Devine Cactus.* Tucson: University of Arizona Press, p. 44.

morning songs and sometimes followed this with instruction, particularly for any younger persons who were present. Afterwards the company would close the meeting and partake of the morning meal that had been prepared by women. Some people would remain until a noon meal was served before returning home. (419–420)

The peyote ritual has a relatively rigid organizational structure. We can even draw an organization chart which indicates the personnel and their function in this ritual. This is presented in table 5.3.

The service follows a rather well-defined ritual pattern, yet it differs from other western churches. The "service" takes place only at night, and it is "sponsored" for different irregular occasions,

Table 5.3.   **Organizational Structure of the Peyote Ritual**

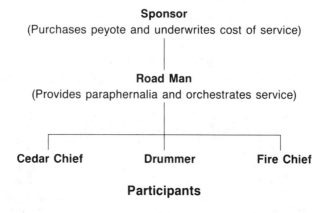

Sponsor
(Purchases peyote and underwrites cost of service)

Road Man
(Provides paraphernalia and orchestrates service)

Cedar Chief   **Drummer**   **Fire Chief**

Participants

such as birthdays or illnesses. In contrast, institutionalized western religions have calendars which prescribe repetitive rituals. The meetings of the Native American Church attract only a few participants; they are not publicly announced; and there is very little public significance attached to them. Those in charge of the ceremony are not full-time specialists. They do not earn a living from their services. Readers might empathize with those state legislators and others who resisted granting recognition to these practices as a church in the European sense. This same concern has been addressed by social scientists. For example, Wilson (1973) defines the Native American Church as an introversionist sect—a contemplative religious movement that emphasizes spiritual inadequacy, a search for spiritual reassurance, along with physical and spiritual well-being (483). Introversionist sects do not usually have formal organizational structures except when threatened. The formation of the Native American *Church* as a religious association is a response to persecution by governmental bodies. Freedom of religion in America is freedom to engage in practices legitimated by a formal organization called church. To the peyotist, the peyote ritual is not separate from everyday life. Its practice, as we have noted, is tailored to conform to the everyday. This is in sharp contract to the Anglo-American separation of church from, let us say, business or education or political life. If one means by "church" a formal organization with a permanent "professional" priesthood or clergy, then the Native American Church is not a church. Its loose-knit structure is more comparable to the traditional practice of shamanism in which an individual with knowledge about religious practices (a shaman) consults with individual practitioners about individual matters of faith or health.

The variations in the ritual and the non-concern for issues such as the inclusion of Christian elements or the presence of women result in a highly variable "religion." The spread of peyotism can in part be explained by the absence of symbolic specificity. Where Western bureaucratized religions failed to attract Amerind converts, peyotism has been successful among rather diverse tribal societies. Peyotism, at least for its practitioners, provides an ethnic identity distinct from the dominant American culture without compromising local beliefs and practices. Peyotism is the source of Indianness, as opposed to tribalism.

The doctrine of the Native American Church offers us an example of **syncretism**, a combination of different beliefs and practices. As Harold E. Driver (1969) reports:

> The doctrine includes the belief in supernatural power, in spirits, and in the incarnation of power in human beings. Spirits consist of: the Christian Trinity; other Christian spirits, such as the devil and the angels; and still other spirits derived exclusively from Indian religions. The Christian spirits tend to be equated with comparable Indian spirits: God is the Great Spirit; Jesus is the culture hero, guardian spirit, or intercessor between God and man; the devil is an evil spirit bent on harming man; the angels are often the spirits of the four winds or cardinal directions, and are sometimes represented as being dressed like Indians. (524)

The ritual is weighted more heavily in favor of Indian traits. The drum, rattle, whistle, gourd, cedar incense, and the peyote all come from an Amerind tradition. The songs and musical styles diffused from one tribe to another (McAllester 1949; Moore 1956). Some early variations of the ritual included a cross or crucifix on an altar. The central participants—the road chief, the drummer, and the cedar and fire chiefs—are all reminiscent of the shamanistic systems of Native Americans.

The values of peyotism may have their etiology in either Western Christian ethics or traditional Indian expectations. Interestingly, they are similar to the values of fundamentalist Christian religions that have been successful in converting Native Americans. They place an emphasis on being friendly, helpful, honest and truthful. Parents should love their children. Spouses should not commit adultery. People should work hard and earn a good living. Most important of all, one should not drink alcohol.

As pointed out in the last chapter, the exact diffusion pattern of the peyote cult from one tribe to another is still in contention. While some cult leaders were known, others have been forgotten. There were changes in its practices as it spread from one Indian culture to another. Some characteristics were dropped; others were added. For example, early practices forbade women to participate in the ritual. Later developing cults permitted women to participate. In spite of these variations, the ritual itself was quite similar from one tribe to another.

What holds these bits and pieces together is peyote. As the "sacred" element of ritual practice and belief, it is not something to be treated lightly. The emic ethics of introversionist movements frequently emphasize inspirationalism. Since inspiration is not available to everyone, the good life can only be known by those who have been charged with divine power. Only from eating peyote can wisdom be acquired. It cannot be described or revealed, because appropriate, descriptive words are not available. Peyote is the teacher, and those that follow the peyote road enjoy a mystic bond. However, peyote is said by some to be "tricky" to use. It is a source of power, and man must lead a straight life or peyote will shame him. It is not easy to eat, and some say that in order to get wisdom one must be prepared to suffer. Thus meetings have some connotations of ordeals, rituals which "test" the capabilities of the participants. Peyote is said to teach man an ethical system, the Peyote Road. The Road stresses brotherly love, care of the family, self-reliance, and avoidance of alcohol. Following the Road leads to bliss in the next life and material well-being, health, long life and tranquility in this one.

This cursory examination of the conditions under which the peyote cult emerged illustrates one type of social movement. Its success depended on two factors. One was the already present practices of Amerinds that emphasized inspiration, protection, and salvation. The peyote cult fit into this pattern—both in the older sense of individual vision quests[1] and in addressing the newly emerged needs to respond collectively to the domination of the Europeans. By the 1880s the old visions—prowess in war, the hunt, or protective medicines—were rendered useless by the imposed "peace" of the Europeans, the disappearance of the buffalo, and other changes. The Plains cultures had institutionalized dreaming, but the culturally prescribed content of those dreams was no longer appropriate and was probably painful to contemplate. The peyote cult did not seek a return to the ways of life before the Europeans. It was not a reform movement. Given their position of powerlessness relative to Europeans, coupled with the values of individual responsibility (including individual shamanism), the practices and the beliefs of the peyote cult proved a successful adaptive strategy for many American Indians.

The Bwite Cult of Fang

Social science literature reveals several different ways to classify social movements. This variation is explained by the number of attributes or variables that are used in constructing the classification. Neil J. Smelser (1962) classifies movements as "norm oriented" or "value oriented." Norm oriented movements direct their attention at changing behavior. In contrast, value oriented movements attempt to change, restore, or create values. Movements might also be classified by the institutional domains within which they are found. For example, there are economic movements, political movements, religious movements, and so forth. If we combined the attributes of norm and value orientation with economic, political, and religious, the result would be six different types of movements—norm-economic, value-economic, norm-political, and so forth. Unless some constraint is exercised, an increase in the criteria used for classification of movements could result in thousands of differently named types. Fortunately, this has not happened. Rather, classifications have tended to reflect the specific research settings which the classifications attempt to explain. In this section, we will review a typology of social movements developed for Africa.

James Fernandez (1972, 238–239) constructed a two-dimensional classification of African religious movements which resulted from cultural contact with the West. These "revitalization" movements all attempt to resolve the dissonance experienced as a result of colonial domination and subsequent changes in traditional cultural adaptations. One dimension is behavioral. Movements vary in their goals from instrumental (adopting behaviors of the colonists) to expressive (withdrawal from the dominant colonial arena). The second dimension reflects variations in symbols. Movements either adopt colonial symbols or retain native (pre-colonial) symbols. The resultant types of movement are illustrated in table 5.4.

Separatist movements have separated from the missionary churches because they object to the differences in power and access to resources between the colonial missionaries and the native population. Their goal is to establish a separate grouping using the models of the West. The messianic movement is one which accepts Western symbolism but does not attempt to alter the differences between colonial and native power. Rather, the emphasis is on reducing this disparity through demonstrating a belief that an external agent—a messiah—will redress the problem. The reformative movement acknowledges the differences between colonial and

Table 5.4. **Types of Revitalization Movements**

	Instrumental Goals	Expressive Goals
Colonial Symbols	Separatist	Messianic
Native Symbols	Reformative	Nativistic

native power and uses traditional symbols to achieve the goal of reducing these differences. The nativistic movement withdraws from this conflict through its use of native symbols. Fernandez suggests that drug use is not widespread within any of these movement types in Africa, but those that do use drugs are most likely to be in the expressive column—the messianic or the nativistic. His own research focused on the Bwite Cult of Fang, who live in Gabon. Bwiti is a night cult which must complete its rituals before the sun rises. As part of their all-night ritual the Bwite Cult members use, in descending order, "eboka," (*Tabernathe iboga*),[2] "alan" (*Alchornea floribunda*), "ayān" (*Elaeophorbia drupifera*), and "yama" (*Cannabis sativa*). In spite of the observation that cults which employ drugs as part of their rituals tend to be in the expressive column, he classifies the Bwite Cult as a reformative movement. He argues that the Bwiti combine two elements of native practices with Catholic evangelicalism. Thus, in spite of attempts to construct all-inclusive typologies of movements, some actual groupings defy being cast into one category. Aside from this analytical difficulty, the observation that social movements that use drugs are most often expressive movements is supported by the data. It cannot, however, be said that all expressive movements use drugs.

The Hippie Movement: Drugs in the 1960s

In the examples of American Indians and the Bwiti, it is clear that both their "ways of life" had been severely disrupted by European intervention. What followed was several different types of social movements that adjusted to those changes. In those cases where most, if not all, the traditional practices were altered, social movements attracted large numbers of members. As dramatic and all-encompassing as those illustrations are, it should be remembered that change does not always affect most people in a society. In large urban societies, changes may only alter the "life ways" of a minority of its citizenry. An illustration of this "small" effect is the so-called "hippie" movement in the United States. This movement began in the mid-1960s and lasted about a decade. One of the characteristics of this movement was the rather rapid diffusion of many non-addicting drugs such as LSD, marihuana, and psilocybin, along with barbiturates, amphetamines, and cocaine. Those attracted to this movement were not subjugated minorities but white, middle-class American youth. If the peyote cult was one possible adaptation to change, what were the antecedent conditions that led to the "hippie movement," and how do we explain this short-lived phenomenon?

Age Grading and Age Grouping: America in the 1960s

All cultures have some system for coordinating and determining the activities of individuals and social groupings. Two human attributes that are universally used to divide activities are sex and age. In all cultures some tasks are considered male and others are considered female. What these tasks are, and the perceived importance of them, varies cross-culturally. The same is true of age. The activities of children are different from those of adults. The importance of age as a contributing factor to the development of social movements was explored by S. N. Eisenstadt (1956). Eisenstadt was specifically interested in the formation of age grading systems. Age grading is the division of people into cultural categories based on their age and is often the basis for the formation of specific social groups—age groups.

In American culture age grading is used as a basis for educational placement. Students are "graded," placed into specific groupings, according to their age. Thus, six-year-olds are placed in the first grade, and one is expected to finish high school by the age of nineteen. A nineteen-year-old in the first grade would be considered "abnormal" and probably cause some concern. Outside the formal school setting, age may be used as a criterion for membership in specific sex groups (Cub Scouts/Boy Scouts or Brownies/Girl Scouts, for example).

Eisenstadt found five basic types of age groups which reflect the organizational principles of five different types of societies. One of these societal types is of interest here, namely, modern societies. Eisenstadt reviewed several different youth movements in modern societies: the Voluntary Youth movement in Israel, the Free German

Table 5.5.

**The Place of Age Grading and Age Groups
in the Levels of Social Science Analysis**

Behavior	Rules
Society	Culture
Associations	Institutions
Age Groups	*Age Grading*

youth movement, the Kibbutz, and the Komsomol in the former Soviet Union. Although the specific histories of these movements were different, there were nonetheless many similarities. In all of these movements age was a criterion for membership, and the age range was from early adolescence to early adulthood. Membership usually terminated when a member married or entered the work force. Some of these age groupings were institutionalized; others were not. Eisenstadt found that the degree of institutionalization was related to the perception of adult society. Those that were informal or semiformal tended to be ambivalent or negative in their relationship to the adult culture. Those that were formally organized exhibited positive orientation toward the adult world. The main question remained: "Why age grading and age groups?" Not all societies have age groups, and age groups appear and disappear over time within a society. In answer to this question, Eisenstadt hypothesized that in modern societies:

> . . . age groups tend to arise in those societies where main integrative principles are different from the particularistic principles governing family and kinship relations, i.e. in societies whose integrative principles are mainly "universalistic." (115)

In other words, the principles that organize the family are not the principles that organize the rest of society. The age groups that emerge as a result of different organizational principles are separated into three types: the educational school system, adult-sponsored youth groups, and spontaneous youth groups. The existence of a school system is evidence that there is some inadequacy on the part of the family as the sole agent of socialization. The school system arises because the family and/or kinship age-heterogeneous relations cannot ensure a smooth and continuous transmission of knowledge, status, or skills of the adult world.

The formal statuses within the educational system are preparatory for the formal statuses of society in general. The school system itself fulfills the function of segregating children from the world of family to the broader social world. In industrialized societies with large numbers of occupational distinctions, the time needed to prepare for full adult status is increased, and social maturity is extended well beyond physiological and sexual maturity.

In spite of careful planning and good intentions, the school system does not or cannot fully socialize youth to enter into the adult world. This gives rise to a proliferation of age groups within different age categories as defined by the educational system. Some of these groups may be formalized and sponsored by adults. Others may be informal and lack adult sponsorship. Regardless of their specific form, the greater the number of these groups, the more diverse will be the symbolic markers that mark the differences between the groups. These markers may include a wide variety of symbols such as clothing, hairstyles, vocabulary, posture and gait, and drug use.

That a youth movement existed in the United States during the 1960s and 1970s is a historical fact. The explanation for this fact is to be found in antecedent social conditions. Eisenstadt has presented a set of general principles by which one could predict a youth movement. But what were the specific conditions that led to this particular movement?

All social movements require personnel, and youth movements require youthful personnel. Thus, one antecedent condition necessary for the formation of a youth movement would be a population of younger people. The study of population is **demography**. Demographers can describe any population with just three variables: births, deaths, and migration. At any point in time, every population is a result of the interplay between these three variables. To understand the youth movement, a review of some demographic data is required. Donald J. Bogue, writing in 1969, noted:

> At the present moment the United States has one of the most extraordinary age compositions in the world. Moreover, it has undergone a very great transformation in the past two decades. ... Never in the history of the world has a nation acquired such a distorted age distribution as a result of fluctuations in fertility. Only a devastating war or wholesale migration has been known to cause greater deviation. (162)

What was Bogue writing about? He was making reference to the proportion of the population in the United States under the age of 20, and the increase in this proportion between the 1950 and the

1960 census. From 1880 to 1940 there had been a steady decline in the proportion of the population at the younger ages. The "baby boom" of 1946–1950 reversed this pattern and was followed by a decline in births. This "lump" of children born during the baby boom came into adolescence in the mid-1960s. Table 5.6 shows this change from 1950 to 1980. The proportion of people in the 15–24 age aggregate increased dramatically during the 1960s. This provided a population base which made the formation of age groups possible.

Table 5.6.

Proportion of the United States Population Ages 15–24: 1950–1980

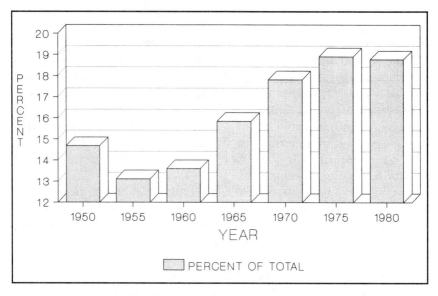

Source: Ottinger, Cecilia A. 1984. *1984–85 Fact Book on Higher Education.* New York: American Council on Education/Macmillan Publishing Company.

The dramatic increase beginning in 1965 of the American population between fifteen and twenty-four years old discloses only that personnel were available within this age interval for a social movement. The population increase provided a **necessary condition** for the youth movement; it was not, however, a **sufficient condition**. Eisenstadt has already suggested the principle. What, however, were the precipitating conditions during this period? William Partridge (1973) suggests:

> The social, political, religious, and economic changes which
> have occurred since World War II in the United States and in

the world have transformed the nature of American society, and with it the socialization and education of the younger members of that society. The central and most momentous transformations have been the industrialization of agrarian America, and the concomitant rapid growth of urban America. The implications of this transformation are broad, but we should be mainly concerned with the impact of this process on the adolescents who crowded into the institutions of higher learning in the 1960s. Some four million strong they came, and the impact of their numbers is only beginning to be felt throughout the larger society. (10–11)

The university curriculum had been established for a rural America and was based on the assumption that decisions about career, marriage, and friendships could be made through leisurely intellectual contemplation. Students under this curriculum, often assured of secure economic futures, selected from a limited number of majors. After World War II, there was an increase in numbers of students in universities and colleges and in the proportion of young adults who attended. This is shown in table 5.7. The post-war population of students did not have the same needs or demands

Table 5.7.

Proportion of the United States Population Ages 18–24 Enrolled in Two- and Four-Year Institutions of Higher Education 1950–1980

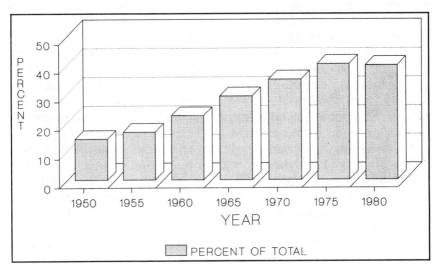

Source: Ottinger, Cecilia A. 1984. *1984–85 Fact Book on Higher Education.* New York: American Council on Education/Macmillan Publishing Company.

of the pre-war student body, however. American society had changed, and that change was in the labor force.

In 1910, slightly over 30 percent of the labor force in the United State was employed in farm work. By 1950, farm workers were only 8 percent of the work force. From 1950 to 1970, the composition of the American work force had continued its change from the turn of the century. In this twenty-year period, white-collar jobs increased 8 percent, while blue-collar work decreased 5 percent. Service work increased 3 percent, and farm workers continued a downward spiral another 2 percent to only 6 percent of the total work force.

The transition from a rural way of life to post-war urban America made many occupations invisible. It is one thing to be raised on a farm where adult roles could be observed directly or in an industrial community where work roles were discussed openly in front of children. It is quite different to prepare one's self for an occupation or job for which the requirements are unknown. It is for this reason that young urban children often express a preference for occupations that are visible to them (such as doctor, nurse, teacher, fireman, policeman), but these occupations are only a small proportion of the division of labor.

These social and economic changes increased demands for more education and training of the work force, a task for which the family was ill-suited and to which higher education had not yet adjusted. As a consequence of longer formal educational requirements, social maturing was further postponed. Adolescence, as a cultural category between childhood and adulthood, was extended to age twenty-one, twenty-two, or even older. "Relevance" became the demand word of many students in higher education, but relevance for what? It was, according to Solon Kimball and James McClellan (1966), relevance in the content of courses which would insure the smooth transition from family life to the public world. "Relevance" was the emic expression for training and information that prepared one for an unseen and uncertain occupational future.

If Eisenstadt is correct, these are the fertile conditions under which one expects to find a proliferation of age groups. Just what the "causes" and agendas of these groups were depended on preexisting patterns of culture. Some groups were political and assumed the opposing poles of the American political spectrum. On the political left were groups such as Students for a Democratic Society (SDS); from the political right emerged the Young Americans for Freedom (YAF). The 1960s also witnessed the emergence of a broad spectrum of religious groupings. According to Harris (1981):

. . . the Children of God, one of the first Jesus freak movements, appeared in California in 1968. "Hare Krishna" started in New York in 1964. Transcendental meditation began to flourish in the late 1960s. Scientology, which had started out as a form of secular therapy in the 1950s called Dianetics, went into eclipse and then entered a period of rapid growth as a religion at the end of the 1960s. The First Unification Church followers of Reverend Sun Myung Moon arrived in America in 1959 but it was not until 1971 that the "Moonies" began to spread. Mararaj Ji's Divine Light Mission was planted in America in 1971. Healthy, Happy, Holy, an offshoot of Indian Sikhism, appeared in 1968. (142)

Added to this list was a resurgence of the "health" movement marked by a proliferation of "health" clubs and spas, exercise groups, and "health" food stores (Dubisch 1981; Berger 1986). Others simply "dropped out" and emphasized the particularistic values associated with family, love, intimacy, communality, and dependency (Partridge 1985; Weakland 1969). This was the hippie movement. The hippie movement never seemed to get out of Blumer's cultural drift. During that stage there is a perception of change, but no clear-cut solution of what to do about it. Groups appeared with quite different agendas for solving "the problem." Some found salvation in nudity or vegetarianism; others focused on drugs and the drug experience, Jesus, Krishna, or music. The media names often associated with the hippie movement, including the poet Allen Ginsberg and the LSD researcher Timothy Leary, were, according to Partridge, never important as prophets or leaders. Cultural drift never became focused. As this youth-age cohort that occupied the mid-1960s to the mid-1970s aged, they left behind the drugs and other symbols of affiliation that marked the different age groups of that historical period. Higher education had caught up with occupational demands, and those coming into higher education were not faced with the same dilemma. The hippie "movement" became an eccentric blip on the American historical horizon.

In reviewing the peyote cult and the hippie movement, several parallels are noted. Both the Amerind and American cultures were faced with changes. For the Amerinds these changes were imposed from outside. For the United States, the changes in age distribution in the 1960s reflected changes in reproductive behavior just after World War II. Neither of these changes were planned, and the consequences of these changes could not be altered. The point made earlier in this chapter that social movements are not determinants of change is illustrated by peyotism and the variety of behaviors subsumed under the general rubric of "the hippie movement." The emergence of such movements is not dependent on the presence of a particular person. Neither Timothy Leary nor the great Comanche chief Quannah Parker were necessary for these movements. There is little need to appeal to psychological or personality variables when discussing the root causes of cultural change. Culture explains culture. Persons who are affected by cultural drift affirm these changes by behaving in ways that are different from the past. Neither Quannah Parker nor Timothy Leary were responsible for those changes which resulted in people becoming powerless or alienated or suspended in adolescence. They merely voiced a particular set of solutions—in this case, withdrawal from what was perceived as the cause of these conditions. The claims that carrying out a set of actions makes one a better person, capable of seeing what others cannot see, is a trademark of all social movements of this type. In some cases, these movements include as part of their trait inventories drugs which enable users to achieve these desired goals. In other cases, they eschew drugs. More importantly, introversionist expressive movements are honest realizations that one cannot change the system.

Ganja and the Rastafari Brethren

The Rastafarians date their origins to 1930, but to much of the Western world the term "Rastafarian" was meaningless until the appearance of Bob Marley and the Wailers in the late 1960s. Their style of music, called "reggae," contained lyrics rich in social commentary and fast became popular in Jamaica, England, and America. Marley himself presented a striking image. Unshaven, with long, uncut and uncombed hair called "dreadlocks," he and the Wailers popularized the Rastafarian movement among Jamaicans and others of African descent. Just who are the Rastafarians, and what is this movement about?

One practice associated with the Rastafarians is the use of ganja, or marihuana, as part of their religious sacrament. In chapter 3, we discussed the use of ganja among working-class rural Jamaicans, some of whom are Rastafarians. Because ganja smoking is widespread among the working-class in Jamaica one cannot argue that this movement, like the peyote cult, is distinguished by that practice alone. Like other social movements it is part of a history of social relationships. To understand this movement, a brief review of Jamaican history is necessary.

Jamaica is an island in the Caribbean Sea, about 480 miles south of Florida. It is approximately 150 miles long and 52 miles wide. Columbus "discovered" Jamaica in 1494. At that time the Arawak Indians lived there. Their name for the island was "Xaymaca," which means "island of the springs." By the time the British conquered Jamaica in 1655, the Arawak were extinct and the island was almost uninhabited. The British imported thousands of slaves to work on the sugar plantations, and the descendants of these slaves constitute 75 percent of the Jamaican population today. Slavery was abolished in 1853, and independence was gained from the United Kingdom in 1962. Today the island has 2.5 million people, 629,000 of whom live in the capital city of Kingston.

Religion in Jamaica has changed since its early colonization. Under Spanish rule there was Roman Catholicism, but few documents exist concerning its practice. The British brought in the Church of England, but slaves were not permitted to participate in the Anglican Church. Although opposed by the established church, various missionary groups, beginning with the Moravians in 1734, followed by the Methodists in 1736, the Baptists in 1783, and the Presbyterians in 1823, made attempts to convert the slave population. Of these, the Methodists and the Baptists were the most successful. When slavery was abolished in 1953, these Nonconformists[3] took credit and their numbers swelled. Between 1860 and 1861 there was a period of revivalism, and thousands of the former slaves flocked to the churches where the services emphasized singing, crying, spirit possession, and loud prayers.

Western revivalism was short lived. The traditional African rituals, practiced so long by the enslaved population, were combined with Western Christian practices to form a variety of Afro-Christian sects. Three groups predominated in this syncretism. Pukumina or Pocomania (a little madness) was the most African of the three; the Revival Cult was partly African and mostly Christian, and the Revival Zion was the most Christian. In 1929, the Pentecostal sects from the United States arrived. The first to arrive was the Church of God, followed by the Church of God in Christ and the Apostolic Faith, and then almost all the other Pentecostals. Some practices were combined with the three mentioned above to form new groups; others attracted converts. By 1930, there were literally hundreds of sects and cults in Jamaica. In November of that year, the Rastafarians appeared (Simpson 1956).

What distinguishes the Rastafarians from the other cults in Jamaica is that they have a political agenda. The freeing of the slaves in 1865 made it possible for ex-slaves to be elected to the legislative council in 1884. Few attempted, however, and fewer succeeded. It was not until the 1920s that the ex-slave political consciousness was raised by the Jamaican-born Marcus Garvey (1887–1940). Garvey's notoriety was gained in the United States. His Universal Negro Improvement Association (UNIA) was founded soon after World War I. This was a period of turmoil for American blacks. Changes in southern agriculture, the migration of blacks to the industrial North, and a post-war depression all contributed to growing unrest that found expression in lynchings and race riots. Garvey's UNIA was the first mass movement of American blacks. He rejected any aid from whites or established black leaders. His appeal was to the common man. He organized black businesses and emphasized exclusive cooperation between blacks. The fundamental principle of the movement was that conditions were so intolerable in the United States that blacks should migrate to Africa. He established a steamship line and appealed to the League of Nations to found a state for American blacks in Africa. Under political and legal pressure, the UNIA went bankrupt, and Garvey was deported. He came back to Jamaica and in 1938 left for England where he died in 1940. The Garvey movement continued in Jamaica with a small number of followers. Among those followers were some who claimed that Garvey had prophesied in his farewell address to America in 1916 that one should: "Look to Africa for the crowning of a Black King; he shall be the Redeemer." (Barrett 1977, 81) In November of 1930, Ras Tafari was crowned Negus of Ethiopia and took the name Haile Selassie. The coronation was well covered by the press in Jamaica and was taken to be the fulfillment of Garvey's prediction. From that time, the movement has identified itself as Rastafarian.

Jamaica in the 1930s was still a colony of the United Kingdom. Political power was vested in colonial overseers, and blacks lived in conditions of absolute deprivation, especially in Kingston. It is not too difficult to understand why the Garvey-Rastafarian message that the white government was responsible for the plight of the underprivileged was appealing to many. Unlike the Garveyites, the Rastafari brethren had no hope of subsidizing their transportation or of earning their keep after relocation to Africa. In spite of this, in 1933, five thousand persons purchased photographs of Haile Selassie, thought to serve as their passports to Ethiopia. In 1955 groups appeared at three piers in Kingston claiming that the ghost of Garvey had announced the availability of shipping. In 1958, many members of the movement from the rural areas of Jamaica sold their belongings and convened in Kingston with the belief that they would embark for Africa. The following year more than 15,000 persons invested a shilling in a card marked "Free" to serve as a ticket for a scheduled October sailing. These responses surely were measures of desperation.

From the mid-1950s to the mid-1960s many Jamaicans, including Rastafarians, migrated to Britain, mostly to the Brixton area of London. In the 1960s there were many converts from Pocomania and Revivalism to Rastafarianism. A momentous event occurred in 1966 when Haile Selassie visited Jamaica. Besieged by thousands of Rastafarians who blocked his exit from the plane, Selassie was eventually extricated and taken to the University where he was given an honorary degree. The emperor gave out medals to outstanding Rastafarians. In the late 1970s, the movement experienced growth among blacks in Britain, the United States, Canada, Australia, New Zealand, Holland and France. This growth was, in part, due to the popularity of Bob Marley.

The Rastafarians today are not a unified group. One branch, the *Niyamen*, use ganja and are militantly anti-white. Another branch is puritanical, renounces ganja, and has a reputation for kindness (Wilson 1973, 66). The common thread that binds these different groups together is their central doctrine or beliefs. These can be summarized:

1. Ras Tafari (Haile Selassie of Ethiopia) is the living God.
2. Ethiopia is the black man's home.
3. Repatriation is the way of redemption for black men. It has been foretold and will occur shortly.
4. The ways of the white man are evil, especially for the black.

(Smith and Nettleford 1960, 53)

The Rastafaris are bitter enemies of revivalist Christian groups who also recruit from the same areas of Jamaica, yet both groups are messianic. The Christians promise that Jesus will return. The Rastafaris maintain that belief in Jesus and Christian beliefs are those of white men and hence represent the very system which put them into the disadvantaged position they occupy. The Rastafaris believe they will return to Africa. They will leave the conditions for which there is no clear solution. In spite of these professed differences, both the Christians and the Rastafaris seek miraculous solutions and have a strong emphasis on Life Hereafter. Viewed as a belief system, they differ very little. The differences are primarily political and social. Rastafarians believe that the activities of whites are responsibile for their plight, and they symbolically reject Western culture through the public use of ganja, marihuana.

There is no precise census of Rastafarians. They live in camps in both urban and rural areas. Most reside in western Kingston, one of the poorest sections of the city. Their "houses" are old automobiles or cardboard and wooden shelters. Their diets are mainly waste vegetables which have been left behind after the close of markets (Kitzinger 1969). Mostly unskilled laborers, the heads of most Rastafarian households are unemployed. In spite of the living conditions in these camps, migrants from the poor rural areas of Jamaica continue to move into them in search of work.

What makes Rastafarians socially different from other Jamaican peasants is their strong anti-white ideology. Consistent with their rejection of "white" culture, there is a rejection of "white" practices. They do not vote, and they do not belong to unions or other associations. They reject any desire for material possessions. They avoid even being touched by a white person. They do not eat food prepared by non-Rastas. Rastas are vegetarians and especially eschew pork. They eat small fish under 12 inches, usually sprat. Larger fish are assumed to prey on smaller fish and hence are cannibals. No salt is used in cooking. When oil is required they use coconut oil. This is known as "ital" food, meaning the essence of things or things in their natural state.[4] They do not consume milk, coffee, or alcohol, nor are patent medicines used. Women may not prepare food during their menstrual periods. They do not permit their flesh to be penetrated for any reason. Rastamen usually have beards and wear their hair in "dreadlocks,"[5] and they will not wear second-hand clothes. Saturday is their Sabbath, and they do not acknowledge death or attend funerals.

Although there have been well-known Rastafarian spokesmen, the Rastafarians cannot be considered to be a church or a formal organization. This is exemplified in the Rastafarian service. For the Nyabingis branch, drum playing is an important element in the service. According to Kitzinger (1969), who conducted field work among Rastafarians, the drums are usually played with the hands and the music is obviously Caribbean in rhythm. The services she witnessed took place in Rastafarian camps in the house or hut of a "leader." Like the Rastafarians themselves, the Rastafarian house is usually distinguished by the presence of the Ethiopian flag or the flag colors, green, yellow, and red. The ceremony started with testimony from the leader, punctuated by enthusiastic responses from the congregation. Much of the testimony was a reiteration of the history of the Rastafarians and comments on the conditions of black people throughout the world. After the leader finished, he turned the floor over to another brother who, when he was finished, passed it on to another until all those who wanted to speak had their chance. Testimony was periodically punctuated by singing or dancing. Kitzinger observed that throughout the service, people were constantly smoking ganja but concluded that changes in the behaviors of parishioners coincided with changes in the music. At various points in the service, the leader would interrupt to read a passage from the Bible and then interpret the passage to the audience. Services such as this may last all day.

The smoking of ganja has received much more attention than it probably deserves. It nonetheless is an important *part* of Rastafarian practices. Ganja, it is believed, helps one to understand God's nature. Alternatively called, "the herb," "the grass," "the weed," or "the wisdom weed," many biblical texts are quoted in defense of its use (Barrett 129). Ganja use also occurs outside of religious services, but not without some acknowledgement of its religious function. Just before smoking, the following prayer is said by all:

> Glory be to the Father and to the maker of creation. As it was
> in the beginning is now and ever shall be, world without end:
> Jah Rastafari: Eternal God Selassie I.

Ganja is usually smoked in a group setting and, like the American practice, shared by members of the gathering. It is smoked either in a pipe or in cigarette form. After several strong pulls of smoke are taken and deeply inhaled, the smoker then passes the pipe or cigarette (spliff) to another person.

Ganja constitutes the only good cash crop for many Jamaican peasants. Police efforts to suppress its cultivation have been largely unsuccessful. Since ganja is essential to the Rastafarians, and they do not want to risk detection by purchasing from strangers, some have become "middlemen"—distributors. Thus, in addition to its sacramental use, ganja distribution both in Jamaica and in other parts of the world provides some Rastafarians with an income. To reduce detection they have fostered intense interpersonal relationships among the brethren.

The practice of smoking and drinking ganja for both recreational and health purposes is widespread in Jamaica. Its definition as an illegal substance is associated with British domination. Aside from the claims that it aids in meditation, the continued use of ganja serves to symbolically separate the African Jamaicans from Europeans. It is clear that the practices of the Rastafarians are in opposition to those of Europeans, but how do their beliefs and practices distinguish their behavior from other poor Jamaicans? In general, the Jamaican poor tend to be women-centered. Women are viewed as the more stable gender. This pattern is found elsewhere when economic conditions are such that men's work is intermittent and unpredictable (Young and Willmott 1957). Rastafarians are characterized by male dominance. In leadership, status, prophecy, and healing, it is men who are dominant. In the other sects, males may be the formal leaders, but women are the most frequent parishioners. Rasta do not formally marry. Among peasant Jamaicans formal marriages may not occur, but it is a desired goal. In many ways, the Rastafarians are marginal to Jamaican society. Women are tolerated and subservient to men. Sons born to women who have relationships with Rastamen are often left in the camps after the mother leaves. Rasta dogma is male-centered and mother-denying. This contrasts with Jamaican peasant culture where women are often required to play both maternal and paternal roles. Without male figures in the family, boys often form gangs within which they achieve a male identity. The Rastafarians are similar to these boys' gangs in their emphasis on masculinity. To the Rastafarian, home is where the father is found, and fathers are generous towards their sons. Fathers replace mothers in providing emotional and financial support. Thus, Rastafarian practices reject both white practices and the practices of other Jamaican poor. They provide a haven within a haven for the conditions of poverty that characterize much of the Jamaican population and a symbol of identity with like-minded practitioners in other societies around the world where social differences in wealth and power are divided along racial lines.

Selassie died in 1975. According to Rasta theology there is no death, only a passing into the spirit world. Rasta is a living belief system and not concerned with death. Reactions to Selassie's death were that he would be closer to Rastafarians now that he was removed from Ethiopia. Selassie is not perceived as the founder of the movement but considered to be God. The real center of the movement is the revelatory dimensions brought about by the impact of the "holy herb." The use of the herb is believed to throw off the shackles of European domination, enabling one to see that Selassie is God and that Ethiopia is the home of the blacks. The herb is the key to new understanding of the self, the universe, and God. It is the vehicle to cosmic consciousness; it introduces one to levels of reality not ordinarily perceived by the non-Rastafarian; and it develops a certain sense of fusion with all living beings (Barrett 217).

The question we asked about the Native American *Church* can also be asked about the Rastafarians. Can the differences in practices be incorporated into a single organization? Have the Rastafarians become a bureaucracy? Barrett (176–185) notes two somewhat different associations of Rastafarians. One is the

Rastafarian Movement Association (RMA) in Kingston. The other is the Ethiopian National Congress (ENC) on the island of St. Thomas. The RMA occupies a two-room building which serves as an office, a workshop for artisans, and a showroom for the wares of these artisans. It was organized in 1969 with the goal of bringing different groups together. Its administrative structure consists of a president, a vice president, and a secretary. They publish a monthly newsletter entitled *Rasta Voice* which includes both editorials and community news and calendars. The RMA supervises a youth program, provides legal advice, and is politically active.

The ENC represents the religious wing of the Rastafarians. It is located in a wire-fenced encampment in the hills outside of Bull Bay on the island of St. Thomas. Run very much like a closed monastery, its leader is Prince Edward Emanuel. Within this group he, Marcus Garvey and Haile Selassie form a religious triumvirate. The organizational structure of the camp is headed by the Prince and his lady or wife, the Empress, who controls the few women in the camp. Below them are priests, apostles, and prophets. The practices of the ENC are different from the RMA. There are special days for fasting and prayers; Sunday is their day of worship; sacrifice is a ritual practice; and there are other practices that are very similar to those of the Pocomania. The ENC, according to Barrett, is the closest of the Rastafarian groups to a church and has very little of the militancy associated with the other Rastafarians.

Drug Subcultures: Evaluation or Understanding?

It cannot be denied that changes in culture may be expressed in the formation of new cultural units, such as age grades, occupational categories, and class structures. We are surrounded by formally named organizations (such as General Motors, the Catholic Church, the Republican party, and Mothers Against Drunk Driving) that have formally defined personnel whose behavior is mandated by formal rules. These visible, named organizations are easily identified, but others are less visible, yet no less structured than organizations with names. The concept often used to describe these units is subculture or culture. One finds the concept of subculture being applied to several different behavioral systems: the culture of poverty (Lewis 1966), the delinquent subculture (Cohen 1955; Miller 1958; Yinger 1960), the culture of unemployment (Schwartz and Henderson 1964), and the black subculture (Valentine 1968). At the same time, it is applied to "quaint" groupings such as the

Amish, the Shakers, American Indians, and so forth. In a not-so-subtle way, the concept of subculture has been applied to a set of behavioral patterns which are assumed to be either in opposition to (contraculture) or as a social problem defined by *The Culture*.

The word "subculture" is a strange term for a social science that espouses a position of ethical neutrality. As Edward T. Hall (1966, 1973) reminds us, Americans use language references to space which serve as social markers. Thus, one dresses *up*, moves *up* in the world, looks *up* to someone. Drugs are claimed to affect the *higher* functions of the brain. Conversely, one gets a dressing *down*, is *downward*ly mobile, and looks *down* on someone. One goes "up" to heaven or "down" to hell. Thus respect, reward, and honor are linguistically signaled by references above the horizon, while dishonor and disrespect are below the horizon. The prefix "sub" in English, when applied to culture, carries with it a pejorative and often moral connotation. Thus, illegal activities take place in the criminal underworld or delinquent subculture; while acceptable but different behaviors are found in the culture *of* poverty, Mexican-American culture, or African-American culture. Whether sub or culture of, this concept is usually applied without comparison to a detailed ethnography of *The Culture*. I would prefer the term "micro-culture" to describe *demonstrable* and clearly different values, rules, and expectations that one might find in pluralistic societies such as the United States and other urban cultures. Currently, however, the prefix "sub" is used to describe enclaves of people whose life ways *appear* different from those of the writer.

In chapter 1, the term culture was defined and briefly discussed. With some variations, the definition offered is accepted by social scientists. This cannot be said of the term subculture. Jack Roach and Orville Gursslin (1967) as well as Charles Valentine (1968) have been critical of the way(s) the term subculture has been used in the social science literature. Roach and Gursslin argue that the study of subcultures assumes that within a subculture there are shared patterns of values, beliefs, and expectations which depart significantly from the core culture. Studies of the poor often assume the existence of such a subculture without sufficient consideration of the concept of culture itself. This same theme is assumed by those interested in changing this culture by altering these presumed cultural patterns.

Roach and Gursslin suggest several analytical problems associated with this concept. One is the tendency to equate one subculture with another. For example, could one equate the black subculture with the culture of poverty, or delinquent gang subculture with the working-class subculture—or are they separate? Another difficulty with the concept is often a failure to indicate the purpose of the concept. "If the purpose is explanation, what is to be explained: group life, personality processes, deviant behavior, the origins of poverty, or the perpetuation of poverty? (386) Is the term simply a convenient descriptive label for the behavior of the poor? A third problem with the subculture concept is what is meant by culture. If culture is a value system, then material descriptions of this subculture would seem to imply that factors such as unemployment, low income, and crowding are part of that culture. As antecedent conditions to the formation of values, these variables might be appropriate, but as values themselves they are not.

Another concern cited by Roach and Gursslin goes back to our discussion of prediction and explanation. They suggest there is often a failure to distinguish between subculture as the "cause" (independent variable) of itself or the "effect" (dependent variable) of some set of conditions. When used as a cause, it must be demonstrated that the values of one generation are passed down to the next, *and* one is obligated to detail exactly how those values being passed down are different from what is passed down in *The Culture*. In other words, what makes the subculture different from The Culture? When subculture is used as an effect of a set of antecedent conditions, it must be shown that these antecedent conditions result in a specific set of values.

One further difficulty with the subculture concept, relative to describing poverty or drugs, is the question of competency. Descriptions of the poor and of drug users are strikingly similar. They both suggest that participants in these subcultures have numerous social and psychological handicaps. Yet nowhere does one find any explanation of how people with these handicaps are capable of perpetuating anything as complex as culture.

This issue of the appropriate use of the term subculture may in large part be due to a failure to distinguish between society and culture. Society is a group of people whose *behavior* is regulated by behavioral *norms*; culture is a system of expectations supported by *values*. When describing American *culture* one might list self-reliance as one of its values. This value is reinforced through several behavioral norms which are consistent with it. For example, children in American culture are weaned and toilet trained earlier than in other cultures where self-reliance is not a value. The object of this is to make the child self-reliant in feeding and bathroom behavior. Self-reliance is also behaviorally expressed in being economically independent. One is expected to earn an income. Whether that income is derived from activities that are licit or illicit is, for our purposes, unimportant. The activities of a Donald Trump or someone selling marihuana on a street corner are both behavioral manifestations of a single value. To speak of a subculture one must demonstrate that the *values* of the subculture are different from the values of the larger culture. A more appropriate name for systems of different behaviors might be subsociety or micro society—not subculture.

Heroin Use and American Values

This distinction between society as behavior and culture as expectations and values is illustrated by a study of heroin users in New England. Harvey Feldman (1973) found that heroin users were persons with the highest "rep" or prestige on the street. The street prestige system recognizes people by their willingness and ability to engage in risk-taking behavior. This behavior includes fighting, verbal attacks, and the use of drugs, beginning with alcohol. Heroin use was considered the most risky, and those who used it were considered to be the most competent. Heroin users were viewed as having:

> positive qualities of creativity, daring and resourcefulness that provide the impetus for the top level solid guys (persons of established high status) to rise to the top of the street hierarchy. Rather than retreating from the demands of their environment, they utilized the risks of heroin to insure (or strive toward) a leadership position. Their use of heroin solidifies a view of them as bold, reckless, criminally defiant—all praiseworthy qualities from a street perspective. (38)

In examining these findings, these behaviors might appear to be quite different from those of "other" Americans. Indeed, the behaviors are different. Only a very small percentage of Americans use heroin. Are these behaviors inconsistent with American culture—that is, are they outside the value structure of American culture? The key to answering this question is found in the rewards given for risk taking. Risk-taking behavior is an outcome of the value placed on individualism in American culture. It is through risk-taking behaviors that one can achieve recognition as an individual. Not many people race automobiles, climb mountains, or invest everything they own in "risky" stocks. By engaging in these behaviors one can accumulate "cultural capital," esteem and prestige. The motivation for risk-taking behavior is reinforced in American lore and history which grants "hero" status to explorers who risked going into unexplored frontiers, pilots who flew across the Atlantic Ocean singlehandedly in rickety airplanes, businessmen who risked their fortunes to open up new industries, and motorcyclists who catapult across the Snake River. Open, oftentimes defiant, behaviors of bank robbers are silently cheered as "daring." Some writers, notably David C. McClelland (1961), suggest that such risk-taking behavior distinguishes the "achieving" societies from those that are stagnant and unchanging. If risk taking is an American norm, then it reflects American cultural values. What Feldman describes in New England is not subcultural at all; it is simply another, albeit different, behavioral manifestation of a cultural expectation. Heroin using is pure American culture. How this value is expressed is determined by specific opportunity structures. Being poor precludes risking a fortune on the stock market, driving a race car, or being a stunt pilot; but, within a particular setting, heroin addiction symbolically represents risky business.

We may now begin to better understand "why" someone would take this drug. The popular notion that heroin is a means of escaping the conditions of poverty cannot be demonstrated by the pharmacological effects of the drug. As Lindesmith (1938) pointed out, the "high" one gets from the drug is short in duration, and many addicted users report no "high" at all. What is reported is the "low" from not having the drug. To avoid the low, the heroin user must obtain funds to purchase the drug, often by illegal and "risky" means. So why take the drug? There is little, if any, long-lasting pleasure from taking it; it is not an escape from reality; and one must work very hard to avoid the displeasure of withdrawal. The answer to this question, I would suggest, lies in the American value system. The same thing that drives people to engage in a wide variety of risky behaviors drives the heroin addict—the social recognition and prestige accorded one who successfully overcomes risks. It is not a defect in character or personality; it is the internalization of culture—American culture.

Unfortunately, the distinction I have just made is not shared by many students of drugs. For example, Goode (1989) is sensitive to the difficulties of drawing sharp lines between ethnic background, age, and type of drug subcultures. However, he insists there are, "at a minimum, the alcohol-abuse subculture, the marijuana subculture, the cocaine subculture, the heroin-injecting subculture, and the multiple drug-use subculture" (67). Note that in each of these descriptions the drug is the adjective which describes the subculture. We might extend this logic to embrace other possible distinctions within American culture such as the bourbon subculture, the scotch whiskey subculture, the beer subculture, the menthol cigarette subculture, the chewing tobacco subculture, and so forth. Obviously, this exercise illustrates the difficulties associated with identifying a culture or subculture with a specific thing. Cultures and subcultures are complex systems of values, rules, and regulations which give directions for, and meaning to, a diverse set of activities. To place the use of marihuana by Rastafarians and by American adolescents into a single cultural category is an obscene misapplication of the concept of culture.

The reader might wonder why so much attention has been given to the subject of subculture. In part, it has provoked the widespread use of "peer groups" to "explain" why adolescents take drugs. The assumption of the peer-group-influence approach is that "individuals" are enticed into drug use because of their desire to be accepted by the peer group. Those that adopt this belief never address the question of the origin of these peer groups. Rather, like their nineteenth-century moralist counterparts, they assume that "the devil made them do it." The devil in this case is the peer group. The "them" are the hapless adolescents. Any argument that uses this "explanation" for drug use among adolescents violates the principles which set the social sciences apart from moral evaluation. Their assumption is that peer groups are pathological and are a corrupting influence on individuals. The "problem" for the peer group advocates is to convert the individual transgressor back to behavioral conformity as accepted by the spokesperson. None of this moralizing leads to an understanding of why, or even if, such groupings exist. When carried out in the guise of social "science," such an approach serves only to further confuse an already skeptical public as to whether social science can be objective.

Conclusion

In this chapter the focus has been on social movements as adaptations to social and culture change. During periods of change, behaviors and beliefs that had been successful adaptations no longer apply to the changed situation. Under these conditions, many alternatives may be tried. The Bwiti illustrated one of many adaptations to colonial domination. Some adopted strategies from outside; they became colonialists. Others blended traditional practices with those of the outside. Still others held to traditional adaptations and withdrew. The transformation from peyote cult to Native American Church represents two adaptations—from initial withdrawal to a mixture of traditional and Anglo-American practices. The Rastafarians were not the only movement that emerged as a result of the tumultuous history of Jamaica. The Afro-Christian sects and the Pentecostals all reflect adaptive strategies by African-Jamaicans. The same may be said of the hippies. Although their presence gained disproportionate media coverage, they were only a minority among the many movements which surfaced during the 1960s. What is clear from our cursory review is that social movements are seldom solitary phenomena. The dislocations—anomie and value conflict—that characterize the change process demand resolution. In the absence of any guidelines, many alternatives may be tried, but only a few survive to become part of the new order.

Why study social movements if most of them turn out not to survive? We study social movements in order to better understand organization as a process—that is, how things get organized. Movements attempt to establish order out of disorder. An understanding of the principles of this process, whether it results in success or failure, is crucial if we wish to understand society or culture. All the parts that make up society or culture are the result of movements. The business corporation, unions, religion, political groups and government, education, kinship and family are all the end products of social movements. Their continued success or failure depends on changes in organization that reflect the organizational process. Both change and adjustments to change are ubiquitous. If we do not understand this process, we cannot hope to understand the unique adaptive strategies that separate humans from all other animals, namely, social and cultural worlds.

Do social movements change the conditions that are responsible for their formation? The hippies suggest that they do not. The changes in demographic, occupational, and educational conditions in the United States were not altered by the hippies. Many of those same conditions exist today. The youth of America are still caught between childhood and adulthood in that cultural category called "adolescence." Youth is still viewed as a "social problem" (Friedenberg 1966). Drug use in American society is still highest among youth. There still exists a discrepancy between information that is learned at home and knowledge necessary to participate in society among some segments of American society.

In contrast to the hippies, both the Rastafarians and the Native American Church still exist. To some extent they have taken on characteristics of a reform movement, especially in the area of lobbying for legislation that would make the use of marihuana and peyote legal (chapter 10). Yet in other ways they remain the same because the conditions which led to their formation still exist. Thus, in spite of the fact that we may focus on the movements themselves, what we are really examining are the organizational principles of the larger society or culture.

If the movements reviewed in this chapter are a representative sample of social movements in general, we might conclude that "movements of the expressive type are more likely to incorporate drug use as part of their trait inventory." However, this statement would be misleading. Had we not focused on drug use, the examples of expressive movements would have included many that not only do not use drugs but are actively opposed to their use. Thus, we are left with the more modest hypothesis that "if drugs are part of the trait inventory of a social movement, then that movement is likely to be the expressive type."

The reader should not be left with the impression that social movements are only found among the dispossessed, the downtrodden, and those out of power. As we will discuss in chapter 10, the social movement model can be used to understand the formation of groupings which are anything but relatively deprived and would be better described as **relatively endowed**. In urban societies there are many interest groups and cultural categories that seek to guarantee their continuity during periods of social and culture change. This is done through the social movement process. Movements are products of change, no matter what segments of society that change affects.

In making the distinction between social and culture change as the difference between norms (behavior) and values (beliefs), the linkage between values and norms is not always clear. I think the New England heroin users described by Feldman and the discussion of subcultures aid in clarifying both the distinction and the connection between these concepts. Values exist as a reference or guide for behavior. They represent the way we "think" about the world. In contrast, behavioral norms represent adaptive strategies to immediate environmental conditions. There is no necessary one-to-one relationship between values and behaviors. The same value may be behaviorally manifested in different ways. The risk-taking behaviors of heroin users are different from the risk-taking behaviors of non-heroin users. That these behaviors are shared among those in the same environments results in a subsociety, not a subculture.

Models of change, especially those that emphasize process, present both methodological and analytic difficulties. Modifications of practices through time and space cannot be described in fractal detail. At some point boundaries must be drawn which encompass intervals of change. Once this is done, that which is being studied most assuredly will have changed. Field researchers must eventually leave the field and analyze their observations. Survey researchers stop their surveying. Studying things "on the move" must eventually conclude. History is never written while it happens, only when it ends. In deference to the obligation to close the research circle, it is understandable that most social scientists have taken refuge in viewing society and culture as static and fixed. In the next chapter we will review the theoretical models and research conclusions of those social scientists who have examined drugs and drug using from this perspective.

Endnotes

[1] The "vision quest" was practiced by Indian tribes that emphasized individual power. The visions were brought about in a number of different ways. Seekers of a vision would fast, induce vomiting, take sweat baths, engage in self-flagellation and/or mutilation, and take drugs such as tobacco. The object of these activities was to induce an altered state of consciousness in which visions were seen.

[2] The *eboka* plant is a shrub that grows approximately four feet high. The main alkaloid—ibogainè—is concentrated in the root bark. The root bark is rasped and eaten directly as raspings, ground into powder and eaten, or soaked in water and drunk. Etically, the effect is said to be "an intense and unpleasant central stimulation and peripheral relaxation and depression (Pope 1969, 178). Fernandez (1990) reports that users usually sit quietly gazing into space and sometimes fall over into a stupor. In lighter doses, users report that it makes the body feel light and helps them through the all-night dancing. Heavy dosages during initiation ceremonies have resulted in death. The reasons for taking eboka vary. Of the 50 "banzie" (angels in the cult) interviewed, the modal reason was because "A dead relative came to me in my sleep and told me to eat it." The second most frequent reason was, "I was sick (or some other physical symptom) and was counseled to eat eboka to cure myself." Of 38 members surveyed, 76 percent reported some kind of vision. The remaining 23 percent reported no visual or auditory effects.

[3] Nonconformists is the name given to any religious group that did not conform to the "established" church—in this case, the Church of England.

[4] The Rastafarians have a distinctive dialect. They use numerous "I" centered words such as "ital" for vital. Absent from their lexicon are diminutives. For example, understand becomes overstand. This argot is consistent with rejection of white culture that is rooted in super- and subordinate relationships, with subordinate reserved for black Jamaicans. More will be said about this in chapter 8.

[5] Dreadlocks is a descriptive term for the hair style of Rastafarians. To achieve this appearance, the hair is not cut or combed. It is washed in water mixed with local herbs, but no chemically processed goods, soap or shampoo may be used. Rastamen who use combs are referred to as "combsome." Those that shave and cut their hair are called "cleanface." Young Rastas who are just beginning to let their hair grow (it takes years to grow dreadlocks) are called "nubbies." The absence of a beard and dreadlocks does not mean that a person is not a Rastafarian. Because Rastafarians are often discriminated against in employment, some Rastamen will cut their hair and shave their beard in order to secure work.

chapter 6

Time Stands Still
The Function of Drugs

B y the end of the nineteenth century the unilineal evolution approach was coming under increasing attack. There were questions that proof of evolutionary stages did not really exist and that detailed field work among real natives could not confirm the evolutionary model. The dean of American anthropology, Franz Boas (1858–1942), rejected the process of grand theorizing altogether. He insisted that the immediate task of anthropology was to gather more information about a larger variety of peoples. Induction, not deduction, was the only method. If historical analysis was to be done, it must be only for a particular society or neighboring societies. Preceding social facts could be used to explain later social facts, but he insisted there was no "grand plan" or "grand schema." His approach was called **historical particularism**, and it became the guiding principle used by his many graduate students at Columbia University.

In Britain, the rejection of evolutionism came from two anthropologists—Bronislaw Malinowski (1884–1942) and A. R. Radcliffe-Brown (1881–1955). Malinowski did extensive field work in the Trobriand Islands of Melanesia, and it is to him that we owe the concept of participant-observation. His long stay, almost five years, permitted Malinowski to study the Trobrianders in great depth. His intimacy with the islanders took him beyond the cataloging of disconnected cultural traits (the units of the evolutionists and the diffusionists) to a consideration of what these traits meant and what they did. He was able to place the many practices he observed into the context of the total Trobriand culture.

Malinowski viewed culture as an integrated system of traits that did not require history to explain. The explanation of culture was in its purpose or **function**. For Malinowski the **primary function** of culture is to satisfy seven basic biological needs of humans—metabolism, reproduction, bodily comfort, safety, movement, growth, and health. In every culture there are practices which function to meet these needs. For example, the biological need to reproduce is satisfied through kinship. Once these primary needs are satisfied, four **derived** needs integrate culture itself. Economic systems (derived) emerge to regulate the production, distribution, and consumption of food, which satisfy the biological need for food (one of the metabolic needs). Systems of social control regulate the relationships between humans. Education guarantees that people are provided with knowledge, and some form of political system is needed to define power and to provide a means for enforcing rules. Malinowski insisted that all traits within a culture have a function that is related to either primary or derived needs. His concern was not how the trait got into the culture but rather how it functioned. In other words, history be damned!

The other figure in British functionalism, A. R. Radcliffe-Brown, was not as consummate a field worker as Malinowski. His "field work" among the Andaman Islanders relied more on the observations made by others, combined with a survey of practices. Unlike Malinowski, Radcliffe-Brown focused on society, not culture. He rejected culture as a useful concept because expectations, rules, and values could not be directly observed. Instead, he suggested that the proper unit for scientific analysis was **social structure**, the organization of people into groups where roles (behavior) could actually be observed. The function of human actions was to support or confirm social structure. The idea that society is what must be explained was borrowed from the French sociologist Émile Durkheim and his students. In this sense, Radcliffe-Brown linked

French sociology with British anthropology. The result is what is now known as social anthropology.

Both Malinowski and Radcliffe-Brown taught in the United States and both influenced American students. While they and their students debated over the relative importance of culture and society, a more subtle message was incorporated into the social sciences—functional analysis.

Functional analysis is not a unique social science strategy. When biologists say that the function of the heart is to pump blood, they are talking about what the heart does. When social scientists say that the function of marihuana is to mark boundaries between social groupings, they are stating what marihuana does. In both of these examples there is an assumption that what is done by the heart or by marihuana is relative to a larger system. The heart is part of the circulation system. Marihuana is part of a system of social differentiation. No matter what the thing or practice, functionalists assume that everything has a function or purpose, otherwise it would not exist. Although Malinowski and Radcliffe-Brown might disagree on whether culture or society is more important, they would not disagree that the function of any practice is determined by the system in which it is found. Thus, function is relative to a whole; and to determine function, it is necessary to study that whole.

Another point of agreement is that the function of a practice can only be determined relative to a whole *at one time*. Thus one must analyze social or cultural functions **synchronically**. A synchronic analysis can ignore history, and it views function within the time interval of the research. This does not exclude **diachronic** analysis, which examines function over time, but always within systems. One final point of agreement is that whatever functional interpretation was made, it had to be rooted in actual observation, not the kind of speculative reconstructions both men attributed to the evolutionists.

The functional approach was by no means the exclusive domain of anthropology. Sociology picked up the banner of functionalism. One of its more articulate representatives is Robert K. Merton (1910–). More interested in what something does than what it is, Merton suggests that the functional approach must distinguish between **manifest** and **latent** functions. The manifest function of something is what is formally stated and widely understood (similar to emic). For example, the manifest function of the university is to train and educate students. In addition to this manifest function, the university has other functions that are not formally intended. One latent function (similar to etic) of the university is to bring people together into a marriageable pool. It is not the manifest function of the university to be a marriage broker, but this is, nonetheless, one of its functions. Note here that the question is not what the university is but rather what functions the university performs.

If numbers are used as criteria, it is clear that most of the social science literature is concerned with the function of this or that practice. Continuity and consensus in social life is the inevitable outcome of the functional approach. This is consistent with the relational characteristic of scientific propositions. A scientific principle or "law" is not bound by time or space. Thus, when writing scientifically it is customary to write in the present tense. Readers not sensitive to this convention often are left with the impression that descriptions of human behavior that may have taken place in the far distant past are part of the time frame in which the reader is reading. This linguistic appearance of stability should not be confused with the absence of change.

Having said this, it must be stated that without "real" continuity and stability, neither society nor culture would be possible. Humans would be no different from other animals in which each generation begins life at the same place as the previous generation. In non-human animal species there is no evidence for learned accumulation of experience over time. Human activities do become institutionalized, and even though the people who engage in these practices die, they are replaced by others who continue these traditions. It is this enduring quality of social life that has consumed the passion of most social scientific researchers. The underlying framework that guarantees continuity is the division of labor.

The Division of Labor

In this chapter the focus is on the parts—**roles** and **statuses**—that make up associations and institutions. The concern here is with the behaviors and the expectations that make orderly social life possible. The emphasis is on the processes of **cooperation** and **competition** as processes of interaction that are associated with consensus—not **conflict**, which is the process that accompanies change. In every society, the activities of people are not left to individual decision making. In order for a society to exist humans must "work" in cooperation with each other. How this "work" gets done, and by whom, is determined by the **division of labor**. There are two human characteristics that are universally used in dividing labor: sex and age. At minimum, males are expected to carry out certain duties that are different from females; and children engage in activities dissimilar from adults. We can visualize this division of labor and the resulting units in table 6.1.

Table 6.1. **Sample Division of Labor**

		SEX	
		Male	**Female**
AGE	**Child**	I	II
	Adult	III	IV

People within a culture with this division of labor would occupy one of these four statuses. They will be either male (I) or female (II) children, or male (III) or female (IV) adults. Each of these statuses would have a set of expectations for what the incumbents could or should do. The actual behaviors of these status incumbents would vary from one culture to another. Therefore, it should be remembered that it is not the content of these categories that is shared, but that these categories are found in all cultures. What would be adult male behavior in one culture could be adult female in another, and vice versa.

Divisions of labor vary in the number of status distinctions. Those that make few distinctions are described as undifferentiated; those that make many distinctions are differentiated. This difference in status differentiation should not be confused with the roles (behavior) that accompany status. For example, in small hunting and gathering societies one may find few status distinctions, but within any status diverse activities are expected. In contrast, in large urban societies one usually finds many status distinctions, but those occupying a status perform very specific tasks.

Émile Durkheim (1947) recognized these differences in divisions of labor and suggested that not only are they recognizably dissimilar, but their underlying principles of organization are distinct. Durkheim used the term **social solidarity** to describe the organizational principles of divisions of labor. For the division of labor with few categories he offered the concept of **mechanical solidarity**; for the division of labor that was highly differentiated, he used the term **organic solidarity**. What binds people together in societies with mechanical divisions of labor is that they are expected to engage in similar behaviors. In contrast, people in societies with organic divisions of labor are highly interdependent because each person makes only a small contribution to the whole and therefore must rely on others. Keep in mind that these different types of division of labor may be found in the same society. A person who installs steering wheels on automobiles on an assembly line is part of an organic division of labor. After work that same person may get together informally with friends to drink beer in a group that is organized by the principles of mechanical solidarity. This is not to say that whole societies are more or less mechanically or organically organized. In the world today there are societies with relatively undifferentiated divisions of labor and societies with highly differentiated divisions of labor. In the following pages we will examine the function of drugs in societies with different divisions of labor.

Ebene and Tobacco Use Among the Yanomamö

The Yanomamö, who number about 12,000, live in the equatorial rain forest between Venezuela and Brazil. They reside in self-contained villages of between 100 and 300 residents that may periodically split when the population becomes too large. These villages are "governed" by a "headman" system in which the "leader" has no formal authority and leads by example. They are, according to their ethnographer Napoleon Chagnon (1983), a "fierce" people. Their continual inter-village warfare and intra-village hostilities, usually over women (an emic explanation), is accompanied by continuous rounds of negotiation between different villages to form shifting alliances for both protection and warfare. They represent a rare case study of a society in which warfare has become a normal part of everyday life, and both their associations and institutions revolve around this activity.

The Yanomamö have a combined economy. They hunt a variety of animal species and gather honey, fruits, eggs, grubs, nuts, tubers, and mushrooms. In addition, they garden plantains, manioc, taro, and sweet potatoes, as well as several nonfood cultigens such as cotton, arrow cane, and tobacco.

The Yanomamö are a male dominated society. Women lack influence and do not participate in decision making within the village. Women are subordinate to their fathers and to their husbands. Women are routinely struck or hit, and sometimes killed, when they fail to follow the orders of males. Girls are expected to help their mothers in household duties, including the supervision of younger siblings. By the end of puberty girls have been promised in marriage, at which time they come under the control of their husbands. Both women and girls are given tasks men do not want. The only time a woman has prestige is when she is old. Old women are not likely to be captured for wives of enemy warriors. They can visit freely within enemy villages and frequently serve as messengers or collectors of the bodies of dead warriors from their own village.

The distinction between male and female is established at an early age. Boys are favored by their fathers and at an early age learn appropriate "fierce" behavior. Girls assume women's obligations earlier than boys become men. Soon after her first menses, a girl moves in with her promised husband and becomes a married woman. Boys earn their manhood gradually and are recognized as adults when they are able to prevent others from using the name that they were called as children.

Both males and females work in the gardens, but only men hunt for meat. Women spend much of their day gathering firewood from the surrounding forest. Males and females cook, but males usually engage in this behavior only in preparation of a feast in which the village plays host to visitors from other villages.

Men's work is ranked higher in prestige than women's work, and there are two statuses within the village that only men can occupy. One is the headman. This status is occupied by a man who has the ability to mobilize the activities of others, a man of influence. The other status is *shabori*, the Yanomamö word for a shaman. Shaman is a Siberian Chukchee word that is used by social scientists to describe a status in tribal societies that has responsibility for diagnosing and curing illness through manipulation of the spirit world.

Among the Yanomamö, one must formally train to be a shaman. This training emphasizes an abandonment of "normal" male Yanomamö life. Because of this, not all males elect to become shamans. The novice is expected to fast and refrain from having sexual intercourse. During this period the initiates are instructed by the older shamans in how they can attract hekura into their chests. *Hekura* are tiny humanoid creatures who are believed to live in different environments—in trees, in mountains, and under rocks. Each hekura follows different trails from its residence. The job of the shaman is to entice the hekura to leave their homes, follow their paths, and enter the shaman through his feet and into his chest where there resides a duplication of these environments, both natural and supernatural. Once the hekura are inside the chest, the shaman directs them to use their special weapons to strike or pierce souls, to cure illness, or to kill enemies.

The Yanomamö use two drugs—tobacco and what they call *ebene*. Tobacco is used by men, women and children, and all are "addicted." Tobacco is not smoked but rather sucked. Each family cultivates and fiercely protects its own tobacco patch. At maturity, individual leaves of tobacco are picked from the plant and are tied together by their stems in bundles of fifteen to twenty leaves. These bundles are then hung over the fire to cure in the heat and smoke. When dried, they are stored in large balls which are wrapped in other leaves for protection. As needed, several leaves are removed, dipped in water, and kneaded in the ashes of a fire. The leaf is then rolled into a cigar shape and placed between the lower lip and teeth. If someone removes the wad from his or her mouth, it might be picked up by another person and sucked until the owner requests its return. The borrower may be anybody—friend, relative, male, female, child, or anthropologist.

The other drug, ebene, is a hallucinogenic snuff. Richard Shultes (1967) suggests that the area encompassing southern Venezuela and northern Brazil represents the center of snuff-taking in South America. Shultes and Holmstedt (1968) go further to claim that the Yanomamö area itself may be where the practice began. There are at least four plants, belonging to three botanical families, that are used to make ebene (Chagnon, LeQuesme and Cook 1971). The most widely distributed source of ebene is the *yakowana* (*Elizabetha princeps*) tree. The soft moist inner bark is dried and ground into a powder. To this is added ashes from the bark of another tree. These ingredients are then mixed with saliva, kneaded by hand to a gummy consistency, and then placed on a piece of heated pot "shard" (a piece of broken pottery). After drying, it is ground into a fine green powder.

The more desirable and more powerful ebene comes from the seed of the *hisiomö* (*Anadenanthera peregrina*) tree. These seeds are skinned and packed in cylindrical wads. The tree is unevenly distributed, and villages near natural groves often specialize in the trading of their seeds. Some Yanomamö have successfully "domesticated" this tree, thus avoiding trade dependency. These seeds are also kneaded with ashes and saliva and then pulverized with a smooth stone or stone axe on a heated shard. Since ebene does not follow any specifically prescribed formula, it is not possible to conclude that it is a particular thing. Rather, its contents vary widely.

Chemical analysis of these ingredients indicates the presence of bufotenine and/or tryptamine, along with several other alkaloids.

There is no evidence that any of these chemicals results in physiological dependency. The Yanomamö may go for weeks without using ebene. This is not true of tobacco. They seldom go without that for more than a few hours.

If available, ebene is consumed almost every day and is accompanied by repeating stories about the cosmos and the origin of the Yanomamö and their practices. According to Chagnon:

> The men usually make a batch of *ebene* every day; sometimes several groups of men in a village make their own batch. It takes quite a bit of kneading and grinding to produce a half cupful, enough for several men, depending upon their appetites and whether it is *hisiomö* or *yakowana*. The men paint themselves elaborately with red pigment, put on their fine feathers, and then gather around the front of the house of the host. A long hollow tube is used to blow the powder into the nostrils. A small amount, about a teaspoonful, is pushed by finger into one end of the tube to load it. The other end, to which a large, hollowed seed has been fashioned as a nostril piece, is put into a companion's nose. The green powder is then blown into the nasal cavity with a powerful, long burst of breath that starts slowly and terminates with a vigorous blast. The recipient grimaces, chokes, groans, coughs, gasps, and usually rubs his head excitedly with both hands, or holds the sides of his head as he duck-waddles off to some convenient post where he leans against it waiting for the drug to take effect. He usually takes a blast of *ebene* in each nostril, sometimes two in each, and "freshens" it with more blasts later. The recipient immediately gets watery eyes and a profusely runny nose—long strands of green mucus begin to drip from each nostril. Dry heaves are also very common, as is out-and-out vomiting. Within a few minutes, one has difficulty focusing and begins to see spots and blips of light. Knees get rubbery. Profuse sweating is common, and pupils get large. Soon the *hekura* spirits can be seen dancing out of the sky and from mountain tops, rhythmically prancing down their trails to enter the chest of their human beckoner, who by now is singing melodically to lure them into his body where he can control them—send them to harm enemies or help cure sick kinsmen. (50–51)

To the functionalist this practice can be understood as one example of the function of ceremonial rituals. Rituals are condensed and somewhat disguised representations of certain aspects of social life, the function of which is to protect the existing social order. This practice by males functions both as a visual demonstration of Yanomamö beliefs, history, and practices, and as a collective enactment of defense by those same males against outside invaders.

At the intra-village level, where interpersonal hostility is expressed in axe fights and chest-pounding duels, ebene use provides for "time out" behavior. Under the influence of ebene, men are granted immunity from acts of hostility against others that might otherwise result in schisms in village integration. Thus, one function of ebene is to offer a safe opportunity to reduce interpersonal enmities.

What, might one suggest, is the function of tobacco? It is clear from the description above that ebene and tobacco are unequally distributed. Adult males grow or gather, process, and use ebene. The manifest (emic) function of this substance is to achieve an altered state of consciousness whereby one can communicate with the hekura spirits, but note that the adult male activities associated with ebene are a collective male activity. Men *gather* the ingredients of the ebene, pulverize the ingredients into powder collectively, and the method of use requires cooperative male activity. You blow it up my nose and I will blow it up your nose! One cannot take ebene alone. Tobacco, on the other hand, is used by males and females, and *grown* in "family" plots. Tobacco functions as a joint activity of the village. Ebene serves to distinguish between adult males and others. In the Yanomamö division of labor, ebene symbolizes the distinctions among adult males, children, and females. Conversely, tobacco serves, in its production, as a distinction between families. In its consumption, however, tobacco marks the integration of men and women and of boys and girls.

Kava Use in Western Polynesia

One of the consistent observations of early European travelers to the South Pacific was the importance some people ascribed to *kava*, a beverage made from the root of the plant, *Piper methysticum* (Lebot et al. 1992). On the island societies of Fiji, Tonga, Samoa, Futuna, and Uvea there are ceremonies in which kava plays a central part (Turner 1986). Although the specifics of these ceremonies differ somewhat, they do have in common some general features which function both to distinguish between the statuses in the division of labor and to order the connections between those statuses. In this section we will explore the symbolic importance of kava in reference to these functions.

James Turner's seventeen-month field study on Viti Levu, the largest of the Fiji islands, included almost daily observations of kava consumption (1986).

Although Fijians use the same word to describe the effects of alcohol and kava, they make a clear distinction between those effects. Alcohol can lead to raucous—even violent—behavior; kava leads to peaceful tranquility. Experienced kava drinkers do make a distinction between the fresh and the dried kava. Fresh kava is claimed to be the stronger of the two. There is still some dispute among pharmacologists about the effect of kava on the nervous system. Experienced users report a loss of voluntary muscle control and numbing of the face, legs, and arms. Different European users did not report these effects. These variations in reported effects may be, in part, due to the variability of kava itself, the method of preparation, and the amount consumed. But whatever the pharmacology of kava, there is no evidence to suggest that its active ingredients define the function of kava use.

Turner reported that kava use was associated with numerous activities. Kava was consumed during kinship and chiefship rituals, before any major undertaking, after any joint effort, at arrivals and departures, at public assemblies, and as a matter of hospitality at social gatherings. In addition, it was part of the treatment for certain illnesses (206). Little wonder that kava was used every day! The activity that is of interest here is the kava ceremony associated with chiefship.

At chiefship ceremonies, seating arrangements are considered important. The spatial arrangement of the ceremony mirrors the hierarchial principles of the chief system. The most senior chief sits at the apex of a circle. He is surrounded to his left and right by lesser chiefs and those related to him through kinship ranking. This same seating arrangement has been reported by most observers of the chiefship ceremony.

Elizabeth Bott (1987) observed both small, informal and large, formal kava ceremonies in Tonga. In informal ceremonies, the chief with genealogical seniority sits at the head of the circle. Next to him are hereditary ceremonial attendants called *matāpule*, who orchestrate the ceremony and are responsible for exchanging gifts. The rest of the circle is made up of other chiefs and non-titleholders. The kava bowl is opposite the presiding chief. In informal kava ceremonies, it may be only a few feet away; in the formal ceremony, two hundred yards away. The kava maker and his assistant sit behind the bowl. Outside of the main circle is a group of people who help make and then serve kava. In large, formal ceremonies, the genealogically senior chief sits at the head of the main circle. The rest of the circle is made up of formally appointed titleholders, chiefs, and matāpule, who occupy alternate seats. The titles of the chiefs in the main circle should be genealogically junior to the title of the presiding chief. The outer group is also ranked. First are the men who hold minor chiefly titles defined as "younger brother" (not genealogically related) to the titles in the main circle. Second are men and women without titles who are the "children" and, in a few cases, the "grandchildren" of the titles in the main circle (187).

In both Tonga and Fiji the function of these seating arrangements is similarly interpreted. On Fiji Turner suggests that:

> The seating arrangement emphasizes a gradation of rank rather than the separation that governed the relationship between ruler and subject in the more highly stratified kingdoms of eastern Polynesia, where the kava ceremony was absent. That difference is the essence of chiefship. It is not simply hierarchy that is underscored in the kava ceremony but also continuity within society. . . . The message of the ceremony is a complex statement of continuity within inequality—a feature of the gradation of rank characterized by chiefdoms—and the spatial configuration of the kava ring is a reaffirmation of both principles. (207)

Bott's conclusions were similar in respect to division of labor. On Tonga, the kava ceremony distinguishes between "titles," not people. The system of title differentiation on Tonga is one of three systems of social differentiation. Paralleling the title system is one based on political power and one based on personal esteem. One's ranking in one of these systems is not necessarily the same as in the other two. Titles are usually inherited through the male line; personal esteem is inherited through both parents. Political power reflects the ability of a man to mobilize family and friends to support his leadership. Thus, a king who had high title rank might have had low political rank. In the traditional system men competed to increase their rank in all three systems. The kava ceremony recognized any changes in rank by a new seating arrangement. In modern-day Tonga the system of personal rank continues as in the past, but education has replaced political rank, with a minor exception. Some of the traditional chiefs were given the European title "noble," with the right to elect seven of their number to the legislative assembly. To keep these systems visible, different ceremonies have different seating arrangements. People in government are seated at governmental ceremonies according to their political (education) rank. At funerals, seating is based on personal and kinships rank. The kava ceremonies functioned to perpetuate the title system of ranking.

A variation on the Tonga and Fiji system is reported by Monty Lindstrom (1982) from his twenty months of field work on Tanna, Vanuatu (previously New Hebrides). He observed that:

> Kava, although suffering prohibition during a period of intense missionary domination of island affairs (1900–1940), continues

to have great ceremonial and everyday significance. Men prepare and drink kava daily at dusk, a period of the day called *einpen se ierema* (the time of the ancestors). Men and boys gather at kava-drinking grounds (*imwarim*) to clean kava root with knives and coconut fibre. They then chew the root, mixing it thoroughly with saliva. The person preparing kava puts several mouthfuls of masticated root into a bit of coconut spathe and pours water onto the kava as he kneads it by hand. Kava infuses in the water and strains into a half coconut shell drinking cup. A drinker takes this to the edge of the imwarim and tosses it down in a long, fast, continuous gulp. (428)

In contrast to the noisy and gregarious kava ceremony of Fiji and Tonga, the behavioral response to kava on Tanna is calmness and silence. After drinking kava the men sit quietly and "listen" to their kava. Note also that kava is prepared by chewing rather than by scraping and pounding. Chewing was the earliest method of preparation but has been replaced by scraping and pounding in all but a few societies. D. C. Gajdusek (1979) and E. F. Steinmetz (1960) suggest that saliva breaks down the kava root more effectively, thereby releasing more of the "intoxicating" ingredients. But whether pounded, scraped, or chewed, ethnographers agree that the degree of intoxication and the behavioral effects are, like other drugs, explained better by the social, not the chemical powers of this substance.

Lindstrom's analysis suggests that the preparation and use of kava reflect socially significant categories. On Tanna, those categories are different from those on Fiji and Tonga. Table 6.2 shows the various steps in the kava ritual accompanied by the division of labor.

The most obvious distinction is male/female. Although women grow kava which they sell for cash, directly exchange kava when their sons are circumcised, and give kava to their male kinsmen, they are prohibited from seeing kava being prepared or consumed. Violation of this expectation may be punished by being hit with a kava branch. In contrast, all males may participate in or at least observe the events of preparation and consumption.

Uncircumcised boys are restricted to only viewing the event. Sometime after circumcision, a boy is encouraged by his father to chew the root. These sexually inactive circumcised boys are considered to be "pure" men. Note that only they are permitted to mix kava by hand. Once they become sexually active they can no longer participate in this part of the kava processing. The drinking of kava does not take place until the male marries.[1] Once married,

Table 6.2.
Distinctive Features of Kava Drinkers on Tanna

	Women	Uncircumcised Boys	Circumcised/ Sexually Inactive	Sexially Active/Un- Married	Married/ Ordinary Men	Old Men, Big Men
	pran	*kapiesi*	*tamarua*	*tamarua*	*ieraman*	*eraghara, iema asori*
Participate in the event	—	+	+	+	+	+
Mix kava by hand	—	—	+	—	—	—
Chew kava	—	—	+	+	+	—
Drink kava	—	—	—	—	+	+

+ = may; — = may not

Source: Lindstrom, Monty. 1982. "Grog Bloung Yumi: Alcohol and Kava on Tanna, Vanuatu."
In *Through a Glass Darkly: Beer, and Modernization in Papua New Guinea*. Mac Marshall,
ed., p. 429. Institute of Applied Social and Economic Research Monograph 18.

males continue to chew and drink kava. As men age, they abandon chewing altogether.

In all cultures, people go through a life cycle in which they occupy different statuses. On Tanna, this process is reflected in the various roles that males play in the preparation and consumption of kava. Although different from Tonga and Fiji, the function of kava is the same. It serves as a visual and behavioral manifestation of those unseen but understood distinctions between statuses that are the building blocks of culture.

The Party: Qat in Yemen

It has been said that if fish were scientists, the last thing they would discover is water. The same might be said of social scientists about the party. Although the social event called a "party" is part of the personal social life of all social scientists, very little has been written on this subject. However, one study (Riesman, Potter, and Watson 1960) did research the linkage between sociability (the success of a party) and the behavior of the "host." David Riesman and his team analyzed eighty parties and discovered that it is difficult to be a full participant in the party and remain totally objective. In spite of this difficulty, they concluded that sociability diminishes when conversation focuses on any one topic. When conversation topics shift and change during the party, it is more likely to be viewed as a success. Since the host or hostess can "guide" conversation topics, they conclude that hosts determine subjective evaluations of parties.

While this study offers some insight into the dynamics of a party, there is one glaring omission from the analysis. Nowhere is offered a definition of the party as a type of social event, nor is the issue of the function of that event addressed. To most of us, the "party" refers to a focused social activity with a rather simple set of statuses—host or hosts and guests. A party takes place in physical space and within a time frame. Parties, at least in American culture, are often named events—that is, they celebrate some culturally recognized marker (a birthday party, graduation party, end-of-the-year party, going-away party, retirement party, and so forth).

The party as a cultural event should not be equated with the party as a social event. As a cultural event it is a learned set of expectations which guide the behavior of hosts and guests. Readers who have attended parties "know" the appropriate etiquette for the party, including when it is over. As an event, the party stands in contrast to "work" in American culture. Work takes place within clearly prescribed times. One may be late for work if one arrives a few minutes past the official starting time. It is not clear when one is late for a party. Party attendance is voluntary (although there may be moral or reciprocal reasons which obligate one to attend a party); work is mandatory. Work is serious; the party is unserious (except perhaps for hosts). There are specified monetary rewards for work; one is not paid money to attend a party. While a theory for the function of the party has yet to be constructed, one insight into the party as both a social and a cultural event is provided by the analysis of everyday qat use in North Yemen.

Qat (Khat) is the Arabic word for *Catha edulis*, an evergreen shrub or tree that is native to Turkestan, Afghanistan, Uganda, Rwanda, Burundi, Zaire, Tanzania, Zambia, Mozambique, and South Africa. The geographic distribution of qat as a cultigen includes: Yemen, western Saudi Arabia, Ethiopia, Somalia, Madagascar, and Kenya. Qat was classified by the Swedish botanist, Per Forsskål, in the eighteenth century. He latinized the Arabic name qat to *Catha* and added the second term *edulis* because it is eaten (Weir 1985, 27). Qat trees reach heights of between five and ten meters and produce leaves for up to 50 years. The preferred leaves for chewing at qat parties are the new shoots that are only a few days old.

The historical evidence for qat consumption is meager. It probably began in either Yemen or Ethiopia in the mid-fourteenth century and was widely consumed by Muslims in the early fifteenth century. The historical data show a close connection with coffee consumption, another diffusion pattern which is unclear. Coffee is thought to have come from Ethiopia sometime in the late thirteenth or early fourteenth century (Ukers 1935).

Shelagh Weir (38–39) insists that Western accounts have greatly exaggerated the physical effects of qat, primarily because it is so pervasive in Yemeni life and because it costs so much. Westerners often assume that it is physiologically addictive or that it gives such intense physiological pleasure that people are psychologically dependent. In contrast, Yemenis regard qat as a mild stimulant. They believe that it increases stamina, concentration, mental alertness, and that it elevates mood. For Yemenis, who are Muslim (either followers of Zaydism, a sub-sect of the Shiah sect of Islam in North Yemen, or practitioners of the Shafì doctrine of orthodox Sunni Islam in South Yemen), the use of qat is not prohibited on religious grounds. Unlike alcohol or other drugs which are *haram* (prohibited by religious law), qat is thought to enhance one's ability to concentrate during long prayer sessions.

Linguistically, qat is neither a drug (*mukhaddir*) like hashish nor an intoxicating liquor (*khamr*). It is placed in its own linguistic category—qat. Qat enthusiasts are known by the term *mowla'i*, which is sometimes translated as "addict." However, it is a complementary term which carries prestige because it indicates that one can afford to consume large quantities of the expensive qat. A better translation would be "connoisseur" or "gourmet." All that has been revealed by the extensive chemical, pharmacological and medico-social research on qat is that it has rather mild stimulant properties and is not addictive in any accepted medical sense of the term.[2] As Weir observed:

> . . . there is no evidence that qat causes dependence or that it is anything other than a weak and relatively innocuous stimulant. . . . Of course the social significance of any institutional indulgence is independent of its physical effects, but the weaker the substance the greater the weight which can be placed on social explanations for its mass consumption. The significance of qat parties in Yemen can no more be understood in terms of the physical effect of qat than the importance of coffee houses in seventeenth-century London can be explained by the effects of caffeine. (9)

Assuming that qat does not cause physical or psychological dependence, further insight might be gained from researching the background of the country in which it is consumed. Yemen, "The

Yemen," or "North Yemen" was officially known as the Yemen Arab Republic (YAR) since the 1962 revolution. (In 1990 the two Yemens were again united.) The total population of North Yemen was a little over 4.5 million in 1975. Most of Yemen is high and mountainous with a temperate or subtropical climate. Until recently, about 90 percent of the population were subsistence farmers living in independent households. Three-quarters of its population lived in small rural settlements with less than 500 inhabitants. In the 1960s Yemen was one of the least developed countries in the world. Most of the population relied upon rain-fed agriculture and animal husbandry. The main crops today are drought-resistant cereals—sorghum, millet, wheat, and barley. Some areas specialize in the production of cash crops, the most important of which are coffee (the famous "mocha" brand named after the port of Mokha), qat, bananas, and grapes (Weir, 17).

In the 1970s there was large-scale migration of Yemeni men to work in Saudi Arabia as laborers in the construction industry. Monies sent home by these workers made it possible for Yemenis to acquire modern amenities and improve the quality of their lives. Associated with this new wealth, there was a rise in consumerism and concomitantly a rise in prices and wages. Many Yemeni farmers moved to towns or abroad because they could not afford increased labor costs. Those who remained, mostly in the rainy areas of Yemen, were able to increase the price of cash crops.

Before the 1962 revolution the organization of Yemeni society was based on a system of **ascribed** statuses that were hierarchically ranked. Ascribed statuses are those into which one is born. Under this system, economic wealth was not associated with birth rights. Thus, one might have little wealth but high social rank. Similar to caste systems elsewhere, rank was occupationally marked. For example, under the traditional system qat sellers came from the lower social ranks and were also poor. The revolution officially dismantled localized systems of birth rank and replaced them with a central government. In spite of the official banning of the traditional system, many parts of the country attempted to retain the traditional political structures based on birth rights. However, increased wealth made it difficult to maintain the traditional system of ranking. For example, qat consumption increased and there was a corresponding increase in prices and profits. By the 1970s, the previously poor and low-ranked qat farmer had become rather wealthy. The combination of government edict and increasing incomes resulted in two parallel ranking systems, one based upon birth, the other on income.

The Qat Party

Before the economic boom of the 1970s, regular and frequent qat consumption was restricted to a minority of wealthy, learned Yemenis. The lower classes limited its use to special ceremonial occasions. By the late 1970s the majority of men and a large minority of women spent their afternoons chewing qat with others in rooms in private homes. The social and cultural aspects of these everyday parties have drawn the attention of several researchers (Kennedy 1987; Shopen 1978; Weir 1985; Frye 1990).

In villages, towns, and cities throughout Yemen, the afternoon hours from 2:00 to 6:30 witness thousands of qat parties. As a social event, one notes that these parties share certain social behavioral features in common. Typically they take place in a room which has been furnished for the purpose. The *mafraj* or *diwan*, the qat room, is arranged with mattresses and cushions along the walls. Long, heavy bolsters serve as back rests. Smaller bolsters are placed at intervals to provide for individual seating. Floors are covered with imported linoleum or Persian rugs. A large brass or aluminum tray stands in the middle of the room, on which there are several "hubble-bubble" tobacco pipes and perhaps pottery or brass incense burners and wooden tobacco boxes. Around the room are various jugs or vacuum flasks of cold water, brass and aluminum spittoons, and ash trays. The host is only responsible for providing drinking water for the flasks and tobacco for the pipes (115–116).

Parties begin between 2:00 and 3:00 P.M. Guests remove their shoes outside the room and acknowledge those who have already arrived. The host either provides each guest with a handful of rosewater which is wiped on the face, or he might waft sweet-smelling incense under the clothing of the guest. After the initial greeting, guests sit on one of the cushions along the walls. The number of guests varies, from three or four to thirty or more. Guests usually seat themselves with the right knee raised and the left leg outstretched. They recline with one of the smaller cushions under the left arm. Each person puts his bundle of qat branches on the floor in front of him or on his lap. A branch is selected; the leaves are then removed and placed in the mouth. When the edible leaves are removed, the branch is thrown into the middle of the room.

After chewing, the leaves are placed in the cheek, where they form a wad. Once the cheek is filled, no new leaves are added. Qat chewing requires frequent sips of cold water to moisten the leaves. Excess juice is spit into strategically placed spittoons. Periodically during the party the long hose of the tobacco pipe is passed from one person to another. Guests carefully cup their hands so the mouth does not touch the mouthpiece. In addition, some men smoke cigarettes.

Observers of these parties note a similar sequence in behaviors. In the early hours guests arrive and are seated. Qat is taken out and the process of chewing begins. Neighbors converse with each other in an outward, animated way. After approximately two hours, the heightened awareness and outward conversation diminish and give way to more inward, contemplative, individual behavior. The room is quieter; men may stare out into space or speak in muffled tones with their neighbors. Finally, the participants get up, put on their outdoor clothing, say goodbye, put on their shoes and depart.

Readers may not find this behavioral sequence unfamiliar. Adult parties begin on a quiet note, move toward a conversational crescendo, and then wind down until all the guests depart. What readers might find different is that at qat parties, guests remain in their "places" throughout the afternoon. It is this aspect of the qat party that informs us of its function and its cultural meaning.

To the functionalist any persistent activity must have a function. Further, that function can only be determined relative to the larger systems within which the activity occurs. One possible function is to affirm existing characteristics of the larger system. This function is obvious when one notes that while males and females have qat parties, males do not attend female parties and females do not attend male parties. Thus, the qat party functions to maintain a cultural difference that characterizes the Yemeni division of labor. Weir notes that qat parties are attended by those who share similar age, occupation, tribal affiliation, political persuasion, religion, and commercial interests.

> . . . each qat party is a microcosm of some section of society and its consuming interests, and the aggregate of qat parties in each community mirrors and manifests its important groupings and concerns. (128)

In spite of official edicts banning the pre-revolution system of ranking determined by birth, guests at qat parties still arrange themselves according to a ranking system. Qat rooms have a *head* and a *foot*. The head of the room is furthest away from the entry door where shoes are placed. At parties where participants represent different traditional ranking, those with the highest rank usually sit at the head; those from the lowest rank, children, and servants occupy the foot. This spatial display of ranking is maintained at parties even where all the guests represent a single ranked category.

At family qat parties heads of households sat at the head. Weir reports that qat parties for physicians were arranged with the senior physician sitting at the head (135). What has changed since the revolution is that the traditional system of ranking is not the only criterion used to determine seating arrangements. Observations of parties with mixed-rank guests often fail to substantiate the traditional seating formula. This, Weir suggests, does not signal the demise of hierarchical principles but rather the emergence of new criteria for ranking (136). Both qat parties and Yemen are hierarchical!

The ranking system employed at qat parties does not define the party as a special type of interaction, nor does the consumption of qat. Qat is also consumed at *ritual* events, such as circumcisions, marriages, and other ceremonial occasions. Unlike these ritual performances, the party has participants whose membership varies from one party to the next. In contrast, qat consumption at ritual events involves participants who are born into families, tribes, or other named groupings. Further, at ritual events qat is provided by the "host"; at qat parties one brings one's own qat. Qat *rituals* celebrate the integration of groups; at qat *parties* individuals compete with each other within a ranking order that reflects individual attainment of an achieved status. Participation in qat ritual is obligatory for group members; at qat parties participation is voluntary—one "chooses" to go to this or that party. These differences clearly distinguish the "party" from other social events.

Returning to our original question—what is the function of the party?—Weir argues that the party functions as a social arena within which individuals can negotiate and achieve a social identity.

> When you step from your house and head for a particular qat party you make a self-conscious public statement of your interests, affiliations and aspirations—to those you join and to those, so to speak, looking on. . . . If you chew qat with the same people repeatedly, the stronger the message becomes to them and to others. You then create facts about your social identity; eventually your status will start being defined with reference to people you habitually choose to mix with at qat parties (whether equals or superiors), and the multitude of everyday encounters and transactions will inevitably be affected. If the people are of much higher status you may not become their equal, but some of their social essence will rub off on you. (144)

This scramble for social identity reflects the reorganization of Yemeni culture as a result of changes in the 1970s. The loss of traditional rankings and emerging new wealth altered the lives of many. The qat party reflects those changes and therefore functions as a testing arena for the new order. At parties participants engage in important business and communications, cultivate relationships, demonstrate affiliations, and compete for rank in a society where prestige and esteem are no longer guaranteed by birth.

The "Great" Transformation: The City and Urban Life

In their search for universal "laws," social scientists have applied the functional model to different societies. To make this model work, it is assumed that whatever practice is the focus of research ventures, it must be understood as part of a system, a functional system. In traditional anthropological research, the limits or boundaries of "the system" are represented by the nomadic band, small village, or community in which field work is done. In the preceding pages, the use of ebene, tobacco, kava, and qat were reviewed as part of a local system, and the function of each drug was determined relative to that system. The ability to specify the boundaries of "the system" is more problematic for the sociologist whose research is usually focused on one specific part of a much larger system with a highly differentiated division of labor. The societies (systems) that sociologists study are different from the societies anthropologists study. Therefore, if one is to accept the function-within-a-system commitment of the functional approach, it is necessary to examine the evolution and distinguishing characteristics of those systems. In the next few pages we will review what social science has to say about the emergence of the type of society within which most sociological research takes place.

For most of *Homo sapiens'* existence, humans lived in small nomadic societies that survived by hunting and gathering. If one makes inferences from observations of contemporary nomadic societies with similar modes of adaptation, the social distinctions made among our ancestors were based on ascribed status, with a few individuals accumulating esteem through personal achievements. In these *societies*, the division of labor was relatively undifferentiated. Their size permitted, and their technology demanded, close cooperative behavior between equals. The reader should not, however, conclude that these *cultures* were "simple"— far from it. When compared to modern cultures, their religion and kinship institutions were exceedingly intricate and complex.

It was not until about 8,000 years ago that some of these nomadic hunters and gatherers settled into sedentary communities made possible by the domestication of plants and animals. This "revolution," as V. Gordon Childe (1948) called it, did not happen overnight, nor everywhere. Where it did happen, the organizational principles that had worked so well for the hunters and gatherers changed to accommodate this new way of life. The obvious changes in material inventories, such as substantial housing, boats, and clay vessels, were accompanied by increased size and density of human settlements. Concomitantly, there was a change in the division of labor. Land became a thing not just to travel over but to own and control. Those who had been heads of kinship groups became leaders and decision makers with authority to implement their hereditary rule. With that came formal authority and the hierarchical society.

Just a few thousand years after the domestication revolution, another change occurred in the organization of humankind. The emergence of central places called cities marked the beginning of **civilization**, the descriptive term for a culture with cities. Unlike the communities and towns that evolved around domestication, these early cities, with populations between 7,000 and 10,000, could not support themselves and relied on the surplus provided by the domesticators. Their central position to several surplus-producing communities provided a location in which goods and services could be exchanged. In order to insure that exchanges could take place among culturally diverse suppliers, a new organizational structure evolved called the **state**.

The state developed as a "problem-solving" organization. The "problem" of diversity in the cultural backgrounds of its citizens was solved in different ways. The assorted languages brought into the city were standardized initially by a *lingua franca*, a common language of trade, and later by formal writing systems that maintained records of transactions between strangers. Money systems emerged to replace time-consuming bartering and to insure a standardized value in the exchange of goods and services; standard measurements for time, weight, size, and distance were instituted. To insure conformity to these norms, the state assumed responsibility for enforcement of codes and rules which not only governed citizens' actions but their relationships to each other. The problem of governing large populations was resolved in what Robert Michels (1959) describes as the **Iron Law of Oligarchy**. This law suggests that when groups exceed a certain size, members are not capable of maintaining communication and interaction with each other. As a result, power and authority are concentrated in the hands of a few, and it was these few who were responsible for insuring that this new system functioned smoothly.

The city as a place (and its concomitant governmental form, the state) had a hierarchical division of labor made up of full-time specialists whose common bond was joint citizenship. Inferential proof for the earliest cities comes from archeological differences between them and outlying communities. In cities one notes large non-residential buildings that could have been used as places of worship, governmental activities, and sports. In addition, there is evidence to suggest roads, markets and parks. The number and placement of houses suggests larger, dense populations. What is absent from this distribution of artifacts is land on which to grow crops or range animals. Cities were and are places in which large populations live by trading goods produced elsewhere in occupations related to the exchange of goods and the delivery of services. In addition to their occupational specialties, residents of cities are part of a new social category, namely, the mass. The concept **mass** is used to describe a heterogeneous social unit that collectively used nonresidential physical structures. They constituted "audiences" at church and sports events, and they traveled over the roads and used the water and sewerage services. At the same time citizens were members of "publics." **Publics** are named groupings with specific agendas and personnel (chapter 10). These groupings might be based on relatively permanent affiliations such as occupation, ethnicity, or class; or they could be somewhat impermanent affiliations that responded to some issue. Unlike the homogeneous communities that contributed labor and commodities to the city and had only a few publics, urban culture was and is made up of many publics. The function of the state is to orchestrate relations among publics and to regulate mass behaviors. With an increase in the numbers of publics and mass behavior there was a corresponding increase in the size and power of states. The interests of the state extended to almost all activities, including drugs. The oldest written record of state interests is the Code of Hammurabi (ca. 1720 B.C.). The Code contained almost three hundred ordinances governing the citizens of Babylon,[3] a city in Babylonia. Of the three hundred, four focused specifically on regulating the distribution of alcohol. According to G. R. Driver and John Miles (1968) these were:

> 108. If an ale-wife does not accept grain for the price of liquor (but) accepts silver by the heavy weight or (if) she reduces the value of beer (given) against the value of corn (received), they shall convict that ale-wife and cast her into the water.
>
> 109: If felons are banded together in an ale-wife's house and she does not seize those felons and she has not haled (them) to the palace, that ale-wife shall be put to death.

110. If a priestess (or) a high priestess, who is not dwelling in a cloister, opens an ale-house or enters an ale-house for liquor, they shall burn that woman.

111. If an ale-wife has given 60 SILA of coarse liquor on credit, at the harvest she shall take 50 SILA of corn. (45)

There is no record of how many women[4] were thrown into the river or burned to death, but the existence of these ordinances is testament to the concern of legislators about the behavior and background of those who operated these places and the customers they served.

The Continuum Tradition

An interest in the social consequences of the transformation of society did not begin with nineteenth-century social scientists. Confucius (551–479 B.C.), Plato (427?–347 B.C.), Aristotle (384–322 B.C.), St. Augustine (396–430 A.D.), and Ibn Khaldun (1332–1406 A.D.) all wrestled with the differences between non-urban and urban societies. In an attempt to understand this transition scientifically, some nineteenth- and twentieth-century social scientists constructed topological continuua of societies. A **continuum** may be visualized as a line the end points of which are idealized types of societies that have been constructed by using a limited number of attributes. Population size, for example, might be one of those attributes. The variable by which one measures size is numbers of people. Thus, on one end of the continuum would be a society with no people (an impossibility); at the other end there would be a society with an infinite number of people (again, an impossibility). Somewhere between none and infinity are actual societies and their populations.

The attributes selected by those in the continuum tradition depended on their specific interests. For example, Sir Henry Maine (1822–1888), an English jurist, traced the change in legal systems from non-urban to urban societies in his book, *Ancient Society* (1906). He suggested that relationships in non-urban societies were based on statuses that were determined by birth. These were replaced by "contract" relationships in which parties could enter freely. Ferdinand Tönnies' (1855–1936) comparison was based on interpersonal relationships. In *Gemeinschaft und Gesellschaft* (1887), he suggests that Gemeinschaft societies were made up of personal and intimate groups whose normative order was determined by custom and religion. In contrast, Gesellschaft societies had impersonal and formal groupings whose order was maintained by legislation or public opinion.

This tradition of classifying societies along a continuum of contrasting types continues in the twentieth century. The words used in these typologies have become part of the vocabulary of social scientists. Thus, we find preliterate or nonliterate-literate, rural-urban, localite-cosmopolite, primitive-modern, pre-industrial-industrial, and so forth.

Perhaps the most ambitious of these continuua was constructed by Robert Redfield (1897–1958). Redfield carried out field work in several communities along the Yucatan peninsula in Mexico. He observed that these communities differed from each other relative to their distance from Merida, the only city in this region. From this observation, he suggested the **folk-urban** continuum. Recognizing an indebtedness to Maine, Durkheim, and Tönnies, Redfield restated their ideas and added to them through his direct observations of real societies (1943). Although he argued that neither the folk nor the urban society actually existed, he nonetheless insisted that any understanding of "ourselves" can only be achieved by understanding societies least like us, namely, the folk society. Redfield incorporated the suggestions of earlier scholars into his continuum. The folk society had few people and an undifferentiated division of labor dominated by kinship rules where consensus and status quo were dominant themes. The urban society had an opposite set of features. Redfield's contribution to the continuum tradition represents one of the last intellectual collaborations between anthropology and sociology. His life, both as a student and later as a faculty member, was spent at the University of Chicago.

During the 1920s and 1930s a dominant figure in sociology was Robert E. Park (1864–1944). Park was a journalist and a student of the German sociologist Georg Simmel (1858–1918). Park argued that urbanism had brough about a new way of life and that the task of sociology was to study that way of life. Park felt, perhaps because of his journalism background, that the methodological approach that best suited this objective was participant-observation of small social units within the city—occupations or neighborhoods, for example. This approach became synonymous with what was called the "Chicago School," and many of the studies that came out of Chicago became classics in sociology.[5] The alliance between Redfield at the folk end of the continuum and Park at the urban end was further cemented when Redfield married Park's daughter.

Both the field work tradition in sociology and the continuum tradition in anthropology have gone out of favor in their respective disciplines. Many sociologists now rely on surveys and mathematical analysis of data; some anthropologists do field work in the city, but the inability to fit the wide variations of societies along a neat continuum has led to an abandonment of this model. Nonetheless, there has been a perpetuation of the assumptions which lay behind the continuum tradition.

In addition to exploring the varieties of life in the city, Park and others shared a common belief about that life. According to C. S. Fischer (1974), this assumption came from Park's mentor, Georg Simmel. Simmel (1906) had proposed that the city with its busy activities, increased nervous stimulation and ultimately produced stress. To prevent a psychic overload from stress, adaptive mechanisms came into play. These included attempts to depersonalize the world and resulted in individual isolation. At the same time, individualization and depersonalization made it possible to engage in the most bizarre behaviors. After all, who was watching! The increase in individual isolation decreased the moral bonds which held communities together. This, coupled with an increased specialization in the division of labor, had an inevitable outcome—a high degree of "disorganization."

In Park's enthusiasm to record city lives, his students were sent out to study the effects of disorganization, the so-called "nuts and sluts" approach. The studies included delinquent gangs, taxi-dancers, jazz musicians, pickpockets, hobos, and others of the "dislocated." The assumption was that the city was pathological and that the behavior of people who lived in cities was a reflection of this pathology. Thus began, and is currently continued in sociology, a tradition of studying social "problems." This tradition is nowhere better illustrated than in some sociological drug research. The underlying assumption is that drug "abuse" is related to poverty, unemployment, divorce, and other "pathologies."

An alternative to this approach is "normal" social science.[6] Instead of urbanism bringing about disorder, the result of this process is simply a different order. The city, with its large and dense population coupled with a division of labor made up of many specialists, makes possible the formation of numerous sub-societies. Fisher employs the concept **critical mass** to explain this process. For example, in a small community with only one lawyer it would not be possible to have a group of lawyers. That same lawyer, however, may belong to a group of model plane enthusiasts or dart players or drinkers if there are others with similar interests. Persons with like interests and concerns have, in the city, a mass of critical size to form those well integrated little societies that early sociologists believed had been destroyed in the transformation of society. These sub-societies exist, not because the social order has broken down, but rather because the order has changed. This is not to say that the process of urbanization does not change the order. Quite the opposite, urbanization has direct consequences for the formation of a different order. To view sub-societies as deviant, pathological, or disorganized is to make a judgement about that sub-society. In the "normal" view, sub-societies can be analyzed as whole units, as little societies in a sea of other little societies, which are linked together in a division of labor that is distinctively urban.

In the first part of this chapter the use of ebene, kava, and qat were examined in small societies or communities. Each of these drugs fit into existing organizational patterns that were neither deviant nor pathological to the users. That a Yanomamö used ebene with his friends and kinsmen is consistent with non-ebene behaviors. That kava use varied by the preexisting orders of Micronesian societies reflects different divisions of labor. And finally, changes in qat consumption are consistent with changes that had happened and are happening in Yemen. The question that must be addressed here is whether drug use in urban societies has the same function as in non-urban societies; or whether it is symptomatic of the disorganization and pathology that was assumed by Simmel and Park. The answers to these questions will be explored in the following sections.

African Beer Gardens

The transformation from non-urban to urban does not take place all at once. One example of this is the changed function of beer drinking in Africa when tribal populations move into cities. In 1970, Harry Wolcott carried out a one-year field study of the beer gardens in Bulawayo, Rhodesia (1974). The research was organized around the seven variables that Bacon, Child and Barry (1965) used to define "integrative drinking."[7] According to Wolcott:

> . . . drinking will be considered integrated in any way that it
> functions to enhance or maximize the survival chances of a
> culture and of the society that practices it. (11)

During this year-long period Wolcott observed the behaviors of customers in the beer gardens, interviewed some of the patrons, and conducted a short survey. In true anthropological fashion, he viewed the beer garden within the larger context of Rhodesian society, both traditional and urban.

When Wolcott studied the beer gardens, Rhodesia was still a segregated colonial society with Europeans in political control over native Africans. In 1965, Rhodesia declared its independence from Britain and retained white rule. It was not until 1980 that black majority rule was achieved and the country name was changed to Zimbabwe. Zimbabwe has a population of approximately ten million, 24 percent of which is urban. The capital city, Harare (formally Salisbury), is also the largest with a population of 720,000. Bulawayo is second with 430,000, followed by Chitungwiza with 202,000. There are eight other cities with populations ranging from 12,000 to just under 85,000 residents. There are two major tribal groups in Zimbabwe. The Shona are the largest with 71 percent of the population; second are the Ndebele with only 16 percent. Other tribal and territorial groups make up 12 percent, and Europeans only 1 percent.

Beer drinking in Africa has a long history. When the Europeans first contacted the Africans, they found them making and drinking beer. As part of a revenue-producing effort, Salisbury (now Harare), founded a municipal brewery in 1908. Five years later, Bulawayo opened its own brewery. Both of these breweries produce beer for the African population living in these cities. The beer they produce is called either African beer, native beer, Bantu beer, or kaffir[8] beer (38). In Bulawayo, the city owns not only the brewery but also the distribution outlets. Beer is distributed through four bar-lounges and one beer garden complex, which includes thirty beer gardens. In addition, there are eleven bottle stores which, along with the beer gardens and the bar-lounges, sell beer for off-premises consumption. The brewery also supplies the Army, prison and local government authorities, several rural African councils, and some large employers who sell beer to their African workers. According to Wolcott, Bulawayo derives a rather sizeable income from the brewery. He estimated the 1970 income to be $5.4 million.

The beer gardens vary somewhat in physical accommodations. They are open-air places with bare earth floors, some trees and/or sheds, and benches and tables. Hours of operation also vary, but with staggered hours for different gardens it is possible to drink from 9:30 A.M. to 10:30 P.M. The number of people in a beer garden will vary by time of day and day of the week. The largest crowds are in the late afternoon and on weekends. In the main beer garden on a hot Saturday payday in 1970, Wolcott counted 52,000 people between 9:00 A.M. and 9:30 P.M. The variation in number of customers is reflected in the quantity of beer sold. Some gardens will serve up to 6,000 gallons of beer per day.

Beer is brought from the brewery to the beer gardens in tank trucks, where it is pumped into overhead storage tanks. The beer is sold to customers at the ground-level serving area in either half- or one-gallon plastic containers ("beer mugs"). The customer hands an empty beer mug with his money to the attendant and is given a measured amount of beer.

Beer gardens are not the only place to purchase alcoholic beverages. There are homes in the African sections of Bulawayo where liquor can be purchased twenty-four hours a day. These places are called *shebeens*. Shebeens are run by a woman, the "Shebeen Queen," who uses one room in her four-room house as a serving area. The price one pays for drinking in a shebeen is approximately double that of the beer garden or bar-lounge. Shebeens have a negative reputation and they are often associated with prostitution, powerful and sometimes lethal home brew, and reports of people passing out and being robbed (43). Wolcott estimated there were approximately 450 shebeens in Bulawayo.

While the beer gardens are a place to drink beer, drinking is not a requirement to be there. Patrons may go to visit, to look, or to listen to music. The music heard varies from "rock" to tribal drumming and may be prerecorded or live. Although drinking is not required, most patrons do drink, usually in the company of others. Individual drinkers are rare in the beer gardens. Drinking is usually done sitting down at one of the tables with friends or acquaintances. These informal groupings are usually made up of persons who share a similar occupation, common language, or residency. Beer is not usually drunk quickly. The customary drinking pattern is to pass the plastic beer mugs from person to person within a group of drinkers. The jug is then set down on the ground after a round of drinking only to be brought back on the table some time later. Wolcott observed that drinking was an adjunct to talking. Conversation within these groups was the primary activity; beer drinking served to fill lulls in those conversations.

One explanation for the leisurely consumption of beer is the beer itself. African beer is not filtered and, if left standing, the solids will settle to the bottom. Many, particularly younger Africans, left beer in the plastic mugs after they finished drinking. In contrast, older Africans drank the thickened beer at the bottom, which they considered to be food. Traditionally, beer was defined as "food" with high nutritional value. This definition is reflected in advertisements for beer which include references to beer being "good for you." The sharing of beer may, in part, be explained by the cost of beer. Draft African beer costs 20 cents per gallon; bottled European beer costs 18-20 cents per 12-2/3 ounce bottle. To many Africans with low income, the municipal African beer is the only beer they can afford. Another factor which contributes to shared drinking is that this pattern is the way beer was consumed in tribal society.

In spite of the definition of beer as "food," Africans do exhibit drunken and/or drinking comportment. This may include such behaviors as singing, dancing, and sometimes fighting. Drunkenness was not denounced. Assistance was usually offered an inebriated customer who might not easily find his way home. Quarrelsome drunken deportment was not excused by drink (time-out behavior); rather, blame was attributed to the drinker. Drinking was alternatively defined as either being a cause of decreased or increased sexual desires. Wolcott observed that Africans make no attempt to hide the effects of alcohol. This was in contrast to Europeans, who attempt to suppress drunken behavior.

The behaviors of those within the garden were influenced by social distinctions outside the garden. Those who met regularly marked off territory which they regarded as their own. The African age-grading system was retained in drinking groups that tended to be age homogeneous. Inside the gardens Europeans remained standing while drinking and did not engage in the characteristic hand-shaking and greetings practiced by Africans. It was considered appropriate for Africans to ask Europeans for money or cigarettes, but it would have been a breach of etiquette for an African to "beg" from another African. Rather, one looked for friends in hopes of being invited to share beer.

Social Categories of Beer Garden Participants

The survey of patrons revealed that the gardens were primarily populated by males who either drank on the weekends only or two or three times a week (a bimodal distribution). Heaviest drinking was done in the afternoons or evenings during the weekend. African beer was the preferred drink, and patrons drank at least 1.5 gallons per week (48–49).

Wolcott distinguishes between two etic categories of beer garden patrons—the **beneficiaries** and the **patrons** or "clubbers" (51). The beneficiaries are those whose work brings them to the beer gardens. This category would include managers and workers, European administrators, the police, representatives of European and African beer companies, missionaries seeking converts, individual entrepreneurs such as women escorts, vendors of food and salesmen, "birds of prey" (such as pickpockets), and the "needy." For these people, the beer garden is a place of work or commerce.

Patrons meet with a predetermined group of others at specific times. Some of these others are members of formal groups who meet at the beer garden. These "clubbers" include drinking "clubs," persons who share some common social bond and collectively purchase and drink beer, or they might be members of sports clubs that periodically meet at the garden. At a more formal level, they might be members of benevolent organizations such as burial societies or *Holisana* groups. These organizations have dues-paying members who pool their individual economic resources to pay a large expense. The burial societies pay the high cost for burial in the city. The Holisana group distributes funds to individual members for expensive items that could not otherwise be afforded. Members of these groups usually meet at the gardens on paydays to collect dues.

Traditional Beer Drinking

Wolcott reports that brewing and drinking of beer in tribal societies distinguished between brewing for work and brewing for ceremony. (For traditional African beer practices, see Netting [1964] and Hagaman [1980].) Brewing for work involved making beer that was consumed as an everyday activity. He suggests that brewing and drinking for ceremonial purposes was more frequent in tribal societies because of a higher frequency of individual life cycle events in small groupings of people. Several occasions demanded ceremonial brewing and drinking of traditional beers. For example, beer was sometimes brewed and drunk to honor a guest or a visit from an *inyanga* (curer) who had been called into the village for some special purpose. Included in the list of events that are accompanied by drinking are

Birth of a first child

Puberty rites for females

Weddings

The payment of *lobole*, the payment made by a suitor to the bride's father

Burials, and a few weeks later when the implements of burial were washed in beer

The *umbuyiso* ceremony, one year after the death of a head of the household when the spirit of the deceased returned to his village and took up residence in the body of an ox (71–72)

The differences in drinking patterns in traditional society and the beer gardens can only be understood when one considers the sexual division of labor of the Ndebele. Activities were strictly segregated by sex. Males and females did not work together but rather maintained quite distinctive statuses. Men worked with men and boys. Women worked with other women or girls. Men were responsible for herding livestock. Their domain was the kraal, the yards where the cattle were tethered. Women were responsible for the household, which included taking care of small children, tending the fields where crops were grown, and brewing beer.

The transition from traditional to urban life changed the function of beer drinking. Urban beer gardens are dominated by younger males. Differences in incomes of urban workers are demonstrated by the brands and the prices of beer consumed. Rather than beer drinking accompanying periodic life-cycle ceremonies, the urban beer drinker's drinking time was determined by the consistency of urban work cycle. Drinking occurs after work or on the weekends. Beer in traditional society was consumed soon after it was produced. In the city, beer was always available within the hours that the beer garden was open, or at the Shebeens if the gardens were closed. In tribal society beer was consumed until it was finished. If someone ran out of beer, it was a measure of his popularity. In traditional societies, the producers of the beer (those who controlled its production by females) consumed the brew. In urban society brewers were primarily European and seldom consumed their own beer. In traditional society, batches of beer differed depending on the expertise of the women brewers. In urban society, there was an expectation that the beer be of equal quality from day to day.

Functions of the Beer Garden

Wolcott argues that the function of drinking in the city differs from that of integrative drinking in tribal society. He suggests that beer gardens provide an arena within which urban information is exchanged. Urban life interferes with **lateral** transfer of information which depends on personal communication between persons who know each other. In urban societies, the kind of information one needs (for example, jobs, availability of women, or crisis situations) is held by strangers, not kinsmen. The gardens enabled individuals to extend and maintain those impersonal networks so characteristic of urban societies. In this setting, personal preferences can be exercised beyond those imposed by work. At work one interacts with others in a structure that is determined by impersonal needs.

In the beer garden, one can dance or sing as a native or as a European; one can sit and talk or just listen; one can drink native or European beer, and one can talk to either men or women.

Because of different timetables and residency, those who share common tribal affiliations are often unable to maintain continual contact with each other. The garden functions as a setting within which there is, or can be, reinforcement of traditional bonds in culture and language. Thus, continuity of tribal identity is maintained in the urban setting where such continuity might otherwise be lost. Recent visitors to tribal communities bring news from home which they share with others, and those returning home take information with them.

From the social science perspective, the beer garden is not just a place to drink beer; nor is it just a business that provides money to the city. Both drinking and income could be cited as manifest functions of the beer gardens. The unintended or latent functions of the beer gardens are that they function to provide a setting within which both the needs for survival in urban society and the maintenance of traditional life can be met.

Opium Dens

The best guess for the origin of opium is Arabia. Arab traders took it to other parts of the world as part of their inventory of trade goods. Opium smoking was first observed in China, and therefore China is thought to be the original center of that practice. Not so clear is where the opium den, as a specialty business, began. In recent history, the opium den is usually traced to China and the Far East. Aside from the most obvious reason for why the opium den exists— to dispense opium for smoking—very little systematic study of these places has been made. What research there is suggests an explanation of the function of opium dens that goes beyond the obvious and points to their possible origins.

Opium Dens in Laos

Joseph Westermeyer (1974, 1982), a physician by training and an ethnographer by choice, collected data on opium use in Laos from 1965 to 1975 and opium smokers from 1971 to 1972. Part of his research focused on the opium den. Westermeyer's research took him all over Laos. He was in refugee camps, in rural areas, and in the cities. One consistent observation he made was that in the villages of rural Laos there are no opium dens. People smoked at home or in the homes of friends. It was only in the larger towns and the cities that one could find opium dens. Westermeyer made detailed observations of three opium dens in the Laotian capital city of Vientiane. This sample was based on his observation that three types of dens operated in the city, and each den selected for the sample represented a different type. In addition to his direct observation of the dens and their patrons, he conducted thirty-five interviews with opium addicts in the Vientiane area. What follows is a description of each den and Westermeyer's analysis of the function of the den.

The first den was also the home of its owner, an immigrant from China. Because of illness, the owner, who had previously been a merchant, was unable to work. His only source of income was the den. The house, which accommodated his wife and eight children, had three rooms and a concrete floor. Customers smoked opium and ate noodle soup in the front room. The middle room, the family's sleeping quarters, housed the smoking paraphernalia. The third room was the kitchen where the noodle soup was prepared. This den's regular customers were employed middle-class Laotian government workers and Chinese merchants. Their visits were restricted to meal times.

The second den was also owned by a Chinese immigrant. This den had a single large room and eight cotlike beds. The floors were tamped earth. A fire was used to prepare meals. Compared to the first den, the customers in this den held occupations that were less affluent. The regular customers were laborers, people on pensions, beggars, and four women. Most of the patrons were Meo[9] men who were refugees from the war in the North. In contrast to the first den, this one was crowded during the latter part of the day.

The third den was a large shed attached to a small house. Its owner was a married forty-year-old Hmong (note 9). The floors were tamped earth; the walls were bamboo matting, and the roof was tin. There were three beds and two double bunks. Food was available from mobile food vendors. This shed also served as a hotel for traveling Hmong. Many of the customers were travelers who used this facility during their stay in the city. Its busiest periods were on holidays and weekends when Hmong men would come by to smoke with friends and relatives.

In spite of their apparent differences in physical amenities and the socio-economic characteristics of their patrons, Westermeyer observed an underlying similarity in the function of the opium den. Regardless of their economic positions, den users were persons who were not part of stable interaction networks, or their participation in those networks had been temporarily interrupted (single or divorced persons, migrants, or travelers). While the American reader may not find the "lone wolf" a particularly distressing image, in Laos one's identity and even survival depends on others. In the rural communities of Laos, kinship groups are bound together in mutual economic, religious, political, and social dependence. Without this superstructure, life is very difficult or impossible. The lone wolf may become a dead wolf, especially if one is an opium addict. In the city no such superstructure exists for many people. The opium den provides a substitute network for those people who have fallen through the rips in the urban social fabric. Westermeyer's description of the behaviors of opium den patrons illustrates just how the den functions for those disengaged citizens.

> The den members were also a human contact for those addicts who had remarkably few friendly human contacts outside the den environment. During many of the interviews and discussions in the dens, an atmosphere of warmth and mutual support was evident. When an addict gave information with which others disagreed, a good-natured teasing gentled the speaker back to more realistic reporting. . . . They sung the praises of good opium and admired one another's analogies in describing opium intoxication. . . . Much of this affable atmosphere occurred among people of varied ethnic groups who, in other settings, might barely speak to each other in a civil manner. (1974, 239)

The opium den in urban Laos provided a place within which intense social interaction could take place. For example, Westermeyer never observed any of the clientele falling asleep while smoking opium. The den is not a place to escape the outside world but, like the African beer gardens, a place for those without social networks to form intimate social bonds, even for a short time. As Westermeyer reminds us, the opium den tells us more about urban societies than it does about addicts and addiction.[10]

Opium Dens in England

One of the difficulties of implementing the historical particularism of Franz Boas was how to add historical depth to the study of a particular culture. In other words, how can one reconstruct the past when that past exists only in the memories of people? **Oral history** offers a solution. Briefly, this involves finding the older members of the society and having them tell their individual history—what they remember from childhood on. It was thought that by comparing oral histories from different members of the same society, it would be possible to reconstruct past cultural practices and arrange these into a temporal sequence. Needless to say, this methodology is fraught with possible difficulties because there is no way to independently verify these remembrances. However, in the absence of any alternative, this method was and is still used. One illustration of this method is a study of opium dens in London around the turn of the century (Berridge and Edwards 1981).

A man, identified only as W. J. C., had grown up in the Limehouse section of London when it was an area known to have numerous opium dens. An extensive audiotaped interview with this man yielded the following information on the preparation and smoking of opium.

> The preparation of the raw opium for smoking was a lengthy process, involving shredding the raw drug into a sieve placed over an ordinary two-pint sauce-pan containing water. This was simmered over a fire, and the essence, filtered through the sieve, fell to the bottom of the pot in a thinnish treacle. Opium was often scraped out of the pipes in the house and added to the raw variety. The pot in which the essence landed would be constantly pushed and kneaded, although in some houses this was done in a different way. "They got a long feather of a bird, a large bird, and they'll just skim the top of the opium, and until that opium is absolutely perfect without a bubble on it, and it's boiled to the amount that they've tested, and that's that . . ." The opium thus prepared was stored in lidded earthenware jars. Sometimes it was sold to outside customers; often seamen would buy it when going aboard ship. (202–203)
>
> A special pipe, about eighteen inches long and often made of dark-coloured bamboo, was used for the actual smoking. One end, hollow and open, served as the mouthpiece. At the closed end, a tiny bowl "made of iron and shaped like a pigeon's egg" was screwed in. Prior to smoking, a small quantity of prepared opium was taken on the point of a needle and frizzled over the flame of a lamp—"twist it and twist it until it becomes sticky, a solid sticky substance . . ." The opium pipe was then placed over the lamp and opium inserted on the point of a needle through a small hole in the bowl of the pipe. The smoker would draw continually at the pipe until the substance was burnt out—"the Chinaman . . . took the bamboo fairly into his mouth, and there was at once emitted from the pipe a gurgling sound—the spirits of ten thousand previous pipe-loads stirred to life." (203)

This description of the **behaviors** associated with the preparation and smoking of opium can be verified through independent accounts. Oral histories generally uncover agreement about past behaviors. But questions directed at interpretation of behaviors are more problematic. For example, Virginia Berridge and Griffith Edwards were interested in why opium smoking in general and opium dens in particular had earned such a negative image. They observed that opium dens and opium smoking in London and other parts of England where Chinese lived never attracted attention until the latter part of the nineteenth century. They measure this change in public sentiment by the increased popularity of novels such as *The Picture of Dorian Gray* (1891), by Oscar Wilde, and the Sherlock Holmes stories. This literature portrayed the Chinese as sinister and opium smoking as a degrading human activity that "enslaved" the user. Berridge and Edwards argue that the acceptance of these novels was linked to the economic decline in the British Empire which resulted in unemployment and increased competition for jobs. Although the actual frequency and amount of smoking was restricted to a small number of people, the fear of corruption, especially among the middle-class, was intense. The working class was most directly affected by the increased competition with Chinese for employment, but fears that it could also occur in the middle-classes—those who read these novels—led to the belief that the same fate awaited them. The Chinese were a greater threat in anticipation of what might occur than they were in fact. The point that Berridge and Edwards make is that the acceptance of fiction is rooted in the experience, real or imaginary, of readers.

Berridge and Edwards, citing newspaper and police reports, found that those who had actually visited these "dens" painted a portrait somewhat different from the novelists. Observers described them as rather poorly appointed social clubs, not dissimilar from public houses (bars) frequented by English persons of the same class. Just as stories of military battles are better told than experienced, the stories of opium dens and opium smoking made the places and practices, virtuous or sinister, larger than life. The function of such beliefs is that they interpret the social world in very simple terms. That the empire was crumbling was due to many factors. Assigning "cause" or "consequence" for the empire falling to the Chinese, to opium smoking, and to opium dens reduces those variables down to a manageable few.

Opium Dens in the United States

The earliest accounts of American opium dens were not until the middle of the nineteenth century. Their appearance was linked to the importation of Chinese workers to meet labor demands in mining, railroading, and other industries (chapter 10). Although opium smoking probably occurred among these migrants in different locations, most of the media focused on dens in cities. Beginning in the 1860s, an increasing Chinese population (coupled with legislation that excluded Chinese from living in non-Chinese neighborhoods) led to the formation of "Chinatowns" in most major western cities. Within these sections of cities, several services were offered to migrants by Chinese merchants and organizations. Among these were opium dens, gambling parlors, and houses of prostitution (Barth 1964).

Popular accounts of opium dens portrayed them as dark, dingy places filled with patrons in various states of opium stupor. In contrast to this view, observers and habitués of opium dens reported that between pipes, the patrons engage in story telling, joking, talking, and even singing (Courtwright 1982, 73). In spite of the common impression that opium dens attracted the least desirable elements of society, insiders described fights and stealing as rare. If either occurred, the participants were disciplined and ejected.

The negative image of opium den patrons had two sources. One was general anti-Chinese sentiment that extended to many Chinese practices, including clothing, food, and life-styles. The other was the allegation that dens were patronized by Euro-Americans with low social standing. As discussed in chapter 4, persons with transient or marginal occupations were among the first non-Chinese to adopt opium smoking. Actors, salesmen, prostitutes, gamblers, and criminals were included this category. Both salesmen and actors were in occupations that required traveling. The "underworld" patrons moved from place to place to avoid police detection and to find new sources of income. For these migrants and their Chinese counterparts, the opium den was a place to mingle with others who shared common interests. The opium den functioned as a social club for those who lived on the edge of "respectable" society, just as it was a social club for Chinese immigrants.

What made opium smoking a social rather than a solitary activity is, in part, explained by the mechanics of smoking. In the description offered above, it is clear that one not only needs equipment but also some level of experience. Unlike drinking alcohol, smoking tobacco or marihuana, or "eating" or injecting opium, the skills needed to smoke opium require some practice. It takes about twenty minutes to smoke a bowl of opium. After a few draws on the pipe the opium turns to a hard crust which must be broken off and deposited on the side of the bowl. If the user did this, it could distract from the effects of smoking. In the opium dens, attendants carried out this task, thus relieving the user of this potential disturbance.

Although conventional wisdom ascribed opium smoking to addiction, descriptions of animated smokers suggests otherwise. While it cannot be denied that some patrons may have been addicts, there are no data on the actual number of Chinese addicts. Many Chinese did smoke opium only during holiday seasons, but this would not have contributed to addiction. The amount of morphine in smoking opium is only nine percent; and for addiction to occur, there must be long period of continuous use. The allegations that opium addicts were the primary customers of opium dens is as accurate as stating that bars serve only alcoholics. If one disregards opium and beliefs about opium, the den is just another place where interaction takes place between those with shared experiences; those experiences need not include opiate dependency.

It is clear from what little data are available that opium dens represent another example of a "public" place. Although their clientele and their activities differ from those of other places, their function does not. They provide a physical setting for people who share similar characteristics. In this case, the characteristic is a migratory life-style. This is what bound Chinese immigrants together with the traveling salesmen, actors, and criminals on the run. Opium dens are not the only public places to attract sojourners. One place that has received much attention in the social science literature is the "bar."

Bars: A Not-So-Neglected Area of Research

One of the unstated attractions of the social sciences is that one can match personal interest with scientific inquiry. It is possible for researchers to analyze social settings in which they are already participants. In reading the social science literature on public drinking places in the United States, one encounters what I call "happy" research. The ethnographic descriptions are almost absent of negative moralizing about the places and the people who frequent those places. Field "work" is more like field "play," and the social scientist gives the impression that he or she might have been in this setting anyway. This is not to suggest that research in bars is any less rigorous than research elsewhere, only that much of the initial uneasiness field workers may experience is avoided because one already has experience in this setting.

Another attraction of the public drinking place is that it is public. Entrance into the field does not require special permission. The behaviors of patrons are visible to all, including the researcher.

Conversations turn into interviews, and the openness of these places often makes eavesdropping possible. The public drinking place offers a setting within which to "test" a variety of theoretical interests. The white-collaring of America is the focus of E. E. LeMasters' (1975) study of a working-class bar. Social class was the topic of David Gottlieb's (1957) comparison of the neighborhood tavern and the cocktail lounge. Women's work is explored in James Spradley and Brenda Mann's (1975) analysis of the occupation of cocktail waitress. Jerald Cloyd's (1976) interest in structural settings which facilitate sexual encounters brought him to the "marketplace" bar. The organization of deviance was the issue for Julian Roebuck and Wolfgang Frese (1976) in their analysis of the after-hours club. Just this brief excursion into the literature is enough to indicate that public drinking places are more than just places to consume alcohol.

Public drinking in the United States occurs in places with distinct names. The names which identify a public drinking establishment vary somewhat from one geographical location to another, but the pool of names is limited. A glance through the yellow pages yields several names, including bar, night club, tavern, lounge or cocktail lounge, pub, and cafe. These names may serve as markers to indicate that alcohol is available. They do not necessarily indicate who frequents them or what kinds of behavior one would expect to observe. To obtain this information one must directly observe the "inside" of the public place.[11]

One of the first systematic classification schemas of drinking places came from a two-year observational study done by Cara Richards (1963) in two Long Island, New York counties. Her data came from observations and casual interviews made while demonstrating a coin-operated miniature billiard-type game she was selling. From 1949 to 1951 she visited 170 drinking establishments. Using eight criteria[12] she constructed four "types" of drinking places. These were: the "night club," the "lounge," the "tavern," and the "dive." She argues that the consumption of alcoholic beverages cannot be the only reason for people drinking in any of these places because there are enough retail liquor stores to supply the entire population. Rather, she argues against the perspective offered by Simmel that cities are impersonal and anonymous places lacking in warm friendly personal groupings of people and that this view grossly underestimates the actual existence of such groups. In contrast to this perspective, observational and survey studies (Axelrod 1956; Dotson 1951; Thrasher 1937; Whyte 1943) do not support the disappearance of voluntary informal intimate groups of people in the city. The tavern, she suggests, is one example of informal congeniality in the urban setting. Others would include juvenile gangs, neighbors, co-workers, clubs, and relatives. The function of the tavern, regardless of its type, is the same. It is a place for people who lack membership in formal voluntary groups.

Sherri Cavan (1966) studied approximately one hundred bars in San Francisco over a two-and-one-half year period. Cavan began with the assumption that what goes on in public drinking places is, for the patrons, non-work, or what she calls, "unserious" behavior. Her question is, "What do patrons expect in these settings for 'unserious' behavior?" Unserious behavior has the character of "play," a voluntary activity within time and space limitations that is different from everyday behavior (Huizinga 1950). In this sense the title of Cavan's book, *Liquor License*, takes on a dual meaning. A liquor license is a formal permit issued by a governmental unit to dispense alcohol. License also means a freedom to act in a way that is irresponsible or without regard to formal rules—in other words, play.

Cavan identified four types of drinking places based on use by patrons. The "convenience" bar is often located in areas where there is already a large public. Shopping areas that have foot traffic might have bars that are used for convenience. Patrons normally spend little time in these bars, just long enough to have a drink and then leave. The open hours of the convenience bar are regulated by the availability of patrons. Thus, a bar might open around mid-day and close in early evening. This does not mean that other types of bars are not used as convenience bars, it only means that this is one activity of some patrons.

Many drinking places provide diversions for their patrons. This includes pool tables, shuffleboard, jukeboxes, dart boards, television, and so forth. In each of these examples, patrons are free to choose whether or not to participate in them. This is not an alternative with Cavan's second type, the "nightspot." In the nightspot the patrons become an audience to a specific set of scripted activities. Patrons may or may not become involved in those activities, but they are restrained from interfering with them. Because patrons are a focused audience, there is little opportunity for contact between the unacquainted. The numbers of patrons varies according to the show schedule.

Cavan's third type is the "marketplace bar." It serves as a center for the exchange of some commodity such as sex, drugs, gambling, or illicit merchandise. The fourth type is the "home territory bar." These serve a more or less permanent set of patrons who define the bar as their "place." In contrast to the British pub, the "local," which is patronized by people in geographic proximity to it, the home territory bar is not restricted by geography. Rather, what patrons share are some common social characteristics—class, race, occupation, ethnicity, school affiliation, occupation, age, or some combination of these characteristics. The behavior in these bars often is based on the distinction between the "regulars" and the "outsiders." Regulars are those patrons who are known by employees and who might receive special services such as check cashing, leaving and receiving messages, borrowing money, and so forth. Among the regulars there are practices, both subtle and obvious, which function to demonstrate territoriality and to intimidate the outsider. Talking pejoratively about an outsider within hearing range or staring at an intruder may result in that outsider using the home territory bar as a convenience bar. Bartenders, managers and owners may also participate in this exclusionary behavior. The regulation of hours to exclude outsiders, slow service, gatekeepers who screen customers, or physical ejection may all insure the homogeneity of the patrons.

These four "types" are not empirical realities. Most public drinking places are a combination of different types. Cavan's concern is with discovering the distinctive behaviors common to all these types which make the bar different from other social settings. She finds a commonality in behaviors which she calls "time out." These behaviors take on an "unserious"⸱ play form. Cavan suggests that unserious behavior establishes a "time out" from the ordinarily regulated set of daily activities. In the time-out settings she studied, people not only expect to but do interact in an unserious way. Should we expect the degree of unseriousness to vary from one bar type to another? According to Cavan, there is no evidence for this.

> The patrons of what might be considered to be middle-class public drinking places were no less mutually open to one another than were the patrons of lower-class bars; nor were encounters in one type of establishment any more or less circumscribed in time and place than they were in the other. Similarly, the latitude of behavior found in lower-class establishments was no broader than that found in middle-class bars. Quarrels of varying intensity, displays of affection, the fabrication and embroidering of biographies . . . were found in both with the same general absence of disapprobation on the part of witnesses. (236)

Cavan suggests that drinking places are not the only settings in which time-out behavior occurs. In American society, vacations, trips to the beach, to amusement parks, to carnivals, to academic and other conventions, public holidays, and so on, are all times in which unserious behavior occurs. Not only is time out a part of general cultural expectations, but the amount of time devoted to this behavior is regulated as well. Too much time in the bar and one is defined as a "barfly" or "alcoholic"; too little time out and one is a "workaholic."

The bar, in spite of both moral and legal attempts, has not disappeared from the American social landscape. The persistence of any practice is viewed by the functionalist as evidence for its having a function—of contributing in some way to fulfilling some social need. Just what those needs are may be debated depending on the theoretical orientation of the observer, but what cannot be denied is that drinking places continue to flourish in American society. As formally regulated businesses they can be counted, taxed, and regulated. As places open to the masses, they are subject to surveillance by anyone, including social scientists. This cannot be said about drinking outside the bar. This same openness is not extended to private or invited events. Yet drinking does occur in these settings and provides us with information on the nature of groupings outside this structured environment.

Bottle Gangs

Cavan's finding that bar drinking is governed by a set of understood norms underscores the social nature of drinking. Although bar encounters may be short lived, tentative, and superficial, they are, nonetheless, a group activity because the interaction between people is governed by shared cultural expectations. Thus, what determines whether an activity is cultural is not the actual length of that activity; rather it is the consensus between participants. That middle-class Americans wait in line, undress for a physician, eat with utensils, and do not speak loudly in elevators are examples of normative behaviors regulated by cultural expectations. As social scientists we recognize that these behaviors are reflections of adaptive strategies. Normative patterns vary in response to environmental circumstances and situations. This variability in adaptive strategy is illustrated by studies of drinking in low-income sections of the city by groups called "bottle gangs."

In low-income areas of cities sometimes called "Skid Row,"[13] bar-drinking norms, in the Cavan sense of "time out," differ little from their uptown counterparts. Surveys of Skid Row residents reveal that their drinking patterns —alone, with others, or both—differed little from residentially stable lower-income non-Skid Row residents (Nash 1964; quoted in Bahr 1973, 162). But Skid Row is a place where a rather unique liquor consumption pattern is found that has attracted the attention of social scientists. This is the bottle gang.[14] Members of these short-lived groupings usually cooperate in the purchase of a bottle of wine, spirits, or some other alcoholic beverage, excluding beer. The gang's life is limited to the consumption of one bottle. When the bottle is empty, the gang disperses until it is formed again. Aside from the obvious economic advantage served by forming a limited-life corporation, some writers have suggested that the gang functions to fulfill social needs experienced by its members.

The bottle gang ranges from three to five in size. James Rooney (1961) distinguishes two types of bottle gangs in Stockton, Sacramento, and Fresno, California.[15] The "permanent" type is made up of two or three men who regularly drink with each other, plus strangers who are recruited for a particular drinking episode. The "temporary" type consists of members who do not know each other.

In spite of its impermanence, the bottle gang has a structure. It has a "leader" whose responsibility it is to provide the initial capital, to supplement the capital if necessary, to arrange the purchase of a bottle, and to act as host. After purchasing the bottle the gang finds a secluded place. The leader opens the bottle and passes it to his left. Each participant takes two swallows and passes it on to the next man. The leader drinks last. After taking his drink, he caps the bottle until the next round. Rooney suggests that the interaction between members of the bottle gang are one of the few instances in Skid Row where men are given personal recognition and esteem. It is an activity that involves trust, a commodity in short supply in this setting. Trust also governs each step in the purchase and consumption of a bottle where each participant is obligated to share resources with other members of the gang.

This obligation to share was noted by Jack Peterson and Milton Maxwell (1958) when they found that those who violated this expectation might be excluded from future participation in gangs. These exclusions were, however, usually temporary. Potential gang members who did not reciprocate in the past could "buy" their way back into the gang at some future date. Permanent exclusions came only from organizations outside the gang. Bars or hotels in Skid Row areas sometimes would ban someone from entering these establishments if their behavior had been disruptive. Bottle gangs were more forgiving of past transgressions.

The solidarity of the gang is, in part, determined by the necessity of maintaining boundaries between itself and non-members. Because the gang drinks in a physical setting that is observable to others, it must be ever vigilant against the possibility that these outsiders might interfere with its activities. The two main interlopers are other members of Skid Row and the police. Other members of Skid Row might attempt to "bum" or "mooch" a drink, a violation of gang reciprocity. The police might arrest all the members of the gang for drinking or drunkenness in public. One might then propose that the intensity of internal solidarity of the bottle gang is a function of the internal norm to share equally *and* the real or potential threat from outsiders. Any understanding of the bottle gang must therefore consider internal cooperation and external threats.

Earl Rubington's (1968) study of bottle gangs on the East Coast of the United States shows how the bottle gang follows a series of stages, each of which is accompanied by a set of rules and sanctions for violating those rules. Although the specific behaviors in his sequence may be somewhat different from those found elsewhere,[16] the general pattern is found everywhere. I have summarized his finding in table 6.3.

An issue that must be addressed in any discussion of the bottle gang, or of Skid Row, is the question of "alcoholism." Does the behavior of those in Skid Row and in bottle gangs simply reflect the actions of alcoholics who are poor? Spradley (1970) reports that his "urban nomads" often drink to "excess," as defined by the larger society. That they engage in group drinking and collective drunkenness does not necessarily mean that the function of drinking is different. Drinking in American society is a symbol of sociability and friendship. Most Americans drink at times and in places that are "appropriate." The places and the times that Skid Row residents drink differ from those of other Americans, but that only tells us that time and ecology are different for Skid Row residents. Peterson and Maxwell (1958) found that only a small percentage of those defined as "alcoholic" live in Skid Row areas. That drunkenness is a behavioral characteristic of some Skid Row residents means only that drunkenness is a behavioral characteristic of this population—nothing more, nothing less. The question for *social* science is the function of drinking and drunkenness for Skid Row residents, or corporate executives, or university professors, or traveling salespeople. What the social scientist wants to know is the symbolic and social significance of drinking in general and bottle gangs in particular.

One possible clue to interpreting drinking in Skid Row comes from Jeff Collmann's (1979) analysis of drinking in the Aboriginal

Table 6.3.
Temporal Stages in the Life of a Bottle Gang

	Organizational Variables		
Temporary Stages	Behavior	Rules	Sanctions
Salutation	Potential members meet and acknowledge each other.	Never snub a friend. Be willing to spend time with an equal. Don't assume familiar relationship when none exists.	**Exclusion**. Rarely applied. **Talk** about violator.
Negotiation	"Leader" determines how much collective money is available for bottle purchase. Panhandling or recruitment of new members provides the needed amount.	Be as ready to offer as to accept a drink. Show your money. Be willing to buy or work your way into the gang.	**Exclusion**. Rarely applied. **Label** violator: "chiseler," "moocher." Those who stand outside and watch are called "merchants," "lap dogs," or "waiters." Those who feign tremors are called "actors."
Procurement	"Leader" chooses one man, the "runner," to purchase the bottle.	Runner should not be too drunk or too shabbily dressed. Make the run quickly. Cover up activity. Have faith in the runner.	Depends on circumstances. Runner may not return because he was arrested. Runner returns, but with open bottle with partially missing contents. If runner is believed to be untrustworthy, he is **labeled** a "Dick Smith," one who has fled with the bottle. This label may **exclude** him from future gangs with the same membership.
Consumption	Runner returns with bottle and gives it to leader. Leader takes two drinks, passes it to runner who passes it one to other members, all of whom take two drinks. Leader holds bottle until next "round."	Wait for leader to open bottle. Wait your turn and match his drinks. Do not drink more than others. Do not attract attention to drinking.	Violator will be **told** not to drink more than others. If his drinking attracts attention by the police, he is more likely to be **excluded** in future gangs.
Affirmation	Gang acknowledges and compliments the leader and the runner.	Follow the leader in topics of conversation. Praise leader and runner. Be critical of persons known to have broken gang rules.	Gang members guilty of incorrect talk or behavior are **labeled** "performers," "wacks," "characters," "nuts," "psychos," or "jail bait." When actions attract police attention, violators are likely to be **excluded**.
Dispersal	Leader decides the time of last round. When bottle is empty it is disposed of and gang either disperses or begins another cycle.	Get rid of the empty discreetly. Say goodbye. Don't beg from, fight with, or steal from gang members.	The more violent or public the violation, the more likely that **exclusion** will be the sanction.

camps around Alice Springs, Northern Territory, Australia. Those living in the Mt. Kelly camp have low income and a low material standard of living. Income sources are from seasonal cattle work, unskilled labor, and social security payments. They represent what many call "detribalized" people. This etic view does not, however, correspond to the emic interpretations of the residents of Mt. Kelly. They pride themselves on having refused alternative housing and not being dependent on welfare, and they insist that large amounts of money flow through the community (209–210). One thing cannot be denied from either the emic or etic perspective. People in Mt. Kelly drink an extraordinary amount of liquor.

Collmann suggests that one can understand this high alcohol consumption by considering the characteristics of the Mt. Kelly residents' economy and corresponding system of "credit." The economy has two sources of income—continuous and discontinuous. Those receiving income from pensions (old men) and social security (women with children) have a continuous income. Others who work cattle and other unskilled jobs have intermittent or discontinuous income. This means that those with discontinuous income must form relationships with those with continuous income. That is, they must establish "credit" from those with continuous income. There are two types of credit—realized and potential. Realized credit is what can actually be received in goods and services from others. Potential credit is the volume of goods and services that could be legitimately acquired if necessary. For any particular individual, the relationship between actual and potential credit is variable and subject to negotiation. There are two sources of credit—specific individuals and general collectivities. The former refers to individuals with whom one has a credit relationship; the latter is reputational and includes those who might be potential creditors. Collmann suggests that these concepts can explain "binge" or "spree" drinking. He suggests that such episodic drinking is one of the:

> . . . appropriate ways of establishing potential credit among a generalized collectivity. They are public affairs in which varying numbers of people accept a highly valued good from an individual, who often makes his "generosity" explicit. Such sprees are rational adaptations to situations in which individuals may experience quite radical changes of personal fortune in the course of their careers. In such situations, individuals must develop credit, deny short-term benefits for long-term opportunities, and commit themselves to the well-being of the community in order to secure their own well-being. (212)

Combining these credit variables results in four theoretically possible outcomes, as shown in table 6.4.

Table 6.4.
**Theoretical Outcomes of the Relationship Between
Source of Credit and Type of Credit**

		Source of Credit	
		Specific Individuals	Generalized Collectivity
Type of of Credit	Realized	I	II
	Potential	III	IV

Let us assume that Collmann's model of credit adequately explains binge drinking among Australian Aborigines. What contribution does this model make to drinking in Skid Row? First of all, both Mt. Kelly and Skid Row areas have residents with intermittent and uncertain incomes. Income sources for the Skid Row residents comes from part-time work, seasonal employment in construction, agriculture and transportation, begging, hustling, and so forth. Some residents do have small but continuous incomes from pensions. From both the residents' and the outsiders' points of view, Skid Row residents are not appealing (Bogue 1963). In both Mt. Kelly and Skid Row, services which represent the outside—governmental agencies, missions, the police and courts—are viewed negatively. In general, communities like Mt. Kelly and Skid Row are composed of isolated individuals, unsure economic outcomes, and distrustful social relationships. Given these conditions, is alcohol simply an escape from this way of life?

Liquor as a thing has some properties which permits it to "do" certain things. Liquor is a fluid substance that can be divided into units with no predetermined size. In the case of the bottle gang, while passing the bottle around, each participant took two "drinks." How much is a drink? Although not specifically mentioned in any of the studies of bottle gangs, one is left with the impression that the "leader" is not left without wine or spirits when the bottle comes around to him for the last time. The numerical unit is two; the amount which can vary is the "drink." In the Australian "sprees" where a communal cup is used:

> An individual may not convert liquor he receives in a *public* distribution into credit of his own with other people; that is he

must consume the liquor on the spot. Unlike the gift of a whole uncooked pumpkin, for example, an individual may not save liquor and pass it on to someone else at the later date. . . . these properties of sharing liquor display the obligations being created in an unambiguous way. (216, emphasis mine)

In the bottle gang if the runner gives away wine to those outside the gang on the way back from purchasing, either as a payment for past or anticipated future obligations, he will be sanctioned. Using Collmann's model, the runner would lose credit of all four types. His actual and potential credit is lost with the gang. If he is labeled a "Dick Smith," he would lose credit with any potential and realized generalized collectivity.

In Mt. Kelly, the type of liquor one drinks serves as a marker for identity and esteem. The specific drinks in rank order are: spirits (rum), beer, port or sweet sherry, and methylated spirits. The studies of bottle gangs suggest a similar ranking. Joan Jackson and Ralph Conner (1953) identified six etic categories of drinkers. They restricted their analysis to the "lush" category. The lushes were described as the elite drinkers, those who could afford to drink in taverns and were only temporary residents of Skid Row. In contrast were the "winos" who consumed the cheapest wine, and below them the "dehorns" or "rubbydubs" who drank bay rum, canned heat, paint thinner and water, or shaving lotion. Peterson and Maxwell (1958) constructed a similar etic distinction between "drunks" and "winos."[17] The drunk was the "spree" drinker who worked between drinking bouts. The wino drinks every day and does not consider himself a worker. Rooney's observations of Skid Row residents does not confirm this distinction. He suggests that many winos still identify themselves as members of the work force in spite of the fact that they have not held a job in a decade. Others have accepted Skid Row as home. In economic terms, the prestige level of drinkers in Skid Row was marked by the cost of what they drank. The same held true for Mt. Kelly.

One distinction between Mt. Kelly drinking sprees and bottle gangs is that in Mt. Kelly someone buys the drink and shares it with others. In so doing the purchaser becomes the "boss." One's ability to buy a bottle and give it away either collectively or individually is a symbol of both affluence and power. At least one ethnographer of Skid Row—Rooney—finds a similar pattern. The leader-host does not underwrite the total cost of a bottle but does exercise authority over the type of wine and regulates both the consumption and the conduct of his "guests." Rooney did find that those who came into money would sometimes pay for the bottle and then share it with his friends. This, he suggests, obligates these same friends to reciprocate. Those who fail to reciprocate soon find themselves defined as "chiselers" and are excluded from further specific "treats" from individuals. The same definition may be earned another way. According to Rooney:

> The obligation of eventual reciprocity can lead to trouble for an individual who wishes to maintain a large number of "treating" relationships but has insufficient income for treating. Financially the most advantageous manner of repayment is to invite former benefactors to share in a corporate bottle and thus to repay with wine for which the reciprocator has borne only part of the cost. That is, a man becomes a legitimate stockholder in a bottle gang by contributing his share toward the purchase of wine, and after the bottle has been purchased, if he meets former benefactors on the street, he invites them to have a drink out of "his" bottle. (455)

Rooney found that the gang often protested this "guest," but he was admitted anyway. The loss of wine, he suggests, is somewhat compensated for by the feeling of collective power or authority over the guest by the gang.

The increase in the consumption of liquor by Aborigines living in camps described by Collmann and the continued high consumption rate of alcohol by bottle gangs in Skid Row cannot be explained in psychological, alcohol "addiction" terms alone. Nor can one accept Bahr's conclusions that participants in bottle gangs, or "drinking schools" as they are called in Britain (Archard 1979), lack organizational structures because they are made up of isolated friendless individuals whose membership in the gang functions strictly to serve utilitarian goals. These conclusions may be accurate when describing individual gang members in jail.[18] They are not warranted when one considers the ethnographic observations of gangs *in vivo*. I would suggest that the model presented by Collmann offers a key to understanding drinking in settings where economic resources are fleeting and unpredictable. To understand the bottle gang it must be placed within a larger context of how all those needs that Malinowski outlined (metabolism, reproduction, bodily comfort, and so forth) are met in these contrasting settings. Bottle gangs are part of a larger set of structural adaptations that have developed to cope with needs such as food, housing, clothing, and health. Among those with few resources, there are striking similarities cross-culturally (Eames and Goode 1988). Drinking in these settings functions as a credit system which binds individuals together, no matter how temporarily, into a general system of mutual obligations beyond drinking. Thus, the symbolic value of liquor is what explains drinking. This is not to say that drinking is the only practice that serves this function, but it is one that, by historical accident, is available.

Conclusion

In this chapter the functional approach to drug use was reviewed. Societies with different divisions of labor were presented in an attempt to uncover an underlying universal function of drugs. This review demonstrated that drug use is not restricted to any particular type of society. Drugs are found in societies with relatively simple divisions of labor (the Yanomamö) to those which stand at the borders of tribal and urban society (beer gardens and opium dens), and in urban societies with their highly differentiated division of labor (bars and bottle gangs). While this excursion clearly demonstrated that drugs can be and have been used in societies whose structures differ widely, it also shows that the function of drugs differs according to how the society was organized. What does this finding say about the functional approach?

To better understand the functional approach in social science it is helpful to distinguish between functionalism as a method and functionalism as a theory. As a method, the functional approach demands that data be collected from a whole system because it is assumed that the function of any practice is in its contribution to that system. For anthropology, the boundaries of the system are usually the whole society or community. In these settings, boundaries are physically observable. The society occupies a geographical territory; the village perimeter is clearly defined. For sociology, the determination of boundaries is somewhat problematic. The large, complex urban societies within which sociologists work often have overlapping communities that are linked together with a multitude of interconnections. This means that only small bits of the total system can be realistically researched. The opium den, the beer garden, and the bar do have a territory even though the personnel may change daily. Thus, instead of the wider, more inclusive society being the basis for determining function, research is carried out in small places, and the system functions are inferred. Regardless of limitations on meeting the methodological expectations of functionalism, there is an attempt to link the activities one studies to some larger framework.

The theoretical difficulties with functionalism are the same, regardless of whether one studies small or large societies. Maintaining that some practice is functionally related to a larger system usually is based on a *post factum* (after the fact) argument. We examine some practice—let us say opium smoking in opium dens—and then suggest a function for this practice. Having suggested the function of the opium den, it is not always clear if we explained the origin of the den, its persistence, or simply what it does. To say that dens emerge to satisfy some "need" does not explain why there was this need, nor is it proof that such a need exists. Even if one were to follow this line of argument, can it be assumed that this need can *only* be satisfied by the opium den, or can other practices or institutions provide a functional alternative? To argue that only the opium den can satisfy this need, even for its particular patrons, one must demonstrate that without dens, the need would not be satisfied. Could one, for example, argue that Yanomamö society would be the same without ebene? Would Yemen be different without qat? Would social distinctions on Fiji disappear if there were no kava? Would there be "bottle gangs" in Skid Row areas without alcohol? These are the kinds of questions that functionalists might find difficult to answer.

Regardless of the limitations of the functional approach, this perspective offers a more comprehensive framework within which to understand both social and cultural phenomena than did the models of the evolutionists and diffusionists. In its insistence on finding the function of every practice, it compels the researcher to consider the possible contributions of socially defined repugnant behaviors. Instead of moralizing about crime or suicide or drug use, the functionalist is forced to examine the potential systemic contributions of these practices.

From our use of the functional perspective in this chapter, it should be clear that drugs, no matter what their chemistry, are only part of the total behavioral repertoire of a people. Unless one purposely focuses on drug use to the exclusion of all other system considerations, it would be difficult to make a case for drugs being dysfunctional or pathological for the society as a whole.

For the most part, this examination has focused on drug use in the secular lives of different peoples. Except for the Yanomamö, whose drug using behavior is part of their religious practices, drugs are just one of many activities in people's lives. However, in many cultures drug use and religion are intimately linked. This linkage will be examined in the next chapter.

Endnotes

[1] Lindstrom reports that some unmarried men do drink kava, much to the concern of their fathers.

[2] The effect of qat is attributed to the alkaloid cathinone, which is similar to dextroamphetamine.

[3] Babylon is an ancient city located 50 miles south of the present-day city of Baghdad, Iraq.

[4] Since the Code only mentions women, one might infer that gender was a criterion by which this occupational specialty was staffed. It might possibly mean that only women publicans were suspected of these practices.

[5] Howard Becker's work on marihuana and LSD, reviewed in chapter 3, reflects the Chicago School tradition.

[6] Fischer has called this approach "subcultural." In keeping with the discussion of problems associated with the concept of subculture in chapter 4, I have renamed this approach the "normal."

[7] The seven variables they used to measure integrative drinking behavior were: drinking as religious ritual; non-religious but ceremonial drinking; ritualized drinking with rules governing time, place, and manner of drinking; quantity of ceremonial drinking; quantity of drinking during religious rituals; approval of drinking by the majority of a society; and the extent of drinking by adults. These seven variables are intercorrelated cross-culturally.

[8] Kaffir is an Arabic word which refers to any native not converted to Islam. It is sometimes used by working-class whites to refer to Africans in general.

[9] Meo and Hmong are the names of tribal and/or ethnic groups in Laos. More will be said about the Hmong in chapter 8.

[10] In 1989 Westermeyer reported in the *British Journal of Addictions* that after several decades' absence, opium smoking among Indochinese migrants in Minnesota has increased.

[11] Being "inside" in a public place seems somewhat of a contradiction. Public is used here to indicate that, for the price of a drink, the public over a certain age is granted admission. Of course there are exceptions. Until recently, women, blacks, Indians, and Mexican-Americans were excluded from some "public" drinking establishments. Other barriers may also effectively exclude some segments of the "public." Having the price of a drink at the Tavern on the Green in New York City might not be enough for one clothed like a homeless person.

[13] According to Peterson and Maxwell (1958), the term "Skid Row" originated in Seattle, Washington. It is derived from Skid Road, an area in which homeless men lived, which had been a logging skid in the early days of Seattle.

[14] Note the use of the word "gang." We might ask, why not the bottle "group," or the bottle "association," or the bottle "club"? In none of my readings did I find any evidence that "gang" was an emic name. Therefore, I assume that is an etic classification used by social scientists.

[15] Rooney lived in the Skid Row areas of these cities for one- to two-week periods. He identified himself as an unemployed traveling worker or "fruit tramp." As a full participant, he was able to both observe and participate in the daily activities of Skid Row residents.

[16] Rooney observed that the "promoter"—leader—drinks last. This author observed the "bottle holder" in Richmond, Virginia to be both the first and last drinker in a "round."

[17] The term *etic* is used here to indicate that these distinctions were those made by inhabitants of Skid Row. Both the Jackson and Conner study (1953) and the

Peterson and Maxwell study (1958) used data collected from inmates in jail to reconstruct street distinctions.

[18] Bahr's conclusion that the bottle gang lacks structure is, in part, a reflection of what units are used as a basis of social science analysis. Surveys of men in prison, health units, and hospitals are sources of data on individuals, not interaction between individuals. Groups, no matter how short their duration, by definition, are both people and their interactions (and the rules governing those interactions). The conclusion that no rules and sanctions exist in bottle gangs, therefore, is more a comment on methodology than an accurate portrayal of those groups themselves.

chapter 7

What Shall We Believe?

Religion and Drugs

In previous chapters the concept **cultural universal** was introduced. A cultural universal is a rule or set of rules found in every culture. Note that I did not say social universal. For example, in every culture there are a set of rules which prohibit sexual intercourse between persons defined as related. These are called the incest taboos.[1] The incest taboo is, therefore, a cultural universal. While the rule is universal, the specific relatives who are considered inappropriate sexual partners vary. The cultural rules of kinship define who is and who is not a relative. These definitions are then translated into the behavioral prohibition of sexual intercourse between those persons defined as relatives. The incest rule is cultural; punishment of the behavior sexual intercourse is social. One also notes that religion is a cultural universal, depending on how the concept of religion is defined. Herein lies a problem.

Within the social sciences many different definitions and classifications of religion have been offered (Wilson 1973). Unlike the specific behavior sexual intercourse, a broad range of behaviors and beliefs has been examined in the social science literature under the topic of religion. These variations are, in part, explained by the variety of cultures and societies examined by social scientists. The solution to this dilemma lies in the process of scientific definition (chapter 1). If we group together all things that share a given relative trait and set apart those things that do not share that trait, it is possible to suggest a definition of religion. Anthony Wallace (1966) observes that those diverse behaviors subsumed under the word "religion" share a single premise, and that premise is that "souls, supernatural beings, and supernatural forces exist" (52). Thus, **religion is any set of practices that are emically explained through belief in the supernatural**, whether that supernatural takes the form of beings or forces. Corresponding to the supernatural reference, there are specific behaviors which define the social aspects of religion, one of which bears directly on our concern with drugs.[2] Wallace proposes that all religions have, either as part of their histories or their present practices, engaged in:

> Efforts to induce an ecstatic spiritual state by crudely and directly manipulating physiological processes. . . . Such manipulations may be classified under four major headings: (1) drugs; (2) sensory deprivation; (3) mortification of the flesh by pain, sleeplessness, and fatigue; (4) deprivation of food, water, or air. (55)

We have already noted a linkage between religion and drugs. Among the Quechua, coca leaves are chewed in the hallpay ritual during which references are made to the supernatural. Tobacco was used by many North and South American Indians to bring on an altered state of consciousness, to cure the sick, or to commune with the supernatural (de Rios 1984). Peyote is used by practitioners of the Native American Church as part of a sacred ritual. The Yanomamö use a snuff they call ebene to contact their hekura spirits, and marihuana smoking is part of the culture inventory of the Rastafarians. As a general observation, the literature which links drugs and "religion" is usually reserved for a category of drugs called **hallucinogens**—any drug which produces altered sensory perception. In this category one finds such drugs as mescaline, psilocybin, bufotenin (found in the skin of toads), *ololiuqui* (the Mexican name for the seeds of morning glory plants), and LSD.

The study of religion has followed somewhat different histories in sociology and anthropology. This difference is tied, in part, to the types of societies studied by these two disciplines. Anthropological inquiry has been worldwide, while sociologists have remained within the confines of Western urban culture. Anthropology has developed schemas to interpret the beliefs and practices of so-called "simple" societies. Sociologists have focused their attention on the behavioral manifestation of religion, namely, the organizational structures of **church**es. In short, anthropology has emphasized the culture of religion, while sociology has viewed religion as part of society. This might be visualized as in table 7.1. Keeping this distinction in mind, it is now possible to review the research of anthropologists and sociologists on the relationship between "religion" and drugs.

Table 7.1.

The Distinction Between Religion and Church

Behavior	Expectations
Society	Culture
Associations	Institutions
Church	*Religion*

The Evolution of Religion

The observation that religion is a cultural universal encouraged many nineteenth century evolutionists to search for the origins and evolution of religion. This in turn led anthropologists to look at those cultures which were presumed to be like those of early humans. Edward B. Tylor (1832–1917) is representative of these nineteenth-century scholars. Religion for Tylor was "the belief in spiritual beings" (Tylor 1871). This spiritualist perspective he called **animism**. He proposed that all religions are attempts to *explain* the unexplainable. Early humans were faced with many phenomena that were not understood. To make sense of such things as echoes, shadows, dreaming, death, and illness, the "soul," or vital spirit, was invented. This soul was a second self that was separate from the corporal body. It would leave the body when asleep and wander around. Thus, the experience of dreaming reflected the wanderings of the soul. At death the soul left the body permanently but then might roam around. When one examines the religions with which readers are familiar, one does note beliefs in spiritual beings—angels, ghosts, or spirits that take on human forms. One also notes a belief in the separation of the corporal body and the incorporeal soul. One can lose one's soul while still having a body. Conversely, souls may remain in the form of ghosts or spirits without physical bodies. Whether this same view of the cosmos is a universal can only be determined through study of "religion" cross-culturally, and Tylor had only a limited amount of information about other cultures. Regardless of the empirical evidence for the universality of beliefs in souls, Tylor's contribution is his attempt to uncover a universal reason for religion.

The Dreams-Drugs-Religion Nexus

The search for the origins of religion is not confined to nineteenth-century theories. Weston LaBarre (1990b) offers an intriguing argument for the "origin" of religion. LaBarre insists that our understanding of religion has erroneously focused on the characteristics of gods rather than the prophets and shamans from whom these gods take their particular forms. Unlike the inaccessible gods whose nature it is to be inaccessible, the "sponsors" or "managers" of gods are available to us as the object of study. Every religion is the beliefs and behaviors of real people, and these people can be studied in secular terms. In other words, one cannot study gods scientifically. One can, however, study people whose behavior or pronouncements are used as a basis for the religion.

Religion for LaBarre is a subjective statement about a world quite distinct from the objective world in which people live. Humans are both **subjective** (sub-jective; literally, that which is thrown under) and **objective** (ob-jective; literally, that which is thrown across) animals. The origins of human subjectivity are to be found in the empirical generalization that all mammals sleep, and during sleep they all experience a state called REM (rapid eye movement). During this stage, it is assumed that dreaming (a subjective state) takes place. What distinguishes humans, as cultural animals, from other mammals is the ability of humans to communicate that experience to other humans through language. Are dreams the only source of subjective states? LaBarre suggests that at least one other source of the subjective experience is drugs—in particular, the hallucinogens.

LaBarre argues that the use of hallucinogens is an old practice, although evidence for their use in the Old World has largely disappeared. Only about 120 hallucinogenic plants have been identified in the world. Compared to the total number of plant species, ca. 800,000, this seems like a minuscule number. However, only about 150 of these species are used by people for food, and most of the world's population is supported by only 12 or 13 plants (LaBarre 271; Davis 1989, 245). The antiquity of the practice of ingesting plants that alter states of consciousness does not rest on the distribution of these plants but rather on the ethnographic observation that the religions of hunters and gatherers, humankind's first cultural adaptation, practiced shamanism. "Shaman" is an Arctic Siberian Chukchee word used to describe a status in band and tribal societies that has responsibility for manipulating the spirit world, curing illness through magical procedures, and diagnosing illness and prescribing cures. The status of shaman is found in almost every New World culture. Associated with shamanism is the use of hallucinogenic plants or some other method of achieving an altered subjective state of consciousness. Since the use of these plants is not widely diffused throughout the Old World, why does LaBarre suggest that shamanism is the oldest form of religion and the taking of hallucinogens the source of religious subjectivity?

LaBarre's argument rests on the use of **cultural survivals**. Shamanistic religions, including their use of hallucinogenic plants, diffused from the Old World. New Worlders' physical characteristics; linguistic similarities; folk tale themes; and the distribution of artifacts such as the bow and arrow, the dog, and the spear thrower demonstrate that the New World aborigine is an Asian transplant. The use of hallucinogenic plants in the New World continued because hallucinogenic plants existed in the New World. In the Old World, climates and cultures changed, leaving the Old Worlders with no hallucinogenic plants and fewer hunters and gatherers. In the New World, tobacco was the most widely used hallucinogen, but other plants having the same effects were incorporated into the cultural practices of shamans.

The first evidence for shamanism in the Old World is found in the appearance of masked figures on the walls of caves dated 20,000+ years ago. LaBarre maintains that these dancing figures dressed in animal skins were, like their New World descendants, users of hallucinogens. He further suggests that shamanism, as a practice, emerged as a means for dealing with crisis or uncertainty. Much of the behaviors of hunter-gatherers is a response to a set of objective physical and natural "unknowns." The altered states of the shaman, like dreaming, hint at another more stable world, albeit one that is subjective. LaBarre argues that:

Every established ecclesia of the majority began in a minority crisis cult of one, in real historic, not supernatural, time; and the cult spread and diffused historically, sometimes until it became the Established Religion, whose priests (as opposed to visionary shamans) are merely the non-ecstatic journeyman officiants of routinized established cults. Every religion, in historic fact, began in one man's "revelation"—his dream or fugue or ecstatic trance. Indeed, the crisis cult is *characteristically* dereistic, autistic, and dreamlike precisely *because* it had its origin in the dream, trance, "spirit" possession, epileptic "seizure," REM sleep, sensory deprivation, or other visionary state of the shaman-originator. All religions are necessarily "revealed" in this sense, inasmuch as they are certainly not revealed consensually in secular experience. (262, emphasis his)

Thus, for LaBarre, as for Tylor, the search for origins of religion lies in the observation that "modern" religions, while staffed by bureaucratic priests, all make references to raising the dead, curing the sick, and hearing and seeing things that others cannot— precisely the kinds of activities that are attributed to shamans in those cultures which still have this form of religion.

Power Without Spirits

As more evidence became available about cultures in different parts of the world, there was increasing skepticism on the universality of the soul. One of the first to question Tylor's assertion was Robert R. Marett (1866–1943). He suggested there was a preanimism stage in human evolution (Marett 1914). This was a stage characterized by **anamatism**, the belief in the inherent power of certain things in nature. Unlike Tylor's idea of a soul which had human characteristics, the power in anamatism was impersonal. Marett based his argument on the assumption that because early humans could not distinguish between natural "orders" (animal, vegetable, mineral, and human) they imbued all objects with "power" or life in a most generalized sense. Marett's illustration of this principle is the Melanesian belief in **mana**, an impersonal power believed to pervade the universe but sometimes concentrated in specific objects or people. When concentrated, either in persons or objects, it could be dangerous and therefore must be treated with caution. As pointed out earlier, members of the Native American Church believe that peyote has power and therefore must be treated with respect, otherwise one could get hurt. In American culture, there is a history of beliefs that drugs *cause* people to behave in a particular way. Marihuana and LSD, as substances, were believed to cause insanity.

Crack, even in small amounts, is believed to cause people to become slaves to its power; and PCP is believed to cause people to become stronger and highly aggressive (Feldman et al. 1979). That these substances do not, in fact, cause these specific outcomes is unimportant. It is the belief in their power that justifies their being classified as objects of animatistic belief. Animatistic beliefs are not necessarily negative. New Age devotees assume that the position of the stars, certain numbers, or rock crystals have certain powers. Many readers might take vitamins based on the belief that taking them will make one stronger, healthier, more virile, or happier than if they had not been taken. However, as with Tylor's animism, a systematic review of the world's religions fails to support the universality of anamatism.

The Function of Religion

Beginning in the early part of the twentieth century, questions about the origin(s) and evolution of religion were replaced by questions concerning the function of religion. One of the earliest contributors to this functional approach was Émile Durkheim (1858–1917). Durkheim rejected the study of Western religions as an appropriate sample of religion and suggested that if religion is to be understood, it must be studied in its elementary form. The elementary form selected by Durkheim was a detailed ethnography of the Australian Arunta (Spencer and Gillen 1968). The Arunta are a clan-based society in which each clan practices rituals and ceremonies which focus on clan totems.[3] Durkheim questions why the totems take on special importance for clan members. He fails to find anything intrinsic to the clan totems that makes them different from other objects in the Arunta environment and concludes that it is not the totem as a thing that makes it special but rather what it symbolically represents.

Durkheim suggests that the practices of the Arunta toward the totem is what defines the totem as **sacred**, and it is this emic definition that distinguishes religion from non-religion. For Durkheim, religion is "a unified system of beliefs and practices relative to sacred things. . . ." (1965, 62). Sacred is anything set apart and treated differently from the secular or profane, or the everyday. Religion consists of two parts—beliefs and rituals. **Beliefs** are an expression of how the world *is*. **Rituals** are the behavioral manifestations of beliefs. Having defined religion, Durkheim addresses the question of its function. Using terms that we have developed in this text, Durkheim insists that all humans depend on culture, but culture is not a thing. Rather, it is a set of rules and expectations which have no corporeal form. The totem is a thing—an animal or some other physical object. The behaviors (rituals) of humans towards that thing (totem) make manifest and visible the unseeable experiences of humans that are determined by culture. Thus, religion, in both its beliefs and rituals, functions to validate culture. Religion is the deification of culture. Religion maintains the values and sentiments of the society through group activity—ritual—and further acts to control behavior through the process of socialization which teaches, through imitation and repetition, rituals and their associated beliefs.

What Durkheim offers is a model for the interpretation of religion in all of its specific manifestations and in all its varied ritual and belief forms. The beliefs and rituals in one society may be quite different from beliefs and rituals in another. The reason for these differences is because each society has a different division of labor. The cultural principles which organize Yanomamö society are different from the cultural principles of American society. If religion is the way these principles are made observable, then one should expect Yanomamö and American religions to be different. Remember that culture is not an object—rather, it is reflected in objects and/or behaviors. One experiences culture, and there is no direct way to display that experience. Religion, for Durkheim, is the collective, shared display of those experiences that make one a Yanomamö or an American.

Durkheim's contribution to understanding religion is his insistence that religion functions to make subjective experiences objective. This insight enables us to use religion as a measure of culture at one time and to explain why religion changes over time. If religion is culture, then its function is to **validate** both stability and change.

Magic and Religion

Some social scientists argue that a useful distinction can be made between religion and magic. Sir James Frazer (1854–1941) observed that both share a belief in the supernatural but differ in the kind of relationships which link humans and the supernatural. In **magic**, humans *manipulate* the supernatural to bring about desired results. In **religion** the supernatural *controls* humans (Frazer 1928). Frazer saw two major principles operating in magic—the "law" of similarity and the "law" of contact or contagion. The principle of similarity is the belief that it is possible to bring about a desired event through imitating that event; this is **homeopathic** or **imitative** magic. The principle of contagion or contact is the belief that things once in contact will continue this bond, even when they have been separated. This belief is the basis of **contagious** magic. Magic, unlike religion, does not bring people together in collectives; rather, it is a response to a crisis. Magical systems are much more individualistic. The magician and those who desire to have magic "worked" have only a fleeting relationship. Under what conditions does one seek magic? As a general observation, magic is employed in situations "out of the normal." Events, either anticipated or real, which interrupt the social "order" are most subject to the believed outcomes of magic. Thus, drought, sickness, war and conflict, barrenness, or loss of hair may be appropriate situations in which to employ magic. In addition, magic may be used in anticipation of future outcomes. Rituals may be carried out to insure the health of a newborn child, the fertility of crops, the success of the hunt, or the growth of hair. Magic is a ritualized activity that emphasizes optimism.

Frazer was part of the evolutionary tradition and argued that magic was the earliest system of supernatural belief and practices. Early humans had only a crude technology for coping with the environment. The assumption that humans could control the supernatural supplemented the inability of these technologies to control or tame the natural world. Magic, according to Frazer, did not always work. It was the failure of magic to bring about desired outcomes that resulted in religion. Instead of defining the supernatural as a force that could be manipulated, religion assumed that the supernatural controlled humans. The behavioral correlate of this change in belief was that in religion, humans "requested" action through prayer, gifts, and other interpersonal techniques.

In reading the social science literature, the distinction between religion and magic is not always clear. Therefore, I have summarized some of the more important differences in table 7.2.

The differences between magic and religious systems reflect the organizational structures of the cultures in which each is found. Cross-cultural comparisons of community organization show a strong linkage to the presence or absence of magic. Charles McNett (1970) found that small communities—bands, villages, and towns—had shamanism, magical systems, individual rituals, no temples, and no religious hierarchy. Conversely, cities and states were characterized by low or absent shamanism and magic. In magic the supernatural is an impersonal (animatistic) force. In this system

Table 7.2.
Comparison of Magic and Religion

	Magic	Religion
Division of Labor	Undifferentiated	Differentiated
Supernatural	Impersonal	Personified
Goal	Control	Verification
Method	Manipulation	Propitiation
Primary Agent	Shaman	Priest
Agent-Patron Relationship	Direct/Individual	Indirect/Collective
Hallucinogenic Use	Permitted	Forbidden

it is assumed that the supernatural can be controlled through manipulation. The designated agent in this relationship with the supernatural is the shaman. According to Jacob Pandian (1991):

> The shaman's role is primarily to communicate *with* supernatural entities and to participate in the supernatural world to help individuals or groups achieve desired goals (divination, sorcery, and healing). Shamans experience ecstasy and transcendence and can achieve trance states with or without the aid of hallucinogenic drugs. (93, emphasis his)

In contrast,

> The role of the priest is primarily to communicate *to* supernatural entities through propitiation and supplication. The authority of the priest stems from their religious training, and they officiate at group rituals and serve as the custodians of sacerdotal knowledge; they interpret and dramatize the mythological charters in public and uphold social conventions and moral order. (93, emphasis his)

It should be remembered that specific societies are not end points on a theoretical continuum between differentiated and undifferentiated divisions of labor. Rather, they may be some combination of these two types. For example, in **peasant** societies one should expect to find both priests and shamans, both religion and magic. Peasant societies are the result of colonialism, where urban societies subjugate folk peoples for the purpose of using their labor to produce needed items. In these societies, both priests (representatives of the urban society) and shamans (representatives of the folk society) are found. Consistent with specialized divisions of labor in urban societies, the priest is a full-time functionary. The shaman, in spite of specialized knowledge, "works" only when required. Priests are usually male in male-dominated urban societies. Shamans may be male or female. The prestige of the shaman is achieved through success in dealings with the supernatural. Conversely, the priest is accorded recognition or prestige because he occupies the status "priest." We can extend this connection between sacred and secular further by noting that so long as the activities of the priest validate secular norms and values, he will remain a priest. When priests break this bond, they often function as shamans, becoming prophets who claim direct communication with the supernatural. Since both priests and shamans reflect the existing order of society, the transformation of priests to shamans is a measure of cultural drift and social change (chapter 4). This is precisely the issue Wallace addressed at the beginning of this chapter.

Shamans are often selected because of some unique physical or behavioral characteristic. Albinos, epileptics, transvestites, and homosexuals are likely candidates for this position. Shamans use several techniques for achieving an altered state of consciousness, including hyperventilation, rhythmic drumming and dancing, fasting, and consumption of drugs. Shamans often "speak in tongues," or through interpreters, or in other languages (Pandian, 95–96). Both their appearance and behavior contribute to a ritual process, the purpose of which is to act on behalf of the client on a one-to-one basis. The use of hallucinogens by the shaman is one method for "seeing" the supernatural cause of the condition the client wishes to correct. The use of hallucinogens in religion is either restricted to some specific segment within a formal hierarchy or forbidden altogether. In non-state societies the shaman deals directly with the supernatural. In state-level societies, a citizen's interaction with the supernatural, like all other power relationships, is through an established formal hierarchy. Just as one must petition authorities through a bureaucratic structure, so too must one petition (pray to) supernatural beings in state-level societies through a hierarchy of religious functionaries. To the shaman, knowledge about the supernatural is revealed through direct consultation with the supernatural, with or without the aid of drugs. Confessions of such direct revelations in state-level societies are likely to be treated as mental illness or blasphemy (treason or sedition) because it violates the established hierarchial order.[4]

Worldview

The discussion thus far has treated religion and magic as a distinct and separate set of activities and beliefs, yet they are part of a larger system that can be called worldview. To the philosopher this is the more complicated German word, *Weltanschauung*. Although the German word freely translates as "world view," the philosopher uses this term differently from the social scientist. Worldview refers to emic definitions of the world. It is how people "think" about the world in which they live. In contrast, *Weltanschauung* is an etic interpretation suggested by the philosopher. Worldview includes beliefs, whether they assume the supernatural or not. Americans, for example, believe in capitalism as the best form of economy and accept the idea that there are job givers and job takers. Americans believe that monogamy is the "best" form of marriage, that people ought to be free to determine what they do (within limits of course), and that the children of incestuous relationships will have genetic deformities. The concept of worldview in social science does not assume the idea of "truth" or empirical knowledge. There is no "scientific" way to determine whether beliefs, ideologies, or assumptions about the "order" of the universe are correct or contradictory. Worldview is the reconstructed logic that is used by a people to define the world and the reality of that world. It is the way order is imposed on chaos. Thus, there are many worldviews. The different definitions of religion offered by social scientists can, in part, be explained by the worldviews at the time they "thought" about this topic. Reservations about the usefulness of this concept by some contemporary social scientists is usually based on methodological concerns. Worldview cannot be measured directly; rather, it must be inferred from observed behaviors. Within anthropology the measurement of worldview has been addressed by the structuralists. In the next section, we shall examine how myths and rituals have been analyzed by these structuralists to reconstruct worldviews.

Religion as Structure: Myth and Ritual

Whether magic or religion, supernatural belief systems universally involve myths and rituals. One approach to the study of religion suggests that these myths and rituals are symbolic representations which dramatize complex beliefs (worldview). The theoretical perspective which focuses on these two activities is **structuralism**.

A major premise of structuralism is that decoding myths and legends will lead to the discovery of the laws of human thought. The acknowledged leader of this approach is Claude Lévi-Strauss (1908–). Using a model developed in structural linguistics, Lévi-Strauss suggests that all cultural activities can be understood as a reflection of how the brain is "wired." The structure of the brain cannot be determined through direct observation of the brain as a biological organ. Rather, Lévi-Strauss argues, the brain's structure can be inferred from an analysis of what the human brain produces. All cultural practices, he insists, have an underlying binary structure, similar to the binary structure of the computer. Further, this binary structure is organized by oppositions, such as yes/no, off/on, either/or. For example, in belief systems, the Durkheimian distinction between sacred or secular might be considered a binary opposition. In culinary systems, the underlying binary opposition is raw/cooked. Lévi-Strauss' analysis of myths, legends, incest rules and other cultural manifestations demonstrate, to his satisfaction, that the human brain is indeed organized by the principle of binary opposition.

Some structuralists have concentrated their attention on ritual and myth as bridges between binary oppositions. Life and death are bridged by a death ritual. Childhood and adulthood may be bridged by a puberty ritual. Religious myths and rituals are a bridge between humans and the supernatural. This in-between characteristic has become the model for analysis of prohibitions. In Mary Douglas' classic study (1966), she proposes a model by which one can make sense of definitions of purity and pollution. She suggests that all cultures have some system of cataloging things and practices into a system of order. One task of the cultural approach is to unravel the underlying principles or rules of that system. Working from the list of prohibited animals found in the Biblical book of Leviticus, Douglas argues that on the surface this listing does not make much sense. What makes an animal "clean" or "polluted" has little to do with human digestion or the edibility of the animal itself. Rather, she argues, the listing outlines a cognitive order that serves to bind Jews together in the way they "think" about the world. Douglas noted three cognitive domains: earth, water, and air. Associated with each domain there are appropriate behaviors. Animals that reside in water should have scales and swim. Based on this rule, clams, lobsters, and shrimp are unclean and polluted because they neither have scales nor do they swim. Land animals may hop, jump or walk; they have four legs, cloven-hooves, and chew their cuds. Animals with hands and feet, such as the mouse or the crocodile, are therefore unclean; pigs are polluting because they do not chew their cud. In the air domain, animals were expected to have feathers and fly. Insects that crawl, swarm, or fly like birds are also defined as unclean. Douglas suggests that only when we understand how worlds are mentally ordered can such definitions of purity or pollution be understood.

The in-between position of ritual and myth also attracted Victor Turner (1969). He agrees with the observation of Arnold van Gennep (1873–1957) that cultures everywhere have **rites of passage** that mark the transition of people from one status to another (1961). He concurs with van Gennep's discovery that these different rites all have three distinct stages. The first stage is **separation**. This is followed by a **liminal** period, and finally by a **reincorporation** ceremony. During the first stage the person is detached from his or her present status. In the liminal stage the person is "betwixt and between," neither here nor there. In the last stage, one is ceremonially installed into the new status. Turner is most interested in the liminal stage because it is this stage that is most often associated with danger, sacredness, or what he calls "anti-structure." Turner suggests that all societies are constructed on the basis of structured differences. This he calls **community**. In the division of labor, for example, distinctions are made between male and female and between children and adults. During the liminal phase of rites of passage these distinctions disappear and give rise to what he calls **communitas**. In communitas there are no structured differences. Those in communitas are equal; and from the perspective of the larger structure, this releases them from the normal controls which insure the continuity of structure. It is this lack of societal constraint that gives power to those in communitas. This liminality may take on different symbolic representations. For example, LaBarre identified drawings of dancing figures dressed in animal skins on cave walls as representations of early shamans. Using Turner's model, these figures represent liminal characters. Are they animals with human features, or are they humans with animal features? For Turner, they symbolically represent neither and both. They are a visual portrayal of a liminal stage between human and animal. The hippie movement discussed in chapter 5 recruited members from a liminal cultural category. Were the hippies children or adults? Just as van Gennep found his three stages in all rites of passage, Turner finds anti-structures in every culture, which becomes the basis for understanding much of humankind's myths, rituals, and art.

The different social science theories of religion are not necessarily mutually exclusive. Even a cursory review of the social science literature on religion reveals that these theories, either singly or in some combination, have been called on to explain various aspects of religion. In the next few pages, a few cases are presented which illustrate the assumptions of these theories.

Values, Norms, and Religion: The Case of Tobi

In the previous discussion of Tobi, it was noted that the symbolic meaning of tobacco was an important, if not central, feature of Tobian secular life. From the Durkheimian perspective, we would therefore predict that this same symbolic meaning would be incorporated into the Tobian sacred. To test this prediction, it is necessary to review religious practices and beliefs on Tobi.

The history of "religion" on Tobi can be divided into three periods (Black 1978). The earliest of these was the traditional community-based religion which placed an emphasis on manipulating supernatural forces under the guidance of a shaman (magic). Tobi emerged from its isolation in the early 1700s when passing European ships began trading metal for Tobian coconuts and other items. Not all passing boats stopped, and Tobians would have to chase them to obtain trade goods. Shamans claimed that they had the power to make these large boats wait for the canoes. In exchange for using this power, they received a share of the bartered goods (311).

By the end of the nineteenth century, many Tobians were "recruited" as laborers on other islands and as crewmen on European vessels. At about the same time they came into contact with Germans who introduced a "plague." Soon after World War I the Japanese brought venereal disease (318). The plague and migration directly reduced the population, while venereal disease left many sterile. This series of misfortunes also disrupted traditional religious and cultural practices. If religion is, as Durkheim suggested, a reflection of cultural patterns, then we should expect religion to change when those patterns change. Black recounts an event that occurred in the early 1930s which marked the end of traditional religious practices:

> Armed with the chief's blessing . . . on a dark night they (the villagers) attacked the chief's spirit house, the women's menstrual house, and the sorcerers' canoe house and burned them all to the ground. This event . . . marks the end of the traditional Tobian order. The old rituals were scrapped, the chief abandoned his exclusive rights to certain foodstuffs, and the great prohibitions associated with everyday life were no longer observed. (319)

This act introduced a short period of secularization, but secularization was no more successful than the rejected shamanism. The population continued to decline and none of the "problems" disappeared. A few years after this open act of rejection, the third period began when Tobians were converted to Roman Catholicism after a short visit by a missionary.

One notes that both the rejection of traditional practices and the adoption of Christianity were responses to crisis situations. Tobi was beset with internal changes as a result of disease, sterility, and outmigration. Contact with the outside world resulted in challenges to those traditional adaptations that had evolved during a long period of relative isolation. The rituals which had protected Tobians at one time could no longer protect them from internal and external forces, and the rituals were abandoned (Frazer's magic to religion).

The arrival of the Catholic missionary offered an alternative to the failure of secularization. The islanders adopted Christianity, but having accepted Christianity does not mean that traditional beliefs were entirely abandoned. Tobians share with other nearby island communities a worldview that includes belief in ghosts. On Tobi these ghosts are called *yarus* and are the most feared supernatural manifestations (320). Tobians believe that there are many ghosts whose ability to do harm is caused by human action. However, the ghosts can be kept in check by rituals. What was introduced by the missionary, and what is practiced by Tobians, is ritual Catholicism. At dawn and dusk the islanders gather in the church to say the rosary. The Catholic birth, marriage and death rituals are thought to be very important. Praying accompanies every meal and women belong to church groups that follow special dietary regulations and extra prayer. In spite of knowledge about and participation in Christian rituals, Tobians retain their belief in malevolent ghosts. Therefore, to understand Tobian Christianity, it is necessary to understand these ghosts. To understand these ghosts, one must understand Tobian culture.

Tobi is an example of forced cooperation. Because of the small number of people living there, it is mandatory that people get along with each other. Yet as Black (1985) points out, "There exists on Tobi a large corpus of conflicts and disputes which divides and subdivides the population so finely that ultimately almost every person is opposed to almost everyone else (272)." These disputes have a long history and may involve land, marriage, and political offices. Thus, much of Tobian everyday life is concerned with managing this undercurrent of hostility. What keeps these hostilities from being behaviorally manifested is the Tobian use of fear as a mechanism of social control. On the surface, Tobians give the impression of being a pleasant, cooperative, and happy people. What maintains this public happy face is fear. Direct confrontation by another is feared because Tobians believe that if such a confrontation takes place it would unravel all the hostility that exists between people. What keeps hostility in check is the belief that those who violate this expectation of outward cooperation will become ghosts.

As previously discussed, Tobian social organization is characterized by the "in-charge" system that is based on the idea of unequal competency. Only older males are viewed as competent; all others are incompetent. Consistent with the norm of cooperation and sharing, all people are expected to share tobacco and competent men are expected to manage tobacco supplies to organize cooperative work efforts (Black 1984). The word used to describe the opposite of sharing—stinginess—is *mwih* and is often associated with an unwillingness to share tobacco. Persons thought to have tobacco but are not willing to share it with others are often the object of gossip and scorn. Black found that when tobacco supplies were low, there was a corresponding increase in gossip about those who are mwih. Tobians avoid being the subject of gossip because continued suspicion of non-normative behavior can lead to accusations that one is a ghost. Ghost accusation does not mean that the person is a ghost but that his true character is ghostlike— evil, dangerous, and powerful. Thus, gossip acts as an effective means by which to insure behavioral conformity to norms and belief in the value of sharing.

Tobian ghosts are both hated and feared—and are the only category of beings toward whom these emotions are acceptable. According to Black,

> These beings are thought to have corporeal reality (eerie and horrible though it is) and to live in the sea off the reef edge. From there they come up onto the island, mostly at night and mostly in the cemetery. Occasionally they roam the entire length of the island and even can be encountered within the village. Most of them are unnamed and only vaguely defined. However, several of them are thought to be deceased islanders whose personal histories are known to everyone . . . There is one, for example, whose presence is announced by the horrible smell of his decaying flesh. . . . An encounter with . . . these . . . beings . . . is extraordinarily terrifying for a Tobian. Although people are quite vague about the actual harm that may result from such an encounter, there is no doubt that it is one of the most frightening experiences of a lifetime. (1985, 274)

The reported sightings of one of these ghosts is linked to the symbolic function of tobacco. When tobacco supplies are low and it is difficult to meet the norm for sharing, this unnamed ghost is frequently sighted in the interior of the island. Black's description of him should make obvious why such sightings occur when they do. This ghost has the:

> . . . habit of simultaneously smoking anywhere from three to ten cigarettes. This tall, frightening figure can be seen from afar at night. His presence is betrayed by the row of glowing tips of those cigarettes, ten to twelve feet above ground. (1983, 485)

Black suggests that religious figures can function to project desired but otherwise antisocial behavior and serve to draw attention to the importance of hoarding tobacco as a possible threat to social integration. Tobacco symbolically makes things happen in their in-charge system of competency. Without that in-charge system, Tobian social order is threatened. The Tobian belief in, and reported sighting of, this ghost validates the fundamental structure on which their continued life depends. The mwih of this hoarding ghost gives a corporeal form to these norms when the value system is threatened by the absence of tobacco. Instead of disrupting social life and relationships, the ghost serves to diffuse potentially conflicting situations.

Siberian Shamans: Separation of the Sexes

Another example of how religious practices reflect the organizational principles of society is found among reindeer herdsmen of eastern and northern Siberia. Highly dependent on reindeer as food and for skins used to make shelters and clothing, these semi-nomadic populations lived in a hostile environment that was covered with snow much of the year. The practice that has drawn much attention is their use of fly agaric (*Amanita muscaria*) as a part of shamanistic rituals.

Amanita muscaria is a highly visible fungus (mushroom). It has a brilliant red cap flecked with white and a snowy white columnlike stalk. It has been known as fly agaric by Europeans since the Middle Ages, when it was observed that if flies sucked the juices from it they became stupefied for several hours (Wasson 1979).

Written documentation of fly agaric use by these herdsmen dates back to the seventeenth century, but it was not until 1905 that the first ethnographic account was published (Jocelson 1905). A consistent observation since then was that fly agaric was consumed only by males, although it was prepared by females. Among the Koryaks, for example, the mushrooms were gathered in late August by young girls who were also responsible for drying them. In other tribes, females were called on to chew the dried mushroom into a ball, after which it was swallowed by males. Females also prepared dried mushrooms for males as a drink, either in water, reindeer milk, or in the juices of different sweet tasting plants. Why was this a male-only practice? One explanation is that the ingredients of *Amanita muscaria* may produce spontaneous abortions (Schultes and Hofmann 1979). Whether this connection was recognized by these tribal herdsmen is not known, nor is it possible to determine if spontaneous abortions were defined as a "problem" by them. An alternative explanation is that the consumption of fly agaric, in addition to other items, functions as a marker in the division of labor. *Amanita muscaria* only grows in specific natural environments. It is found in association with birch and fir trees. The Siberian environment is not conducive to the growth of large forests with these trees. Even where this environmental prerequisite is found, this fungus is relatively rare. This natural scarcity, coupled with the fact that several mushrooms must be taken to produce a desired altered mental state, restricts their use to a limited number of people. Cultural distinctions everywhere recognize sex and gender differences. Thus, one could argue that the consumption of this naturally rare item provides a convenient visible marker between males and females.

Taking this interpretation somewhat further, one notes that a male-female distinction in the consumption of fly agaric is only a first, and rather crude, distinction. Between males its use was generally reserved for tribal elders and, more specifically, shamans. Thus, both age and status further restrict its use. Its consumption was believed to aid in communicating with the supernatural to predict the future or cure illness. The Koryaks believed in harmful spirits called *nimvits*, who can only be controlled by shamans who had taken fly agaric. Non-shaman males also ate the mushroom, but the powers they received were restricted to explaining illness, interpreting dreams, or revealing aspects of the upper and lower universe (de Rios 1984, 33). Other herdsmen societies in this area had visions of mushroom men whose numbers equalled the number of mushrooms eaten. Whatever the particular vision, the shared belief among these peoples was that the power to "know" or "see" beyond the objective world was attributed to the ingredients of the mushroom.

The use of fly agaric among Siberian shamans, in their role of "doctors," is quite different from the use of "drugs" in Western medicine. In Western *medicine* the physician diagnoses an illness and then may prescribe "drugs" as a course of treatment. In shamanism, it is the shaman who takes a drug or uses some other technique to alter consciousness. In this altered state he consults with the supernatural about the cause of the illness and the course of treatment. This information is then passed on to the patient. Spencer Rogers (1982) reports that the typical Yakut healing ceremony has three parts. After taking fly agaric, the shaman first attempts to bring down his spirit guardian. He sits, smokes, sings and bows to the four sides of the universe. The second stage is more active. During this stage he dances, jumps, sings, and beats a drum continuously. It is during this stage that he determines the cause of the illness. In the final stage, he exorcises the evil spirits which have caused the illness by frightening them and by sucking the afflicted part of the patient's body. The disease is then spit out, kicked, and driven away by the shaman. Finally he sits down and decides what sacrifices are needed to reward the spirit guardian who has cured the sufferer.

The problem of a limited supply of fly agaric was solved by some Siberian herdsmen. This was the discovery that the intoxicating ingredients are excreted in only slightly less potent form in the urine of the user (Schultes 1969). R. G. Wasson (1979) reports that urine was the preferred beverage, and the potency was usually gone by the fifth generation of drinkers.[5] Schultes and Hofmann (1979) maintain that poorer people waited outside the huts of those using the mushroom and, when the mushroom eater came out to urinate, they caught the urine in wooden bowls for their own use.

One might ask how this recycling was discovered. One possible explanation is that, because herdsmen rely on the reindeer, they have accumulated detailed information about their behavior (Wasson and Wasson 1957). For example, when reindeer eat lichen their appetite for human urine is increased, and they are attracted to areas close to dwellings where urine is deposited. The Koryak even carry a vessel on their belt to store urine. When they wished to attract reindeer, they emptied the contents on the snow. It is possible that users of the fly agaric noticed that when reindeer ate their yellow snow they became intoxicated. Of course, we will never know the answer to this question, but such questions can lead to some rather lively academic speculations.

The larger issue here is the function of using hallucinogens as part of shamanistic practices. Not all shamanistic religions employ drugs, but they all require shamans to achieve an altered state of consciousness when rendering decisions involving the super-natural. Since consciousness is subjective, evidence for an altered state is change in behavior. By all accounts, there are rather dramatic changes in behavior associated with fly agaric. Within a half hour after being ingested the user falls into a deep sleep from which the inebriant cannot be awakened. This lasts about two hours. After waking, there is often twitching and trembling of the limbs accompanied by a state of euphoria that lasts another three to four hours. This period is sometimes accompanied by confessions and the performance of extraordinary physical feats. While these out-of-the-ordinary behaviors clearly function as markers which distinguish shamans from non-shamans, can we conclude that hallucinogens are the source of shamanism as suggested by LaBarre? That is, are hallucinogens determinants of shamanism or is shamanism a necessary condition for the adoption of any hallucinogen? Depending on one's theoretical orientation, shamanism, like religion in general, functions to explain, predict, or control forces not otherwise understood. The marker for those functionaries through whom explanation, prediction, and control take place can be any characteristic that distinguishes them from others, including altered behaviors attributed to drug use, but one must exercise caution in concluding that drugs are responsible for shamanism.

Spirits for the Spirits

Siberians used fly agaric as a vehicle to converse with the supernatural. This practice disappeared with the sovietization of Siberian peoples. The drug used today is commercial vodka, and it has no sacred function. Seth Leacock's (1964) analysis of the Batuque, an Afro-Brazilian cult in northern Brazil, examines the use of alcohol as part of religious rituals. In contrast to the Siberians' use of fly agaric, the Batuque define their drinking as a directive from the supernatural.

The Batuque are a loosely knit group with no rigid procedures for membership and variable expectations for spirit possession. Their rituals and ideologies were brought into the New World by African slaves but have been greatly modified by Amerindian practices. The principal ceremony is a public performance during which members of the cult dance to the rhythms of drums, sing songs designed to call down the gods, and enter trance states which are interpreted as possessions by the deities (344). It is during these ceremonies that members drink alcoholic beverages. However, members deny that they drink. They insist that drinking is actually being done by the deities who possess them.

The Batuque have several deities, including spirits associated with animals. These deities have Portuguese names and are known collectively as *encantados*, or enchanted ones. Most of the Batuque are also Catholic but make a distinction between the encantados and Catholic supernaturals. The latter they regard as rather remote. Unlike the Western definition of the supernatural as a world of "good" *or* "evil," the encantados have a wide range of motivations and desires. It is believed that they like to dance and sing, smoke cigars, and drink alcoholic beverages. When people permit these spirits to fulfill their desires, the deities must reciprocate by doing favors. These include helping to cure illness, increasing economic prosperity, and favorably forecasting the future. If cult members become good at these activities they can become leaders and open up their own cult center.

Cult leaders are also curers. The techniques of curing show a striking similarity to the curing rituals found throughout the Amazon Basin. One exception to this similarity is that Batuque curers have substituted alcohol for the plant hallucinogens used in native ceremonies. Another distinction is that native curers use hallucinogens to induce possession, while Batuque drink alcohol after possession by the spirits. Leacock describes a typical curing session:

> A curing session begins with a brief period of singing and shaking the rattle, after which the cult leader is typically possessed by a steady stream of encantados, none staying over two or three minutes. Most of the encantados demand cachaca (white rum), and the curer drinks almost continuously for the hour or so that the session continues. He also smokes cigars, cigarettes or pipes, according to the preference of the encantado, and if a child encantado should descend may be given a soft drink. From time to time patients come forward for treatment and are whisked with the macaw feathers, saturated with smoke, and sometimes sucked as a prelude to being shown some object supposedly causing the trouble. Curing is always a solo performance, with only the curer being possessed and drinking. (346–347)

In addition to alcohol being consumed during curing rituals, the Batuque also drink at public meetings that are held every few weeks. The meetings attract both male and female "mediums" who begin to dance and sing about 9:00 in the evening. Cult leaders are usually the first to be possessed. They are followed by the mediums. Several encantados may be called during the meeting, at which time the dancer becomes possessed. Occasionally, members of the audience become possessed and join the mediums. The first encantados are usually the more important ones. They stay for a short period and do not drink. Later in the meeting the fun-loving encantados appear. They stay longer—several hours and sometimes several days—and like to drink. By three or four in the morning the dancers are usually in high spirits and the ceremony takes on an air of gaiety and fun.

Regardless of the amount of alcohol consumed, no "hangovers" are reported, even by those who do not normally drink outside of the ceremony. Drinking is prohibited on the day of the meeting. This is consistent with the belief that it is the spirit who does the drinking, not the drinking that brings on the possession by the spirit. The alcohol consumed at the public meetings may be provided by the cult leader, but more often each participant brings his or her own bottle. Those who have alcohol rarely share it with others. As Leacock notes, drinking is individualistic. Some members drink prodigious amounts; others abstain. Whether drinking or not, individual cult members behaved the same when possessed by the same spirit. Thus, there were no noticeable effects of alcohol on behavior.

From the description of the public ceremony one might conclude that the function of alcohol is to integrate the membership by facilitating interaction. However, as Leacock notes, the behavior of people in these ceremonies is the same, with or without the alcohol. Possessions are not aided by alcohol; and it could be argued that the music and dancing provide a greater stimulus for integration than does alcohol. Horton's suggestion that alcohol reduces anxiety is one alternative explanation. Cult members do have concerns about their economic and personal well-being but believe that the powerful encantados are watching out for them. Therefore, one might argue that it is this belief, not alcohol, that functions to reduce anxiety. Another possible explanation explored by Leacock is that the function of alcohol in this setting is related to the disparity between competency and expectations during the trance state. In the trance state, a person is the encantado. During the trance, one is supposed to answer questions, forecast the future, and solve problems. In addition, one is expected to display competency in speaking. To those with little education, these may be expectations that are difficult to achieve. Therefore, might alcohol function to reduce anxiety at public speaking, thus making it possible to meet these expectations? Unfortunately, this too fails as an explanation. In the sequence of possessions, the most articulate and most powerful spirits appear first. It is only later, when the fun-loving spirits arrive, that alcohol is used.

Leacock's study was presented here as an illustration of what can happen when one focuses on a single behavior. Had he been concerned with the function of religion rather than the function of drinking, could he have been more resolute in explaining the function of drinking? In all fairness, he does hint at a possible function, but it is cast in psychological and individualistic terms. He suggests that people with drinking "problems" can justify them as the actions of spirits. I would suggest that had Leacock begun his observations and analysis with the Durkheimian explanation of religion, he might have looked for parallels between the variety of spirits and the organizational principles (culture) of the participants. This, I maintain, would have encouraged him to compare the drinking practices within the public ceremony to drinking practices in general. Unfortunately, we are not privy to this information, but its absence only illustrates how important theory is in directing the range of observations that are made. In spite of this shortcoming, the comparison of Batuque and Siberian practices demonstrates how emic explanations of drugs vary as either a "cause" (independent variable) or "effect" (dependent variable) of supernatural intervention.

Ritual: The Huichol Peyote Hunt

The Huichol (wee-chol) live in the Sierra Madre mountains of western middle Mexico. The archeological record suggests that the Huichol or some other culture has been in this location at least 2000 years. Historical records indicate that they were first contacted by the Spanish around 1520, and the Spanish settled among them in the middle 1700s. Phil Weigand (1978) suggests that the area in which the Huichol live has historically attracted refugees escaping from Spanish and missionary control. Therefore, any consideration of *The* Huichol must acknowledge the influence of the Spanish, even though others have concluded that they represent a pristine culture (LaBarre 1990). The effects of Spanish colonialism can be seen in several of their practices, both sacred and secular. The present-day Huichol, like many other cultures, possess a composite of aboriginal and urban practices, along with cultural traits that have developed to cope with both internal and external conditions.

The Huichol numbered somewhere between thirteen and fourteen thousand in 1977 (Weigand, 102). Although there were probably fewer in the past, accurate estimates are not available. Even when contemporary census data are used, there are questions of validity. The Huichol live in an area surrounded by other Indian and Mestizo groups whom census officials often include in the Huichol population, and many Huichol have migrated into urban and town areas some distance from where they were born. Regardless of the accuracy of population estimates, the Huichol have been the subject of rather intense anthropological inquiry.

The first Western observer was Carl Lumholtz at the end of the nineteenth century. Lumholtz made three visits to the Huichol to collect symbolic and decorative art for the American Museum; he was followed by the German ethnographer Konrad Preuss, who spent nine months in 1906–07. In the 1930s, Robert Mowry Zingg and Otto Kleinberg carried out additional field work. They were followed by Barbara Myerhoff and Peter Furst in the 1960s. The one theme that binds all these research ventures together is an emphasis on religious life and practices. Furst (1978) suggests that this is more than idle fascination and is an accurate reflection of Huichol life. He argues that they do not make the same sacred-secular distinction found in Western culture. All their activities are imbued with some reference to the sacred, and this sacred reference has persisted from pre-Columbian times. Even formal Catholic Church practices cannot be understood without reference to Huichol interpretations. While there is no formally stated definition of religion, Furst equates Huichol religion with what exists in the heads of the Huichol—their worldview—not in ceremonies or practices which we, as outsiders, can observe.

The Huichol are subsistence agriculturalists. They use a slash-and-burn system for land clearance. Crops are interspersed within rows. Corn is mixed with beans in the same hole, with every fourth hole reserved for squash. The corn stalk serves as a pole for the beans. Family plots are worked together with friends, neighbors, and relatives. Varieties of corn are planted, depending on altitude and soil conditions. Planting begins in June, and weeding is carried out for the next six weeks. Crops are harvested in November. This planting cycle is accompanied by ardent ceremonies which formally focus on corn and squash. In addition, the Huichol raise cattle. In the past, cattle raising was not considered a safe investment. Periodic epidemics often resulted in whole herds being decimated. Today, because of vaccines, fewer animals are lost, and "cattle wealth" is becoming an indicator of social rank. In spite of the prestige value of cattle, meat is not part of the daily diet. Cattle are used as part of the fiesta system in which sponsors are required to sacrifice an animal. Thus, social rank is accumulated by sponsoring a feast, not just owning cattle.

The residential unit is a scattered system of rancheros organized into *comunidades*. The ranchero is a family unit, which at minimum consists of a man, his wife or wives, and their children. Some rancheros include extended kin as well. Inheritance rules make gender distinctions. Older sons inherit from fathers; older daughters inherit from mothers. Land use and farmsteads always go to the son of a man's first wife. Land itself cannot be owned and is controlled by the right of **usufruct**. In usufruct systems, land is held in common, and permanently abandoned land can be used by anyone. As long as the land is being used (even if it is temporarily abandoned because of their system of farming), land use is inheritable. That is, sons inherit the use of the land from their fathers, not the land itself. Women may own cattle that they have obtained through gifts or inheritance, and some women control large numbers of cattle.

The traditional political system has four offices: Gobernador, Juez, Capitan, and Alguacil or Alcaide. The Gobernador is the "mayor" and has decision-making powers in community matters. He and Juez preside over trials. The Capitan is the "police." He and his two assistants take orders from the Gobernador. The Alguacil or Alcaide and his assistants are the jailers. The "election" of these officers to their one-year, non-paid office is determined by the "dreams" of the *kawitero*, a man who knows everything. The kawitero is given a bottle of liquor and told to dream who the successors of these officials will be. His decision is final and never questioned.

In addition to these secular authorities there are five "Mayordomos," whose duty it is to carry the saints to and from the various festivals. Except for the Mayordomo del Cristo, who serves a five-year term, each official serves a one-year term without pay. They are "elected" to office through the dreams of the kawitero's two assistants. The mayordomos are present at trials and are part of all communal decisions.

This reliance on "sacred" personnel to determine governance personnel is guided by the belief that such decisions are made through—not by—traditional "holy" people. This same belief underlies the fiesta system, which is, in part, determined by formal Catholic traditions. Fiestas are hosted by an individual or a communidades but are open to all. Sponsoring a fiesta is one way to accumulate prestige. The host is required to sacrifice an animal, usually a cow. Even if the fiesta is community sponsored, someone is designated by the *Cantador* or shaman as host, and he is expected to sacrifice a cow. Shamans "dream" a host, and those so designated do not refuse. To do so, it is believed, would result in illness or death.

The fiesta system, as outlined by Otto Klineberg (1934), marks a series of events associated with agricultural cycles, the Catholic calendar, and traditional belief systems. He notes the following yearly fiesta cycle.

July: **Fiesta de la Virgen de Guadalupe**. Begins in the evening and lasts through the next day. Eating and drinking. Cow sacrificed in evening of first day. Chicken sacrificed the following morning.

August: **Fiesta de las Aguas**. Purpose is to control rain. Same as above but includes prayers to rain.

September: **Fiesta of the Squashes**. Young squash not eaten until after fiesta. Squash first offered to saints. No feasting the next day.

October: **Fiesta of the Green Corn (Elote)**. No new corn can be eaten prior to this fiesta. Must first be offered to saints. Men dress as children at dawn, followed by communal bathing. Eating and drinking throughout day.
The Peyote Hunt: Fifteen days' journey each way on foot (see details below).

November: **Fiesta of the Harvest**. Corn offered to saints. Eating of corn tortillas.

January: **Fiesta of the Peyote (Hikuli)**. Singing throughout night. Eating of peyote that was collected in October and preserved in the ground.

Huichol religion is a combination of traditional beliefs and Catholic practices. Traditional beliefs include several deities—God, the Sun, the Earth, the Moon, Fire, Water, the Sea, Corn Mother, and the "saints." (447) The most important saints are La Virgen de Guadalupe, La Purisima, Maria Soledat, San Sebastian, San José, San Antonio, Jesus, Santo Cristo, and San Isidro. No fiesta is held unless the saints are present.

Furst (1978) argues that the presence of Catholic saints in fiestas and other activities of the Huichol does not mean that the Huichol are Catholic.

A number of Christian observances have been incorporated, with major modifications, into the culture, but not, at least in the tradition-minded *comunidades*, at the expense of the indigenous ceremonials that, if not purely pre-Hispanic, at least bear a strongly pre-Conquest flavor. Ceremonies of Christian origin, such as holy week, have added to rather than replaced the great body of traditional ritual. Christian deities and saints,

often acknowledged and included in shamanic recitations and
ritual drama even outside of Catholic origin, have not displaced
but only augmented the indigenous pantheon. (22)

That Huichol religion reflects both traditional beliefs and catholic
practices should not surprise the reader. Rather, this **syncretism**
only reminds us that cultures that have been dominated by colonial
powers often adopt practices that have been thrust on them. The
process by which the powerless give the outward appearance of
assimilation to the more powerful but at the same time retain their
own practices is called **accommodation** (chapter 10). The earlier
discussion of the Native American *Church* illustrates this social
process. The test of traditional versus Hispanic-Catholic influence
comes not in the manifest presentations of saints and saint's days,
but in the worldview of practitioners.

To the Huichol, there is no distinction between "religion" and
everyday life. Natural phenomena such as rain, air, and fire are
personified as spiritual beings, as are animals and plants that are
part of their lives. These deities may be appealed to at any time for
a variety of reasons. As Myerhoff (1974) reports:

> . . . any deity may be asked for all that is necessary to life.
> Requests are usually specific and basic for good health, good
> fortune, children, safety, and so forth. A cumulative principle
> here is detectable in that the more deities one addresses and
> gives offering to, the better one's chances for success. (94)

These deities are bound together in a trinity that reflects both
history and present. The Huichol were, like all other North
American aboriginals, a hunting and gathering society. According
to their origin story, they originally lived in Wirikuta, some three
hundred miles south of their present location. Their ancestors lived
a life of harmony and tranquility in this location until they were
driven out. The trinity which represents this history is deer-maize-
peyote. The deer was the animal on which they depended for their
existence in their original home. Maize is the food on which they
presently depend. Peyote mediates between former and present life.
In other words, it is liminal.

These three elements are bound together by the Huichol to
explain life and success. Both maize and peyote are believed to have
been given by the deer. In order for maize to be grown, rain is
needed. Rain is obtained by Grandfather Fire (Tatewari), who must
be given peyote to carry out this task. However, peyote cannot be
"hunted" without first sanctifying the maize with deer blood; and
deer cannot be hunted without first consuming peyote.

Peyote, "good" or "proper" peyote, can only be obtained in one place. In October of each year there is a pilgrimage to Wirikuta to "hunt" this good peyote (*hikuri*). The pilgrims, or *peyoteros*, include only a small number of Huichol. This group includes both males and females and the old and young. The leader of the group is a shaman, a *mara'akáme*. The decision to join the pilgrimage is individual, as is the decision to participate in only part of the journey.

> Some participate in the rituals before and after the journey and take peyote at the various ceremonials, but are not willing to submit themselves to the intense hardships . . . required of the peyotero. . . . Others have gone five, ten, even twenty times. . . . Some go to Wirikuta in fulfillment of a vow, perhaps made in a moment of stress, or at the behest of a shaman when someone in the family fell ill. . . . The pilgrimage helps one attain whatever one desires—health, children, rain, protection from lightning and sorcerers, or divine intervention. . . . Above all, one goes to attain visions of great beauty, to hear voices of the spirits, the divine ancestors, and to receive their guidance. (Furst 1990, 150–151)

Others go to fulfill a requirement for becoming a mara'akáme. In addition to learning the details of myth and legend, to become a mara'akáme, one must make at least five journeys to Wirikuta. The number five is sacred to the Huichol. It signifies the four cardinal points and the sacred center, and it stands for "completion" (Benítez 1975, 68–69).

The three-hundred-mile trip was done on foot before modern transportation. Even with modern transportation:

> . . . they cover a terrain in which the most minute geographical features are known, given Huichol names, and completely incorporated into the religion. Mountains, caves, groves of trees, water holes, springs, rivers, and rocks, are among the "sacred places" visited by the Ancient ones during their exodus according to Huichol oral literature, and revisited by the present day (1966) Huichol during the peyote hunt. (Myerhoff 1974, 56)

The actual pilgrimage takes about two weeks, during which they stop at specific places where it is believed that the "First People" did various things. The Huichol believe that the journey is fraught with danger; therefore, the pilgrims must trust each other and the mara'akáme. During the pilgrimage the participants become deities and restrict earthly needs such as eating, drinking, sexual intercourse, and excretion. To become gods they must be pure. To accomplish purity they confess their transgressions before leaving and are renamed. Each confessed act is symbolized by tying a knot in a rope. Before leaving, this many-knotted rope is thrown into the fire. Their dependence on each other is ritually manifested by each participant tying one knot in another rope shortly before leaving. This rope is kept by the mara'akáme during the pilgrimage, and on return the knots are untied and the participants become mortal again.

Just prior to arriving in Wirikuta:

> . . . everything is equated with its opposite and reversed. The known world is backward and upside down: the old man becomes the little child; that which is sad and ugly is spoken of as beautiful and gay; one thanks another by saying, "You are welcome"; one greets a friend by turning one's back and bidding him or her good-bye. The sun is the moon, the moon is the sun. (Myerhoff 1978, 57)

This use of **cultural inversions**, or oppositions, are common to many religious rituals. The "normal" secular world is turned upside-down to remind participants of their liminal status as part of a ritual. On the peyote pilgrimage, the old become babies and male and female distinctions disappear. Behaviorally and symbolically the world is temporarily reversed (Babcock 1978). In Victor Turner's model, this is communitas, or anti-structure.

Having arrived at Wirikuta, the pilgrims begin their "hunt" for peyote. They stalk the peyote as one would a deer. Once sighted, the mara'akáme shoots it with an arrow, after which offerings are presented.

> . . . if one did not leave gifts and propitiate the slain Deer-peyote (just as one should propitiate the spirits of animals one hunts, the maize one harvests, and trees one cuts), Elder Brother would be offended and would conceal the hikuri (peyote) and withdraw them altogether, so that the next time the seekers would walk away empty-handed. (Furst 1972, 180)

The peyoteros weep with joy at having attained their goal, and with grief at having killed their brother. The roots of the plant are cut away and buried later; the peyote is removed and sliced by the mara'akáme, who gives a piece to his companions. The hole left by the absent peyote is then surrounded by offerings. After this initial ritual, the process of gathering peyote begins. The plants are dug up and placed in a basket or bag. At the end of the day, the pilgrims sit around the camp fire and eat segments of the best peyote. The visions they experience usually include vivid dancing colors, moving deer, spirits, saints, or some combination of these images. The specific visions are idiosyncratic, but the peyoteros would agree that whatever is seen places him or her into the divine scheme of things. In this experience one finds oneself and knows what it is to be Huichol. When enough peyote has been collected the pilgrims return home.

Peyote is usually eaten or drunk for ritual purposes during the dry season of the year. It is also used as a general-purpose medicine. It may be used to decrease pain or a fever, as a poultice for a wound, and to give one energy, endurance, or courage. Peyote may be given to a child over three years of age to predict whether they might become a mara'akáme. Peyote is also used as a trade item with other Indian groups. When used ritually, only a small amount is consumed, usually not enough to bring on visions. In this ritual context, it is accompanied by maize and deer meat or blood. Lastly, it may be consumed nonritually to produce visions, although this practice is mostly confined to shamans.

The reader should not conclude from this description that the Huichol are a peyote-centered society. Not all Huichol consume peyote and, for experienced users, peyote is reserved for special ritual occasions. Symbolically, peyote is an important *part* of Huichol worldview, but only when linked to maize and deer. Behaviorally, peyote gathering and consumption are a reflection of another part of their worldview that organizes cycles of activities into a calendar. Whether user or non-user, peyote is part of a consciousness which defines the boundaries between being Huichol and not being Huichol.

Ritual: The Organizational Charter

Thus far, the discussion of religion and magic has been illustrated by practices which have some reference to the supernatural. In each of the preceding examples, belief in supernatural forces or beings has functioned to explain or validate existing secular activities. However, not all cultural rules find their correspondence in belief and behavior systems that refer to some specific supernatural entity. How do we explain all those other beliefs or practices which make no claim on the supernatural? If one insists that belief in the supernatural defines religion, then the Huichol have more religion than Americans—or do they? This was one of the questions that led the structuralists such as Lévi-Strauss, Douglas, and Turner to focus on universal behaviors associated with both religion and the secular. Although Wallace suggested that religion always has ritual, this does not mean that **ritual, as a collectively prescribed repetitive set of behaviors**, is restricted to religion. Durkheim was correct in assuming that the rules of culture are made manifest in religion, but not all of those rules are expressed as religion. Depending on the culture, expectations may find expression in different institutional spheres. Therefore, it is necessary to go beyond the restrictions of the supernatural definition of religion if we are to understand culture.

Rituals are markers between human activities. Rituals may mark the transition of individuals from one status to another. This might include the movement from childhood to adulthood, from single to married, and from alive to dead. In American society, which is age graded, birthday rituals are performed to mark someone's acquiring a new age. We have identified this type of ritual as a rite of passage. Rituals also accompany transitions in activities that affect large numbers of people in a society. In American culture these rituals are called "holidays" (holy days). Some holidays are religious rituals. Others, such as Thanksgiving, Super Bowl Sunday, or the Fourth of July are not. Since the function of these rituals is to validate or explain the general or common rules of culture (the shared worldview), they have been named **rites of intensification**, or **rites of solidarity** (Chapple and Coon 1942, 507–528). Rites of passage may occur at any time. Birthdays and deaths are individual observances. In contrast, rites of solidarity are usually calendrical events. For example, the fiesta calendar of the Huichol accompanies agricultural transitions, from sedentary behavior to planting, from tending to harvesting, and then to resting. Fiestas, holidays, birthday parties, curing rituals, and church services are obvious examples of ritual performances. However, I would argue that there are other rituals that are equally important as markers between activities which can be called the rhythm of culture.

The Rhythm of Culture: The American Case

Human behavior is repetitious, and repetition makes human behavior predictable. In all cultures, people are permitted to do whatever they want, so long as what they do is not different from what other people do. When individuals behave outside of the expected normative framework, some social mechanism is brought to bear to "encourage" the transgressor to conform. More will be said on this topic in chapter 9; but for now, it is enough to state that these repetitive behaviors change over time as humans shift from one set of activities to another. For example, in American culture there are several behavioral calendars. A day may be divided into activity periods. Meals follow a set pattern: breakfast comes before lunch, and lunch precedes supper. Accompanying this eating cycle are appropriate foods. There is no nutritional reason that one could not eat mashed potatoes, green beans and salad for breakfast, but they are considered more appropriate for lunch or supper. Conversely, cereal, juice, bacon and eggs are considered "right" for breakfast. Breakfast is eaten to "get you going." Lunch is eaten to "keep you going." Nutritionally, these two meals make sense as a source of energy needed for future physical activity, but what of dinner or supper? Is there another calendar operating that has nothing to do with nutrition? In American *culture* there is another daily calendar based on activity. This might be envisioned as: non-work::work::non-work. Breakfast marks the boundary between non-work and work. Lunch divides work into two segments equidistant between the two non-work segments. Finally, dinner or supper marks the transition between work and non-work. Thus, the evening meal can be explained by a cultural fact, and one need not appeal to biology.

What if we add the drug alcohol into this calendar? In contemporary America its consumption is defined as appropriate or inappropriate depending on *when* it is consumed. It is appropriate to consume alcohol after work, not before. In American culture, those who violate this rule are defined as having a drinking *problem*. This time schedule and resulting definitions of deviance have not always characterized America. Joseph Gusfield (1987) argues that before the 1830s, drinking had a place in both the work and non-work settings because this distinction of time did not exist. With the industrialization of America, cultural time changed. Industrialization brought about fixed time distinctions between work, home, and leisure. Work took place in rigid organizational structures identified with controlled, orderly, and "rational" behavior. Leisure became the opposite of work. It was unserious, playful, "free" time; and it was only during this time that drinking was appropriate. Gusfield argues that this distinction between work and leisure is not uniformly observed in American culture. As he notes, there are certain occupations in which pre-industrial forms of organization still exist. In the construction industry:

> Drinking is more likely to occur within the work period. Beer and whiskey, but not wine, may be used during work time in any quantity and are not always seen as antithetical to the day's activity. Such occupational worlds have only partially "surrendered" to the routinized and controlled arenas of bureaucratic organization and factory discipline. (87)

Different types of drinks are also used as markers in the ritual of the evening meal. This meal requires a sequence of foods served on separate plates. The meal opens with soup or salad, followed by solids, and finishes with sweets. When alcohol is added, one notes a parallel sequence. Before the soup or salad, it is appropriate to drink distilled alcohol—the "cocktail" or aperitif—along with hors d'oeuvres.[6] During the meal, it is appropriate to consume only fermented alcohol, beer or wine. On completion of the meal, the circle is closed with the after-dinner distilled drink, which would include a sweet liqueur. When appropriateness or etiquette is considered, one can understand the meal as a ritual, the parts of which are marked by the consumption of different "things." This could be visualized in table 7.3.

Table 7.3.

The Evening Meal as Ritual

Time Periods		
Before Meal	**Meal**	**After Meal**
Little foods distilled alcohol	Soup or salad—solid food—sweet fermented alcohol wines appropriate for the solid food	No food distilled alcohol often sweet

Not all evening meals of all Americans follow this pattern. I would hypothesize that a survey of American households would reveal that the cultural expectations for the meal ritual are more closely followed in practice than the alcohol ritual. Yet Americans would not find the above alcohol sequence to be bizarre or "abnormal," even though they never practice it themselves. Cultural rules exist as part of a worldview. These are rules which guide how we think about the world as an orderly place. When behavior is called for, they guide the actions of people.

If we go beyond the daily calendar to the weekly calendar, one notes that drinking is most frequent on the bridge between the work week and the non-work weekend. Friday night is the drinking night.[7] Just as breakfast bridges non-work/work and does not involve alcohol, Sunday night bridges a weekly non-work/work cycle and is not a drinking night. Underlying this pattern is the rhythm of drinking in American culture. Drinking is appropriate in the transition from work to non-work. Drinking is inappropriate during the non-work to work transition. The uncovering of this rule by the social scientist is not, however, always recognized by participants. In other words, this rule is not recognized as an emic explanation. Etically, one observes that drinking is not random. It follows a pattern, the violation of which results in emic sanctions. It is the sanctions or the morality of drinking that are recognized within society, not the underlying rule itself. Those who drink outside ritually prescribed cultural times violate a ritual expectation. Punishments for this violation may vary. Offenders may be fired, shunned, or sent to therapy or to jail. Whatever the specific sanction, an understanding of the drinking ritual brings us closer to understanding societal definitions of deviance. Deviance is not the act of drinking in and of itself but rather a violation of the "normal" times for drinking, which are themselves liminal or in-between times.

The explanation for drinking offered above could well be extended to the yearly calendar in the United States. For example, whether one drinks or not, New Year's Eve is recognized as a time for drinking and drunkenness. The "office party" which usually takes place at Christmastime is another event where drinking and drunkenness are excused. One does not have to be Irish to know that excessive drinking is permissible on St. Patrick's Day. University students are, of course, aware that drinking is associated with Spring break. The most colorful display of "time out" is officially celebrated in three states—the event of Mardi Gras.

Mardi Gras, or Carnival, is a festive occasion which is celebrated in many parts of the Western world. Although associated with the Christian observance of Lent, it is not, strictly speaking, a religious event. Historically, Carnival was a time of jubilation at the new year. The old lunar calendar did not correspond to the solar year. Because of this, it was necessary to insert extra days in December. These days were literally "outside of time." During this "time out," ordinary customs and laws did not apply. For example, during the Roman feast of Saturnalia, masters and slaves traded places and feasting, revelry, and drunkenness contributed to the mad pursuit of pleasure. Although Mardi Gras (Fat Tuesday) applies literally only to Shrove Tuesday (the day before Lent), the celebration begins eleven days earlier and ends on Tuesday. This eleven-day period is an example of Turner's communitas. During this period of anti-structure, normal constraints and expectations are suspended. If sobriety is the norm, then drunkenness prevails. If clothing is the norm, nudity is encouraged or tolerated. The masks worn by revellers hide their community identities and often mock figures in positions of power or prestige. In community, gender is acknowledged in clothing. During Mardi Gras, cross-sex dressing is permitted without sanction.[8] Of course, on the Wednesday after Mardi Gras things return to community.

In American culture, there are other calendrical periods of liminality. Thanksgiving, not an official religious holiday, marks the end of the growing season and the beginning of death. While drunkenness is not a characteristic of this holiday, another inversion is practiced—namely, gluttony. Religious Christmas, which under the old calendar corresponded to Saturnalia, was a celebration of birth, complete with fertility symbols associated with contemporary secular Easter (for example, rabbits and eggs). Secular Christmas is marked by several inversions from community. Trees normally grown outside the house are brought inside at Christmas. People usually enter and exit a house through the door, but Santa Claus makes his ingress and egress through the chimney. In community, goods and services that are normally exchanged for a price are given away at Christmas. The point is that all cultures have periods that are neither one time or another—periods that are "betwixt and between." Drugs may or may not be used during these periods, but one might suggest that where drugs are available, the frequency of their use will vary according to the timetables of that culture.

One final issue on American drinking practices is where drinking occurs. Ray Oldenberg (1989) argues that cafes, coffee houses, and bars are "a third place" between home and work—that is, they are neither home nor work, with all the behavioral expectations each requires. We have already noted that qat parties take place either in a specially prepared room in one's house or in a room that has been specially built for this purpose. Beer gardens in Bulawayo are set apart from home or work, while shebeens, with their negative reputation, are part of someone's house. Ndolamb Ngokweay's (1987) description of palm wine consumption among the Lele, who live in the Kasai region of the Republic of Zaire, illustrates the linkage between drinking and space. Palm wine and water are the main beverages of the Lele. Palm wine is made by tapping the crown of the palm tree. The sap is naturally converted into wine (Obayemi 1976). Both the production of wine and access to the trees are defined as a male domain. Palm wine is drawn twice daily—once in the morning and once at night. It is brought back to the village in the late afternoon or evening, the appropriate drinking time. Lele divide time into work/leisure, and it is appropriate to drink only during leisure time. The work activities include agriculture, hunting, weaving, and house-building. Wine may be consumed while making combs or carving bowls, activities the Lele define as taking place during "spare" time.

The Lele do not drink while eating, but they do at social events and during visitations by traditional chiefs, administrative officers, and military or police officers. "Ordinary" drinking occurs at the *mapula*, a small cleared area in the forest or savannah. At this "third place," all-male groups meet after drawing palm wine and before returning to the village. These informal gatherings stand in contrast to the *mabandna*, a formal meeting called to discuss issues of importance to larger social units, such as the village, clan, or lineage. These meetings are defined as "work," and hence no drinking occurs at them.

The identification of drinking as an appropriate activity for in-between time is reflected in the appropriate physical location of drinking places. Why might Americans become quite exercised if someone were to propose putting a bar in a residential neighborhood or in the work "place"? The allocation and use of space is as much a part of worldview as are beliefs and values. The study of the cultural meanings of space is called **proxemics**. Although a somewhat new specialization, it promises to add yet another instrument to unlock the rules which govern both actions and beliefs.

Religion and the Churched

Social scientists have suggested several alternative schemas for the social manifestations of religion, the organizational groupings of people into church(es). Max Weber (1963), the German sociologist, suggested a simple typology ranging from sect to church. The **sect** is a voluntary adult grouping, in which membership requires the adoption of a particular doctrine or practice. In contrast, **church** is a more inclusive grouping that encourages membership from society in general and requires very few commitments to specific doctrines or practices (65). Since Weber, others have elaborated on these simple distinguishing criteria and have added the term "cult." The popular definition of the cult is a small religious group having occult ideas, lacking a formal or bureaucratic structure, and led by a **charismatic** leader. Charisma is a Greek word meaning gifted. A charismatic leader is one who is believed to have special powers to control the members of the cult. This definition of cult is the least acceptable among social scientists, as it is the one most frequently used by the American press to describe "bizarre" group practices. For some social scientists, the cult is a loosely knit *urban* group made up of persons who share some common view of some *specific* aspect of the supernatural. In this definition, a charismatic leader is not necessary, and members may simultaneously belong to conventional churches (the Batuque offer an example). A third perspective views the cult as the beginning phase of an entirely new religion. Charles Glock and Rodney Stark (1965) define the cult as:

> religious movements which draw their inspiration from other than the primary religion of the culture, and which are not schismatic movements in the same sense as sects whose concern is with preserving a purer form of the traditional faith. (245)

This definition has gained acceptance by many sociologists of religion. The emphasis on change and evolution of new groupings is certainly consistent with the recent history of "religious" movements within the United States. The emergence of groups such as the Moonies, Hare Krishnas, Transcendental Meditation, Scientology, Black Muslims—not to mention the large number of television evangelists—seems to suggest that Established Religion is being challenged by alternative belief and behavioral systems. The research questions most asked from this typology are the social correlates of membership in church, sect or cult. The general finding is that membership in these three types are correlated with social class. The higher the social class, the more likely one would belong to a church. The lower the social class, the more likely one would belong to a sect or cult (Stark 1972; Demerath 1965).

Underlying the research findings of correlations between membership in specific church types and social variables (such as income, education, age, gender, and so forth) is a more general theoretical question. Durkheim's observation that "religion" mimics and verifies culture suggests that the organization of society is the independent variable that determines the dependent variable, namely, religious beliefs and practices. In contrast to that view, Max Weber (1958) suggested that it is religion that determines society, or at least some parts of society. Weber's thesis was that the shift from Catholicism to Protestantism was accompanied by a different view of the world that made capitalism possible. In Weber's view, Protestantism is the independent variable and capitalism the dependent variable.

At a more abstract level in this debate between the Durkheimian and Weberian views of religion is the question of the priority of thought or action. Does what we believe determine what we do, or does action determine belief? This question underlies much of the research on American adolescent drug use and religion. A review of this research illustrates the difficulty of determining which of these models is more accurate.

Drug Use and the Churched

The concern about drug use among American youth emerged as part of a larger interest in delinquency. Until the 1960s, drug use among adolescents was low and therefore attracted little interest. With the increased use of drugs beginning in the 1960s, drug use was incorporated into existing measures of delinquent behavior. The pre-1960s research failed to support any influence of religion on delinquency. Religiosity is measured by frequency of church attendance. Therefore, knowing how often one attends church does not enable one to predict delinquent behavior. Travis Hirshi and Rodney Stark (1969) confirmed this general finding but did observe that acceptance of conventional authority and moral values was negatively related to delinquency. Thus, it is not low or infrequent church attendance (behavior) that determined delinquency, but acceptance of secular authority (beliefs). This conclusion was challenged by Steven Burkett and Melvin White (1976), whose research focused on religion and the use of alcohol and marihuana. They found that the higher the church participation (behavior), the lower the use of alcohol and marihuana (behaviors). In addition, they found that all three of these behaviors were related to the belief that the use of these substances was "sinful," a belief that was more strongly related to "belief in the supernatural" than it was to worldly authority. If the reader is now thoroughly confused by these findings, he or she should not feel alone. In reviewing the social science literature, one is often confronted with similar conflicting or contradictory conclusions. It is precisely this kind of reporting that contributes to the social scientists' well developed tolerance for ambiguity.

One way to resolve differences in these findings is to recognize that those small pieces of behavior or beliefs measured in surveys are but part of a larger complex system. The United States is an urban society, and urban societies are characterized by variations in behavioral and belief systems, some of which are expressed in different "religions." As previously noted, the definition of alcohol use changed in the United States from the Colonial Period to the middle 1800s. That broad change was reflected in anti-drinking doctrines of some churches (Gusfield 1963). Today this proscriptive stance is found among sectlike Protestants, Baptists, and Methodists. In contrast, Catholics, Episcopalians, and Lutherans have adopted secular drinking practices. Because there are variations in doctrine between religious groups, the obvious question is whether drinking behaviors vary by church membership.

Hart M. Nelson and James F. Rooney (1982) surveyed 4,500 high school seniors from six northeastern states. Their survey instrument contained questions on religious affiliation and drug use. The affiliation responses were divided into three categories. "Proscriptive Protestants" included Protestant sects such as the Black Muslims, along with Baptists and Methodists. All these churches expressly forbid drinking. Churches that do not have formal drinking prohibitions where divided into two categories. Members of the Lutheran, United Church of Christ, Presbyterian, and Episcopal churches were designated "Other Protestant," while Catholics, Jews, and those who indicated no religious affiliation were assigned the "Other" designation.

Nelson and Rooney hypothesized that those affiliated with proscriptive protestant churches, who attended church more frequently, would be less likely to drink alcohol. Other Protestants and Catholics, because of the church's neutral or secular stance on drinking, would have increased drinking patterns. Attendance was divided into three categories. "Low" attendance was less than once a month; "moderate" attendance was at least once a month; and weekly attendance was classified as "high." Drinking was measured by asking whether the respondent had ever used beer or hard liquor. Table 7.4 shows the relationships between attendance and affiliation on the consumption of beer and hard liquor.

The general finding is that as attendance increases, the percentage of those who drink beer or hard liquor decreases. In addition, as attendance increases for Proscriptive Protestants, the percentage of beer and hard liquor drinkers decreases more dramatically when compared to Other Protestants. The only deviation from this general finding is the Episcopalians. Eighty-three percent of the low attenders drink/drank beer compared to 90 percent of the high attenders. But note that some of these changes are rather modest when contrasted to the overall use. With only a few exceptions—high attendance sectlike and Baptists—considerably more than half the respondents drink/drank beer and hard liquor.[9] If one disregards church affiliation and participation, the cultural pattern is some experience with drinking, regardless of "religion."

Table 7.4.
Percent Reporting the Use of Alcohol (ever) by Combined Categories of Religious Preference and Attendance

	Percent Reporting the Use Of:					
	Beer			Hard Liquor		
Religious Preference	Categories of Attendance			Categories of Attendance		
Proscriptive Protestant	Low	Moderate	High	Low	Moderate	High
Sectlike (293)	85	76	43	77	55	43
Baptist (270)	86	86	47	71	64	43
Methodist (328)	88	77	60	74	65	48
Other Protestant						
Lutheran (188)	87	81	81	75	71	56
United Church of Christ (119)	89	83	68	86	63	68
Presbyterian (172)	86	80	81	75	77	69
Episcopal (125)	83	88	90	80	79	79
Other						
Catholic (2976)	89	90	83	79	80	70
Jewish (88)	76	55	100	83	64	67
None (269)	89	79	64	79	71	18

Source: Hart M. Nelson and James F. Rooney. 1982.

The variations between church categories offer some slight advantage when predicting drinking from attendance. The variation in drinking beer for Proscriptive Protestants can be explained 14 percent of the time if we control for attendance.[10] For other Protestants and Catholics, this prediction is less than 1 percent. For hard liquor use among Proscriptive Protestants, it is possible to predict drinking with 7 percent accuracy by knowing attendance. In this same category, both Catholic and Other Protestant drinking can be predicted with only 1 percent accuracy. Obviously, something other than these two variables is contributing to an explanation of drinking by adolescents. In the debate between the Durkheimian and the Weberian models, these findings suggest that "religion" and "church" doctrine do not determine drinking behavior. Conversely, it is not possible to conclude that drinking behavior determines doctrine. Thus, we are left with the uneasy interpretation that the overlap between doctrine and drinking is accidental or spurious.

Conclusion: Drugs and the Sacred

A theme that runs through the observations of religion is that drug use is restricted to specific statuses within the institution of religion. In shamanistic religions, it is usually the shaman, or those who are potentially shamans, who consume drugs. For whole cultures, drug use is often confined to those periods that fall between or outside the "normal" time sequence of activities. On close examination of drug "time" or drug-taking status, one notes that each is a reference to times or statuses that are set apart in some way from the "normal" or everyday. This distinction defines, both for participants as well as students of religion, the sacred dimension of life. Just as drugs may be required substances for the sacred, so too may drugs be prohibited. In cultures where drugs are rare or out of the ordinary, their use by sacred statuses or during sacred periods serve to distinguish them from the ordinary. Where drugs are a part of the ordinary, their use may be prohibited by sacred doctrine. For example, the prohibition of alcohol or tobacco by Proscriptive Protestants is an inversion of the "normal" in American culture. In either case, the reference is to drugs.

The drug-sacred linkage is only one of many possible ways to mark the boundaries between religion and the "normal." Out-of-the-ordinary behaviors such as music, dance, clothing, and rituals have been, and are, used to serve this same function. This also applies to non-drugs as well. The prohibition of certain foods, dancing, musical instruments, hair styles, jewelry, and other traits is another way of stating that these activities are different from the everyday and "normal." Thus, in spite of the attraction of citing drugs as part of magic and religion, it must be acknowledged that they are not universal markers. When drugs are already part of a culture's trait inventory, they may serve this purpose. If they are not, other practices or things may perform this same function.

In summary, belief in the supernatural is a cultural universal. Humans live in both objective and subjective worlds, and much of the subjective may be incorporated into a culture's "religion." However, religion is only part of the total cultural experience. To expand our understanding of culture, it is necessary to explore the objective dimension of the human condition and how drugs fit into behaviors related to "making a living." In the next chapter we shall address those activities which make up the economic system of a culture.

Endnotes

[1] The concept "taboo" is used in reference to any act the commission of which is believed to result in automatic punishment. Violation of the incest taboo in modern American culture is believed to result in children with diminished capacity, either physical or mental. This taboo is automatically enforced by a belief in the "laws" of genetic inheritance, even though these may be imperfectly understood by those who evoke them. The result is that most Americans do not violate the incest rule.

[2] The others are prayer, music, physiological exercise (the one in which we are interested), exhortation, reciting a code, simulation, mana, taboo, feasts, sacrifice, congregation, symbolism, and ritual.

[3] The clan is a unilineal descent group in which kinship ties, and hence group membership, are determined by a shared ancestor. The clan is different from a lineage. While both use unilineal descent principles to determine relatedness, the clan's ancestor is a plant or animal. This is the clan "totem" or symbol of identification. Membership in the clan is periodically reinforced by gatherings which celebrate the clan totem.

[4] The astute reader may find this discussion revealing about contemporary American society. "Cults" proclaiming direct communication with the supernatural, holistic medicine with its rejection of the separation of mind and body, channelling, appeals to self esteem and self actualization, parapsychology, out-of-body experiences, and the use of hallucinogens (to name but a few) are all behavior manifestations which reject the established order and science as a representation of that order.

[5] Wasson reports a second method for obtaining second-hand fly agaric. When a reindeer is found that shows signs of having eaten this delicacy, it is held down until the behavioral effects disappear. Then it is killed and eaten.

[6] As Gusfield reminds us, the word *hors d'oeuvres* literally means "outside the main work."

[7] An interesting aside that requires observation is the designation of Wednesday evening as an occasion for drinking. "Over the Hump" or "Hump Day" is celebrated at parties or public drinking places and marks the bridge between the first and second part of the week.

[8] A rather amusing note appeared in the newspaper reporting the arrest of a drunken man who was walking nude in a New Orleans street. The police commented that if he had waited one day for the beginning of Mardi Gras, he would not have been arrested.

[9] A puzzling finding is the "None" religious preference category. No explanation is given by the authors in reference to attendance by these no-preference respondents. Nonetheless, only 18 percent of the "nones" who were high attenders had used hard liquor.

[10] The percentage figures presented here are for the Eta correlation coefficient. This coefficient is similar to r, as discussed in chapter 2. Predicting one variable from knowledge of another can be expressed as a percent if the Eta coefficient is squared.

Quechua couple (chapter 3) chewing coca and sharing *chicha* (chapter 9). Photo by Catherine J. Allen.

A Tobi chief (chapters 4, 7) rolling a cigarette. Photo by Peter Black.

Patrons in an opium den (chapter 6), New York City, c. 1925. Photo: UPI/Bettmann.

Members of a burial society at the beer gardens in Bulawayo (chapter 6). Note containers of beer. Photo by Harry Wolcott.

Huichol *peyoteros* (chapter 7) collecting peyote at Wirikuta. Photo by Peter Furst.

Ban Lum villagers (chapter 8) preparing a field for opium poppy planting. Photo by E. Paul Durrenberger.

A Jamaican harvesting ganja (chapter 8). Photo by Melanie C. Dreher.

Making a Living
The Economics of Drugs

he constant interplay between theory and research has several consequences. The theory may be accepted or rejected, or the theory might be revised to include contradictory research findings. The unilineal evolutionary theories of the nineteenth century were rejected at the beginning of the twentieth century and replaced by historical particularism and functionalism. Evolutionism lay dormant for the next forty years until it was "rediscovered" and revised. The most articulate proponent of the "new" evolutionism was Leslie White (1900–1975). White argued that there is a direction to **general evolution**, and this direction is provided by technology. Technology is the system by which energy is extracted from nature. Accumulated innovations through diffusion or independent invention led to greater control over energy, which in turn modified behavioral norms and cultural values. White's (1949) "law" of cultural evolution states:

Culture has grown as the amount of energy harnessed per capita per year has been increased. But amount of energy is not the only significant factor in cultural development, although it is the most important and fundamental one. The means by which energy is harnessed is also significant. This factor is expressed in the efficiency of tools and machines, and in the social organization of their use. With the amount of energy remaining constant, the amount of needserving goods and services produced will vary with the efficiency of expenditure of the energy. (377)

White's argument is that not all parts of culture are equally important, and in a causal sense, some parts determine others. Unlike the nineteenth-century evolutionists, White rejected the idea that there were specific stages of evolution or that specific parts of culture (religion, political organization, or kinship, for example) followed any particular predefined evolution. Instead, he insisted that variations in culture reflected incremental changes in the ability to harness and control energy. The result was a wide variety of cultural adaptations which White argued could be explained by one general theory.

White was not the first to propose a theory which placed technology and the means of production as the independent variable. A consequence of eighteenth-century European industrial change was reflected in several theories that emphasized evolution and competition. Darwin's theory of natural selection was one product of the nineteenth century. Karl Marx (1818–1883)[1] was another. His classic work, *Das Kapital* (1867), argued that history is divided into stages that reflect dominant modes of production. The mode of production includes three parts: technology, the division of labor associated with that technology, and the associated relationships between people in the division of labor. Marx's theory of economics assumed that the mode of production determines all other relationships within a society. He observed that humans differ from other animals in that they are capable of producing what they need to survive (technology). At the same time humans share a characteristic with all other animals, namely, they compete with each other for scarce resources. The function of the division of labor was to increase the productivity of technology, thereby reducing scarcity and ultimately eliminating competition.

Marx's analysis was limited to historical Western Europe. He noted that during the period from feudalism to capitalism different "economies" were linked to different governmental systems. What these governmental systems had in common was that each had a ruling class that controlled the mode of production. This led to the division of society into two broad "classes." One class, the **bourgeoisie**, controlled the means of production. The other class, the **proletariat**, were subservient to the bourgeoisie. Underlying this division is the assumption that competition between these classes for control over the means of production is inevitable. The eventual outcome of this conflict is the emergence of a new non-class, non-competitive governing system.

Marx's model has been adopted by some social scientists in a form known as **conflict** theory or the conflict model. In contrast to the functional model, the conflict model assumes that society is unstable. Because the means of production is regulated by those who do not produce, there is a constant effort by those in control to exploit workers (the proletariat). Because workers lack control over the means of production, they experience alienation from their work. For Marx, and the contemporary students of Marx, the social world is little more than the projection of an unsubstantiated view of nature as gnashing teeth and claws dripping with blood, a view that reflected the confusing and anomic state of a changing nineteenth-century Europe where "survival of the fittest" was taken literally. When this perspective is applied cross-culturally, it falls far short of having universal explanatory value. Yet, in spite of these shortcomings about human "nature," Marx was one of the earliest to systematically explore the hypothesis that technology determines cultural configurations. I will return to this model in chapter 10 where we explore explanations for legislation prohibiting the use of drugs.

Leslie White's revision of evolutionary theory influenced several social scientists. Julian Steward (1902–1972) proposed a theory of change that emphasized the relationship between technology *and* local environments as the crucial linkage for understanding **specific evolution**. This he called "cultural ecology" (Steward 1955). In contrast to White's general theory of evolution, Steward was concerned with the cultural consequences of adaptations to local environments. Those practices which permit people to deal effectively with local environments he calls **cultural core**. These would include technology, division of labor, practices related to land use and settlement, and any other activities which directly relate to exploitation of local environments. Outside of these practices are others which are less important as adaptations. These would include legends, myths, clothing styles, and decorations. The term he used to describe these practices is **secondary features**. Because both technology and local environments can and do vary, Steward suggested that evolution is **multilineal**—that is, different cultures experience different evolutionary histories. Although different, what one notes in the theories of both White and Steward is an agreement that the way(s) technological systems extract energy from environment(s) is the prime mover of culture change.

The most recent contributor to the materialist approach is Marvin Harris (1979). He calls his theory **cultural materialism**. He accepts the priority of technology as the prime mover and adds population size to the equation. He suggests that modes of production determine modes of reproduction. As production increases, so does population size. Increasing population size in turn puts more pressure on the mode of production, which results in greater environmental exploitation. This intensification of production results in new social practices and cultural patterns which are supported by changes in beliefs, values, and ideology. In other words, what people think is a consequence of what they do to balance out the demands of population and the abilities of technology. Harris suggests a cost benefit model as the basis of change. Changes occur when they offer an adaptive advantage to culture, when they ". . . increase the energy flow per capita and/or reduce reproductive wastage" (1979, 71). If the change results in a reduction of costs, then it is adopted. If not, then "traditional" practices will continue.

Harris' view that beliefs and thoughts are the result of materialistic concerns stands in bold contrast to models which suggest that thinking determines behavior. For example, Mary Douglas (chapter 7) interpreted Hebraic prohibitions against eating pigs as a reflection of cognitive or "thinking" categories. Because pigs did not fit these mental categories they were defined as "dirty" or "polluted." Harris rejects such "mentalistic" explanations and insists that food prohibitions reflect materialistic concerns. Pigs are prohibited because they compete with humans for certain scarce resources (they eat the same foods as humans and hence are competitors). Harris uses this same model to explain "sacred" cows (1966). The Hindu prohibition against eating meat is an emic justification for the cost benefits which come from not eating cattle. Cows are not competitive with humans. They do not eat human food. But the milk they provide is consumed by humans, and their dung is used as fuel. Thus, a live cow produces a continual supply of energy while eating the cow has only short-term energy benefits.

The attraction of the materialistic theories of culture is that they can be tested through empirical methods. Energy can be translated into calorie units. "Work" can be measured by hourly or daily inputs. Environmental energy potential can be estimated and populations can be counted. These are variables that can be translated into numerical values and thus have the potential for constructing probability or causal models.

In spite of some differences, the materialistic approaches share several assumptions in common. The most fundamental of these is that culture is the adaptive strategy employed by humans. In other animals, adaptation takes place through genetic selection for characteristics that fit the animal for its environment. In humans, technology manipulates environments to make them consistent with genetic characteristics. Thus, humans are able to live in a wide variety of environments because their modes of adaptation go beyond the limitations of genetic determination. Human adaptation is therefore **extrasomatic** (outside the body). From this it follows that variations in culture are a reflection of this process. At the most fundamental level, the mode of production (technology) determines the mode of reproduction. The number of people in any society is a direct result of the ability of technology to produce food and energy sources. If this system fails, the population will not survive. If there is an increase in food and energy, the population will increase. However, the other parts of culture—the institutional arrangement of statuses, ideologies, beliefs, and other practices—must be consistent with the basic relationship between technology and environment. Thus, for the materialists, technology is the independent variable that determines and explains all other non-technological practices.

The difficulty with the materialistic perspective is that it may exclude a wide variety of human behaviors. In previous chapters, it was noted that drug use occurred in a variety of settings. As a non-food, non-energy trait, drug use does not appear to qualify directly as an adaptive practice. This also may be said of other practices such as games, play, art, music and other manifestations of what may be called expressive culture. In and of themselves, these practices do not seem to contribute to effective or cost beneficial adaptive strategies, yet they persist as cultural practices. Because we do find continued drug use, and on the surface these practices seem to contradict the materialistic perspective, we are obliged to examine in more detail how drugs fit into the adaptive strategies of different cultures. In compliance with the scientific method, we must attempt to falsify the materialistic perspective. That humans engage in practices that are both "rational" (directed at maximizing adaptive efforts) and "irrational" (non-cost benefit) can be tested by examining that institutional arrangement most closely aligned with the technology-environment nexus, namely, economics.

Formal and Substantive Economics

Formal economic theories (those reflecting the worldview of industrialized urban societies, or more specifically the **market mentality**) is based on three assumptions (Beals and Hoijer 1971, 316). One is "maximization." This assumption is that people will seek to get the highest rewards or benefits from production. Further, maximization will be achieved through "rational" means. Lastly, supply and demand determine the value of what has been produced. While these assumptions may be useful in understanding economic systems in industrial Western cultures, the question is whether they can be applied to non-Western and non-industrial societies. In cultures without markets regulated by formal money systems, the *business* of culture must go on, or they will become extinct. Karl Polanyi (1947, 1957) was the first to inform social science of another type of economics that does not assume a market mentality.

> The substantive meaning of economics derives from man's dependence of his living upon nature and his fellows. It refers to the interchange with his natural and social environment, in so far as this results in supplying him with the means of material want and satisfaction. . . . The latter (formal economics) derives from logic, the former (substantive economics) from fact. The formal meaning implies a set of rules referring to choice between alternative uses of insufficient means. The substantive implies neither choice nor insufficiency of means.

In contrasting these two economic models, George Dalton (1961) suggests that the formal model developed in nineteenth century Western culture where selling and buying took place in the market. The market during this period was unregulated by any principle other than supply and demand; there was no organized labor; and the economic units (individuals, firms) were decentralized. Where this model fails as a cultural universal is when applied to cultures without markets, or more specifically, those without the market mentality. Both in non-market systems and some "economic" activities in Western culture, the substantive model can be used. In non-market systems one finds either special-purpose money or no money at all, in contrast to all-purpose money that is used in market systems. Non-market systems lack a combination of external and internal trade within the same market, and there is no market for labor or land. This is not to say that goods and services do not get distributed in these kinds of cultures, only that this distribution is not determined by an impersonal market characterized by maximizing profits, rationality, and the forces of supply and demand.

Economy as Culture

From the social science perspective, economy refers to a range of human activities directed at the production, distribution, and consumption of goods and services. In contrast to the formal models and deductive theories of Western academic economics, which frequently assume psychological and individual motivation, social scientists are concerned with how each of these activities is organized, what they mean to those engaged in them, and how they articulate with the society or culture within which they are practiced. In this sense, all cultures have economies, but not all cultures have specialized and separate economic institutions. For example, the Yanomamö produce ebene in groups of village adult males. It may be distributed as part of political alliance or as a trade good, but its consumption is part of the religious domain. The distribution of tobacco for Tobians is part of their worldview which distinguishes competent from incompetent people, just as kava is an important symbol of inherited political distinctions for some Polynesian societies. Because the "economics" of non-urban societies is not emically distinguished from other activities, when social scientists refer to economics they use an etically derived distinction, based on rules and expectations, that focuses on goods and services. Thus, economics is one institutional arrangement of culture, whether or not it is recognized as such. This can be analytically and behaviorally separated from the social groupings whose behavior reflects these rules. In some cultures these groups may be family or kinship based, church based, or based on age groups. In other societies, such as Western urban societies, these groupings may be observed in factories, sales organizations, advertising firms, stock markets, and other specialized associations. To understand economics in this broad sense, it is necessary to look beyond the social manifestations of cultural rules. All societies have rules governing the production of goods and services—whether or not they have factories. That some societies have formal markets and money while others lack these traits does not mean that one regulates distribution and the other does not. That some societies have formal written rules governing consumption and others do not is not evidence for the conclusion that some societies fail to regulate the consumption of goods and services. As used here, economic systems are a cultural universal. We can visualize this in table 8.1. With this distinction in mind, we can now review some of the social science research on the economics of drugs in different cultures.

Table 8.1.

The Place of Economy in the Social Science Model

Behavior	Expectations
Society	Culture
Associations	Institutions
Social groupings such as family, age and church groups, factories, and so forth whose activities are concerned with production, distribution, and consumption of goods and services	*Economy, Rules governing exchange*

Production

At the core of every culture is a set of regulations and expectations regarding relations with the environment. These regulations focus on the process of extracting energy from the environment to meet human needs—from basic biological necessities to derived cultural requirements. The means by which this is done is through technology. **Technology**, in its most fundamental sense, is the means by which humans modify or alter environments to suit human needs. It includes both the tools (physical traits) and the organizational principles which guide those who use tools (cultural expectations). The latter dimension of technology has already been discussed as division of labor. In this case, that part of the total division of labor that organizes the use of tools for extracting energy from the environment is part of the technological system. This division of labor dictates what social categories are responsible for what activity and how the activities are linked together.

The technology and the division of labor associated with the production of drugs will depend on the natural state of the drug itself. Many drugs can be consumed in their natural state. Some species of fungus or mushrooms, succulents such as peyote, or plants such as the coca shrub require no elaborate transformations in order to be used. Other drugs are the result of controlled natural processes. One process is fermentation which occurs naturally under certain conditions in natural items that contain sugar or starch. This process has been applied to a wide variety of natural items such as grain, fruits, honey, sugarcane, cactus, and even milk (*kumiss* of Central Asia). The result of fermentation is the production of alcohol. Two products result from this process, wine and beer. **Wine** is produced from natural substances which contain sugar. **Beer**, on the other hand, is made from plants that contain starch which is converted to sugar through the action of enzymes. These enzymes may be found on grains in their early sprout stage of development, or they may be added.[2] Distillation is another step removed from nature. This is a process of vaporization which extracts and concentrates the alcohol that has been produced by fermentation. This process reduces any food value that might have been present in the fermented beverage and can raise the alcohol content to over 90 percent. Other drugs, such as cocaine and heroin, require more elaborate chemical processing. The furthest from nature are the synthetic drugs such as LSD, methamphetamine, and the barbiturates. One might visualize this relationship to nature as shown in table 8.2.

Table 8.2.

Nature-Culture: Transformation of Drugs

Technological Transformation

	Direct	⟶		**Synthesized**
	Peyote/Mushrooms	Ebene		LSD
N		Fermentation	Distillation	
A	Coca Leaves/Qat		Cocaine/Crack	
T	Opium Eating	Opium Smoking/ Morphine	Heroin	Methadone
U				
R		Marihuana Smoking	Hashish	
E	Tobacco Eating	Tobacco Smoking		
				Methamphetamine Barbiturates PCP, etc.

The production of any of these substances will be accompanied by various divisions of labor. At the direct end of the nature-synthesized continuum, the drug is a natural substance that requires no transformation. The mushroom is picked and eaten;

leaves are removed from the coca plant and chewed. Obviously, natural drugs require only a simple division of labor to be produced. Drugs that are synthesized may require elaborate, interconnecting, and specialized divisions of labor. Even the simplest and most direct method of production is accompanied by a division of labor. For example, Huichol peyote harvesting is not the work of an individual producer but is accomplished through a division of labor that regulates when it is gathered and who goes to gather it, along with rules governing how many buttons are taken. Other natural attributes that should be considered are variations in durability and quality. Opium will store for extended periods without losing potency. Palm wine becomes lethal if it ferments too long, while qat and marihuana decompose in a relatively short time after harvesting or gathering. Whether gathered or grown, processed or synthesized, there are cultural rules which dictate the organization of this "work."

Distribution

The division of labor that produces a drug may be different from the division of labor that distributes or consumes the drug. Distribution is the way goods and services are exchanged between social units. One of the earliest commentators on this exchange process was Émile Durkheim's nephew, Marcel Mauss (1872–1950). In his now classic essay, *The Gift* (1954), Mauss explores the principle underlying the moral obligation to repay a gift that has been received. He suggests that one can understand this obligation through what he called **total prestations**. Total prestations are not limited to the distribution of "things" but rather are the underlying principles which explain how cultures work.

> In the systems of the past we do not find simple exchange of goods, wealth, and produce through markets established between individuals. For it is groups, and not individuals, which carry on exchange, make contracts, and are bound by obligations; the persons represented in the contracts are moral persons (cultural units)—clans, tribes, and families; the groups, or the chiefs as intermediaries for the groups, confront and oppose each other. Further, what they exchange is not exclusively goods and wealth, real and personal property, and things of economic value. They exchange rather courtesies, entertainments, ritual, military assistance, women, children, dances, and feasts; and fairs in which the market is but one element and the circulation of wealth but one part of a wide and enduring contract. Finally, although the prestations and

counter-prestations take place under a voluntary guise they are in essence strictly obligatory, and their sanction is private or open warfare. (3)

Mauss observed that in modern societies, things and persons may be distinguished from each other; but gift giving, which makes no such distinction, has survived. Things received carry with them a moral obligation to pay back at some future time. Invitations to rituals, such as weddings, funerals, and parties, are either an obligatory act of reciprocity for some past ritual or initiation into a relationship. These **norms of reciprocity** go beyond any monetary or market considerations of profit. Rather, they mark boundaries between "friends" and "enemies," between stranger and acquaintance. The exchange of goods symbolizes obligatory relationships through things. From the formal economic perspective, such exchanges have "zero sum" outcomes. Nobody profits or loses from the exchange. For example, in a study of a small Scottish fishing village, Ed Knipe (1984) found that fishermen often "stood their hand" for drinks (bought drinks for others) in the local pub. Viewed only as a single act, this might be interpreted as a profit for the recipients and a loss for the one who paid. However, systemic observation over an extended period found that those who had received a drink paid back an equal or near equal number of drinks. Thus, nobody won or lost in this transaction.[3] Exchange marked the boundaries between groups of men bound together by similarity of age and occupation. Within these "drinking circles" drinks were exchanged; outside of these circles, drinks could be refused. Alcohol thus served as a contract that marked the borders between groups of men with shared characteristics.

Mauss' discussion sensitizes us to one type of distribution found in every culture. However, there are other systems. Considering no other variables, cultures differ in their technologies and the environments in which those technologies are applied. This fundamental relationship either limits or requires alternative systems of distribution. The economist Karl Polanyi (1893–1964) recognized three distinct types of distribution (1944). The first of these is **general** or **balanced reciprocity**.[4] This is the moral form of exchange outlined by Mauss. In this system, distribution either reinforces established relationships or marks new ones. For example, Yanomamö alliances between villages (established or new) are marked by the exchange of items that each village can and does provide for itself. Dogs, ebene, tobacco, baskets, pots, and other items are given, either to initiate an alliance or at the feast where alliances are formally recognized.

The second type is **redistribution**. In redistribution, a central agent (religious, political, or social) collects goods and then redistributes them back to the population. Often part of what is contributed is kept by the central agent. For example, readers may be familiar with a "bring a plate" party at which each guest is expected to bring something to eat. For this "gift," guests are entitled to eat what others have brought. Taxation in state-level societies is another example of redistribution. Taxes are paid by the citizenry to a central agent. These monies are used to underwrite the costs of running the government, including services that are beyond the capability of any one citizen, such as police, military, education, transportation, and so on. Religious festivals and feasts may also function as a system of redistribution. The last system is **market exchange**. In this system there are no moral, kinship, or friendship obligations to reciprocate. Rather, goods and services are exchanged through **barter**, in which prices are negotiated, or **money**, which serves as a state-backed system of value. Markets are impersonal systems of exchange in which participants can purchase from anyone, including strangers. Cultures vary in their use of any or all three of these distribution systems depending on the technology/environment relationship. In societies where technology produces only enough for local consumption (a **subsistence** economy), we find general reciprocity is the most common form of distribution. In contrast, when the technology-environment relationship produces more than can be consumed locally (a **surplus** economy), market systems regulate most distributive activities.

Consumption

The category consumption includes the everyday consumption of goods and services such as food, shelter, and clothing, along with ideas about ownership and property. As previously noted, in some societies the units of production may not be the units of consumption. Among the Koryaks, fly agaric was gathered by women but consumed by men. On Tanna, kava was grown by women who were prohibited from consuming it. Among Americans there are appropriate ages and times for drinking and appropriate types of drinks for different occasions. Patterns of consumption are not a direct reflection of biological needs for food and shelter but may be used as exchange for power, authority, or esteem. Whatever the consumption pattern, it is another part of that area of study we call "economics."

Opium Production

Much of the present-day supply of the raw material to make morphine and heroin is produced in the **Golden Triangle**. This area encompasses a vast region of Southeast Asia along the border of China and includes parts of Burma, Thailand, and Laos (Inciardi 1986). To understand why this area of the world is a major producer of opium, a cursory review of Asian history is necessary.

Opium was probably diffused into China by Arab traders in the eighth century. At that time, it was cultivated on a small scale for medicinal purposes. Opium has several properties that make it attractive as part of "medicine." As an analgesic it is very effective in relieving pain. Opium is also an anti-diarrhetic and is instrumental in relieving other gastrointestinal disorders. In addition, it is an effective anti-tussive that prevents coughing. Since pain, digestive, and respiratory disorders afflict all human populations, it is understandable why opium, if available, might be adopted as part of curative practices.

In China, the earliest method of consuming opium was to eat it. Because of its unappealing taste, it was not widely used until American seamen introduced the practice of smoking during the seventeenth century. After that, opium consumption increased to include non-medicinal use (Scott 1969, 8).The increase in opium smoking was accompanied by legislation against opium in China, the first of which was passed in 1729. This legislation included severe punishment for operating or working in an "opium shop." Owners were strangled; assistants were whipped and then banished for at least three months (Scott, 12). Addicts were not punished. In spite of these efforts, opium use increased and provided a market for opium grown in China. To meet the increasing domestic demand for opium, some Chinese merchants illegally imported it from India through Western contacts, notably the British East India Company. The British East India Company wanted to purchase tea, silk, and other items from the Chinese for an increasing market in Britain. The Chinese, however, did not want goods from Europe and would not accept European currency as payment. This meant that some alternative trade good had to be found. Because there was widespread local demand for opium, the East India Company attempted to use opium as a trade item. The Chinese did not want to accept opium, which it had formally banned in 1800. This led to the so-called "Opium Wars" in 1839–42 and 1856–60. After the first "war," the Nanking Treaty of 1842 forced China to accept opium in exchange for other goods. In 1858 opium was legalized and taxed by the Chinese. By 1883 Chinese home production had increased to twice the amount imported, and British imports began to decline.

The increased market for opium proved a boon for "hill people" living between the Chinese border and the Southeast Asian lowlands (Wolf 1982). These peoples, including the Hmong, the Iu Mien, and the Lisu, had been driven out of China in the late seventeenth century. The marginal, high altitude lands onto which they had been forced were not very productive. The swidden[5] techniques they employed led to depletion of the already poor soil. One consequence of this practice was that whole villages had to move to new locations after only a few years, but one species of opium (*Papaver somniferum*) would grow in this environment and had a ready market in China. To realize the economic potential of this crop and to overcome the limitations of swidden practices, many of these hill peoples added the opium poppy to the inventory of crops they grew.

Opium is a labor intensive crop. The production of opium requires that land be cleared and then tended. Opium is a difficult crop to grow in a high altitude environment. The plants are delicate, and too little or too much rain can result in a lost crop. When the flower petals fall from the poppy, the capsule must be carefully scored to entice the flow of opium resin. The resin is then scraped from the capsule and packaged. This is a time-consuming task. A single worker would take over a month to harvest one *rai* (2.4 rai = 1 acre). Once harvested, opium sap is durable. It lasts a long time compared to other crop products. As a trade good (it serves as a general purpose money in this part of the world) opium can fetch a higher price per weight than any other crop and can be exchanged with traders for subsistence crops. Traders will offer food now for future opium production (Tapp 1986).

The adoption of opium by the hill peoples did not result in dramatic changes in local cultures. There was no opium revolution. Rather, opium became part of local economies in different ways, depending on the preexisting cultural patterns. To illustrate this, we focus on two of those local cultures, the Lisu and the Hmong.

Ban Lum, A Lisu Village

The Lisu are Tibeto-Burman hill people who live in Southern China, Northern Burma, and Northern Thailand. Paul Durrenberger (1976) conducted fieldwork in the Lisu village of Ban Lum in Northern Thailand between November 1968 and September 1970. His research during that period revealed four "sectors" in their "economy." These are

1. The subsistence sector: rice the main commodity
2. The reciprocity sector: pigs which forage for food during the day and are fed at night to guarantee that they come home
3. The consumption sector: purchases in cash or opium for labor, purchases from lowland markets, medical costs, and traveling peddlers
4. The reinvestment sector: very low because of right of "usufruct," no rents paid for land not being used, and tools for this type of adaptation are low in cost.

In Ban Lum, the household is the producing unit. Durrenberger conducted weekly surveys of households to determine how much time was invested by each household in the three main sectors, how much money was spent, and how many pigs were slaughtered for what purposes. He found that the average number of person-days a household spent producing rice was 164.35; opium, 364.75; and growing corn and getting other food for pigs, 53.65. The price of a *joy* (1.6 kilograms) of opium was 1,800 baht (1 baht = $.05)[6]; the lowest price for a *phit* (basket) of rice was 30 baht. The mean value of rice produced was 3,647 baht; for opium, 3,131 baht; and for the pigs that were slaughtered, 1,423 baht.

If one accepts the assumption of maximization of formal economics, the question is, "Why spend more time producing opium than rice?" The average value of a day's work producing rice is 23.26 baht, and for opium it is only 9.45 baht.[7] What about pigs? The baht value of a day's work devoted to pig raising is 26.51 (figures mine). From the standpoint of modern formal market economics, these villagers are not rational. Durrenberger argues that an understanding of Lisu economy does not come from simple monetary computations. Economic transactions for these villagers are not just the transfer of commodities (labor for money) but rather are imbedded in the mode of production coupled with social relations and cultural obligations.

The Lisu grow rice for subsistence. That is, most of the rice produced by the household is also consumed by that same household. Durrenberger found that the average adult working-age male consumes 453 kilograms of unhusked rice in a year. Adult women are .8 consumer units and therefore consume 362 kilograms per year. Children, depending on their ages, consume even less. From these consumption estimates, one can estimate total household requirements. The mean proportion of rice subsistence requirements by each household is 94 percent of total household production. Therefore households produce enough rice for subsistence needs, with only a small 6 percent surplus.

The Lisu cultivate upland rice on swiddens some distance from the village of Ban Lum and close to their neighbors, the Karen. Of the two crops, rice and opium, rice depletes the soil faster than poppies. If the Lisu were to grow only rice, this would lead to land shortages and ultimately less rice. Thus, the production of rice as a cash crop is a very direct threat to the production of rice as a subsistence crop (636). The alternative is to grow the poppy and sell it for money. Opium has a ready market; rice does not.

Durrenberger suggests:

> ... that Lisu produce opium as well as rice simply because they do not have to spend all of their labor at the task of providing themselves with subsistence, or in some cases the land is so infertile that such labor would be unrewarded. In remote hill villages, where oxen to transport rice from fields to the village houses have to be hired from tea-growing Karen, surplus rice has little value; it cannot be readily converted into money. Opium, on the other hand, can be easily converted into money. The argument, then, is that there is a surplus of labor, beyond the needs or possibilities of subsistence agriculture. This surplus labor can be most easily converted into surplus capital by cultivating poppies, and producing opium. After a household's subsistence requirement of rice has been produced, the value of more rice is negligible, but the value of opium is at least something. The opium market, then, provides a means by which surplus labor can be converted into surplus capital. (636)

The labor to which Durrenberger refers is household labor. The Lisu have a system of labor that is based on the cultural principle of balanced reciprocity. If a Lisu from one household contributes labor to another household, that labor must be paid back in equal amounts, but not all households have equal amounts of labor to contribute. This means that those with little or no surplus labor are at a disadvantage in fulfilling the moral obligation to reciprocate. One available alternative is to "buy" labor from outside the moral boundaries of the village. In this case, labor is recruited from among the opium addicts living in the nearby Karen village. Although there are opium addicts among the Karen, they do not grow opium. Rather, their cash crop is *miang*, pickled tea (Durrenberger 1974). The Karen addicts are paid in opium for their labor with the result that reciprocity is maintained. Thus, we note that poppy growing has importance beyond being a cash crop that can supplement subsistence shortfalls. It is a product that can be used to meet reciprocity obligations. With social units in balanced relationships, the village remains egalitarian. It is only under conditions of unbalanced reciprocity that hierarchial structures with ranked differences can exist. When social units are unable to repay, they are subordinate to those that they owe. Opium thus prevents the establishment of a formal leadership system with power.

Opium money is used to make other "purchases." The villagers rent oxen from the Karen to bring the rice from the field to the village. Consumer goods are purchased from itinerant peddlers. Among villagers, money is used to purchase liquor and pigs at a prearranged, fixed price. Neither pork nor liquor are consumed by individuals. Rather, they are necessary items for feasts that accompany rituals. Feasts are part of the reciprocal sector. Guests are morally obligated to invite their hosts to any future feasts that they sponsor. Failure to do this would result in losing "honor." Therefore, one keeps pigs and purchases liquor.

The other item in the Lisu economy is corn. Like the opium poppy, it is transformed rather than used directly. Corn is grown in the poppy fields and fed to pigs which are then either consumed by the household in feasts based on reciprocity or sold to others in the village at a fixed money price.

As Durrenberger points out, the village is dependent on the opium market in other ways.

> Social and political relations within the village take their form from the economic conditions, which depend on the demand for opium, the markets which supply lowland goods, and the availability of wage labor.
>
> But these relationships with various markets are motivated by internal social and political considerations in the village— the ideology of "honor" and "respect" and the importance of reciprocity in this ideology. In this sense, "external trade and money uses. . . are derivative expressions of reciprocal . . . modes of transaction" (Dalton 1971, 75). The markets make possible the social and political forms. Reciprocity, informed by an ideology of "honor," "potency," and "respect," which is a consequence of social and political relations, motivates market interactions. (643)

To the formal economist, the sale of opium for cash and the purchase of goods from outside the village may give the appearance of a market economy. From the substantive perspective, Ban Lum may be monetized, but it does not have a market economy. The principle which dominates the organization of work is the principle of balanced reciprocity, not profit, and not supply and demand.

The Hmong: Opium Users

Durrenberger's research did not include reports of opium users or addicts in the village of Ban Lum. The absence of opium users does not, however, describe some village communities in Northern Thailand. Among the Hmong, for example, village addicts may consume up to 60 percent of the local opium production (Tapp 1986). In one village, eight out of twenty-five household heads were addicted. These addicts were typically male and over the age of thirty-five, and their addiction was the result of using opium for medicinal purposes. In spite of this high addiction rate, addicts do not form any special interest or subgroup, and their addiction does not interfere with performing normal behaviors. We might ask whether addiction is the primary reason why the Hmong grow opium poppies.

The Hmong number six million and live in the northern parts of Laos, Vietnam, and Thailand. Their origin is shrouded in some debate. One view is that they migrated north from Indonesia. Their origin legend, however, hints at a migration south from Northern Asia. Whichever history is correct, Chinese records indicate contact with the Miao or Meo[8] in the second century B.C. Continued southern expansion of Chinese empires forced the Hmong into the mountainous environments of Vietnam, Laos, and Thailand. Although their history includes bloody confrontations with state-level societies, the Hmong have no political structure beyond the village. They are organized into patrilineal, exogamous clans which provide the basis for residence and political organization. The ideal settlement pattern is the village compound composed of a lineage belonging to a clan. The more usual arrangement is that two or more different clans reside in the same village. This serves to facilitate marriage. Disputes, usually over land or marriage, are settled by regional clan elders whose decisions usually favor the majority. The basic principle of Hmong social organization is, like that of the Lisu, communal and egalitarian.

Women do most of the work among the Hmong. They may own poultry and poppy fields, but their status ranks below that of males. Females are expected to tend the fields, take care of household animals, and do most of the housework. Even though their prestige ranks below males, women actively participate in informal meetings and often act as mediators in times of crisis. In addition to gender, age has prestige. Male heads of households have the final word on most matters. The only exception to this principle is if the male is senile.

The producing unit is the household, which averages from eight to ten members. The household may be composed of the oldest son, his wife, his parents, and any unmarried siblings. After the birth of one or two children to the oldest son, he will move out and establish his own household. The Hmong permit polygyny (a man may have more than one wife), but only if a man can afford the expensive bridewealth for the second wife.[9] In polygynous households, the first wife accumulates increased esteem because the second wife assumes the field-tending responsibilities and the first wife is then able to remain at home.

The yearly horticultural cycle begins in January. Land is cleared and the scrub is burned off using the slash-and-burn technique. Dry rice is planted in the ash-fertilized soil in May or early June. Planting is simple. Men use a dibble stick[10] to open a hole in the earth. They are followed by women who drop five or six seeds in each hole. Maize is planted sometime before the rains in May. Other domestic crops are cabbage, spinach, beans, and gourds, as well as fruit trees, bananas, and bamboo. After the maize is harvested in September, the opium poppy is seeded. The rice is harvested in December. The time-consuming task of incising and scraping the opium poppy is carried out by women soon after New Year, and the planting cycle is repeated.

Rice is grown for local consumption, while maize is used primarily as fodder for pigs and chickens. The opium is sold to Chinese and Thai traders who transport it to lucrative markets in the south. Opium sales provide cash to purchase supplemental rice from lowland wet-rice farmers. These monies are also used to purchase silver rupees which are melted down and provide the major item of the bridewealth payment.

The only specialized status is that of shaman, which may be occupied by either males or females. Shamans go into trance states to communicate with the "other-world" where they are expected to bargain with hostile spirits for the release of the captive souls of the living. Sickness and other misfortunes are believed to be the result of loss of several soul-essences. During the rather elaborate curing rituals, chickens or pigs are sacrificed and then eaten by the family. Aside from their religious significance, these rituals are an important source of protein, as meat is only consumed at these curing rituals and major celebrations.

Returning to our question of why the Hmong grow opium, Tapp suggests several reasons. One of these is related to **carrying capacity**. This is the number of people that can be supported by a technology in an environment. The lands on which the Hmong live, coupled with swidden practices, are not capable of providing prolonged subsistence needs. In contrast, opium grows well in soil with low fertility. Unlike other products, such as perishable food-stuffs and livestock that have to be transported down to the lowlands and sold at low prices, opium attracts traders who will travel to the villages. These same traders bring rice, which they sell on credit to the villagers. Thus, rice shortfalls are made up through opium sales and carrying capacity is increased to maintain population size.

Opium is a general purpose money that can be used to purchase utilitarian items, such as salt and iron, from diverse ethnic groups in the region. What is left over after consumption by local addicts is exchanged for silver. Silver is a special currency that is used to satisfy the bridewealth. Without silver to pay the parents and relatives of the bride, marriage would be impossible. Without marriage there would be no children, and without children there would be no clans. Although the household is the basic social unit, the kinship principles by which the clan is organized provide the master plan for community and alliances between communities. Thus, the payment of bridewealth does not constitute an impersonal accumulation or loss of capital in the Western economic sense but rather serves as the symbolic glue that binds Hmong culture together. Without it, there is no Hmong culture.

Opium is widely used in many hill tribes, including the Hmong, as treatment for illness, recreationally, and when socially mandated (Suwanwela et al. 1980). The only exception to satisfying these needs locally is the Karen. Peter Hinton (1983) suggests that differences in Hmong and Karen social organization explain why the Hmong grow opium and the Karen do not. He found that Karen social structure developed in response to extensive agriculture. The Karen producing units are independent nuclear families, and they have strong prohibitions against remarriage, adoption, premarital sex, and polygyny. This form of structure does not "fit" the intense labor requirements associated with opium production, nor is it successful when used to organize intense agriculture on marginal lands. In contrast, the Hmong and others have social structures that enable them to recruit and organize the labor necessary for opium growing. This comparison illustrates why we find cultures characterized by "disorder." The adaptation to one ecological situation may not be preparation for another ecological situation. The Karen's subordinate position to the Hmong and the Lisu is demonstrated by their reliance on them for opium and their willingness to exchange labor for opium. Hinton's analysis reminds us how fragile the connection between organizational characteristics and survival can be, and how this fragility may be the impetus for adoption of different practices—culture change.

Distribution: Band and Peasant "Markets"

Distribution refers to the movement of goods or services within and between producing units. For folk societies, the production and distribution often have overlapping personnel. That is, those who produce are also those among whom the goods and services are distributed. Yet even these subsistence economies recognize exceptions. Within families, children are provided with goods and services they did not produce, and there may be elaborate rules on the ordering of distribution according to kinship, age or gender. At the other end of the continuum, urban industrial societies make sharp distinctions between production and distribution systems. Those who produce goods may be prevented from using them. Not all workers in the Mercedes plant own a Mercedes! Even if the producers are also part of the distribution system, what is produced is more than the producers need. In such surplus economies, specialized producers receive money for their productive labor which enables them to procure the surplus that others produce. In this section we review two examples of distribution systems. One is a band-level (folk) society. The other is an economic system midway between the influences of folk and urban society—the peasant society.

Pituri: An Australian Aborigine Hallucinogen

The popular image of small hunting and gathering societies as isolated social units is not supported by the empirical evidence that shows that their nomadic way of life often brings them into contact with others through trade networks. The Australian Aborigines illustrate this observation. In the late 1700s, when Europeans first made contact with the aborigines, there were hundreds of different, small, nomadic societies that formed a large distribution system. One item used in this system was *pituri* (*Duboisia hopwoodii*), a hallucinogen that had the added benefit of reducing the effects of thirst and hunger.[11] Bags containing the leaves of the pituri plant were traded for food and manufactured items, such as boomerangs and spears, over vast areas of the desert. Although the literature is sparse, de Rios' (1984) review found several uses of pituri: as a symbol of friendship between strangers, as a social lubricant, as payment in circumcision and subincision[12] rituals, as an intoxicant to trap birds and animals, and by old men to obtain power and riches (23). The natives had well traveled pituri "roads," and the only system of writing known to the Aborigines was incised wooden sticks that served as a mnemonic device for messengers who were sent out to purchase pituri from neighboring groups.

Conquest by Europeans had rather dramatic consequences for the Aborigines. Brady (1991) reports that estimates of the Aboriginal population in 1788 was 750,000. By 1986 it had declined to 206,000. Depending on the territory, more than half of the Aboriginal population lived in cities in 1986. The present-day Aborigines have higher disease rates and lower life expectancy than the Europeans in Australia. The use of pituri and other pre-contact drugs has been replaced by substances such as alcohol, kava, chewing and smoking tobacco, and the sniffing of solvents such as gasoline, methylated spirits, and methanol.

The Rastafarians: Adaptation to Change

In chapter 5, the antecedent conditions which gave rise to the Rastafarian brethren were discussed. Their beliefs and practices not only set them apart from the dominant Europeans but also from other working class Jamaicans. Lewis' (1986) analysis of the Rastafarians departs somewhat from that taken by others and suggests that the movement was primarily an adaptation to changing economic conditions.

Under the system of slavery, slaves operated "free" markets authorized by plantation owners. These markets served:

> ... as a means of subsistence for the slaves. ... These higgler markets, as they were later called, released the slaves, albeit for a short time, from the domination of their owners. The free markets operated on Sundays and were a system of exchange for the entire population, free as well as slave. ... Through them the slaves learned how to be free producers. (8–9)

With the abolishment of slavery in 1834, the freed slaves developed free markets in which they distributed their products. Although the producing units were extended families, women conducted most of the marketing activity. The result was a self-sufficient peasantry whose "economies" were localized.

Beginning in the 1920s, this peasantry declined as a result of efforts by Europeans and Jamaican mulattos to modernize the economy. By the 1930s, labor unions and wage labor had replaced the peasant system of production and marketing. Kinship and self-sufficiency were displaced by a money economy, and local production was tied to international markets. In spite of efforts to convert all the peasants to this new economy, some resisted. They argued that the peasantry enjoyed a relatively steady, albeit low, income while wage laborers were forced into conditions of abject poverty because of the Great Depression.

Much of the literature on the Rastafarians links Marcus Garvey's Universal Negro Improvement Association movement to the beginnings of Rastafarianism. Garvey, along with the Europeans, attempted to convince African Jamaicans to become part of a "rational" economic system. According to Lewis, the connection between Garvey and the Rastafarians is spurious. Although they, like Garvey, accepted African exclusiveness, they rejected Garvey's insistence that Africans adopt capitalism and industrialism. Consequently, they rejected both labor unions and capitalism and maintained the peasant mode of cooperation and exchange.

Rastafari operate small-scale businesses such as craft shops, clothing stores, fishing, and the illegal sale of ganja.[13] These are all controlled through familylike local cooperatives which circulate wealth through gifts and parties. The result is the peasantlike practice of **leveling**, a highly controlled system in which members share equally in all resources. Instead of adopting a competitive capitalist system with its corresponding hierarchical structure with ranked differences, Rastafarians maintained a cooperative peasant economy. This leveled out economic fluctuations that resulted from changes in international markets. From the standpoint of formal capitalism, this system produces no great wealth. As the Rastafari realize, however, there is no poverty either. This is Harris' sacred cow in operation!

The use of marihuana by Rastas fits in with other cooperative ventures. Because it is illegal, each neighborhood must maintain contacts with the producers and distributors of the holy herb. Even the recent stepped-up efforts by the American government to stop its production, including armed confrontations with drug agents, further legitimates independence from the dominating system. When viewed as an adaptation to a vacillating and precarious economic structure, the Rastafarian practice of smoking ganja takes on a new meaning, not as an escape from the everyday need to "make a living," but as part of an active participation in an alternative economic strategy.

Distribution: A Subsistence Marihuana System

During the height of the "hippie" movement in the 1960s, marihuana became a symbol, along with other "drugs," of the movement itself. The research during the 1960s on marihuana users was confined to young Anglo high school and university students. In these settings, dealers sold small quantities in a secretive and unsystematic fashion, for minimal or no profit, to friends or acquaintances (Fields 1984). The process by which these "sales" were made has been outlined by James Spradley and David McCurdy (1975).

Spradley and McCurdy are interested in unraveling **folk taxonomies**, the categories that map cognitive worlds (worldviews). One dimension of cognitive order is inclusiveness. For example, the word automobile is more inclusive than Ford or Chevrolet. For American users of the 1960s and 1970s, "marihuana" or "dope" is a word that includes Colombian Gold, Thai Stick, or homegrown. Thus, "marihuana" is the more inclusive term.

The construction of folk taxonomies begins with soliciting verbal emic categories which are then ordered into etic structures. Methodologically, the process of constructing folk taxonomies requires asking informants a series of questions. The answers to these questions should yield responses that identify the words and definitions of these words in an **argot**, a specialized vocabulary. Further probing should reveal the logic by which words are linked into a taxonomic structure. For example, in questioning informants about how they acquire marihuana, one answer might be, "You score (acquire) dope from a dealer." This response would prompt the question, "Why?" The answer might be that one "scores" because of the fear of being "busted" (arrested) and that the chances of being "busted" are greater if you are caught "holding" (having marihuana). The way to get around being "busted" is to "score" small amounts. Then how does the "deal" work? Spradley and McCurdy reconstruct a taxonomy based on a temporal sequence (table 8.3). All the meanings one derives from this process might be hidden, and the goal of this exercise is to uncover the underlying structure.

In this process, larger amounts of marihuana are held for only a short time (steps 4 to 5) because one only buys enough to satisfy existing orders (steps 1, 2, and 3). This reduces high-risk exposure for the group purchaser. Only step 4 requires contacts outside of this system, but since the purchase is immediately redistributed,

Table 8.3.

Steps in "Making a Deal"

Steps				
1	2	3	4	5
Check for interest among customers	Check with contacts	Quote prices to customers	Score dope	Get rid of dope

risk is reduced. Viewed holistically, what Spradley and McCurdy described is a subsistence system governed by balanced reciprocity. It is not a formal economic transaction that involves any profit, other than free marihuana for the dealer, and even this he or she is expected to share with others. The dealer serves as the conduit between this system of redistribution and the one outside that is the source of marihuana. Although one could accrue some personal esteem by achieving the status "dealer," this recognition carries with it the expectation that one conform to egalitarian values. Profit is not a motive and there is a rejection of the market mentality. This practice further reinforces the rejection of wider values and practices. To those outside, this inversion of the "normal" was used as evidence that hippies were "crazy" or communists!

While anthropologists have been concerned with the rules of economic life, sociologists have often viewed drug worlds as structurally similar to licit businesses. Within formal organizations (bureaucracies), specialized offices or statuses are linked together both vertically and horizontally. Within this structure, the movement of a person vertically from one office to another is called a **career**. Such movement, and hence a career, is only possible when an organization makes vertical distinctions. Therefore, the question of whether those involved in the distribution of drugs have careers depends on demonstrating that drug organizations with vertical distinctions exist and that persons within these structures are able move from one office to another. In the following sections we explore this issue further.

Distribution: Cannabis Careers

Allen Fields (1984) carried out a participant observation study of marihuana sales in a low-income urban black community in northern California. Within this area he identified three distinct neighborhoods. One was a middle-class neighborhood of home-owners; another was not as affluent and contained a public housing project with a reputation for high crime. The third neighborhood had deteriorated public housing and was often assumed to be the source of crime in the community.

Fields' study area was one of the main business streets of this community. This street had a large volume of pedestrian traffic. Shoppers made purchases both in stores and from the many vendors who lined the sidewalks. Others used the street as a place to just "hang out." Fields describes the street as having an open-air bazaar atmosphere complete with music, dancing, eating and drinking. On three of the corners along the street, young males sold marihuana to pedestrian and vehicular customers. These males, and the organization of their sales, were the focus of Fields' research.

One of the difficulties of doing field work is establishing legitimacy. Informants often question why the field worker is there and why the study is being done. When the activity studied is illicit, these questions from informants are based on real concerns about detection and arrest by authorities. It is therefore important that the field worker assure informants that he or she is sympathetic and will not report anything that might harm them. Public marihuana sales were conducted by young black males who knew each other through school, neighborhood, or family ties. Being black, Fields fit in with the ethnicity of the street, but he was not young. To legitimate his age he "hung out" in a pool hall along the street and at a community gym a few block away. In both of these establishments, there were males in their forties. From the pool hall, Fields was able to observe marihuana transactions, and his walks to the gym took him by the corners where sales took place. The last difficulty, his lack of identity or legitimacy, was overcome by talking to and befriending individual sellers during his three years in the field. This extended stay enabled him to interview, both formally on tape and informally, several marihuana vendors.

Fields discovered three dealing networks. Each network consisted of a small number of youths who were part of a larger organization structure that occupied separate street corners. In each of these networks there were four distinct statuses, or occupational specialties: employer, marijuana entrepreneur, rider, and runner.

Employers were usually older males who lived in their own accommodations. They were rarely seen on the corner, preferring to conduct their business in secrecy. Employers, as the name implies, hired people to make the actual street sales. Their source of marihuana was through contacts outside the community. Depending on how many employees they had, their income ranged from $1,000 to $2,000 per day. Since their incomes depended on the quantity of marihuana sold by their employees, they had to be careful about whom they hired and how they managed these workers. In order to motivate their personnel, employers adjusted the supply of marihuana and the commission rate for sales. Employees whose sales were high were given more marihuana and paid higher commissions. Those with less exemplary sales records were fired. Leaving aside the fact that what was sold was illegal, Fields' description of the management duties of the employer would apply to selling brushes, vacuum cleaners, or encyclopedias.

Marihuana entrepreneurs were somewhat younger than the employers. Some lived with their parents; others were on their own. Unlike the employers, they conducted direct sales on the street corners during established "business" hours. Entrepreneurs had their own suppliers outside the community, but because many lived with families or relatives, they often had a problem storing larger amounts of marihuana. One solution to this problem was to exchange marihuana for storage space from friends, which added to the costs of doing business. Fields reported that they made less than $1000 a week. For this lower income the entrepreneur did not have staffing problems, but he was exposed to a greater risk because he made direct sales in the street and had to compete directly with other street vendors.

Two types of employees were identified by Fields—riders and runners. Riders ranged in age from seventeen to twenty and usually lived at home with their parents. They developed an exclusive relationship with one employer and earned between $2.00 and $2.50 for each bag sold. Depending on the demand, a rider could make as much as $60 a day. The relationship between the rider and the employer was often tenuous. Good riders, those who sold more, could negotiate a higher commission from an employer by threatening to go with another employer. Employers would therefore have to weigh the possibility of reduced sales against increased commission costs in making their decision to retain or lose the rider to a competitor. Good riders were committed to the "work ethic," and employers continually sorted their work force on this criterion. Riders not willing to work hard were fired, and ideally each employer wanted his riders to make many sales.

Runners are temporary employees, usually hired for some special events (for example, a sports event, or a concert). They are younger, fourteen to seventeen years old, and are still in school and living at home. They are given fewer bags to sell and make less per bag

($1.00–$2.00). Runners are at a competitive disadvantage to riders and entrepreneurs who have regular customers. They usually compete among themselves for unclaimed customers. Theirs is an activity that brings in "extra" money, rather than being a steady source of income. Fields' description of marihuana street sales suggests a shallow organizational structure that might be pictured as in table 8.4.

Table 8.4.
Organizational Structure of Marihuana Street Sales

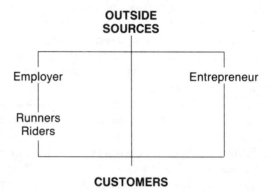

The term used by dealers for street sales is "slinging weed." Slinging weed is a set of behaviors and rules for selling marihuana *and* procedures for reducing risk. Sales take place in open public places during business hours, from 9:00 A.M. to 5:30 P.M., Monday through Friday. There are few sales on weekends. The price per unit is fixed. Thai Stick (Buddha) is $10 a bag (approximately one gram); Columbian Gold, Sinsemilla, Indica, and Homegrown are $5 per bag.[14] The openness of sales serves several functions. It signals potential buyers that marihuana is available. Selling on a street corner is also safer than selling from an automobile or a fixed dwelling, because there are more escape routes in the event of attempted apprehesion by police. Lastly, public sales enable sellers on different corners to warn each other if the police are in the area or if a seller on one corner has been "ripped off" (robbed) by someone in an automobile.

The simplest sales are between dealers and their regular customers. One finger is raised by the buyer if interested in buying one bag. An open hand held high signals the customer that $5 bags are available. Opening and closing the hand twice indicates the availability of Buddha. A feigned handshake conveys several bags to the consumer for inspection. Another handshake returns the unaccepted bags and money. The transaction is then complete, and the customer leaves. Transactions among dealers and unclaimed customers are somewhat different. There is an underlying agreement among dealers that one does not sell to another's regular customer. With unclaimed buyers, there may be rather vocal competition among dealers. Once a buyer decides to buy from one dealer, however, the competition ends.

Selling to customers in automobiles can present several problems. One, the expectation that customers can inspect the merchandise may hold up traffic and draw attention from the police. Another is the possibility that these "customers" will drive off with the marihuana without paying. To reduce this risk, there is cooperation among dealers on the three corners. Maintaining a tough reputation may prevent this from happening, but if someone does try to "burn" (steal from) a dealer, the other dealers from the other corners will pursue the offender, reclaim the stolen bags, and usually inflict physical damage on the offender(s) and the car. This action is, however, not without its hazards as it too may alert the police.

Fields' description of slinging weed demonstrates that organizational structures and divisions of labor are not always formally prescribed. The behavioral repertoires of and among sellers and the evolution of a specialized communication system are both adaptive strategies for adjusting to environments. The primary environmental constraint in this case is that selling marihuana is illegal. The behaviors he describes are all in some way related to maintaining secrecy while being in public. Although he does not indicate whether the organization of dealing can constitute a career, he is clear that slinging weed is an attractive occupational alternative that can, and sometimes does, lead to a full-time job for young males. For the older employers and entrepreneurs it has all the characteristic features of a nineteenth-century market economy— no organized labor, competition without restraints, and an unregulated market. For them, this is raw entrepreneurial capitalism!

Distribution: Heroin in Detroit

A distribution system similar to that reported by Fields was studied in two major inner-city housing projects in Detroit. Thomas Mieczkowski (1986) spent three months formally interviewing fifteen heroin dealers. This information was supplemented by his long residence in the city and by his acquaintanceship with people whose occupations brought them in contact with the illicit drug market. This study is somewhat different from other analyses of heroin sales in that members of this distribution system were not themselves heroin users, rather they were functionaries in a for-profit business.

The early type of heroin distribution in Detroit was the "dope-pad system." These were rather conventional retail outlets that had a fixed physical location. Heroin was purchased in bulk from wholesalers and then "stepped on," or "cut" with fillers such as quinine, and then repackaged in bags for retail sale. In this system there was a "boss" who was in charge of two or three employees and "steerers," who advertized the location of the pad and the quality of the product. The employees provided security and were also salesmen. Depending on the operation, the dope-pad provided several services in addition to direct sales. One could rent or buy the "works" (the needle, spoon, and heat sources), or one could pay to have heroin injected.

Beginning in the early 1980s, a new system for distribution was introduced. This was called the "Young Boys, Inc." (YBI). Instead of having a fixed location, the YBI brought heroin to customers through the runner system. The runners were male, black, usually young, and non-addicts, although they might use some drug or drugs. The mean age was 19.3, and the mean age at which they began selling was 16.6. Their self-reported incomes ranged from $25 to $3,000 per working day. These figures may be somewhat misleading if one projects them to an income-per-year base. Heroin sales are similar to other illicit activities in that they often result in income that is irregular. Thus, these figures are only for those days worked.

The YBI structure is similar to the employer-runner/rider system described by Fields, with some exceptions. Runners work in "crews" which range in size from three to twenty-five. Each crew has a crew boss who acts as a sponsor for the runners. Above him is a "lieutenant" who manages several crews and in turn reports to the "big man," the representative of a heroin syndicate. According to Mieczkowski, the syndicate controls about 60 percent of the heroin trade in Detroit through YBI. The organizational structure can be diagrammed as in table 8.5.

The runner engages in the actual selling of heroin to customers. Mieczkowski found the mean number of customers for these runners was 135. To protect the runner in small crews, the crew chief will act as a "gun." The gun is expected to help the runner if he has problems with a customer or if someone tries to "rip them

Table 8.5.

Organization of YBI

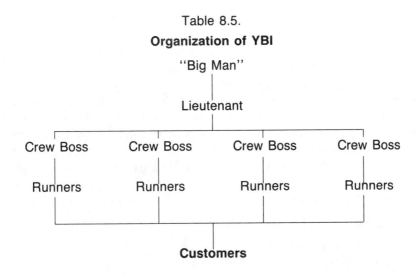

"Big Man"

|

Lieutenant

Crew Boss   Crew Boss   Crew Boss   Crew Boss

Runners   Runners   Runners   Runners

Customers

off." In larger crews, there are designated guns who perform this function. Payment schedules vary. Runners, for example, are paid in one of two ways. They are either paid on commission on sales, or they earn a fixed amount at the end of a "shift." A shift ranges from two to seventeen hours per day, with the standard being ten and one-half hours. Each runner is given his consignment of heroin at the beginning of the shift from the crew chief. Periodically during the shift the chief visits the runner to collect some or all of the sales money. Some runners may attempt to increase their income through deceptive techniques. One such method is skimming. A small amount of heroin is taken from each packet sold until there is enough to make up extra packets. These are then sold and the proceeds kept by the runner. Another technique is to fake being robbed by an accomplice. Although these practices can increase income, they are not without hazards. If a customer complains to the crew chief about the purity or quantity of his purchase, the runner might be dismissed or beaten or both. If he fakes being robbed, and the crew chief recognizes the conspiracy, a similar fate awaits him.

One observation of heroin sales in the United States is a linkage to "violence." Mieczkowski did report the use of physical force by crew bosses as punishment for thefts by runners. We will have more to say about this in the next chapter, but the application of rather severe punishment for stealing can, in part, be understood from a strictly economic standpoint. The crew boss purchases heroin from his contacts. He hires and supervises his crew and provides them with protection. In addition, he must protect himself against theft of his heroin stash and the possibility that he may be robbed of the cash he collects from crew members. To insure that his crew members do not skim, he may employ direct punishment of a specific crew member who steals, or he might take the loss from all members of the crew in the form of reduced commissions. Whatever the particular method used, the crew boss (or anybody else in this system) has no access to third parties (police, courts) that could resolve any dispute that arises in the daily functioning of this "business." Crew bosses must, in threat or in fact, adopt a strict disciplinarian management style. Mieczkowski reported a hierarchy of disciplinary methods used by bosses. These are

1. threats of violence
2. active intimidation
3. inflicting a beating without weapons
4. inflicting a beating with a weapon
5. wounding with a gunshot
6. killing with a gunshot (659)

Crew bosses have alternative methods for encouraging compliance with expectations. One is through the use of bonuses. Crew members who perform well may be given cash or expensive gifts, or the crew chief may lend his automobile to a productive crew member. The purpose of either the carrot or the stick is the same: to maintain a well-disciplined and highly motivated work force.

Upward mobility is possible within this structure. Initially, crews are recruited from among friends, relatives, or others who are known and trusted. A crew member can become a crew chief if he can accumulate enough cash to purchase heroin in large amounts; or he can develop a trusting relationship with a lieutenant who would become his patron and thereafter provide a steady source of heroin. To maintain this higher paid position, the chief must demonstrate that he can maintain an efficient crew.

This study casts additional light on the process of heroin distribution. We note a highly structured system, even though the actual membership in this structure often has very short tenure (usually less than one year). It also illustrates that, at least for Detroit, the street sales of heroin are carried out largely by young non-addict males whose participation is viewed as just another job. Mieczkowski argues that this structure is more efficient than the older dope-pad system. By being mobile, it avoids police surveillance. By taking business into the streets, a larger volume of trade is possible in less time. Lastly, by using non-addict minors, risk is reduced for adult syndicate administrators.

Distribution: Relationships Between High-Level Dealers

Much of the social science research on the distribution of drugs in American society has focused downwardly on those with the least amount of social power. The poor, minorities, and those out of power have been overrepresented in the literature. The explanation for this lies in the relationship between science as a social activity and the hierarchical structure of urban society. Scientists either come from or become part of the middle to upper middle levels of urban stratification. Social scientists are keenly aware of their position within the structure of society and have availed themselves of the benefits that this ranking provides. Research funding is seldom provided to study the sponsors of that funding. Social science research is more likely to be supported, whether privately or by government, *if* the research focuses on those least able to resist. Thus, high school and college students, peasants, hunters and gatherers, the unemployed, and ethnic minorities are more likely targets for social science research than are the rich, the professional, and the politically powerful. Patricia and Peter Adler offer an example of "studying up" the organizational hierarchy of drug distribution. While their work carries with it the same methodological problems as "studying down," they offer a rare glimpse into a world about which little is known.

In a series of articles, the Adlers report their findings based on a study of "Southwest County," a large metropolitan area in Southwest California (1980, 1982, 1983, 1989). The Adlers literally fell into this study. They were living in a neighborhood where many of their neighbors were involved in smuggling and dealing marihuana and cocaine. Through social contacts they were able to gain the trust of these neighbors, who in turn introduced them to others. Using both participant-observation and unstructured taped interviews, they were able to gather data on sixty-five dealers and smugglers along with other members of the local drug "world" over a six-year period from 1972 to 1980.

The upper-level dealers and smugglers described by the Adlers are another link in production—street-level system of distribution of drugs in the United States. The smugglers brought marihuana from Mexico[15] and cocaine from Columbia, Bolivia, and Peru in large quantities.[16] These upper-level dealers then "middled" these drugs to lower-level dealers. The lower-level dealers "cut" (added adulterants to) cocaine and separated marihuana into smaller sale units. Unlike the street-level marihuana salesmen described by Fields or the heroin street salesmen discussed by Mieczkowski, dealing and smuggling was a full-time occupation. Of the sixty-five smugglers and dealers studied, about half earned up to $750,000 per year. The other half either lost money or were just barely getting by. Another contrast to the street-level studies just reviewed was that the upper-level dealers and smugglers were mostly white, came from middle-class families, and ranged from twenty-five to forty years of age.

Entry into the upper levels of dealing and smuggling was similar to other occupations. In spite of the American "dream" of working your way to the top, the Adlers found that only 20 percent of upper-level dealers began at the low or street level. They argue that low-level dealers lacked the social connections necessary to acquire large quantities of drugs. Most upper-level dealers (75 percent) came from the middle level. These were people who, through social contacts and friendships, were given an opportunity to deal in larger quantities of drugs. Many had been in a non-drug related occupation such as bartending, acting, real estate, graduate school, construction, and other intermittent or low-income occupations which required entrepreneurial skills. The Adlers argue that the crucial independent variable for entry into high-level dealing or smuggling was social, not technical skills. Therefore, training in how to deal and smuggle often took place on the job. Approximately half of the smugglers, for example, were recruited from the drug social scene and had no previous experience in the distribution of drugs. The other half came from middle-level drug dealers.

The Adlers suggest that the social world of upper-level dealers and smugglers consists of a series of linking and overlapping relationships, from small relatively intimate partnerships to a reputational sphere. Some dealers may work alone, but smuggling demands cooperative efforts among a few specialists. Within partnerships there is almost daily contact between members. Relatives are the most trusted partners, and recruitment into dealing may follow family ties. Some partnerships are formed between friends. These are usually pragmatic and businesslike and reflect the division of labor of dealing or smuggling. In either case, partnerships with relatives or friends serve to reduce possible risk because of pre-existing moral bonds. Long-term partnerships are related to success. Less successful dealers or smugglers are more likely to have fleeting or transitory partnerships which last for a few "deals." Some of these long-term partnerships may evolve into what the Adlers call a family. One of these smuggling families had eight members. Table 8.6 shows the family and the responsibilities of each member.

Table 8.6.
The Smuggling "Family"

"Family" Member	Number	Activities
Family head	1	Coordinated "family" activities, including: buying and selling connections, financing, supplying equipment (such as planes, vans, radios), recruiting and supervising "family"
Driver	2	Brought goods from point of entry to "stash" house
Pilot	1	Flew plane in and out of source country
Co-pilot/driver	1	Co-piloted plane and occasionally drove
Pilot/smuggler/ wholesale dealer	1	Part-time pilot who was also an independent smuggler and dealer, supplied by family head
"Stash house" distributor/ enforcer	1	Lived in house where marihuana was stored and distributed it to customers. When needed, used force to extract payments
Business manager	1	Handled finances, laundered money, operated legitimate "front." Also arranged for legal counsel when needed

Not all members of the family were paid the same. Pilots were paid $10,000; drivers received $4,000. Members could also be paid in marihuana which they then could deal. Membership in a "family" is sponsored by the head or boss. Recruits are taught the varied activities that are necessary for successful smuggling. In exchange for being accepted, recruits are usually loyal to their sponsor. This loyalty could eventually lead to having one's own "family," either because one mastered all the social and technical skills or through inheritance if the family head retires. Since success as a dealer or smuggler depends on personal contacts with suppliers and distributors, socialization into a "family" includes learning how to develop and maintain social networks, or connections.

Connections include a wider network of relationships that link the family or partnership to a larger vertical organizational world. This includes supply connections or foreign brokers (from whom marihuana or cocaine is purchased) and lower-level dealers (to whom it is sold). Connections with suppliers are relationships between near equals. Novices will cultivate connections as they learn the business and will retain them if they contribute to their success. Connections to lower-level dealers are somewhat different. They are less permanent. This temporal impermanence is explained, in part, by the "market." The demand for drugs is always higher than the supply. High-level dealers have many alternative low-level dealers to whom they can sell. What accounts for any sustained relationship between these two levels is the need for secrecy. A known low-level buyer presents less risk than a stranger. Thus we note that the high-level dealer is part of a hierarchical structure. With those above him, he will develop strong permanent ties. With those below him, ties will be more transitory.

Beyond connections, dealers and smugglers are part of friendship networks, membership in which goes beyond drug business considerations. The basis of networks is shared interests and life-styles. The major activity of the network is the party, at which large quantities of drugs are consumed. At these events, ideas and information about business are shared. The network provides a setting within which to maintain and cultivate friendships and to receive support. As with other voluntary friendship-based groups, membership is often very fluid because interpersonal relationships change.

Two levels exist beyond networks. The Adlers call these levels "tribes" and "umwelt." Tribes are composed of acquaintances whom participants see on various occasions and about whom they have general information. From the standpoint of any particular person, the boundaries of tribes vary and overlap. In large part, tribal worlds are a reflection of residential propinquity. Because dealers and smugglers live within a relatively small geographical area, the daily routines of people often bring them into contact with "neighbors." These contacts are periodically reinforced through common participation in social events, such as weddings and parties. The umwelt level describes a world that is constructed from reputation. It is based on what is known about a person rather than actually knowing the person. This reputational world may, however, present a dilemma. One's reputation in the umwelt can work against the necessity to maintain secrecy. Whatever the personal consequences, umwelt serves as a boundary marker between the drug world and the non-drug world.

The social worlds of dealers and smugglers are, because of the illegality of their work, ones that are circumspect. The Adlers' analysis does not portray a rigid bureaucracy, nor is it "organized" in the conventional wisdom sense of "organized crime." Dealing and smuggling require cooperation, but it is maintained through a complex set of social relationships. The Adlers describe a world in which leisure pursuits and business requirements overlap and mutually reinforce each other. Unlike the formally organized structure of bureaucracy where prestige is accorded to the office one holds, this is a world of the entrepreneur where recognition is given according to how well one achieves. Perhaps for this reason, both dealers and smugglers find it difficult to get out of the business. Attempts to "go straight" are usually not successful. Being accustomed to this way of life, those who leave often return or continue dealing on a part-time basis. The "deviant" career, once entered, is not easy to abandon.

Consumption: The Economics of Qat

In a survey of 439 men and 364 women in Yemen, respondents revealed that a high proportion of household expenditures was spent on qat regardless of income (Kennedy et al. 1980). In households with moderate or heavy users, expenditures on qat were 30 to 40 percent of household income for lower- and middle-income families. Among upper-income families, 20 to 30 percent of household income was budgeted for qat. Although upper-income families spent proportionally less than lower-income families, they nonetheless spent a larger amount of money. In general, higher expenditure for qat was negatively related to expenditures on meat and other foods. This finding disturbed many Western observers who concluded that the Yemenis spend such a high proportion of family income for qat because it is addictive. Yet, as previously noted, there is no pharmacological or any other evidence to suggest this conclusion. Why do Yemenis spend so much of their income on qat?

According to Shelagh Weir (1985), the high price paid for qat cannot be entirely or even mainly explained by its stimulant effects. There is an important distinction to be drawn between the reason something is consumed and the reason for placing a high monetary value on it.

> An alternative view is that the high expenditure on qat and its increasing popularity are better understood if they are seen less as a reflection of the value Yemenis place on qat's stimulant effects and more of the value they place on the social effects of being a qat consumer. (53)

To better understand the cultural value of qat, a review of qat as a thing and of how that thing is produced and distributed is necessary. Qat is a bush or tree that is grown for its leaves. Leaf colors range from pale green to dark green and red and vary in flavor as a result of soil type, age, and amount of watering. Thus, there is variability in qat as a natural product. Qat is picked in the morning. Branches with a good growth of new leaves at their tips are broken off about a half meter down from the tip and laid out in cowhide bags or plastic sheets. At midday the branches are carried back to a house where they are packed. Just prior to packing, old leaves are stripped from the branch around the new shoots. Old leaves are left on the lower part of the branch for aesthetic purposes. Two to four of these branches are then bunched together. These small bundles are tied in threes to make a larger bundle, and two of the larger bundles are tied together to make the trade bundle (*guruf*). This is then encased in banana stems to keep it from drying (93–94).

Qat is sold at the marketplace in bunches call *rubtah*. These bunches are prepared by landowners or specialized qat traders before being transported to retailers, who sell directly to customers. Although rubtah vary in the way they are packed from region to region, their size is tailored for one day's usage by a customer and is approximately 100 grams. Qat is purchased either the day before or on the day of consumption.

Because there is variation in qat, competition between producers is based on the characteristics of the leaf itself. This makes qat quite different from other drugs such as heroin, methamphetamine, alcohol, and cocaine which, as things, do not vary. Freshness is another attribute by which qat is judged; therefore, qat farmers must get qat to market as soon as possible to insure a high price.[17]

The distribution system for qat was altered in the 1970s as a result of improvements in the infrastructure of transportation. The building of roads, the acquisition of motor vehicles, and the extension of rail lines greatly increased the size of potential markets. However, as Weir points out:

> Improved infrastructures and marketing were not the sole contributors to increased qat consumption in Africa and Arabia. They only made qat more readily available in areas where it was already consumed or where there was a local cultural potential for qat consumption. The demand that already existed could be more easily met, but new demand was not created. What in fact was created, or increased, were changes in economic and social conditions, which *coincided* with improvements in transportation facilities. This needs stressing because the

diffusion of qat consumption and analogous consumption practices are often described as though they were diseases which only require carriers in order to spread widely and indiscriminately in any population. But the host culture must be receptive to the adoption of such a complex practice as qat chewing. It is hard to imagine that it would catch on, say, in Edinburgh parlors or Paris salons, however many planeloads of qat leaves were imported. (30)

The price of qat is not directly related to production or transportation costs. As Weir reminds us about the price of anything:

What ultimately determines both the high price of qat and the range of prices at which it is sold is customer preferences and what they are able and prepared to pay. The crux of the matter is that *people do not pay as little as they can, but as much as they can afford.* Forces rooted in the context and meaning of qat consumption push the expenditure of each customer to a personal ceiling determined by his income. This dynamic is what makes qat so expensive (99, emphasis hers).

This same principle can be applied to food. One cannot assume that those who spend proportionately more on qat have diets that lack nutrition. The price of food does not necessarily indicate nutritional value. Monied Yemenis will buy local foods which are more expensive, although imported and equally nutritious foods are less expensive. The buying of expensive foods is another way of garnering prestige. Choosing to buy qat over expensive foods is an indication that one may only be able to compete for prestige in one of these areas (food or qat), not that families or people are suffering non-nutritious diets in order to consume qat (108).

Probably the most important function of qat is as an article of **conspicuous consumption**, the ostentatious display of wealth in order to acquire prestige. Hosted rituals, such as weddings and circumcisions, where hosts are expected to provide qat yield very little prestige because providing qat is obligatory. Conversely, the daily qat parties are mechanisms by which one can earn more prestige. As a product, qat qualifies as a prestige item. On the symbolic level, it is a green substance in an environment where drought and famine are part of the historical consciousness. It is also a luxury in that it has no food or survival value or any practical use (this can be said of most drugs). Because of its expense, it is a clear indicator of economic and hence social differences. The visible differences in the size, shape, and color of the leaves are recognized and valued by consumers. Yemenis can tell the quality and can estimate the cost of another man's qat from across a room.

Thus, qat serves both to affirm one's social standing in the community and as a means by which to "buy one's way" up the social ladder (159–161).

What about the argument that scarcity determines value? Here one must consider whether the item is naturally scarce or socially scarce. Weir argues that in Britain when most could afford only beer, wine indicated high prestige. When wine became more available, rare and scarce wines distinguished the rich. Originally tea was the mark of upper-class standing. When it became readily available, distinctive brands, fine china and silverware marked the upper-class consumer. Rarity, either socially contrived or due to natural distributions, transforms an item into cultural capital. Qat consumption, for example, involves a gamble with expendable income that can result in prestige. Those who must struggle financially to compete are viewed in negative terms. Those who spend without concern for other needs are acknowledged in positive terms.

Weir's analysis of qat consumption illustrates how "things" may take on cultural meaning, irrespective of the characteristic of the thing. Readers may find this argument convincing, but what about things that are addictive? Conventional wisdom suggests that drugs which are addictive must be treated differently than those, like qat, which are not addictive. The next section addresses this question.

Consumption: Taking Care of Business—Part I

A study that has become a classic in the drug literature was done by the anthropologist Edward Preble and the economist John Casey (1969). Preble spent time in bars and in the streets of four lower-income communities in New York City, where he was able to establish longtime relationships with heroin addicts in their environment. In addition, they interviewed patients in a drug addiction unit of a hospital. In total, they were able to use data from 150 informants. Most of the prior studies of addicts had taken place in organizational settings such as hospitals, clinics, and prisons. Not surprisingly, addicts in these settings were not different from their fellow patients or inmates. Addicts in mental hospitals were described as having various mental pathologies; addicts in clinics were viewed as having medical problems, while addicts in prison were defined as criminals. The picture of the addict world presented by Preble and Casey was quite different from these other models. They described them as alert, purposeful, and resourceful persons who were pursuing a meaningful way of life, albeit behaviorally different from the life-style of other Americans. They found that:

> Their behavior is anything but an escape from life. They are actively engaged in meaningful activities and relationships seven days a week. The brief moments of euphoria after each administration of a small amount of heroin constitute a small fraction of their daily lives. The rest of the time they are actively, aggressively pursuing a career that is exacting, challenging, adventurous, and rewarding. They are always on the move and must be alert, flexible and resourceful. The surest way to identify heroin users in a slum neighborhood is to observe the way people walk. The heroin user walks with a fast purposeful stride, as if he is late for an important appointment—indeed, he is. He is hustling (robbing and stealing), trying to sell stolen goods, avoiding the police, looking for a heroin dealer with a good bag (the street retail unit of heroin), coming back from copping (buying heroin), looking for a safe place to take the drug, or looking for someone who beat (cheated) him—among other things. He is, in short, *taking care of business*, a phrase which is so common with heroin users that they use it in response to words of greeting, such as "how you doing?" and "what's happening?" *Taking care of biz* is the common abbreviation. *Ripping and running* is an older phrase which also refers to their busy lives. For them, if not for their middle and upper class counterparts (a small minority of opiate addicts), the quest for heroin is the quest for a meaningful life, not an escape from life. And the meaning does not lie, primarily, in the effects of the drugs on their minds and bodies; it lies in the gratification of accomplishing a series of challenging, exciting tasks, every day of the week. (1969, 2–3)

Preble and Casey point out that the heroin user must become involved in heroin distribution because the quality of street heroin is low and the price is high. This had not always been the case in New York City. Between the world wars, heroin use was limited to people *in the life*—show business people, thieves, gangsters, prostitutes and pimps. The major ethnic groups associated with heroin use were Italian, Irish, Jewish, black, and Chinese. The market was controlled by users, and there was little public acknowledgement of its use. During the Second World War, supplies of heroin were cut off and there was, for all practical purposes, no use at all. After World War II, there was an expanding population of users. From 1940 to 1960 blacks who migrated from the south increased the black population twofold, and the Puerto Rican population increased over eight times. These newcomers filled the ranks of the lowest economic levels. Along with other slum dwellers, the Italians and the Irish, they became the heroin users. Heroin was sold in capsule form during this period. Each cost about one dollar and would get two to six people high. A common practice was for several people to contribute toward the purchase of heroin and use it communally.[18]

> Sometimes as many as twenty people would get together and, in a party atmosphere, share the powder contents of several capsules, which were emptied upon a mirror and divided into columns by means of a razor blade, one column for each participant. The mirror was passed from person to person and each one would inhale his share through the nose by means of a tapered, rolled-up dollar bill which served as a straw, and was called a *quill*. (1969, 5)

Because the price was so low and the quality so high, heroin addicts could afford to support their habits, even in low paying jobs. As a result, there was little illicit behavior associated with being a heroin addict. This began to change around 1951 when heroin became popular with young street gang members. The more respected members of these gangs were the first adopters of heroin. They were soon followed by other gang members. This increased demand and resulted in higher prices. With fewer work skills and a history of illicit activities, these gangs expanded their illicit "work" to underwrite the cost of heroin. Corresponding to the upward spiraling of heroin use and illegal activities by these youth, law enforcement efforts intensified and there was pressure put on legislators to pass anti-drug laws.

In November 1961, there was a severe shortage of heroin. Although it lasted only a few weeks, the demand was so high that many distributors were able to reduce the quality of the heroin they sold and double or triple the prices. This lesson in free-market economics, coupled with subsequent short-term shortages over the next few years, resulted in even higher prices. Preble and Casey report that in 1969 it cost the user $20 a day compared to $2 a day in 1949. Corresponding with this price increase, the social cohesion that had characterized the addict in 1949 was replaced by competition among users. Instead of a community of users bound by common interests, the user in 1969 formed temporary partnerships with other addicts to engage in illicit activities or to share in the purchase of the drug and the paraphernalia of use. Heroin use became a "central life issue," where the activities of users focused on the acquisition of the drug. Heroin was now a business—or a least the basis for business.

Preble and Casey observed that most heroin users in low-income neighborhoods engaged in illegal activities to support their heroin use. This included a wide variety of criminal activities such as burglary, hustling, shoplifting, and robbery. In general, they avoided crimes that did not result in financial gain. Crimes against persons, such as felonious assault, were rare and usually occurred only when the addict sought cash as an outcome. Crimes which resulted in cash, such as robbery, conning, or selling heroin, were preferred over crimes that resulted in property because having property increased one's risk of detection. Unlike money that can be concealed, stolen goods must be carried around in search of a direct buyer or a "fence."[19]

The Heroin Addict as Redistributor

Preble and Casey discovered a system operating in low-income neighborhoods where otherwise law-abiding citizens could purchase goods at discount prices from heroin users. They report that:

> Housewives will wait on the stoop for specialists in stealing meat (known as *cattle rustlers*) to come by, so that they can get a ham or roast at a 60% discount. Owners of small grocery stores buy cartons of cigarettes stolen from the neighborhood supermarket. The owner of an automobile places an order with a heroin user for tires, and the next day he has tires—with the wheels. At the Easter holidays there is a great demand for clothes, with slum streets looking like the streets of the Garment District. (19)

Preble and Casey's observation describes a **redistribution** system. Although the reader may accept taxation as a necessary but genteel way of redistributing income, there are alternative methods for accomplishing the same goal, especially for the poor. As Brinkley Messick (1978) points out: "The poor are never capable of operating in a system of power and influence controlled by the rich . . . because they do not have the money to buy influence, nor the influence to be paid money" (212). An alternative system for redistributing income is theft—one way the poor can extract taxes from the wealthy. As part of the economic structure of the low-income neighborhood, the heroin user provides an economic service to the community. Goods are usually stolen from more affluent neighborhoods and brought back into the low-income neighborhood. In spite of criticisms from residents of low-income neighborhoods about the drug addict, they nevertheless purchase items from these discount salesmen. In this milieu, the addict can garner prestige from other addicts and non-addicts in the neighborhood as a result of success in this system of redistribution.

The term *real hustling dope fiend* (a successful burglar, robber, con man, and so on) is a mark of respect. Those addicts who remain in the neighborhood begging for money or renting out needles are negatively viewed as *non-hustling dope fiends* (20). What we note in this description is not that much different from descriptions of other careers. Hard work, ingenuity, and skill are rewarded in both licit and illicit professionals. As Preble and Casey state:

> The activities these individuals engage in and the relationships they have in the course of their quest for heroin are far more important than the minimal analgesic and euphoric effects of the small amount of heroin available to them. If they can be said to be addicted, it is not so much to heroin as to the entire career of a heroin user. (21)

Addict Careers

The "career" to which Preble and Casey refer includes several services or tasks related to the marketing of heroin. Within this marketing system, users are seldom specialized—that is, they move freely from one task to another. For example, one week a user might be a *tester*, one who can test the quality of heroin that is being sold by a *dealer*. In exchange for this service one might receive drugs, money, or both drugs and money. The next week this same person might be a *juggler*, one who sells directly to other users; the profits are then used to support his own habit. The movement from one of these specialized activities to another illustrates the versatility of the heroin user. Unlike his middle-class counterpart who specializes within a complex division of labor, the drug user from a poor neighborhood is a generalist who moves from one specialized position to another within a complex division of labor. The same holds true of criminal activities. Although some addicts do repeat the same criminal offense, others are *flat-footed hustlers*—persons who, when presented with the opportunity, will engage in almost any crime. Whatever the "career" of the user, whether within the drug distribution system or in the non-drug illicit market, the goal of their activities is to obtain money with which to purchase heroin. Just how much money and how it is distributed is the subject of the next section.

Consumption: Taking Care of Business—Part II

Preble and Casey's seminal findings encompassed a wide number of varied topics, many of which were later studied in detail by other researchers. For example, one study focused on the issue of the economic contribution of addicts to the wider community in which they live (Johnson et al. 1985).

Johnson's team, like Preble and Casey, took to the streets. They set up two field offices or research stations. One was in East Harlem and one in Central Harlem. East Harlem, or Spanish Harlem or El Barrio, is predominantly Hispanic (66 percent). Central Harlem is 95 percent black. Using ex-addicts/offenders as their staff, they were able to interview 201 street addicts. The final sample was 75 percent male. Fifty-five percent were black; the remainder were Hispanics. Sixty-three percent were thirty-five years old or younger. Sixty-three percent were daily heroin users; 50 percent had used heroin for 10 or fewer years. Forty-four percent engaged in theft as the principal support for drug use, while 23 percent earned their income from drug business. Sixty-two percent had been incarcerated. Each addict was interviewed for five consecutive days and then once a week for four weeks. Additional cycles of interviews were carried out in East Harlem where respondents were asked to return every three to six months.

The goal of the interviews was to collect detailed information about the daily activities of drug users. They measured earnings from both legitimate (family, welfare, friends, and legitimate work) and criminal activities, type of criminal activities (drug or non-drug related), arrest information, and a detailed accounting of living expenses (rent, food, legal expenses, transportation, and so forth). The interviews resulted in a total of 11,417 person-days of data.

The major advantage of this study was that data were obtained from drug users rather than official reports. Income from illicit activities are often underreported because the "crimes" themselves are not reported. Monies from con games, prostitution, and pimping are almost never reported. The Internal Revenue Service would be quite surprised if they received a tax return that included revenues from drug sales or thefts! Other crimes, such as stripping abandoned buildings for copper wire, usually have no victims and hence are not reported. Even such crimes as burglary, robbery, and forgery may go unreported or underreported, especially if the victims are heroin users.

Johnson found that daily heroin users had the highest income from both licit and illicit sources— $18,710 per year. Irregular users averaged $5,867 per year. These totals considered both cash and non-cash activities. Included in this latter category was "income" from avoided expenses, such as fare evasion on the subway and shoplifting for one's own use. In comparing cash income from all sources to cash expenditures for drugs and non-drugs, it was found that regular and daily users had no surplus to their economies. What they "earn" they spend.

Analyses of costs linked to heroin use often emphasize "social costs" (103). These are costs associated with enforcement of drug laws, incarceration and/or treatment of drug users, and indirect costs (such as lost productivity due to incarceration or treatment). Another social cost included in these formulations is victim losses. Johnson's team argues that including this as a cost of drug use is misleading. Victims seldom know who stole their goods; therefore, it is impossible to calculate whether or not they were taken by heroin users.[20] Even if theft by a heroin user is known, victim loss fails to recognize that stolen goods do not disappear—rather, they are transferred from one party (the victim) to another party. Goods stolen by drug users may not be available to the victim, but they remain in the market. They argue that the only way to determine the social costs of theft is through analysis of individual data on economic transfers. This is precisely the data that the Johnson team collected.

The study found that goods stolen by heroin users are redistributed back into the community at discounted prices. The data indicated that television sets were the most frequently stolen item. From their sample of 201 users, they estimated that approximately 1,000 television sets were stolen in one year. The official data would report only the number and the value of the television sets as social costs. Johnson's team, however, maintains that the "real" calculation must include other variables. For example, they write the following scenario:

> . . . we assume that the typical stolen television was a color set purchased about three years prior to the theft. The owner (individual victim) paid $400 for the set, and it was worth $200 after three years of use. . . . The individual suffered a $200 monetary loss. . . . But the victim also had an unexpected monetary cost of $450 for a new set. He purchased a comparable replacement set for $450 from a local store after the theft. Thus, an equivalent color television actually *cost* the victim $600.
>
> The purchaser of the television stolen by our subject was typically a low-income worker who already had a color television but wanted another. He was unwilling to pay over $100 for a second set, so effectively, he had zero demand for a retail color television. After laying out $50 in cash to the burglar for the television, the purchaser had a new capital asset and a net economic gain of $150 that the crime *paid* to him.
>
> . . . The burglar then purchased three bags of cocaine and three of heroin ($60 value) for $50 and injected them as a speedball.[21]

The heroin abuser faced the risk of arrest, incarceration, and confrontation with the victim in committing the burglary. He invested about an hour of time in planning and committing the crime and another hour trying to sell the television set. For his risk and time, he received only $50 in cash. Although he got the drugs he desired, he was soon without cash. . . .

The retail merchant selling the new television had an indirect gain from the burglary. The previously no-demand (for a new television) victim immediately became a high-demand customer, and the merchant gained a $450 sale.

In sum, one person—the individual victim—had a substantial economic loss, but that loss was offset by the direct and immediate gains to four other parties: the burglar, the purchaser of the stolen television, the retail merchant, and the drug seller. (116–117)

If we take this example and multiply it by 1,000 television sets, the resulting figures become quite large. In addition, the effects of these transactions extend beyond the local community. Manufacturers had to produce 1,000 more televisions to replace those that were stolen. To accomplish this, either additional employees were hired or present workers worked more hours. This increased income paid to workers was taxed by local, state, and federal governments. And finally at the sale end of replacement, merchants collected taxes that were paid to the state.

Another economic benefit to the community came from shoplifting. Shoplifted goods are high priced items that could be sold fast. Thus, the cattle rustler stole steaks, not hamburger, and the booster lifted expensive clothing. Even though customers in low-income neighborhoods paid more for goods because merchants increased their prices to offset losses from shoplifting, those higher costs could be corrected through purchases on the illicit market.

Further economic benefit came from the sale of heroin. According to William Chambliss (1977), heroin addicts spent over $30 billion in 1970 for heroin, an amount larger than gross sales of the 10 largest multinational corporations. Because the street-level price is at least 15 times greater than cost, this represents profits for someone, profits that could be invested in legitimate banks and businesses. If we add to this equation monies spent for law enforcement, drug research, therapy, and home security, the drug business may be the largest industry in the world! Given all these considerations, we can conclude that both licit and illicit economies gain from the activities of the heroin users.

The Johnson analysis of the "economics" of heroin use in Harlem forces us to consider markets other than those defined as legal. The "underground" economy is as much an adaptive strategy as the formal economy. For example, Gretchen Herrmann and Stephen Soiffer (1984) estimate that "garage sales," a legal activity, generated nearly one billion non-taxed dollars in 1981. They argue that the increased frequency of these sales is but one survival strategy used by working- and middle-class Americans in response to a decline in real disposable income (wages and salaries adjusted for taxes and inflation). Other strategies include baby-sitting, crafts, lawn care for money, and labor exchanges which function to evade the formal economic sector. In places like Harlem, with its high numbers of unemployable and high rates of unemployment, there are limited alternative strategies. Heroin users who took care of business earned, on average, about the same as their low-income, minority counterparts in the licit economic system—$12,000 a year. In addition, they contributed to increased production of goods and services in both the underground and the licit economy. Johnson's team estimated that the victims of the crimes committed by heroin users lost, on average, about $14,000 a year. The heroin user received about $5,800 in cash for these crimes. The purchasers of the stolen merchandise thus gained $8200 worth of products they otherwise could not afford (184–185). The loser in this venture was the heroin user. The underground economy, including the heroin-distribution industry, were the winners.

Consistent with the social science approach, Johnson's analysis of the consequences of heroin use is systemic, not individual. By incorporating heroin use into the economics of low-income neighborhoods, he avoids legalistic and moralistic concerns. Heroin use, when viewed this way, is neither an individual pathology nor an idiosyncratic behavior. Rather, it is an adaptive strategy for the redistribution of goods. On the cultural level, the behavior of the heroin user is consistent with the general value placed on "hard work" and, as previously discussed in chapter 5, "risk taking."

Have Economies No Limits?

Johnson's study introduces an interesting issue, namely, what are the limits to economy? In this chapter, we have reviewed the economies of villages and neighborhoods. Yet at the same time we have noted that these local economies may be and sometimes are linked to larger global economies. Jack Rollwagen (1980) suggests that treating villages, communities, and neighborhoods as autonomous systems with self-contained adaptive strategies reflects an isolationist position that violates the social science principle of holism. He argues that in the last 100 years or so, economies have become increasingly worldwide. Marihuana grown in Jamaica by Rastafarians may find its way into junior high schools in Minnesota. Opium harvested by Ban Lum villagers will, through a series of transformations, become heroin on the streets of New York City or Detroit. These examples need not be restricted to drugs. The economics of American culture have been affected by manufacturers' decisions to move their production facilities to Korea, Poland, Mexico, Taiwan, or any other place where labor is less expensive. This, in turn, has altered distribution networks and consumption patterns. The result of these decisions is that local economies, both in the United States and in other countries, have been changed.

In answer to Rollwagen's charges, I would agree that international economies have emerged over the past century, and I would agree that these *may* have cultural characteristics distinct from the cultures that make up that global economy. However, any understanding of that "culture" must come from the same concerns and variables used to study local economies. Neither Leslie White's "law" of evolution nor the principles of cultural materialism proposed by Marvin Harris came from the study of *a* global "culture." Rather, they were constructed from multiple observations of specific cases in different cultural settings. At the level of theory, the concern is with explaining variations in production, distribution, and consumption by a limited number of attributes or variables. The process of theory construction leads to an understanding of the general, not the particular. This does not mean that global economies cannot be studied as social and cultural *systems*; but it does not follow that they will be any different, insofar as the rules by which they operate, than the economies of villages, communities, or neighborhoods. If they are, our theory must be reworked.

One additional difficulty associated with the global approach is the possibility of neglecting the holistic approach. For example, in this chapter we have reviewed opium production in Southeast Asia and the distribution and consumption of heroin in the United States. From this discussion, one might conclude that there is an opium/heroin economy. However, to infer this would deny the assumptions of substantive economics. Economies are not the production, distribution, and consumption of a specific thing but rather a complex system of adaptation. Although our focus has been on drugs, it should be remembered that drugs are one trait among many. For example, opium production is one item in the economy of the Lisu and the Hmong. Marihuana is one trait in an inventory of traits for the Rastafarians. Heroin distribution and consumption are a part of the adaptive techniques used in Detroit and Harlem. The boundaries between the economies of a Lisu village and their Karen neighbors are not determined by the fact that the Lisu produce opium and the Karen do not, just as the boundaries between residents of Spanish Harlem and middle-class New Yorkers are not marked by the presence or absence of heroin. Concluding that there is a drug economy presents us with the same problem as concluding that there is a drug culture or subculture—namely, the assumption that the effect of adaptation is also the "cause." That economies are linked cannot be denied, and that economies are linked by drugs cannot be ignored. However, saying that the cigarettes smoked by Tobians joins them with workers in a cigarette factory in Virginia or North Carolina ignores the fact that Tobi and the United States have quite different substantive economies as adaptive strategies to different environments.

Economy as Adaptive Strategy

Economy, as we have used the term here, refers to rules governing activities that reflect adaptive strategies to environments. Those environments may be physical, social, or some combination of the two. The Lisu's organization of labor to produce opium is, in part, explained by the "natural" relationship between opium as a plant and the ecological zone in which it is grown. In contrast, organizational structures that sell marihuana and heroin in the United States are responses to an environment that defines this activity as illegal. In both cases, different cultural rules evolve as a response to environmental demands.

A cursory review of the different economies in the world would reveal that the resources and the technologies to exploit those resources are unevenly distributed. Some economies reflect rich resources; others have only meager environments to exploit. The Lisu and the Hmong live in an area of the world where it is necessary to exercise caution in using their environment. The economies of these two societies reflect adaptive strategies that efficiently exploit those environments, not by specializing in the growing of opium but by using opium as one of several different sources of support. The adoption of opium growing by these mountain tribes is not something they sought. Rather, the adoption of opium occurred at an "optimal moment" in their history. The **optimal moment**, according to Benjamin Higgins (1963) is a short period where a favorable coalescence of conditions occur that are conducive to the adoption of a trait or practice. If there had been no market for opium among the Chinese first, and had that market not continued in other parts of the world, the Lisu and Hmong would be just another example of tribal societies with horticultural technologies.

In constructing a theory that is based on adaptive strategies, one first reviews different specific studies of adaptation and then constructs a typology of environments and the corresponding adaptive strategies. The typology is then used to construct an explanation. One example should illustrate this process.

We might ask, "How do the poor adapt to the conditions of poverty?" Using cross-cultural data, Edwin Eames and Judith Goode (1980) found that people in urban industrial societies with low cash incomes that are intermittent and sporadic have developed similar adaptations to this environment. They found that the primary mechanism for survival under these conditions is conservation of resources. For example, insurance is provided through kin or quasi-kin; capital is stored in goods that can be sold or pawned, and goods are recycled. Because of low cash reserves, the diets of the poor consist of low-cost, starchy foods such as potatoes, rice, and corn. Purchase of these items is in small units, not only because small units are affordable at the time of purchase, but because the poor often lack storage facilities. Cooperative meals and purchases from street vendors or "fast food" outlets is another conserving practice. Cooking food for only one family or other small units requires more energy (kerosene, electric, gas) per household than when such costs are distributed or borne by many others. Housing needs are met by sharing. This leads to the observation that the poor live in high-density areas. Depending on the culture, this may be in squatter sections of a city, in rented facilities, or in the street. Clothing is obtained by directly searching garbage for castaway clothing, through secondhand vendors, or at "thieves' markets."

Corresponding to the intermittent cycles of income, some items may be obtained during high-income periods as a form of savings that can be converted to cash when income is low. This may be viewed as "irrational" or "irresponsible" by outsiders; but refrigerators, television sets, and automobiles may provide cash when needed to meet out-of-the-ordinary expenses.[22] The purchase of expensive items is often cited as "proof" that the poor are unable to defer gratification. Yet, as we have noted, this is simply an alternative method of savings. The practice of consensual or common-law "marriages" is judged to be evidence of an inability to control sexual urges. Yet when one considers the cost of marriage and the possible cost of divorce, not being married is one way of conserving scarce resources. Conditions that lend themselves to stable "families" include both potential and real access to economic resources. With low and intermittent income, especially for males, husbands and fathers can be economic liabilities. The large proportion of female-centered households in low-income areas of cities around the world is not evidence for "pathology" but rather an efficient adaptation to real economic circumstances.

We have already noted that the distribution and consumption of some drugs in the United States is a behavioral characteristic of the young, primarily the male, in low-income neighborhoods. From an adaptation perspective, young males are the most affected by intermittent and low income. Cross-culturally one finds gangs of young males in all large cities. For them, entry into even the most unskilled jobs is difficult. One response to this condition is to participate in the "underground" (from the standpoint of those in the licit economy) economy, including street sales of marihuana, cocaine, and heroin; theft; gambling; pimping or other illegal activities. While the dominant society may view these behaviors as "antisocial," "deviant," or "pathological," from a systems perspective they are effective strategies both for the participants and the community as a whole.

Whether drugs are part of the economy of the poor depends on the optimal moment. As an item that can be sold in a money economy or traded in a barter economy, they are likely to be adopted and incorporated into the local distribution system. It is not the drugs that "cause" the conditions of poverty but rather the conditions of poverty that encourage the adoption of drugs if they contribute to economic needs.

Conclusion

The use of the social science economic model, coupled with ecological or materialistic considerations, further expands our understanding of practices associated with the production, distribution, and consumption of all goods, including drugs. The application of the substantive economic model requires us to include systems of relationships into any explanation of economy. However, it would be imprudent to conclude that we can halt our search into the human condition by appeal only to *Homo economicus*. The behaviors of humans are collective. They are governed by a system of sanctions that insure predictability and conformity to expectations. Just how order is maintained in societies is our next topic.

Endnotes

[1] White did not cite Marx in his writings, but White's biographers suggest that Marx's "historical materialism" was well known to White. One might suspect that White avoided specific references to Marx because of the political climate of the 1940s and 1950s. There were strong negative sentiments against communism which became manifest in the 1950s with the McCarthy hearings in United States Congress. Everyone was suspect, including academicians. White himself was attacked by some anthropologists who were probably incensed by his materialism and attempted to have him disbarred from anthropology because of his "communist" leanings.

[2] One interesting way that this is done in some parts of the world is through mastication. Saliva contains enzymes which when added to starchy plants will result in fermentation.

[3] This was true within established circles. For those who wished to get into one of the circles, it was necessary to maintain the zero-sum. If one did not have the resources to reciprocate, he would either drop out or assume a subservient position to other circle members.

[4] There are some social scientists who separate generalized and balanced reciprocity. Generalized reciprocity is viewed as a pure gift that carries with it no expectation to directly reciprocate. Thus, parents have costs associated with raising children. This "moral" obligation does not carry with it the expectation that children repay these costs. In the short run this is true, but what obligates people to have children anyway? The payback, the reciprocity, for having been raised by one's parents or kin group is to have children yourself. This is a "system" requirement that keeps family and kinship going over time. To distinguish this form of reciprocity from balanced reciprocity in which there are clear obligations to repay in kind and in value within a specified time limit only makes a distinction between emic explanations of the individual parties involved at the expense of etic explanation of how systems operate. It is this latter consideration that distinguishes the social sciences from the individual consequences of social processes.

[5] Swidden (shifting) cultivation is a term used to describe the practice of clearing and burning vegetation and then planting on the burnt fields. This is sometime called slash-and-burn.

[6] In addition to the Thai paper baht, French Indo-China silver dollars and Indian gold rupees are found in the village. The latter two are used as a measure of wealth for such practices as the bridewealth, and as such are valued as metals.

[7] Durrenberger points out that other observers have put the price of opium higher and the labor inputs lower, resulting in opium having a higher return than rice production. If one accepts these figures, then the question becomes, "Why grow rice?"

[8] Meo or Miao are pejorative terms still used today. They mean savage or barbarian.

[9] The bridewealth is a payment to the family of the bride.

[10] The dibble stick is a pointed wooden shaft.

[11] Pituri contains the alkaloids scopolamine and hyoscamine.

[12] An initiation practice found among Australian Aborigines which involves slitting or perforating the urethra along the bottom of the penis.

[13] Although marihuana is not produced exclusively by Rastafarians, Jamaica was the third largest producer in 1985. Somewhere between 1,500 and 3,000 tons per year are estimated to be grown in Jamaica, with only 20 percent consumed locally (Taswell 1985).

[14] A gram is .03 ounces. Thus, the price of Thai Stick was $333 per ounce. The others were $165 per ounce.

[15] This was true until the mid-1970s when the U.S. and Mexican governments began spraying marihuana fields with paraquat. Southwest County's proximity to Mexico no longer had an advantage, and local dealers and smugglers had to compete with others for high-quality marihuana from Central and South America.

[16] The units used by smugglers and dealers were kilos (2.2 pounds) of marihuana and cocaine.

[17] In recent years, the qat market has expanded beyond Yemen. Qat is now exported by air to London, New York and elsewhere for consumption by emigrant Yemenis and Somalis.

[18] Note the similarity to the description of bottle gangs in chapter 6.

[19] One who knowingly purchases stolen merchandise.

[20] We will come back to this measurement dilemma in chapter 10. Briefly, the concern is with what is called the "ecological fallacy." If heroin use increases at the same time that crime rates increase, can one conclude that heroin users are responsible for crime? With just those two bits of data the answer is "no." There is the possibility that *both* heroin use and crime rates are the result of another variable and that heroin users and those responsible for the increased crime rates are two different populations.

[21] "Speedball" is the street name for injecting a combination of cocaine and heroin or amphetamine and heroin.

[22] This same function can be met by cooperative mutual aid groups of friends or kinsmen. One example of this is the burial societies in Zimbabwe that were discussed in chapter 6.

chapter 9

Social Control and Drugs

A constant theme throughout this book is that drug use must be explained as part of larger and more inclusive social and cultural frameworks. We observed that marihuana was a marker between age categories in 1960s America; that Yanamamö shamans were separated from non-shamans through their use of ebene, and females were prohibited from using kava as part of the division of labor in Tanna. In each of these cases we noted the existence of rules governing the use and meaning of different drugs; and in each of these cases, shared meanings and behaviors resulted in the construction of a predictable universe for the participants. The processes by which these universes are maintained is the subject of the social science approach toward understanding the rules governing social order. In this chapter we will review how drugs and drug use contribute to those orderly worlds within which humans live.

Socialization and Enculturation

One inescapable conclusion from observations of the human condition is that no society or culture has survived an extended period of anarchy or anomie. By definition, what we call a society or a culture can only exist when there are *shared* rules and norms. What accounts for this sharing was addressed by Durkheim (1938) when he wrote about the process by which social facts are inherited.

> To confirm ... the social fact ..., one need only observe the manner in which children are brought up. Considering the facts as they are and as they have always been, it becomes immediately evident that all education is a continuous effort to impose on the child ways of seeing, feeling, and acting which he could not have arrived at spontaneously. From the very first hours of life, we compel him to eat, drink, and sleep at regular hours; we constrain him to cleanliness, calmness, and obedience; later we exert pressure on him in order that he may learn proper consideration for others, respect for customs and conventions, the need for work, etc. If, in time, this constraint ceases to be felt, it is because it gradually gives way to habits and to internal tendencies that render constraint unnecessary; but nevertheless it is not abolished, for it is still the source from which the habits were derived. (5–6)

The terms used in social science to describe these processes of teaching are socialization and enculturation. **Socialization** refers to the process of learning appropriate social (behavioral) norms and behavioral strategies. **Enculturation** is the term used to describe learning cultural values and rules. Consistent with the distinction made throughout this book, we can visualize these two processes as shown in table 9.1.

Table 9.1.

The Place of Socialization and Enculturation in the Social Science Model

Society	Culture
Behavior	Expectations
Norms	Values/Rules
Socialization	*Enculturation*

Both enculturation and socialization are necessary components of the human condition. It is through socialization and enculturation that we learn to speak a language, to adopt a particular worldview, to behave correctly, and to avoid thinking or acting inappropriately. Thus, socialization and enculturation channel the human dependency on learning to a specific set of societal norms and cultural rules. The primary function of these processes is not to create separate and distinct *individuals* but rather to create social and cultural *persons*. Social and cultural persons share cultural values and social behaviors. This joint sharing validates the processes and defines the boundaries between "we" and "they" in organizational terms.

Variations in the content of socialization and enculturation are a reflection of the division of labor. Where the division of labor recognizes few distinctions, there will be fewer social persons. In contrast, where there are many distinctions, the outcome will be wider variations of social persons.[1] Yet, whether the variations in the division of labor are few or many, what results is *a* culture or *a* society, a common core of shared values and norms.

Neither socialization nor enculturation stop with childhood. Rather, they are continuous processes. Unlike genetically programmed behaviors which are fixed, learning permits modification and adaptability. The flexibility of learning allows for change and, as noted elsewhere, change is constantly occurring.

The reader might conclude that enculturation and socialization operate in a consensual way. People willingly adopt a particular set of values and behaviors. Yet even casual observation confirms that infants do not voluntarily give up breast-feeding, nor do adults voluntarily conform to speed limits on the highways. Acceptance of norms and values does not rely solely on voluntary actions. Rather, conformity to norms and acceptance of values are enforced through the use of sanctions.

Sanctions

The term **sanction** describes a wide range of rewards and punishments. In other words, sanctions vary. Some of these variations are outlined in a guide for field workers studying childhood socialization and enculturation (Whiting, Child, and Lambert 1966). Under rewards, they include the giving or showing of emotional support, acceptance, material objects, and various privileges. Rewards may be direct or promissory as, for example, when rewards are withheld until some expectation is met. More neutral techniques are distraction from an offending behavior, instruction or teaching, coaching, and demonstrating. Included under punishment are physical injury or threat of physical injury, ridicule, denial of privilege, and withholding support (41–42). Regardless of which sanctions are used, the function is the same. Sanctions insure conformity to norms and values.

In Durkheim's statement, we note that the application of external constraints results in "habits and to **internal tendencies** that render constraint unnecessary." Durkheim recognizes that while norms and values are initially learned from others, they eventually become internalized—that is, they determine how we "think" about the world or are the basis of emotional states that "tell" us about the propriety of our behavior. Thus, the norms and values that are imposed from outside become self-reinforcing. We have already noted this internalization in previous discussions. The Lisu keep pigs as a demonstration of one's ability to repay a debt and hence protect one's "honor." Tobians report that they avoid outward displays of aggression because they "fear" ghosts. Internal states such as embarrassment, guilt, humility, and anger have been reported as effective deterrents of untoward behavior. In contrast, other emotions signal rewarded behaviors. Love, pride, affection, trust, elation, and contentment are among those internal states that mark the fulfillment of norms and values.

Internal constraints operate as sanctions in all cultures. One way they are emically expressed in sanctioning systems is through references to some "others." Readers will be familiar from their own experience of different emic explanations for conformity to norms. One may avoid engaging in some behavior for fear of "what people might *think*[2] of them"; or there may be an expressed concern for "what people might *say* about them." Taking this one step further, people may fear what others "would *do* to them" if an expectation were not met. Thus, we note that internalized sanctions are arranged along a continuum from passive to active sanctions, as shown in table 9.2.

It is clear that sanctions vary when expressed emically. In addition to their being positive or negative, they also vary in intensity. Thus, the penalty for using the wrong fork is not as severe as the penalty for murder (wrongfully killing someone). Both actions may result in embarrassment, shame or guilt. Both may elicit gossip, and both may result in something being done. The German social psychologist Ralf Dahrendorf (1964) suggests that one way to measure the importance of expectations is through sanctions.

Table 9.2.

References for Sanctions

Levels of Sanctions		
Passive ◄————————————————► Active		
Thinking	Saying	Doing
Internalized sanctions guilt, shame, honor	Gossip, scandal	Physical action, force

Although his model focuses on explaining specific statuses[3], I would suggest that it can be used at the more inclusive level of culture. Table 9.3 shows the linkage between expectations and sanctions.

Table 9.3.

Hierarchy of Status Expectations and Associated Sanctions

Level of Expectation	Kind of Sanction	
	Postive	**Negative**
"Muss"—Must or Mandatory	——	Formal punishment Loss of a status
"Soll"—Should or Preferred	Social Acceptance	Social Exclusion
"Kann"—Can or Permitted	Praise	Dislike

From Dahrendorf's general model, we can analyze specific cases. For example, in chapter 8 we reviewed Mieczkowski's analysis of Young Boys, Inc. (YBI), a heroin distribution system. The YBI had a division of labor which linked "runners" to a "crew chief," who in turn was tied to a "lieutenant." In this system crew chiefs used sanctions as a way of rewarding or punishing runners for conformity to or violations of expectations. At the "muss" (or must) level, the expectation was that runners must not steal from the crew chief. Runners who did not steal were neither rewarded nor punished. For those runners who stole or were suspected of stealing, there was a range of punishments from "threats of violence" (saying) to "killing with a gunshot" (doing). When stealing was confirmed, runners at minimum lost their status and at maximum lost their lives. Either way, they were no longer incumbents of the position runner.

At the "soll" (or should) level in Dahrendorf's model there are both rewards and punishments. For runners, the reward for exceeding expectations was recognition in the form of cash bonuses and gifts. In addition, "good" runners received higher commissions and more to sell. Continued exemplary performance carried anticipatory rewards, such as moving up to crew chief. In contrast to rewards for incumbents of the status runner, those whose performance fell below expectations were punished by being given lower commissions and less to sell.

Expectations at the "kann" (or permissive) level represent a range of alternatives. Although one notes both positive and negative sanctions, they are at an interpersonal level. The options for runners are options of "style" rather than content. The methods used by runners to make sales through interpersonal skills may be praised or disdained by chiefs without any necessary connection to actual sales.

Although Dahrendorf's model was constructed for the analysis of specific status systems, it could be applied to shaman-client systems, family structures, or work groups such as the YBI. By ranking expectations we are able to isolate the core requirements for any specific status and thereby reconstruct how these systems operate. This hierarchical perspective is not unique to Dahrendorf. In fact, it has a long history in the social sciences. William Graham Sumner (1906) used this approach to identify the boundaries of a culture. His term **mores** (plural of mos) describes mandatory expectations that are shared by all statuses. For example, in American culture one must not appear in public without certain areas of the body covered, regardless of one's status. There are no rewards for conforming to this expectation, only punishment if it is violated. At the "should" level, the kinds of clothing that one wears to cover those parts will be dictated by different settings and situations. While a bathing suit is appropriate for the beach, it may be inappropriate for other settings. Sumner suggested the term **folkway** to describe this level of expectation. Folkways are appropriate behaviors, conformity to which brings social approval or acceptance. Failure to meet these expectations would result in some form of social disapproval. At the cultural level, the least imperative of the expectations are **alternatives**. It is at this level that we can acknowledge choice or "free will." Carrying our clothing example further, we may note that when the body parts are covered (mos) and the style is appropriate for the situation (folkway), there are choices between different colors, patterns, or fabrics. The "freedom" to select from among these alternatives is evidence that these behaviors have no consequences for defining the boundaries of culture. This same "freedom" does not, however, extend to the mores or the folkways, the violation of which results in negative sanctions—either internalized or imposed from outside.

In summary, the attribute "expectations" is a cultural universal. And in every culture these expectations vary along a continuum from more to less imperative. This does not, however, mean that the content of those expectations is universal. What is an imperative expectation in one culture may be an alternative in another. The question we have to answer is, "Why do expectations exist at all?" Humans are born without a set of instructions on appropriate behavior. We are not preprogrammed to express specific emotions, avoid punishment, or seek rewards. The processes of socialization and enculturation impose those instructions on us, and it is variations in those instructions that we have to explain. One suggestion is that sanctions exist to insure conformity that maximizes individual survival—but no individual survives. Instead, societies and cultures survive. Therefore, sanctions must exist to insure the survival of social and cultural systems. In order to answer the question of why sanctions are universal, we must first determine how social and cultural systems survive.

The Survival of Social and Cultural Systems: Alliance and Descent

The survival of any association or institution must consider two independent, but related, necessary activities. One is the continuity of order *within* the unit; the other is the establishment of order *between* that unit and others. The maintenance of order within and between kinship associations has been a central theoretical issue in the study of kinship rules (Buchler and Selby 1968). The associational or social unit is some form of kinship group (for example, family, lineage, or clan). The institutional or cultural unit is a system of kinship rules and expectations. The question of how continuity is maintained over time comes under the general title of **descent**. At the simplest level, families (social units) reproduce themselves under the guidance of kinship (cultural) rules. Parents not only have children but also pass on the rules by which these children will someday become parents. These rules of descent act as charters or guidelines which perpetuate a particular descent group—a family, a lineage, a clan. For example, in American kinship, kinship rules give children membership in both parents' families. This is reflected in naming rules. For example, the name "uncle" describes a male sibling of one's parents and identifies both a mother's brother and a father's brother. Thus both sides of the family are united by shared names. In other systems, such as lineages or clans, children belong to the groups of one parent or the other. Depending on rules of descent, the brother of a mother would have a name that is different from the brother of a father. The name would thus preserve the descent rules. Whatever social form kinship groups take, the rules governing membership in those groups must provide for descent or the groups will disappear.

In addition to rules which perpetuate descent, kinship systems everywhere have rules for forming **alliances** between different kinship groups. This is reflected in marriage rules. Kinship systems everywhere prohibit marriage between persons who hold membership in the same kinship group. This is incest, and those who violate this expectation are severely punished. What defines incest, therefore, will depend on the rules of descent. In the American system, the descent rules are the basis for kinship groups whose organizational structure is expected to have two parents, four grandparents, eight great grandparents, and so forth. Consistent with this expectation, marriages between persons who share the same parents (brother and sister) or grandparents (cousins) are prohibited as incest. Although emic explanations for this prohibition are often couched in terms of genetic consequences, the organizational explanation is that children from marriages between siblings or cousins will not have an organizationally "correct" kinship group. Children of brother-sister marriages would only have two instead of the expected four grandparents; children of cousin marriages would only have six of the organizationally expected eight grandparents. If the organization of "family" is to continue, the rules governing who marries whom will prohibit marriages that fail to replicate family organization. What survives if these rules are followed is not an individual but an organizational structure.

The study of how various kinship systems operate reveals that while variations exist, each system has rules which contribute to the survival of the system itself. If we extend these same principles to non-kinship groups we note that they too must address the question of alliance and descent. Whether we focus on church, government, school, military, or family, the continuity of any association depends on organization principles that are self replicating. At the same time, no association stands alone. Rather, all associations are linked in some way to others. What determines those linkages are alliance principles.

Our discussion of sanctions now begins to take on meaning far beyond a focused analysis of a few statuses. Sanctions are a surface manifestation of underlying structural principles of descent and alliance. I would suggest that the severity of sanctions is a window into the structural arrangements of society or culture. Where the practices are central to meeting alliance and/or descent functions, sanctions will be at the "must" level. When expectations have little or no consequences for alliance and descent, sanctions will be personal or absent. Thus, the study of sanctions and their variations is one way to gain an understanding of the principles that make society and culture possible.

With this framework in mind, we can now review some cases of how sanctions measure the organization rules governing descent and alliance.

Drinking: Sobriety, Insobriety, and Change

Sobriety and Control in an Egalitarian Village

It is rare that one finds an exact correspondence between enculturation and socialization. It is more common to expect and then find that the rules for behavior, while understood, are violated because environmental forces demand other behaviors. Stanley Brandes' (1978) study of a small Castilian village offers us a rare example of a community in which drinking expectations are identical to drinking behavior.

Spain ranks fourth in per capita consumption of alcohol among European nations. In spite of this high consumption (twice that of the United States), Brandes did not find any instances of drunkenness in his study of Becedas, an agricultural community with a population of 800. These villagers drink a wide variety of alcoholic beverages, including beer, wine, brandy, and an anise-flavored liqueur. This list is expanded further by inclusion of *aguadiente*, a home-brewed distilled wine. Alcohol is an accepted part of everyday practices. Both white and red wine accompany the midday and evening meals (on average, two liters a day for couples without children). In addition, certain foods are cooked in brandy or wine. Alcohol is an obligatory offering to visitors. Guests expect something to drink, as well as an assortment of sweet snacks that contain aguadiente, anise liqueur, or white wine. All rituals, such as baptisms, first communions, and weddings, require that alcohol be served.

Alcohol is also part of the ethnopharmacology[4] and ethnomedicine in Becedas. Hot milk, mixed with brandy, is given to people with colds; the pain of a toothache is relieved by a mouth rinse of aguadiente, and a stomachache is cured by multiple ingestions of whatever distilled beverage works.

In addition to home and ceremonial drinking, Becedians also consume alcohol in the village's three bars. Although they are open during the week, the largest number of customers are found on Sunday afternoons. After mass, women return home to prepare dinner and men gather in the bars. This drinking usually takes place in small groups where men reciprocate in buying each other drinks. The amount consumed therefore varies by the size of the group in which a person has membership. After dinner the men return to the bars to play cards. In contrast to the reciprocity which characterizes the pre-dinner drinking groups, the loser of the card game is "invited" to buy drinks for the other players. Brandes observed that if a man was not part of a drinking group or a card game, he would seldom order an alcoholic drink. Thus, the norm was that one only drank with others.

Brandes argues that the absence of drunken behavior can be explained both normatively and in reference to Becedian values. As previously reported by MacAndrew and Edgerton (1969), drunken comportment (behavior) is not linked directly to the amount of alcohol consumed but rather is learned. Drunken behavior is a consequence of socialization. With no drunks after whom to pattern appropriate drunken behavior, Becedians simply do not know how to behave in a drunken manner.

The value ascribed specifically to alcohol varies contextually. When taken with meals, it serves to enhance food; when consumed as a cure, it has medicinal value; and when ingested with friends it enhances sociability. In other words, the value of alcohol has nothing to do with alcohol or any physiological effect of alcohol but rather serves as a symbol that is used to achieve desirable or valued goals. Consistent with this, drunkenness (non-contextual drinking) is condemned outright.

Beyond specific references to alcohol and drunkenness, Brandes argues that sobriety is part of a larger system of values and expectations for Becedians. The village has no formal hierarchy of authority, and cooperation among households is highly valued. The source of the value on cooperation comes from economic necessity. As Brandes observed:

> Farming in Becedas is labor intensive. Because the surrounding countryside is hilly and rocky, the possibilities for agricultural

modernization have been limited. The quality of soil is generally poor. . . . Not only is much of the land terraced, but also orchards are interspersed with treeless parcels, a situation that creates difficult obstacles to the concentration of plots. (11)

Under these conditions, families must cooperate with each other in order to maximize each family's earnings.

One part of the general value system in Becedas is the belief in individual accountability. In reference to alcohol, there is no idea that one is "born" with a predisposition to drink. Drinking, or not drinking, is believed to be an act of free will. This same master value on accountability is the basis for a belief in economic self-reliance. While households provide some of their own resources, such as firewood and soap, total economic self-reliance is not possible because of the environment. Each household is expected to contribute one adult male to help clean communal irrigation ditches, clear communal roads, and maintain communal threshing floors. In addition, families exchange labor during haying and during the collection of apples and pears. Supporting the formation of these essential communal work groups is the belief that a man who lacks self-control when drinking cannot be relied on for necessary reciprocal and cooperative activities. Drunkenness is therefore a sign of one's violating not only the value of individual self-control but also the value of economic self-control. Avoidance of drunken comportment thus serves to preserve both of these values and contributes to the economic continuity (descent) of the village itself.

Brandes' study illustrates the importance of both alliance and descent for the survival of this community. Drunkenness has the potential to interrupt the formation of alliances which insure continuity in village life. Intolerance of drunken behavior is not therefore the condemnation of an individual transgression but rather a recognition of very real organizational needs. Under these conditions, shared internalized sentiments insure that norms and values correspond without the benefit of formal sanctions.

Obligatory Drinking in a Ranked Community

Just as sobriety is a learned behavior which contributes to the continuity of an egalitarian village, drinking and drunkenness may serve this same function in hierarchical communities. Stephen Bunker's (1987) analysis of Pumamarca, an Andean pueblo of 800, focuses on pressures to drink as part of social and economic life. In this village, alcohol is readily available. It is sold out of large drums in local shops. In addition, beer, wine, rum, and a homemade corn beer—*chicha*—can be conveniently purchased. Drinking occurs during rest periods between and after work, when buying and selling animals, and at church festivals. Bunker observed widespread encouragement to drink, to offer others drink, and to accept drink when offered. Paralleling this expectation were voiced concerns about drinking too much and about the "feelings" of obligation to drink, even when drink was not wanted. It was this ambivalence between normative expectations and vocal reservations that Bunker addressed in his research.

Like many other Andean communities, the village of Pumamarca was organized into two ranked social categories. In the upper rank were the *mestizos*, public service outsiders and descendants of large landowners. The lower rank was populated by peasants and small-scale agriculturalists whose labor was organized by households and exchanges between households. Before the land reforms, peasants were part of the hacienda system in which they were resident employees of landowners. Under this system, part of their wages was paid in *ch'akipa*, a predetermined amount of liquor, and they were provided with chicha during work breaks.

The expectation that workers receive alcohol is found today in association with cooperative unpaid projects, such as collective harvests. In both traditional and contemporary settings, a similar ritual is followed. Alcohol and chicha are served to workers from one container. After one man finishes his drink, the container is refilled and passed on to the next man. Refusal to accept the first drink of alcohol or chicha is rare. Verbal urgings from the server and other drinkers usually insure initial acceptance. If a second drink is offered and refused, there is less pressure to accept. Although the traditional and contemporary rituals are similar, Bunker suggests that they have different functions and meanings. Drinking while engaged in cooperative ventures represents sharing and mutual obligations. Under the traditional system, it was considered part of a payment by wealthy landowners for work done.

Drinking is associated with interregional economic exchanges. The mountainous area surrounding Pumamarca contains several distinct ecological zones. In each, different crops are grown and animals raised. As part of bartering practices between representatives from different regions, buyers are expected to offer alcohol. An initial step in the bartering process is the acceptance of alcohol by the seller. This is followed by negotiations on price and amount. When an agreement is reached, a final drink marks closure of the negotiations.

Drinking accompanies hosted religious events, such as fiestas, as well as individual rites of passage, such as weddings, funerals, and birthdays. During these events, one is obligated to accept whatever is offered in whatever amounts. To refuse is considered an insult to the host. Bunker interprets this response by hosts as a reflection of the alcohol-power linkage in this community. In addition to the mestizo-peasant distinctions, Pumamarca has a ranked system of power and wealth. Differences in wealth also mark differences in power. Sponsors of fiestas, by definition, are men of wealth. One demonstration of that wealth is the ability to offer drink. Refusal to accept a drink is interpreted as a challenge to the power of the giver and frequently results in anger. According to Bunker, sponsors are more insistent with some celebrants of fiestas than others, even to the point of getting them very drunk. Those to whom this zealous hospitality is directed are usually those who refused a request for contributions to the fiesta and therefore challenged the sponsor's authority. Since drunkenness is viewed negatively within the community, those who accept too much to drink are viewed with disapproval. In this way, those in more powerful positions can sanction those who do not contribute and, at the same time, confirm their own power.

While humans may intend their actions, they do not always intend the consequences. In addition to being the givers of drink, persons with high rank could not refuse an offer to drink. As a consequence of this obligation, Bunker notes several cases where persons in highly ranked positions lost money, and hence power, because of continued drunkenness. The expressed ambivalence about drinking was a reflection of this organizational characteristic of Pumamarca. Working one's way up the hierarchical ladder required purchasing and accepting alcohol. The higher up that ladder, the greater this obligation and the greater potential for losing power.

Ritual as Social Control

In chapter 7, we discussed the function of ritual in religion. We also noted that ritual analysis could be extended beyond the religious domain. If we define ritual socially as a predetermined, repetitive set of interlocking behaviors, we can add another function of ritual, namely, control. Ritual prescribes what participants must do, and order is established as a consequence of those prescriptions. In both Becedas and Pumamarca, drinking was part of a ritual performance. Not only were there expectations for when and with whom alcohol was exchanged, but the outcomes (drunkenness or sobriety) were part of ritual itself. It was on the basis of these expectations that participants were judged or sanctioned by others. It was the ritual that defined "drug abuse." These specific observations are confirmed in a cross-cultural review of drug use which found that emic definitions of "drug abuse" did not exist in traditional societies before European contact (de Rios and Smith 1977). This is attributed to the ritualization of drug use.

> In many traditional societies where ritualized drug use has occurred without evidence of abuse (either in terms of negative health considerations or social mores), the introduction of foreign drugs such as distilled alcohol, without any accompanying ritual, caused subsequent abuse that was of major social, political, and economic consequences. (16)

The conclusions of Marlene de Rios and David E. Smith offers us an insight into the drug use/drug abuse/ritual linkage, but it does not inform us about the organizational basis of rituals themselves. In his review of the ritual literature, William L. Partridge (1977) argues that ritual is employed by social scientists in two different ways. One is the "system transformation approach"; the other is the "structural redundancy approach." The system transformation approach defines ritual as a regulatory device which serves as a mechanism that guides individuals or societies through transitional stages or liminal periods (Turner 1969). This includes both rites of passage and rites of solidarity. The structural redundancy approach interprets ritual as a condensation of cultural information without interference (Leach 1966). Taken together, these two models address the issue of alliance (structural redundancy) and descent (system transformation).

In both its transitional and redundancy functions, ritual serves to maintain order. As a collective repetitive event, it publicly demonstrates those invisible obligations which bind people together into associations. In other words, rituals transform everyday variability in interpersonal relationships to both behavioral and symbolic order.

Partridge tested these two models in his analysis of the *chagua*, a pre-Colombian work ritual still practiced in contemporary Colombian communities. Traditionally, these work parties— chaguas—were used to accomplish different goals, such as caring for the aged, weeding, transporting produce, and house building. Under the Spanish, communities would meet their tax obligations through the chagua. This system was even adopted by African slaves who later used it in their free towns to organize collective labor. When wage labor was introduced by international corporations such as the United Fruit Company, most workers were organized into work gangs that used the chagua system. These were called *macheteros* and were formed to engage in seasonal work. The macheteros were day laborers hired to carry out temporary work assignments for cash wages. In these work gangs Partridge observed the ritual use of cannabis.

> Cannabis smoking diffused to Colombia only during the last 50 years and became customary only in these work gangs. Life histories reveal that smoking begins at the stage in the life cycle when adolescent males adopt adult work patterns, between the ages of 12 and 22, and that initiation into cannabis smoking invariably begins in the work gangs out in the fields and pastures and not in leisure activities. Informants have between 11 and 31 years of smoking experience, and no informant reports that his father used the drug. Rather, it is members of the nonkin based work group who initiated the neophyte. (64–65)

Partridge argues that under the traditional chagua systems, alcohol was consumed; but because of its expense, cannabis became the substitute for these day workers. What developed was a system of permanent reciprocal exchange between workers who shared cannabis with each other. Those who violated the obligation to reciprocate were labeled "vivo"—intelligent but unscrupulous and untrustworthy. The label of vivo may have negative consequences, especially in a highly competitive job market. When work gangs had too many members for a labor contract, those defined as "vivo" were excluded from the gang and therefore lost work and income.

The consumption of cannabis has various explanations. The emic explanation by participants defined it as an energizer. Cannabis was believed to increase work stamina, and it was used to relieve joint pains and to calm crying infants. These are the same explanations once ascribed to tobacco when it was part of chagua ritual. When viewed as a symbol, cannabis served to mark initiation into and integration of the chagua. New members were "tested" by their willingness to participate in cannabis sharing, and the boundaries of group were symbolically marked by who shared with whom.

The chagua was one of several different groups in which males held membership. The family and church were two others. Colombian males were expected to become "padre de familia," or head of a household. In order to achieve this status, men were expected to build their own houses. During an earlier period, help in building a house came from kinsmen, but changed work patterns resulted in the migration of kin and a weakening of kin obligations.

In place of the vanishing kinsmen, members of the chagua who participated in the cannabis ritual helped each other meet this expectation. In addition, ritual participants supported church obligations by becoming godparents to other members' children and also helped underwrite religious commitments. In contrast, those outside the cannabis ritual—those who were "vivo"—had to fulfill the same church and family obligations without help from their work mates. Thus we note that the practice of cannabis smoking symbolically bound non-kinsmen into obligatory relationships that maintained traditional cultural expectations outside of work. The ritual not only insured descent within the work group but provided personnel to aid in the descent functions of family and church obligations. The alliance between work, family, and church mutually supported each social unit. In Partridge's terms, this ritual served as both a mechanism for system transformation and structural redundancy. In our terms, this ritual has both alliance and descent functions.

Gossip as Social Control: The Newfoundland Case

In his classic statement on the function of gossip and scandal, Max Gluckman (1963) points out that these two activities are universal to humankind. If one goes behind the emic level—the topics of gossip and content of scandal— one notes that each functions to mark the borders among social groupings. With whom and about whom one gossips clearly distinguishes between a "we" and a "they." The obligation to participate in gossiping marks one's membership in a grouping of people. In short, the function of gossip is to mark alliances.

John Szwed (1966) used Gluckman's observations on the function of gossip to analyze changes in drinking patterns within a Newfoundland parish. This parish of 1,800 was divided into eight smaller sections resembling villages. Until the 1920s, the economy was mixed fishing and agriculture. The products of each of these activities were locally consumed—a subsistence economy. In the 1930s, logging was combined with agriculture to replace fishing. Construction of a United States Air Force Base during World War II increased the price of agricultural products and also absorbed surplus local labor. After 1949, Newfoundland became confederated with Canada. Farm prices lowered dramatically, and farming returned to its previous subsistence level. The expansion of employment opportunities, such as road building and railroading, reduced reliance on agriculture; and males became more oriented to outside labor markets where they competed for a few temporary but highly paid jobs.

The primary mechanism for disseminating information and maintaining social control in this parish was gossip. Gossip served to relay information about people who were not present and as a mechanism for assessing and determining public opinion. Gossip, as a continuing form of socialization, functioned to inform people how to behave in social groupings and to protect them from violating expectations. Szwed argues that this traditional communication system became less effective when males were forced to work outside the community—and therefore were not subject to continued internal surveillance. Because they were absent from the parish, males were less subject to the control function of gossip. This difference was marked by changes in drinking behavior.

Before the advent of the air force base, beer was brewed at home for special events, such as cooperative work parties and weddings. During the Christmas season, rum was smuggled in for the one period of sustained drinking. When beer was consumed at home, it was part of a food exchange system that linked households into alliances that bound sections together. These household alliances took the form of visiting between households. During these meetings, women in the host household were obligated to serve tea and bread. Visits usually involved both men and women from different households. However, even on those occasions when women and men met separately, women were responsible for providing the customary tea and bread. These visits not only served to link households but were the settings within which gossip occurred.

Military personnel introduced United States drinking patterns and commercial beer to the parish. The result, according to Szwed, was that alliances between households changed from male *and* female household activities to male-only or female-only events, with male alliances marked by beer consumption.

> Whereas men once sat in the kitchen and talked over their tea, the automobile and truck have tended to alter this pattern to the point where one now sees cars along the road in which the driver and his friends are drinking commercial beer by the caseful. . . . most men carry several bottles of beer in their parkas when they go out . . . . Men in cars and trucks invariably carry a case in the trunk. . . . Beer is never far away. (437)

While beer became a symbol of male friendship and reciprocal obligations, one cannot conclude that beer was the causal factor.

The air force base was only one of several contributing factors to employment changes in the parish. The change from stable households, with their obligation to host visits, to a migratory male work force had other consequences. Under the traditional household alliance system, food was prepared by women. In order to meet this exchange expectation, males were "encouraged" to marry. When the symbol of exchange changed from tea and bread to beer, wives were no longer necessary to maintain a reciprocal set of ties among males from different households. Drinking patterns changed from being limited to a few special occasions to a standard accompaniment for almost every male gathering—sacred and secular, public and private.

Changes in the structure of this parish altered the contribution of gossip toward social control. Male absenteeism from the parish and the increased competition for employment removed males from the information-gossip flow which had contributed to leveling out differences between individuals and households. It was replaced by two different networks of control, one for males and one for females. Females, who remained out of the public arena, maintained the traditional network of gossip-information through household visits where tea and bread were consumed. In contrast, males participated in a new system of reciprocity and leveling marked by drinking. In the public arena, conflict was reduced between potential or real competitors through mutual drinking. In fact, public meetings became small drinking groups where interpersonal relationships were on a friendly basis and where there were few social distinctions. In addition, alcohol consumption could be used to "explain" dissent. Outbursts of hostility were simply explained as the result of having too much to drink. Thus, we note that control had not disappeared but rather had been transformed to confirm broader changes. For both males and females, mechanisms existed which insured the leveling of differences. Females relied on household alliances maintained by gossip; male alliances were maintained through drinking beer.

In these four cases we observed that the meaning and function of different drugs could be understood as contributing to both the alliance and descent functions within different social and cultural settings. It was not the drugs or any physiological response to these drugs that imposed order but rather the meanings that were imposed when these substances were shared. The tea served by women in Newfoundland had the same organizational consequence as the beer drunk by men. Cannabis replaced alcohol in the changed chagua system, but it did not change the function of that system. Organizational necessities explained both sobriety and drunken behavior. Underlying the use of these different drugs was a structure or system whose survival or extinction depended on meeting alliance and descent requirements. One should not, therefore, conclude that these drugs were the agents of control. Rather, they are physical traits which serve as symbolic markers for alliance and descent.

While most behaviors and beliefs within a society or culture are regulated through continuing socialization and enculturation that has been internalized, there are always situations in which disputes arise. In those cases, settlements may have to be imposed from outside for the sake of alliance and descent. When order is imposed by a third party, we consider this sanction to be part of the legal domain. In the next section we review the social science approach to law.

The Law and Social Control

When disputes or arguments occur between either individuals or associations, they may threaten or disrupt social order. William Haviland (1993) suggests three possible processes by which disputes can be resolved. One is though **negotiation**. Here both parties deal with each other directly and, when each is satisfied, the dispute is resolved. Another is **mediation**. In mediation there is a third party who assists the disputants. Third parties are presumed to have no stake in the outcome, nor can they impose a resolution. The third process is **adjudication**. Similar to mediation, the third party in adjudication listens to the disputing parties and then makes a decision that is binding on both disputants. Law, as we shall use it here, is a system of adjudication that sanctions one or both of the disputing parties.

A search of the social science literature reveals that defining the "law" offers us an example of an unresolved dispute. While there is general agreement that deviations from the norms are rare in all societies, there is less agreement on what specific social form the "law" takes in insuring order when violations do occur. Nicholas Timasheff (1976), for example, insists that attempts to maintain order are universal, but "law" is found only in some societies. The order to which he refers falls under the category of alliances, or what he calls "coordination." He reserves his definition of law to societies that have shared norms for coordination enforced through a centralized power. Thus, law reflects alliance norms and, at the same time, is their perpetuator. Using this definition, he concludes that societies with centralized authority that impose norms different from the collective norms are "lawless." Further, he rejects the application of the concept "law" to societies that have shared norms but no centralized power. In short, Timasheff restricts his study of "law" to state-level societies that are "democratic." In these societies we note the existence of courts, judges, and prisons which function to uphold consensus.

In contrast to Timasheff's insistence that law exists as a phenomenon (courts, police, and so on), Leonard Pospisil (1968) argues that "law" is a concept. He notes that although societies may be leaderless (no centralized authority), order is nonetheless maintained through consensus, and there exists some system of decision making by which disputes are settled. Pospisil draws on Karl Llewellyn and E. Adamson Hoebel's (1941) analysis of the Cheyenne to identify three different manifestations (phenomena) by which law might be defined as a concept. These are: abstract rules which may be written or spoken, the behavior of people, and principles abstracted from decisions which resolve disputes.

In its first manifestation, law is a mechanical guide for adjudication. This is the approach to law suggested by Timasheff and comes primarily from the sociologist Max Weber (1960). Weber linked law to bureaucracy and its "rational" system of rules and principles. He states:

> The "rational" interpretation of law on the basis of strictly formal conceptions stands opposite the kind of adjudication that is primarily bound to sacred traditions. The single case that cannot be unambiguously decided by tradition is either settled by concrete "revelation" (oracle, prophetic dicta, or ordeal—that is, by "charismatic" justice) or—and only these cases interest us here—by informal judgements rendered in terms of concrete ethical and other practical valuations. This is "Kadi-justice," as R. Schmidt has fittingly called it. Or, formal judgements are rendered, though not by subsumption under rational concepts, but by drawing on "analogies" and by depending upon and interpreting concrete "precedents." This is "empirical justice." (167)

According to Weber, the bureaucratic form of organization represents the most efficient and hence the most "rational" form of justice. "Rational justice" only exists when bureaucracy provides technical means and rational, but abstract, rules which reduce the possibility of individual variations in dispensing justice and in the enforcement of laws. It is only under these latter conditions that one can talk of "law." Pospisil rejects this definition of law because it is applicable to only a few societies.

Pospisil also rejects any definition of law that reflects modal[5] behavior. Defining law as what most people do (norms) can lead to abstracting "rules," but it denies the realities of social life. Even in non-bureaucratic, non-state-level societies, some individuals are more important than others. The "good" hunter or gatherer, the "expert" gardener, and the "gifted" shaman are not part of some abstracted "average" from group behavior. Hierarchy is a behavioral universal. If "law" is an abstraction from modal behavior, then law is not necessary since the behavior that defines it already exists. Systematic observation of any society would find that behavior often violates "law." If this were not the case, then "crime" could not exist. One notes that "legal norms" and "behavioral norms" are often not the same. For example, most adolescents in the United States consume or have consumed alcohol, yet legal norms prohibit its use in this age category. Speed limits may be set by "law," but modal speeds often exceed these limits. For both adolescents and drivers, legal norms are acknowledged but do not necessarily have behavioral consequences. Concluding that "law" functions to validate modal behaviors denies our observations of behavior everywhere.

The third way to define law is to identify principles of social control that are upheld in the process of settling disputes. Pospisil notes that in all societies there are arguments, disagreements, and violations of expectations. In all societies there is some organizational unit—a court, a chief, a shaman, a priest, a jury, councils—with the responsibility for adjudication of disputes. The principles by which disputes are settled, regardless of the specific organizational unit that has this responsibility, can be induced from observations of adjudication proceedings. Instead of defining law as formally written or spoken statements (the approach of Timasheff and Weber) or recording modal behaviors that are often inconsistent with "legal" expectations, this approach defines law as part of a larger system of decision making. Since these principles are constantly being applied, one does not have to consider "laws" that formally exist but are not enforced. In contrast to the analysis of **formal law**, which may be found only in some societies, Pospisil argues that the principles of adjudication define **substantive law**, and this concept can be applied universally.

From a methodological point of view, substantive law is determined through the process of induction. Decisions are recorded in specific cases, and then a limited set of principles or rules are developed to reconstruct the logic by which these decisions were made. In contrast, the analysis of formal law is deductive. Decisions are justified because they "fit" formal law. United States constitutional "law" offers many examples of this difficulty. The principles of the constitution were used to justify and then abolish slavery, to prohibit and permit universal suffrage, and both to ban and to allow abortion. Obviously something other than the "principles" of the Constitution were at work. From the substantive definition, law is an adjustment to changes in culture, not a determinant of culture.

As one contributor to social control, the principles of substantive law are part of public knowledge. These principles are not vaguely stated, and they are understandable to a wide audience. As shared principles by both adjudicating parties and possible litigants, their consequences for social control form part of consensual agreement. Thus, substantive law is acknowledged, even when violated, and violators know how and by whom sanctions will be administered.

Formal definitions of law are based on the existence of specific bureaucratic associations that have specific powers to enforce decisions. To Westerners, the enforcement power of courts to levy fines, impose prison sentences, or assess damages is often cited as part of a definition of law. In other cultural settings, enforcement is based on following decisions made by authorities who do not necessarily have any formal authority to "force" compliance. There are no "courts" and no "police," yet Pospisil would insist that within these systems there is some system of law—substantive law.

In contrasting the formal and substantive definitions of law, it is clear that substantive law is more in keeping with the social science tradition of determining "social facts." Law from this perspective is a cultural universal. As part of culture, law reflects values, not norms. Perhaps more importantly, the substantive definition makes cross-cultural comparisons possible. Formally, then, substantive law is defined as *one mechanism of social control that is reflected in the cultural rules by which disputes are settled.*

To illustrate how this substantive definition applies to different societies, we will review three studies. One study is of a society that is "lawless" from the formal perspective. The other two show how substantive law can be used to explain behavioral outcomes in a society with a formal, bureaucratized system of "law."

The Tobacco-Law Connection: The Case of the Kuikuru

Gertrude Dole (1964, 1986) studied the Kuikuru, a Carib-speaking community of horticulturalists in Central Brazil. Kuikuru society consists of a single settlement with 145 members living in nine multifamily houses. There is no formalized leader with powers to enforce normative rules. In fact, no system for punishing violations of most norms exists. Thus, theft, adultery, and other forms of "deviance" are not controlled by any formal mechanisms. The Kuikuru appear to lack formal law. How, then, do they maintain a system of cooperation and peaceful coexistence?

One practice which contributes to the stability of Kuikuru society is found in procedures which combat witchcraft. The Kuikuru believe that witchcraft is the cause of death, illness, crop failure, and accidents. When these events occur, someone is either suspected or accused of being a sorcerer. In one case, a man thought to be a sorcerer was left alone in a multifamily house. The others moved out. More grievous accusations of sorcery may result in the alleged sorcerer being killed. Yet both of these sanctions are in opposition to the Kuikuru value of cooperation, amiability, and generosity. How can these sanctions be explained?

Even without formal controls and sanctions, the Kuikuru nonetheless have a system of social control and substantive law. Their division of labor lacks any formal institutional arrangement called law. There are no courts, judges, or police. Rather, their system of control is managed by shamans.

> The primary function of a shaman is medical; he is hired to cure illness which does not respond to herbal remedies that are common knowledge. A second important function is divining[6] to determine the causes of illness and other misfortunes. The principal techniques used are removal of intrusive objects and trance induced by smoking native cigarettes. (1964, 55)

Shamanism is an achieved status. One is "called" to be a shaman. Those wishing to become shamans apply to a master shaman. If accepted, the novice is secluded in the shaman's house and tutored in the skills of shamanism. One of these skills is learning how to induce a trance state through smoking tobacco. It is believed that the smoke-induced trance enables the shaman to communicate with spirits and to see and hear things that are hidden from others. As one test of competency, the novice shaman goes through an initiation ordeal which requires going into two smoke-induced trances without vomiting.

In spite of their view that the universe is a cooperative place, the Kuikuru experience illness, crop failures and other misfortunes. When these occur, a shaman is summoned to determine who caused the problem. Since all misfortunes are the result of sorcery, the shaman is called to determine the sorcerer. After the shaman goes into a trance by inhaling tobacco smoke, the name of the guilty party is revealed.

Dole's examination of cases of sorcery determination uncovered one constant theme. Those accused were either violators of the expectation that they be cooperative and friendly or were close relatives of the uncooperative and unfriendly. Identification of a specific person by the shaman reflected public suspicions about the responsible party. Thus, divination or tobacco-induced states only confirmed what was already collectively determined.[7] The consequence of this process insured continuity (descent) in the cooperation value by removing transgressors through procedures which themselves confirmed cooperation.

What we note in Dole's description of Kuikuru society is that even with the absence of any formal law, there is a system by which disputes are adjudicated and order is maintained. In other words, substantive law is practiced by the Kuikuru.

Beating the Drunk Charge

Public drunkenness is the most frequent "crime" in the United States. There are more than one million arrests each year for public inebriation (Reid 1988; 287, 295). It is estimated that between 25 and 40 percent of all inmates in jails are there under the charge of "drinking in public."

Advocates of the formal law approach might predict that sanctions for violating the drinking-in-public law would reflect a "rational" set of procedures for disposal of such cases. There is an ordinance prohibiting a behavior (drunkenness in public); the defendant has been arrested and brought before a judge; the accused is found guilty or not guilty and then sentenced to jail or set free. James P. Spradley's (1970, 1974) study of those he calls urban nomads, or the emic name "tramps," revealed that the process of sentencing followed a set of principles that were not specified by formal law. Rather, the dynamics of decision making in the court were governed by conformity to, or violations of, values shared by both judges and tramps.

Tramps are citizens in a world where adaptive strategies (behaviors) have evolved to meet real environmental needs. These include "making a flop" (finding a place to sleep) and "making a dime" (earning a living). In this world another adaptive strategy has resulted from experiences that are somewhat unique. This involves a set of behavioral repertoires designed either to avoid or to reduce sentences for public drinking. In their own terms these techniques are described as "beating the drunk charge." Spradley reported several adaptive strategies that were used to achieve this goal. They include:

> Bail out; bond out; request a continuance; hire an attorney. Have a good record, or use an alias.

> Plead guilty and request the treatment center for alcoholics. Plead guilty and make a statement.
>> Talk of family ties.
>> Talk of present job.
>> Talk of intent to work.
>> Tell of extenuating circumstances.
>> Offer to leave town.

Accompanying each of these alternatives, Spradley constructed a list of possible costs or risks associated with successful avoidance of or reduction of sentence. For example, making bail, posting a bond, or hiring an attorney all have a cost—that is, they require money. Asking for a continuance to get money or hiring an attorney requires someone on the outside willing to help. The best way to avoid sentencing is to have a good record or to invent a good record by using an alias. However, having a good record requires not drinking for an extended period, and this had a social cost. As Spradley noted:

> The life-style of urban nomads, with its drinking rituals, provides men with a group of friends wherever they go, men who accept them as they are. If a man stops drinking and sharing drinks, he cuts himself off from the most valuable of all resources, human companionship and acceptance. (1970, 177–178)

Spradley noted that formal "law" should dictate that those charged with drinking in public and having a prior record of the same offense should be given the same sentence for each charge. Yet he observed that sentences varied by conformity to American values—not by charges or records. Being arrested for *public* drunkenness (as well as other acts, such as urinating, defecating, or sleeping in public) is a violation of the American value on privacy. In sentencing, the values involved are materialism, moralism, and work. These values also serve as guides for "punishment rules." The general substantive rule for sentencing is: "The less a man conforms to other American values, the more severe his punishment" (381). Thus, not only had the formal "law" been violated, but a broader set of unspoken values was used as a basis for sentence length.

Corresponding to each of these values are substantive rules. For example, "When guilty of public drunkenness, a man deserves greater punishment if he is poor" (382). The bail for public drunkenness is $20. In most courts if the $20 is paid, the accused is set free and scheduled for a later hearing. Generally, if the accused did not appear in court no arrest warrant was issued. In contrast, those without money "paid" for their offense by "doing time." Thus, money demonstrated conformity to the value on materialism.

The second substantive rule is: "When guilty of public drunkenness, a man deserves greater punishment if he has a bad reputation" (383). In American culture those accused of a crime, regardless of whether they are ever convicted, are stigmatized. Judges follow this rule by increasing the length of sentences for repeat offenders. The tramp knows this rule and attempts to "clean up" his past arrest history by moving from place to place or creating an alias with no prior arrests. In addition, he can plead guilty, publicly state that he has a "problem," and then ask for "treatment." Although he does not avoid incarceration, going to a treatment center for four months is viewed by some tramps as "beating the drunk charge" because it is an easier place than jail to "do time."

The third substantive rule, derived from the general value, is: "When guilty of public drunkenness, a man deserves greater punishment if he does not have a steady job" (383–384). The American value on work is applied equally to the "idle rich" or the "idle poor" and is distinct from materialism. Tramps often work as day laborers, by selling junk, or by panhandling. None of these "jobs" is evidence for steady work. In recognition of this value, tramps develop ingenious ways to prove they have a job. Spradley cites one case in which a man wrote a letter to himself indicating that he was an employer in another city who wished to employ the inmate. The letter was taken by a recently released inmate to the other city and mailed. The inmate then used the letter to convince the judge that he had been offered a steady job, with the result that he was given an early release.

Spradley's analysis of sentencing further illustrates a point made throughout this book, namely, that behaviors are adaptive and situational. In and of themselves they have no meaning. That drinking in public is an offense depends on who is drinking. In public parks and on beaches throughout the United States people drink and do not get arrested. Picnickers and bathers may be formally enjoined from drinking, but enforcement of no-drinking ordinances is selective. Arrests depend on appearance and, as Spradley documents, incarceration depends on acceptance or use of understood and shared values. The adaptive strategies employed by tramps do not deny those values; rather, they use them to avoid sanctions which they find unappealing. The recognition of those values does not predict norms. The behaviors of tramps are adaptations to conditions of low income, intermittent employment and other "real" social conditions, just as the decisions made by judges are consistent with their "real" social conditions. That both judges and tramps acknowledge the same values only serves as guidelines for adjudication that is understood by both parties. This is what Pospisil meant when he pointed out that the principles of substantive law in any culture are known and accepted by all parties. Bums and barristers are part of a value system where consensual agreement enables the adjudication process to work as one form of social control.

The Impact of Changing Values on Legal Sanctions

Spradley's study illustrates how substantive law operates within a system of values during one period. He is not concerned with the origin of those values but with the behavioral effects within a formal legal system. Yet even the most casual observer will note that values change. The consequences of these changes for legal sanctioning was investigated by the criminologist John Hagen (1989).

Hagen observed that the field of criminology has recently become dominated by "conflict"[8] theory. Conflict theory assumes that society is characterized by competition for scarce resources. This approach is informed by selected writings by Karl Marx and insists that norms and values are controlled by the self-interests of the more powerful in a society. Writers such as Richard Quinney (1974) argue that one way this is done is through the passage of legislation which protects the self-interests of the more powerful. By defining the behaviors of the less powerful as "crime" and then punishing crime, those in power are able to sanction—and therefore control—those out of power. If we apply this model to the United States, one might hypothesize that, all other things being equal, blacks should receive more severe sentences than white offenders for the same crime. This conflict theory hypothesis is based on the observation that whites have more power than blacks. Confirmation of this hypothesis is not, however, borne out by empirical studies of sentencing by ethnicity. Some studies do find that blacks receive longer sentences for the same offense; others find just the opposite. These inconsistencies intrigued Hagen and prompted him to analyze time-sequence data on sentencing as a test of the single-variable (ethnicity) model of conflict theory.

Hagen's answer to conflict theory is the structural-contextual model. This approach assumes that legal sanctioning, as measured by sentence length, is a dynamic process that must consider both changes in the definitions of the social characteristics of offenders and the specific behavior that is being punished. For him, sentencing is:

> ... not a matter of individuals being processed through the criminal justice system. Both the individual and the system occupy variable positions and locations within a social structure. (71)

Hagen notes that public concerns and legislative controls on drug use historically were directed at minorities. (More will be said about this in the next chapter). This, he suggests, reflected the absence of drug use among the largely white middle class. Beginning in the early 1960s, however, drug use dramatically increased among middle- and upper-class youth. This disparity between norms (increased use) and values (anti-drugs) was resolved by redefining the drug "problem." Those who had been defined as "villains"— addicts and the crimes "caused" by addiction—now became "victims" of "organized crime" and high-level dealers. This supply-side view of the drug "problem" excuses not only the white drug users but also the traditional minority drug user. Consistent with this new definition of the problem, the Comprehensive Drug Abuse Prevention and Control Act was signed by President Nixon in 1970. This act decreased sanctions (sentence length) for drug users and increased sanctions for traffickers.

Hagen systematically reviewed media coverage of drugs and found a dramatic increase beginning in the late 1960s. He argued that this reflected a changed definition of the drug "problem." To measure this change, Hagen and his colleagues measured both content and number of pages in the *New York Times* and other national periodicals devoted to the topic of drugs, as well as the results of national public opinion polls and legislative activities. On the basis of these measurements he identified three distinct media periods: 1963–1968, 1969–1973, and 1974–1976. The first and last period ranked low in media and public concern. The middle period, 1969–1973, ranked high. In addition to quantitative changes from 1963 to 1974, content analysis of the media indicated a change in descriptions of users and dealers. He labeled the 1963–1968 period "user-as-villain," the 1969–1973 period "trafficker-as-villain," and the 1974–1976 period "post-trafficker-as-villain."

To test whether these changes in definitions influenced sentencing lengths for blacks and whites, Hagen reviewed sentencing records of 4,371 drug offenders in the Southern Federal District of New York City from 1963 to 1976. These data provided measures of twenty-two variables that could be used to determine sentence length. Over these three periods there were several consistent observations. "Big dealers," those convicted of having more than 100 pounds of drugs, received longer sentences than did users; black offenders received lesser sentences than did white offenders; and middle-class membership reduced the likelihood of imprisonment.

Hagen found statistically significant differences in sentencing length when he compared these periods. From 1963 to 1968, black offenders' sentences were, on average, 8 months shorter than those of white offenders. From 1969 to 1973, however, the difference was more than 18 months. In the post-period, it dropped slightly to a difference of 17 months. For big dealers there was an increase in the middle period from 46 months to 86 months. It then declined to 55 months in the post-period. Consistent with these findings was that middle-class white youth were given lower sentences in the middle and final period. Hagen argued that changed definitions during the middle period explain the overall decrease in sentence lengths for blacks. Blacks and other minorities are more likely to be users than big-time traffickers. This reflects their inability to acquire the necessary capital to get into the distribution of heroin and other drugs, such as cocaine. Thus, the calculation of average sentencing by race showed increases for white users.

The analysis of sentence lengths for big dealers by race showed that blacks received sentences 19 months longer than did whites. Hagen argues that this is consistent with changes in the definition of victims and villains. Blacks who were big dealers were viewed as even greater villains because they preyed on an already highly victimized population.

Spradley's analysis of sentencing for public drunkenness found that those who entered not-guilty pleas were given longer sentences. Hagen's analysis revealed that the not-guilty plea resulted in longer sentences for both users and dealers. Over the three periods, users who pled not guilty received sentences that were more than 36 months longer than those who pled guilty. For dealers this difference was even greater. Those who pled guilty received sentences that were 136 months shorter. Within the three periods, these differences increased. Hagen argued that the legislation under which judges decided sentence length encouraged great latitude and discretion in the 1969–1973 and later period. A plea of guilty and subsequent negotiation of sentence was a public admission of villainy or victimization. Conversely, the plea of not guilty denied either label. Public confession was an expression of conformity to the changed definitions and was rewarded by a decrease in sentence length.

Social Control: Some General Observations

The study of processes by which social order is maintained does not constitute a separate subject in social science. The processes— both subtle and obvious—are a necessary part of what makes society and culture possible, and they permeate all of the activities in which humans engage. The most important consideration when studying control processes is the way that they contribute to alliance and descent functions—whether those alliance and descent concerns are part of religious, economic, or kinship systems. The observation and recording of praise and encouragement, teaching and coaching, aggressive physical punishment, or substantive law is an invitation to examine these more fundamental prerequisites to order. The way that drugs fit, or do not fit, into this scheme will depend on the specific alliance and descent needs of particular societies and cultures. Drugs, in and of themselves, neither deter nor contribute to order. As noted here and elsewhere, drugs have been symbolically interpreted as a necessary component of order. In other settings drugs have been considered a source of disorder. If we have been challenged to determine the contribution of drugs to alliance and descent functions, we should also be challenged to explain why drugs and drug use have been defined as "problems." In the next chapter we accept that challenge when we focus on the etiology of "social problems."

Endnotes

[1] The emergence of a belief in "individualism" with its corresponding emphasis on individual legal, economic, and social responsibilities is a direct result of changes in the division of labor. In cultures with undifferentiated divisions of labor, an individual's actions are more likely to be the responsibility of collectivities.

[2] I recognize that "thinking" is an inferential state. The only way to measure "thought" is by speech. Therefore, one can "say" what one "thinks," but by so indicating thought, any explanation of thought is filtered through the structure of language. This is why I constructed this continuum on the basis of emic explanations that are understandable to the reader.

³ As a sociologist, Dahrendorf uses the term "role." See chapter 1 for a discussion of the ambiguity of this concept as it is used by sociologists and my suggestion for clarification.

⁴ Words with the prefix "ethno" are used in the social sciences to describe everyday practices and beliefs of informants. Ethnomedicine refers to practices in reference to illness, disease, and health. Generally, "ethno" words describe practices that are carried on through an oral, rather than a written, tradition.

⁵ The word modal is used here in the statistical sense. The mode of a distribution describes the most frequent entry. When used to describe social behaviors it simply means the behavior or behaviors in which most people engage.

⁶ Divination is the practice of using impersonal objects to obtain information, including the determination of guilt or innocence. For example, in American society, the so-called "lie detector" could be considered a divination instrument. The use of this instrument serves to distance accusers from those accused in such a way that a decision can be made.

⁷ In contemporary urban societies this same process takes the form of public opinion polls. The purpose of these polls, with their accompanying "scientific" ritual, is to tap collective sentiments for various purposes.

⁸ The use of the term "conflict" by these theorists is not the same as the definition of conflict that I suggested in chapter 1.

chapter **10**

Political Systems and Drugs

![I]

n the last chapter some of the techniques by which societies and cultures insure compliance with norms and values were reviewed. In that discussion we noted that the purpose of these efforts was twofold: first, to maintain a state in which there was consensus in behaviors and beliefs during any particular time period; second, to serve as ways of perpetuating consensus through time. This temporal continuity of norms and values we labeled descent, and we noted that if the organizational basis of human life is to continue, the issue of descent must be satisfied. In this chapter we shift our attention to an examination of the other necessary condition that contributes to survival, namely, alliance. Alliance refers to how order is maintained among the units which make up a society or a culture. Within the social sciences the study of associations and processes which address the issue of alliances and alliance formations at the societal and cultural levels is usually identified by the adjective "political" (for example, political science, political anthropology, political sociology). While there are variations in the foci of these disciplinary distinctions, they nonetheless share a common interest in unraveling how political systems work. Therefore, if we are to understand the linkage between drugs, drug use, and political systems, we must begin by defining concepts used in social science to identify political processes and the associational forms of political systems.

Understanding Political Systems

Political systems are those rules, procedures, and policies which function to maintain order between several **publics**. A public, according to Smith (1963), is a **perpetual group** with distinguishable boundaries and membership, internal organizational rules, and procedures which regulate external relations with other publics. Thus, a public is a named group, the organization of which must address the dual functions of alliance and descent.

Publics should not be confused with culture categories. **Culture categories** are emically recognized distinctions within a culture. Depending on the culture, different criteria may be used as a basis for cultural categories. These include sex, age, ethnicity, common property interests, ritual and belief, occupation, residency, language, and class. While culture categories may provide a basis for publics, it is not until they acquire a name and an organizational charter that they become publics. Thus, people named Smith are not a public, but the Smith Clan is. The wealthy are not a public, but the Republican party is. Workers are not a public, but a union is. Sociologists and anthropologists are not a public, but the American Sociological Association and the American Anthropological Association are. The boundaries between publics are reflected in names which mark common membership and also identify a distinct group to those outside its membership. Words such as "association," "company," "party," "club," and "clan" may mark different publics within a society. At a more inclusive level, "American," "German," Yanomamö," "Huichol," and "Apache" provide this same identification at the society level. When these name distinctions are coupled with the existence of rules and regulations governing internal descent and external alliance, we have identified a public.

Political Processes

Because political systems function to integrate different publics, they must be superordinate. This has suggested to many observers that what distinguishes political systems from other systems is their ability to employ force as a mechanism of control. If **force** is broadly defined as "the ability to mobilize the actions of others, even when those others do not wish to be mobilized," then we note that force is not limited to the political arena. Parents may "force" their children to engage in appropriate behaviors; crew bosses employ several methods to "force" runners to conform to expectations (chapter 8); teachers "force" students to take exams; and bullies force anybody they can. The more appropriate terms to describe the means by which political systems maintain order among publics is power and authority (Cohen 1974).

Political **authority** describes the rules, traditions, and precedents for alliances which are shared (accepted and understood) by different publics. Thus, political authority describes the management of relationships among publics when there is joint agreement on the rules of alliance. In contrast, political **power** is employed when the rules governing alliances among publics are not consensual. In short, power is used when conflict exists in interpublic alliances. Using this distinction, one measure of societal consensus or conflict is the proportions of political power and political authority used in a political system.

Government and Governance

Political systems are a cultural universal. That is, every culture has a set of rules and expectations that regulate alliance formations among publics. However, these rules and expectations may take several different associational forms. If we focus on the social manifestations of political systems, we study government. Even a brief review of governments, either historically or cross-culturally, reveals rather wide variations. Governments may have temporary or permanent organizations; they may have full-time or part-time functionaries. These variations in government are, in part, explained by the number of publics in a society. As a general rule, the greater the number of publics, the more likely a government will be a permanent organization with a full-time staff. This observation is based on the mathematical principle that as the number of publics increase arithmetically, the number of real or potential alliances among those publics increases geometrically. For example, in a society with two clans, there is only one possible alliance. With the addition of one more clan, the number of alliances increases to three; with four, the resultant alliances are six; with five, ten, and so forth.[1] If this mathematical model holds true, we should not only expect government to change when there are increases or decreases in the number of publics; but where the number of publics is small, one might conclude that there are societies without government. Indeed, this conclusion has been drawn by some who have attempted to impose Western models of government, with their many publics, on societies with only a few publics. Regardless of its form, government, like political systems, is a universal.

Government as a social form can be distinguished from governance. While governments vary according to number of publics, variations in governance reflect consensus in alliance rules among publics. **Governance** refers to the specific procedures or rules by which public groups are integrated. Governance may be democratic or totalitarian; it may have leaders that are charismatic, elected, appointed, or it may lack any clearly identifiable leadership. Using the distinction between power and authority, we note that governance by "power" (dictatorships) reflects an attempt to integrate publics which lack consensus on alliance rules. In contrast, where publics agree on alliance rules, governance is by "authority" (democracies).

When we combine the measure of government (numbers of publics) and governance (consensus or conflict in alliance rules), the resultant "types" of political systems can be enormous. In an attempt to summarize the possible combinations, social scientists have offered many taxonomies to describe political systems. One finds references to bands, tribes, chiefdoms, peasants, pre-industrial, industrial, post-industrial, and the state as possible types of political systems. None of these distinctions has proved efficient, primarily because there is often as much variation within the types as there is between types. What I propose is that we view variations in political systems as a result of processes directed at "problem solving." When the number of public groups is small and there is consensus among the groups, there are few "problems" to solve. In this instance, government will be a temporary organizational structure whose functions are primarily ceremonial. In contrast, when publics are many and there is little consensus among them, governments will be permanent structures with adaptive strategies for problem solving that emphasize power.

Because a political system is one part of a larger cultural arrangement, government will reflect characteristics of that larger system. When those larger systems are organized by bureaucratic, formal, literate traditions, the political system will mirror this organizational model. This association form is described as **formal government**. If the political system is part of a culture that is non-literate and makes few status and institutional distinctions, political activities will be incorporated within the boundaries of those institutions and statuses. For example, in kinship based cultures, older clan or lineage members may form interlinking councils. In religion based cultures, shamans or priests may be called upon to perform alliance activities when needed. This non-differentiated form of government can be described as **substantive government**.

Data sources for the study of formal and substantive government come from different sources. In formal governments the political process is reconstructed through an examination of legislative activities carried out by full-time politicians. In political systems with substantive government, data can only be obtained through direct observations and interviews with informants. Regardless of our data sources for government, we as social scientists are obligated to explain the political process as a consequence of attempts to form alliances between publics.

In keeping with the distinction between culture and society, we can summarize the distinctions made thus far in table 10.1.

Table 10.1.
The Place of Government and Political Systems in the Social Science Model

Society	Culture
Government	**Political Systems**
Publics	Cultural Categories

Political Action, Drugs, and Social Problems

Throughout previous chapters we have noted that drug use takes place in various social settings without being emically identified as a "problem." Within those settings, the regulation of drug use is not a concern of the political system. In other societies, drug use is defined as a "problem" and is subject to governmental action. If our argument on the function of political systems is correct, then we would predict that this "problem" definition is the consequence of alliances among publics. Therefore, if we wish to offer a social science explanation for drugs as a "social problem," our task is to work backward from political actions which assume drug use to be a "problem" to the antecedent alliance arrangements among publics. Perhaps the most convenient sample for testing the linkage between political action and public alliances is in historical societies. Within these societies social scientists have recorded, time-sequenced data available for analysis and interpretation of changes in publics along with formal statements of "problems" and their proposed "solutions."

The Political Foundations of Drug Legislation

A search through the social science literature reveals several different interpretations of drug legislation. At the most inclusive level, legislation has been viewed as both an independent and a dependent variable, as both a cause and an effect. Depending on the theoretical orientation of the researcher, legislation has been viewed either as a reflection of consensus or the imposition of self-serving interests of the powerful on the less powerful. In this section, we will examine legislation as a political activity: a recognition of boundaries between public groups and an attempt to implement alliances among those groups. Legislation is therefore a process that is both static and dynamic. When public groups are in alliance there is little legislative activity. Conversely, when the numbers and kinds of public groups increase there is greater demand for alliance through legislative activities.

In previous discussions of drugs, we have gone beyond the narrow confines of Western culture to illustrate the variability of human behavior. In reviewing the relationship between religion and drug use we looked specifically at those cultures in which drugs were incorporated into religious practices. When examining the drug-economics nexus, we included a broad range of economies. As part of the social science venture, we wish to know about the human condition from an all-encompassing perspective. We therefore study ritual in ritual-rich cultures and kinship in cultures where kinship is *the* basis for organization. If we apply this same principle to the study of the relationship between social conditions and drug legislation, we need not search very far. The United States is one of the most drug legislated countries in the world. Cities, states, and the federal government have each contributed to an abundance of prohibitions against substances defined as "drugs."

U.S. Drug Legislation: A Brief Review

Historically, most anti-drug legislation in the United States belongs to the twentieth century. A scan of legislation at the federal level reveals that the first attempt to regulate drugs was the Pure Food and Drug Act of 1906. This act required manufacturers of so-called "patent" medicines,[2] food, and drink to list the ingredients in their products. Although primarily aimed at food, this act was the first to acknowledge the use of opiates, cocaine, and cannabis in various products sold in the marketplace.

The first comprehensive federal legislation specifically directed at drugs was the 1914 Harrison Narcotics Act. This act introduced the word "narcotics" in reference to the opiates. It mandated that only those permitted to "own" narcotics—physicians, veterinarians, and dentists—register with the Internal Revenue Service, the agency responsible for enforcement. Since its enactment, it has been amended over sixty times. Each of these amendments banned opium and heroin and set restrictions on the distribution of morphine.

Limitations on importing opium and coca leaves for medicinal purposes were set by the Narcotic Drugs Import and Export Act of 1922. The Heroin Act of 1924 further restricted the manufacturing and possession of heroin to government controlled research. These acts imposed fines and prison sentences for importing and/or possession of prohibited drugs. The sentencing of those found guilty under these acts dramatically increased the federal prison population. In response to this, in 1929 congress authorized the building of two federal narcotics hospitals charged with "treating" drug users as an alternative to prison.

In 1937, the Marijuana Tax Act was passed. It placed a federal tax on marihuana and imposed prison sentences or fines on those who did not register. Beginning in 1951, several more amendments were added to the Harrison Act. The Boggs Amendment mandated minimum and mandatory sentencing for violators. This was followed by the Narcotic Drug Control Act of 1956 which increased sentences and prohibited parole or probation for violators. It assumed that persons caught with only small amounts of narcotics or marihuana were pushers, and selling heroin to a person under the age of eighteen was a capital offense. The most recent legislation was the Comprehensive Drug Abuse Prevention and Control Act of 1970. As the name implies, it was an attempt to bring together under one act the growing diversity of drug legislation. Under its broad provisions, funding was provided for the study and treatment of drug users; there was increased latitude in sentencing (Hagen, chapter 9), and it established a drug category system (Schedules) based upon actual or potential for "abuse."

This brief chronological sketch of drug regulations reveals little about the process of legislation. If we view legislative action as part of a political process carried out by government, then as social scientists we must analyze this history as a reflection of attempts to establish public policy which address the dual issues of alliance and descent. Since twentieth-century anti-drug legislation is an appendage of the 1914 Harrison Act, it would be instructive if we start with the antecedent social conditions that contributed to this legislation. In the following sections I will review three "critical events" which led to this legislation. These are: the immigration of Chinese and their subsequent unwillingness to join the newly emerging labor unions, the emergence of new professions, and international governmental concerns. In each of these, we will examine how public groups attempted to encourage the passage of the Harrison Act as a means by which to insure their own descent functions.

The Chinese and the Harrison Act

The history of legislative actions against drugs in the United States begins with municipal ordinances. In 1875, San Francisco prohibited opium smoking and operating opium dens. A year later, Virginia City, Nevada passed an ordinance against opium smoking. In 1877, Nevada banned the sale of smoking opium; four years later, California passed similar legislation. At the federal level, Congress raised the import tax on smoking opium from six to ten dollars a pound in 1883. In 1887, Congress passed legislation that specifically prohibited Chinese from importing smoking opium. This was amended in 1890 to restrict the manufacturing of opium to American citizens. Tariffs on opium increased an additional $2 in 1890. Suspicious that opium was being illegally imported to avoid this high tax, Congress reduced the tax to $6 in 1897. This resulted in an increase in recorded imports and a corresponding increase in tax revenues. The 1909 Opium Exclusion Act banned the importation of opium but permitted domestic production. Further restrictions on one type of opium were enacted in 1914 when Congress imposed a prohibitive tax of $300 per pound on smoking opium.

Antismoking-opium legislation during the late nineteenth and early twentieth century is linked to an increasing Chinese population. In 1860 there were only 35,000 Chinese in the United States, most of whom resided in California. Thirty years later the population had increased threefold to 107,500. Can one, therefore, conclude that this legislation was simply a case of sanctioning Chinese rather than an attempt to suppress drugs such as opium? To answer this question, it is necessary to examine Sino-American relationships before 1914.

The United States is a nation of migrants. Beginning on the east coast, early migrants came primarily from northern Europe. By the middle of the eighteenth century the bulk of the population still lived in the eastern half of the country. Although some eastern states were becoming industrialized, much of the technology in the United States was labor intensive. This requirement for labor was met in a variety of ways. Indentured servants, slavery, and relaxed immigration requirements brought labor to work in farming and industry. The settlement of the West Coast lagged behind that of the East Coast. The first American ship to reach California arrived in 1796. In the 1830s, settlers, miners, trappers, explorers and soldiers from east of the Mississippi River were pouring into this new territory. However, the new settlers could not satisfy the labor needs of the expanding California economy. Early attempts to harness the labor of American Indians, southern slaves, and Mexicans either proved ineffective or unconstitutional, so employers looked west toward China. Between 1820 and 1840 only forty-three Chinese had immigrated into the United States. In the next decade over 36,000 Chinese entered western ports. This migration was legitimated in 1868 with the signing of the Burlingame Treaty between the United States and the Emperor of China. This treaty recognized the right of voluntary migration by both Chinese and Americans and guaranteed mutual privileges, other than naturalization. Despite protests from California against free immigration, the Chinese population increased to over 100,000 in the 1880s.

Acculturation and Assimilation: Alliance Functions

The consequence of two previously different cultures or societies coming in prolonged direct contact with each other is described in the social science literature as either acculturation or assimilation. A 1974 review of these concepts as used by social scientists reveals that they share some common attributes, but are nonetheless different (Teske and Nelson 1974). Both describe a process resulting from direct contact between different social or cultural units where one of those units has more power than the other. The concepts differ in the resulting relationship between the units. Acculturation describes non-acceptance by the dominant unit with little or no changes in the values of less dominant unit. In contrast, assimilation measures value changes in the less dominant unit and acceptance by the dominant unit. In short, **assimilation** is a process by which less dominant units are accepted by and become integrated into more dominant units both socially (behaviors) and culturally (values). In contrast, **acculturation** describes the process where subordinate units maintain their social and cultural identities independent from the larger society and culture.

In a very real sense, both assimilation and acculturation describe a process of change and reciprocity between social units. The end product of assimilation is a loss of past social and cultural identity of the less dominant unit. Acculturation describes a continuation of a past identity. Since both terms describe a process rather than a "thing," the application of either concept is always relative to time. Thus, to understand the Chinese experience in the United States one must examine both the cultural backgrounds of those Chinese who migrated to the United States and the social and cultural dynamics of America before and after their arrival.

Pre-migration American Exposure to Chinese

Stuart Miller's (1969) analysis of the popular media suggests that Americans were exposed to certain aspects of Chinese culture prior to their actual immigration. He found two major sources for this information. One came from Protestant missionaries whose vivid and negative descriptions of life in China supported the need for missionaries; the other was the coverage of the 1839–1842 "Opium Wars." One constant theme in the popular press was opium. Americans were given

> Detailed descriptions of the mechanics of smoking the drug (opium) and its degenerating effects . . . in American magazines after 1840. The opium pipe became as much a symbol of Chinese culture as the queue (pigtail) or the tea cup, and the mass media gave the impression that Chinese adults of all classes were universally addicted to this pernicious drug. (148)

At an intellectual level, scholars in the 1850s were debating whether "races" had sprung from a single origin (monogenesis) or had followed separate evolutionary lines (polygenesis). Although the former view was eventually accepted as correct "science," the latter became the basis for public sentiment and legislation prohibiting **miscegenation**—marriage between "races"—which included the Chinese as part of the Mongolian "race."

By the 1870s, when Chinese immigration was on the rise, both the medical world and the popular media were debating "germ" theory. Germ theory, the idea that disease is spread through contact, won out and soon became a metaphor for the negative consequences of contact with "others."[3] There were reports that Euro-Americans had caught a virulent form of syphilis from Chinese prostitutes and that one could "catch" leprosy from cigars wrapped by Chinese workers.

The Chinese did not enter American society in a sentiment vacuum. Awaiting their arrival were popular views that were predominantly negative. Assimilation requires the host unit to either accept or be neutral toward the new unit if the process is to be successful. Thus, for assimilation of the Chinese to occur, some or all of these preconceptions had to be neutralized.

Encouragement to Migrate

According to S. W. Kung (1962), there is historical evidence for migration during various earlier Chinese dynasties, but large-scale emigration did not begin until the outbreak of the Taiping Rebellion (1850–64). During this period, a mass exodus occurred in spite of formal discouragement by the Manchu throne, including a declaration that forbid emigration and threatened emigrants with prosecution as traitors (7).

The argument that economic hardship was the "cause" of migration cannot, however, explain why migration occurred or where these migrants went. Bernard Wong (1988) noted that in addition to an economic "push" in China, there were "pulls" provided by international labor brokers who were active in two coastal regions of China: Fukien and Kwangtung. Through their recruitment efforts, Chinese labor contracted to work in several parts of the world. The first shipment of these Chinese laborers was to North Africa in 1845. Two years later, eight hundred left for Cuba. During the ensuing years, a half-million left for Cuba, Peru, Chile, California, Canada, the Philippines, and Australia (Kung, 16).

The recruitment of Chinese labor followed three patterns (Barth 1964). **Indentured immigrants** were underwritten by Chinese merchants under the credit-ticket system. Passage was reimbursed by the emigre's family or their future employers. Until the loan was repaid, the migrant worked for whomever extended the credit. **Contract laborers** were recruited to fill specific contracts for employment by importers and Chinese middlemen. **Coolies** formed the bulk of migrants to the West Indies, Latin America, and the Indian Archipelago. These laborers were either kidnapped or decoyed and then sold into service. Most of the Chinese migrants to the United States were indentured to labor merchants in the United States, who either employed them as their own labor or sold their lien to other employers (55–56).

Chinese Order in the New World

What is striking about Chinese migrants worldwide is their tendency to establish similar systems of order, in either expatriate communities or "Chinatowns." It has been suggested that in the United States these organizational adaptations were a combination of traditional structures and a response to anti-Chinese legislation and sentiment (Ma 1991; Lyman 1977; Barth 1964). For example, in San Francisco between 1860 and 1882, ordinances restricted residential areas for Chinese, denied Chinese access to public education and the San Francisco City Hospital, banned the carrying pole for Chinese vegetable peddlers, increased taxes on laundries that used the pole, prohibited firecrackers and ceremonial gongs, required that all city prisoners have their hair cut within one inch of the scalp, and imposed special licenses and restrictions on laundries (Courtney 1974). At the California state level, legislation and court rulings prohibited immigration into the State, placed special bonds on Chinese, ruled that Chinese could not testify against non-Chinese in court cases, and taxed or limited employment of Chinese. This list of examples could be further extended if one considered similar legislation in other Western states. The assumption that punitive legislation was one of the "causal" factors contributing to the organizational features of Chinese in America leaves out other possible contributing factors. Paul Siu (1952) suggests that most Chinese immigrants viewed their residency in the United States as temporary. His term for this type of resident is "sojourner."The sojourner's goal was to earn enough money to return home to China relatively wealthy. If the worldview of Euro-Americans included assimilation of immigrants, then some of that legislation can be understood as an attempt to force compliance with that objective. In addition, immigrants brought with them a system of ranked "racism" from China (Ma

1991). The adaptive strategies of Chinese migrants had been worked out long before their arrival in the United States. Whatever the contributing factors, the fact that Chinese immigrants formed associations that borrowed traditional Chinese forms as effective adaptive strategies for the very real situations in which they found themselves cannot be denied. The three types of associations identified with the Chinese in America are: secret, surname, and regional.

Secret associations are what some Westerners called triads. According to Stanford M. Lyman (1977), the term "triad" originated from the belief of their members in the three basic elements— heaven, earth, and man. The Chinese use the word *T'ang* to identify this type of association and it became anglicized into the popular name "Tong." In China, the rise of secret societies is associated with periods of imperial domination over the citizenry. In response to this domination, two forms of secret societies evolved. One form withdrew into other-worldly religious orders (an expressive movement); the other practiced "social banditry" (a reform or revolutionary movement). In both their expressive and active forms, what taxonomically binds these groups together is their emic emphasis upon secrecy. What distinguishes T'angs from temporary and informal groups that emphasize secrecy (such as gossip and scandal groups) is that T'angs have formal names end organizational rules. In other words, they are public groups.

T'angs were active in southern China up until 1949. Today they are found only in large urban areas such as Hong Kong, Singapore, and Taiwan. They first appeared in San Francisco in the 1850s, but unlike their Chinese counterparts they functioned as "political," benevolent, and "criminal" associations (Lyman, 89). The "political" functions included support of the traditional activities of T'angs in China. The benevolent functions provided protection from outsiders, companionship in a hostile environment, and a sense of community. The "criminal" T'angs were the source of illicit services to Chinese immigrants—prostitution, opium dens, and gambling.

People with common or select surnames were organized into surname associations. Known in the United States as "family associations," they had a long history in Kwangtung province. In China, however, they ranked below clan and lineage associations, both of which required members to demonstrate kinship affiliation. Their prominence on the American scene reflected the demographic characteristics of migrants. Most were single or were married but had migrated without their wives or families. Surname associations relaxed the rule for demonstrating kinship ties between members and used shared surnames to link members together. Since migrants came from a few regions with a limited pool of surnames, the formation of alliances based on names was simplified. Surname associations in San Francisco made their initial appearance in the 1870s. They functioned to find jobs for members, obtain loans, meet funeral expenses, and provide some housing and food services. In the 1890s they took on the additional task of providing their membership with protection from Euro-Americans and other Chinese associations.

Most migrants prior to 1914 came from an area within two hundred miles of Canton. In this region there are several dialect districts. This distinction became the basis for membership in various *huiguan*, or regional associations, in the United States. All migrants belonged to a huiguan, which made them the largest and most powerful public groups in Chinatowns. They provided legal services for members, acted as guarantors for repayment of debts, encouraged Chinese employment agencies to use their headquarters to find laborers for American employers, maintained rooming houses for newly arrived or transient members, and assisted in burials and in shipping the bones of the deceased back to China. Although the actual number of huiguan varied in the latter half of the nineteenth century, an alliance between six huiguan was formed in 1882. This union became known as the "Chinese Six Companies" or the "Chinese Consolidated Benevolent Association" (CCBA). In New York City the CCBA was composed of seventy representatives from different associations, nineteen of whom served on a standing committee. Both the representatives to and the leaders of the CCBA were identified as *Kiu Ling*—leaders of overseas Chinese, known informally as "big persons" (Wong 1988, 110–111). Barth (1964) reports companies called *kongsi* in Malaysia which performed similar alliance functions, with some local variations.

The CCBA operated as both the law and government in Chinatowns. Their legal functions included mediating disputes between individuals and other associations, and sanctioning those who did not follow their decisions. As "Chambers of Commerce" they were recognized as being "legitimate" community organizations by the dominant Euro-American political structure and thus provided a base for alliances outside the Chinese community. Within the Chinese community they maintained traditional practices (descent functions) through their support of religious temples and sponsorship of festivals celebrating Chinese holidays. The CCBAs, unlike the T'angs and family associations, exemplified an intermediate form of both assimilation and acculturation. They had associational characteristics that appeared American, combined with organizational principles that were Chinese.

Membership in the different associations was not mutually exclusive. One could belong to all three types. The number and types of organizations depended upon population size. In larger places, such as San Francisco or New York City, there were many associations which often competed with each other for membership and control over resources. This competition sometimes led to violent confrontations known to Westerners as "Tong Wars," even though the antagonists might not have been T'angs. When disputes occurred, the rules for settlement were often misinterpreted by outsiders, hence the epithet "wars." To those involved, however, the obligatory rules of conduct were well understood. Lyman's (1977) description of San Francisco Chinatown illustrates how "government" worked to handle the often fragile relationships between different public groups. Chinatown was

> . . . neither ruled by mobs nor orderly and peaceful. Conflicts between the several associations were not uncommon. Fights arose over scarce and valuable "resources"—power, wealth, and women. In these fights, erroneously called "tong wars" . . . The recourse to violence, the mode of fighting, and the institutions for peacemaking were all regulated by custom understood by the opposed parties. Indeed, early Chinese communities in America were "united" by the conflicts within them, which made no sense to non-Chinese outsiders and therefore isolated the contending parties and bound them together in "antagonistic cooperation." (90)

Although bound by shared language and cultural rules, Chinese immigrants nonetheless retained traditional organizations that reflected schisms and histories brought with them from their homeland. Their sojourner status made them different from other immigrants whose native organizations were similar to those found in the United States and who were committed to assimilation. The formation of cultural islands, where all things Chinese where obtainable, further reinforced the differences between this temporary population and American institutional arrangement. Part of that rejection involved the use of opium and the use of the opium den.

Sex, Gambling, and Opium

From the social science perspective, social behavior is an adaptive strategy. For Chinese migrant workers there were several activities that came under the supervision and coordination of the T'angs. Originally emerging as contra-government organizations in China, the T'angs adapted their goals to include prostitution, gambling, and operating opium dens. Although defined as inappropriate by the dominant Euro-American society, these activities were responses to a specific set of environmental conditions faced by Chinese migrants. Prostitution was a response to the demographic characteristics of Chinese migrants, most of whom were younger males, either unmarried or married but without their wives. In 1870, the **sex ratio** (number of males per 100 females) was 130 to 100. By 1880 it increased to 210 to 100 (Helmer 1974, 23). This imbalance led to the importation of Chinese females who became prostitutes. Prostitution appears to have been a temporary adaptation. Lyman noted that by the 1930s, when the sex ratio was closer to 100, prostitution had all but disappeared.

The study of games and their linkage to other cultural practices has intrigued some social scientists. With only rare exceptions, all cultures have games, and there is general agreement that games contribute to both socialization and enculturation. Games reward certain attributes or behaviors, pass on values, and teach interpersonal skills. John Roberts, Malcolm Arth, and Robert Bush (1959) proposed a threefold classification of games: games of physical skill, games of chance, and games of strategy. Using these distinctions they employed data from the Human Relations Areas Files to determine correlates of types of games. They discovered that games of strategy (games such as chess where participants are rewarded for competitive strategies) are dominant in highly stratified societies (states) that have clear class boundaries. Games of physical skill have a higher frequency in societies that emphasize individuals and individual achievement. In contrast, games of chance have their highest occurrence in societies characterized by uncertainty. Kung (1962) reports that the lottery and fan-tan (games of chance) were popular in Kwangtung. Thus, one could argue that gambling simply diffused with these migrants along with food and dress preferences. On the other hand, classification of games suggests a broader interpretation. The Chinese in America were a transient population whose lives were directed by others—both Chinese and Euro-American. Under these conditions, gambling as a game of chance is one expression of that uncertainty.[4]

The third adaptation was opium smoking and opium dens. According to Elmer Sandmeyer (1973), the earliest Chinese migrants were not opium users. They were representatives of the entrepreneurial classes in China—farmers and merchants. In China the practice of opium smoking marked class distinctions. Wealthy merchants did not smoke. It was not until the peasant opium smokers arrived in large numbers that a Chinese-Opium connection was observed directly. Thus, it could be argued that opium smoking, along with food, clothing, and other traits, simply diffused from China and contributed to acculturation. Yet in chapter 6 we noted that opium dens, like bars, are temporary public places which serviced transient populations. The Chinese were double transients. They had migrated from another culture, and they commuted to work sites in mining, farms, railroads, and factories in the United States. The only anchors to their internal migration were the larger urban hubs within which "Chinatowns" had evolved. Even there, residency was often temporary. In this situation, opium symbolically provided a traditional Chinese trait, but the opium den was the adaptive strategy. Within it, differences in surname and huiguan affiliations disappeared, at least for a short time. Patrons were Chinese. If prefectoral and surname associations made distinctions between migrants, the T'angs functioned to dissipate those differences in prostitution, gambling, and the opium den.

Chinese Consumption of Smoking Opium

If smoking opium was imported only to meet the demands of the Chinese, then one would hypothesize that the quantity of opium imported would vary according to the size of the immigrant population. In table 10.2, we do note a parallel increase in numbers of Chinese and amount of imported opium between 1870 and 1890. This observation seems to support this hypothesis. After 1890, however, we note a decline in the Chinese population and corresponding increase in pounds of imported smoking opium. This increase in opium imports continues until 1909 with the passage of the Smoking Opium Exclusion Act. After that date, no official data are available on opium imports.

If one begins with the assumption that only Chinese smoke opium, this finding suggests two possible explanations for increased importation after the turn of the century. One is that the absolute number of smokers increased. Another is that the population of users remained constant, but the per capita consumption increased. One difficulty with both of these explanations is that they cannot be tested. No data are available to measure how many Chinese smoked opium or how much opium was consumed by Chinese. We can, however, estimate a frequency range of users. Edward Brecher (1972) estimated that opium smokers consumed two and one-half

Table 10.2.
**Chinese Population in the United States: 1860–1950
and Pounds of Smoking Opium Imported: 1860–1909**

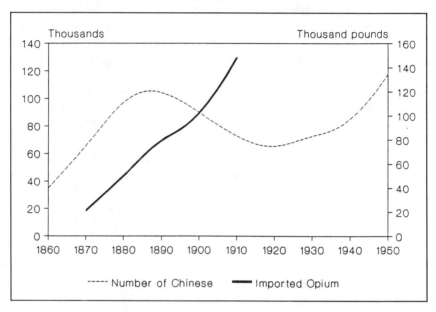

Source: Brecher, Edward M. (1972:45)

pounds per year (45). In contrast, Barth (196–197) referenced one case where a sugarcane planter in Louisiana included a ration of six pounds of smoking opium per person per year as an inducement to attract Chinese laborers. Using these two tables, it is possible to estimate the number of Chinese opium smokers. This is shown in table 10.3.

Obviously, the two estimates of yearly consumption are at variance with each other. Using Brecher's estimate, 83 percent of the Chinese population in the decade preceding the Opium Exclusion Act would have been smokers. In contrast, Barth's estimate predicts only 14 percent of the Chinese as regular users for this same period. The overall percentage range also varies, from a low of 2 percent (Barth) compared with 13 percent (Brecher). This exercise illustrates how "data" can be used to justify any "problem." For anti-opium activists, Brecher's figures are the "truth." For smoking advocates, Barth's estimates show how small the "problem" is. Obviously, data can be forced to dance to anyone's tune. In contrast to both these estimates, John Helmer (1974)

Table 10.3.
Estimated Number of Opium Smokers

Source: Distilled Spirits Council of the U.S., Inc., September 20, 1991.

suggests that the amount of smoking opium imported had little to do with domestic consumption. Rather, it reflected speculation by Chinese merchants on the international opium market in an attempt to recover losses they suffered during the depression years at the end of the nineteenth century.

There is ample evidence for anti-Chinese legislation and sentiment in the United States before 1914. This does not, however, support the conclusion that the Harrison Act focused on curbing a practice associated with the Chinese. Nor can one dismiss this factor as a condition contributing to legislative action. In expanding our explanation beyond single causes, one must explore other possible influences on this legislation.

Organized Labor and Anti-Chinese Legislation

In the last quarter of the nineteenth century, two major institutions were evolving in America. One was the business corporation, which through permissive legislation was able to amass large amounts of capital to invest in manufacturing. Sheltered from individual financial responsibility by the limited liability clause of general incorporation and capable of entering into diverse economic ventures for an unlimited life, "big" business was born. Paralleling this development was the rise of big unions. To legitimate themselves as public groups, unions relied on the control of a resource needed by the manufacturing corporation, namely, labor. The two mechanisms they used were recruitment of workers and the strike. Success in negotiating with management depended on recruiting all workers in an industry or factory, along with their ability to withhold that labor if negotiations failed.

A consistent interpretation found in the literature is that unions were influential in the passage of anti-Chinese legislation (Kung 1962; Barth 1964; Chen 1980; Miller 1969). This conclusion does not mean that unions were the only supporters of this legislation, but as visible publics they had a resource that could be exchanged with legislators. This resource was votes—block votes. In California, the major political parties were equally balanced. In some cases, elections were won by only a few votes. Taking advantage of this situation, the unions offered votes to candidates who would sponsor and support legislation to exclude Chinese migration and restrict Chinese labor. The successful result of this lobbying led to the interpretation that unions were primarily responsible for anti-Chinese legislation. Yet before the existence of unions, there is evidence for rejection of Chinese emigrants.

Many of the early Chinese immigrants were miners. In fact, they constituted the largest ethnic category in the gold fields. As early as 1849, reports ranging from individual beatings and killings to riots and forced expulsion of Chinese appeared in the press. There is no evidence that unions sponsored these hostilities. Rather, they were spontaneous community reactions against Chinese miners (informal government). Even without a strong union presence, in 1850 California passed the Foreign Miners' License Tax. This act imposed a tax varying from $3 to $20 per person on Chinese, Chilean, Mexican, and Australian miners. In 1852, several localities banned Chinese miners altogether and raised the foreign miners tax to $4 a month. Additional legislation taxed, limited, or excluded Chinese fishing and forbid the hiring of Chinese by municipalities. While most of this legislation was either repealed or ruled unconstitutional, local and state governing bodies continued to pass restrictions on Chinese labor without the direct influence of labor unions.

Gold mining in the 1850s was becoming increasingly mechanized. Smaller entrepreneurs were being replaced by large corporate mining operations. As a result, many miners left the fields to work on the railroads. The increased demand for labor to build railway lines in the mid-1860s was satisfied by Chinese and American labor merchants. Some railroads even recruited directly in China. Agents of the Central Pacific Railroad drafted workers from the mountain districts of the Pearl River Delta. They paid for outfit and passage. In return, each draftee signed a promissory note for $75 in United States' gold coin that was secured by family or friends. The contract called for regular installments with completion of the total obligation in seven years.

Chinese were not the only foreign labor recruited by the railroad. For example, in 1869 Cornish miners were specifically engaged to do rock tunneling. In spite of their expertise they were unable to compete with Chinese workers. Their response was to form the "California Workingmen's Society," a union whose charter stated that "all those of Mongolian origin should be prohibited from entering California" (Chen 140).

Chinese laborers from Cuba worked in the cane fields of Louisiana in the middle 1860s. A few years later, colonies of Catholic Chinese from the Philippines reached the American South. Most of these workers deserted the plantations after a year or two. Many went to California where they could earn higher wages; some remained to become independent fishermen and truck farmers for the New Orleans market (Barth 196). It was not until the late 1860s that Chinese laborers appeared in the Northeast.

If the rise of unions is linked to anti-Chinese sentiment, the rise of the corporation and "big" business is not. While entrepreneurs employed Chinese workers in the West, management in the East hired them as strike breakers. It was in this capacity that the first Chinese traveled to the Northeast. In North Adams, Massachusetts, Belleville, New Jersey, and Beaver Falls, Pennsylvania, factory owners responded to strikes by bringing in Chinese workers (Barth 197–198). North Adams received its first shipment on June 13, 1870. Seventy-five Chinese arrived as strikebreakers for the Calvin T. Sampson's Model Shoe Factory. The union was the Secret Order of the Knights of St. Crispin, which at that time was the largest labor union in the United States. The arrival of the Chinese brought strong negative reactions from both politicians and the press. However, the American, Irish, and French-Canadian Crispins viewed the Chinese strikebreakers in North Adams as potential new union members (200). Their previous experience had been that strikebreakers soon became loyal union members. Anticipating this same response from the Chinese, the Crispins offered to organize a local Chinese lodge and to negotiate for a daily wage of $2. The Chinese rejected the union's offer and never became union members. Although the Chinese left within a decade, the union's failure to organize them turned Eastern workingmen into determined opponents of Chinese labor and ardent advocates of Chinese exclusion (Barth, 202).

Responses to Chinese labor differed from one coast to the other. In the West, anti-Chinese sentiment came after competitive experiences in the gold fields and the railroad. In the East, the history of Sino-union relations was relative to strikebreaking. The result, according to Miller (1969), was the adoption of a siege mentality among unionists. The most prominent labor spokesmen of the time were all anti-Chinese. Virtually every labor newspaper and organization opposed Chinese immigration after 1870. Even the Negro delegates at the first Colored State Labor Convention in Baltimore in December 1869 passed a plank in favor of Chinese exclusion (Miller, 196).

The official positions of unions on both the Atlantic and Pacific coasts made the Chinese issue national. Further, at the national level, the balance of power between the Republicans and the Democrats was held by the Pacific states where anti-Chinese sentiment had been the most intense. Unions had the ability to deliver needed votes in this situation, and they were able to influence Congress to pass The Chinese Restriction Act in 1882. This act effectively banned Chinese immigration for ten years, with options to extend the exclusion. The Act was not repealed until 1942.

Union opposition to Chinese workers included support of anti-opium legislation. The ability to work longer hours for less income was often attributed to the drug itself. Even the Irish-American press in New York City took a strong stand against the Chinese in words that had been applied to the Irish by English-American editors only a few decades before. The only difference was that opium smoking replaced whiskey drinking. Public sentiment linking substances to social categories was not restricted to the Chinese. The belief that the opiates in general were responsible for an assortment of social ills was widespread before the Harrison Act. As David Musto (1987) reports:

> By 1914 prominent newspapers, physicians, pharmacists, and congressmen believed opiates and cocaine predisposed habitués toward insanity and crime. They were widely seen as substances associated with foreigners or alien subgroups. Cocaine raised the specter of the wild Negro, opium the devious Chinese, morphine the tramps in the slums; it was feared that use of all these drugs was spreading into the "higher classes." (65)

The belief that these substances contributed to social disorder led to the question of control. Opium, morphine, and cocaine were easily available through numerous sources, both licit and illicit. The political solution to this "problem" was about to arise at the turn of the century with the birth of a new American institution that lobbied for ownership of "drugs."

The Harrison Act and Health Professions

David Musto (1987), a physician and medical historian, suggests that the passage of the Harrison Act was influenced by the emergence of two professions—medicine and pharmacy. According to Musto, at the turn of the century:

> . . . both suffered from weak licensing laws, meager training requirements, and a surplus of practitioners. (13)

The chaotic state of medicine reflected a larger debate about disease etiology. During the nineteenth century there were few remedies for communicable diseases. Without cures, physicians and druggists administered opiates to relieve pain and discomfort. Beginning in the mid-nineteenth century, there was increasing acceptance of germ theory by American physicians, but its full endorsement did not occur until the success of diphtheria antitoxin in 1895 (Rothstein 1972). The application of germ theory to everyday maladies such as diarrhea and dysentery, along with knowledge about the bacteria that caused tuberculosis, diphtheria, and cholera, reduced the use of opiates. With improvements in diagnostic procedures, the benefits of vaccination, and the accidental discovery of the analgesic properties of aspirin in 1889, "modern" medicine emerged as an opiate-free discipline (Courtwright 1982).

Corresponding to the success of medical practices was an attempt to legitimate the medical "profession." Founded in 1847, The American Medical Association (AMA) was one of many competing medical public associations. At the turn of the century it had only 8,500 members. By 1913, membership had increased to 36,000 (Musto, 56). As part of its efforts to represent medical practitioners, it formed a special committee to review legislation that might affect physicians. Although lobbying efforts were primarily directed at establishing unified standards for medical training (socialization) and the professionalization of physicians through strict licensing procedures, the AMA was also concerned with drugs. Its first success in this area was the passage of the Pure Food and Drug Act in 1906.

The American Pharmaceutical Association (APhA) dates from 1852. It was one of many competing associations concerned with the manufacturing, importing and exporting, and dispensing of medications. Pharmacists who defined themselves as professionals became members of the APhA. The APhA did not support narcotic use for other than medical purposes, and it fought proprietary (patent) medicines along with the AMA. Several reasons were offered for their position. One was that drugs are dangerous and that self-medication carries with it an inherent risk. Another reason was economic. Legislation which restricted dispensing drugs only to pharmacists would reduce competition with grocery stores, mail-order houses, and other sources.

The first attempt to control drugs at the national level did not win approval in Congress. In 1910, the Foster Bill was introduced to Congress. It permitted small amounts of narcotics in patent medicines but had rather rigid requirements for licensing and record keeping. Both the AMA and the APhA lobbied against this bill, especially its provisions for record keeping. The first draft of the Harrison Act appeared in 1912. It differed only slightly from the Foster Bill. Noting the inevitability of some sort of federal legislation, the AMA and the APhA formed an alliance, the National Drug Trade Conference (NDTC). Made up of representatives of the drug industry and medicine, the NDTC opposed the initial wording of the Harrison Act, again citing excessive record keeping as a central concern. One of the issues that emerged in the NDTC was who would dispense drugs. The pharmacists lobbied to limit the issuance of drugs only to patients who had been diagnosed by physicians. This restriction came in response to experiences with dispensing physicians who sold medications to non-patients as an income supplement. However, as a result of the AMA's previous efforts to professionalize medicine, physicians' incomes dramatically increased, and this practice had all but disappeared. This issue was easily resolved by an agreement that physicians would diagnose and prescribe, and pharmacists would fill the prescriptions. With this accord in hand, the chairman of the NDTC signed a draft of legislation on June 10, 1913 that would soon become the Harrison Act.

This brief review of how physicians and pharmacists contributed to the passage of the Harrison Act illustrates the function of government and legislation. The function of legislation is to integrate different publics. The NDTC was the public association that represented an alliance between two other public associations, namely, the APhA and the AMA. In concert with unions as publics and the State Department (discussed below), the NDTC was able to influence the wording of the act to benefit both the APhA and the AMA.

We have already discussed the linkage between unionization and the rise of the corporation. But what explains the emergence of the AMA and the APhA? Why was this legislation so important for them? From the social science perspective, legislation not only recognizes publics and attempts to integrate them but also reflects structural changes that have occurred in society itself. Thus, legislation must be viewed within the larger social context. During the nineteenth century there was no separate recognizable health institution in American culture. By 1913 there was. One possible explanation for this change is found in a model proposed by Norman Storer (1966). He defines institutions as clusters of rules that regulate the exchange of a commodity. The commodity can be any "thing," but must be some "thing" defined as valuable. For example, in contemporary American culture, the institution of economics regulates the exchange of money; the commodity regulated by the institution of religion is salvation; and education sets forth the procedures regulating how knowledge is acquired. Storer is not concerned with why a commodity becomes valuable. Rather, he would argue that because money, salvation, and knowledge are commodities which define the boundaries between institutions in American culture, they are therefore valuable.

Rules governing the exchange of commodities may require different behaviors. One works to get money; one prays to achieve salvation; and one studies to gain knowledge. In spite of these different behaviors, Storer argues that there are three general principles which regulate all exchanges. These are

1. The commodity is wanted—that is, participants in the exchange assume that others also want the commodity. In other words, there is agreement that the commodity is valuable.
2. The commodity can only be obtained through exchange with others.
3. Different exchange systems must not be compromised. For example, money cannot be used to purchase salvation, knowledge, or sex. (pp. 38–39)[5]

During the nineteenth century there was little to hold doctors together. Surgeons competed with other curers, and knowledge about the cause and cure of the diseases that brought patients to physicians was, for all practical purposes, unknown. What unified medical practitioners was the use of drugs to cure disease. This commodity took on special value as a "thing" or "things" which defined the institutional boundaries of "medicine." But drugs could only retain their value if their distribution was restricted. The involvement of the AMA and the APhA in passage of the Pure Food and Drug Act served to demonstrate that "drugs" were widely available. Everybody had access to opiates and cocaine but nobody had proprietary rights to these substances. The Harrison Act granted "ownership" of drugs to bona fide members of the health care system—physicians, dentists, veterinarians and pharmacists. They had exclusive "rights" to exchange those substances defined as "drugs" for health purposes. To insure exclusivity in the exchange of drugs, the Act imposed penalties on those outside this system if they exchanged these commodities for money (economic institution), or sex (kinship institution), or salvation (religion), and so forth. On the surface, the Harrison Act focused on a few commodities—morphine, cocaine, and heroin. Symbolically, it legitimated medicine as a new institution within American culture.

To argue that the Harrison Act was a response to changes in medical knowledge and the rise of a medical institution as well as to popular perceptions that associated drugs with those outside the mainstream of society is in part true. However, there is one more alliance that we must consider—an alliance that was international in scope.

The Harrison Act and International Treaties

That government, as the social manifestation of political systems, functions to adjudicate disputes between publics is clearly illustrated for both unions and medicine. However, government is itself a public with its own rules regulating internal descent and external alliances. A contributing factor to the passage of the Harrison Act was an attempt by the American government to form alliances with other nation states. This came about as a result of a change in the position of the United States in the international community as a consequence of the Spanish-American War (1898). This four-month war ended with the United States gaining control of Puerto Rico, Guam, the Philippines, and Cuba. After this war, the United States became a colonial power.

The colonial powers of the United States were resisted in the Philippines. Philippino loyalists who fought with the Americans against the Spanish believed that the islands would be given independence at the war's end. When this was not granted, the loyalists became "rebels" who directed their military efforts against American forces. It was not until 1902 that these rebel forces were brought under control. With its colonial domination established, the United States then faced an opium "problem." Under Spanish rule there was a government controlled monopoly of opium. Merchants paid taxes to the Spanish for the sale of opium to Chinese-Filipinos, the only people permitted to purchase it. With the end of Spanish control, opium imports increased. A cholera epidemic in 1902 raised the demand for opium among the general population. This widespread use of opium was viewed as a "problem" by American emissaries. In 1905 Congress passed legislation ordering an immediate prohibition of opium except for medical use. The only exemption was to Chinese males over the age of twenty-one. They were granted a three-year extension of the ban during which they could obtain a license to purchase smoking opium.

A second alliance focused on Sino-American relations. At the end of the nineteenth century, after centuries of isolation, China and the Far East opened to American financial interests. This market was viewed as having the potential to overcome many of the losses American firms experienced during the 1893 depression. Since the late eighteenth century, there had been some international trade between China and other countries. India, for example, derived much of its tax revenue from opium shipped to China. Although the British expressed moral concerns with this trade, they feared that prohibition would have negative financial consequences. Either Iran (then called Persia) or Turkey would increase their exports to China, or the Chinese would increase their internal production. These concerns were resolved in 1906 with an agreement that the Chinese would decrease internal consumption and India would reduce shipments at a rate of 10 percent per year.

The opium-reduction agreement was facilitated by the defeat of the Boxers in the Boxer Rebellion of 1900. The Boxers were nationalists who opposed any foreign intervention in China. In 1899 the Boxers attacked Christian missionaries and Chinese converts. Soon after, all aliens became targets for Boxer hostilities. In response, an allied army composed of United States, British, German, French, Russian, and Japanese troops was sent in to restore order. Within a few months this army had subdued the Boxers. In opposition to the Boxers was the Liberal party. It welcomed both the technologies and practices of the West and Japan and believed that China's problems stemmed largely from opium addiction. The Liberal party's victory in the 1906 elections signaled the beginning of a successful and sometimes brutal program to eradicate all opium from China.

The experience of the United States in the Philippines and China led to the formation of the First International Opium Congress in 1909. Thirteen nations were present at the Shanghai meeting. Both Turkey and Persia (Iran) declined official participation. Although interested in the issue of narcotics control, most of the nations were not supportive of the United States' position that non-medical use of opium was evil and immoral (Musto, 36). The United States insisted that it had a "problem," and this problem was not of its own doing. Since opium and coca were not large cash crops in the United States, the only solution to the problem was to convince other nations to stop production and export. This proposal was questioned by the delegates from other nations. How could the United States—with no general anti-narcotic legislation of its own—ask others to do what it was not willing to do? This meeting adjourned with only four non-binding resolutions.

The leader of the United States' delegation in Shanghai argued that control of the drug trade was an economic issue. The regulation of drugs could be achieved by taxation. All drugs would require a tax stamp, and the possession of any drug without it would be punishable. States could control the import and export of drugs simply by increasing or decreasing taxes. This idea was incorporated into the 1910 Foster Bill. It proposed a tax on drugs, and it answered those international critics who had questioned the sincerity of the United States.

In 1912 the United States returned to the second international convention, this time in The Hague. Again only twelve nations participated. The leader of this convention was The Right Reverend Charles Henry Brent, the first Episcopal bishop of the Philippines and an international leader in the anti-opium movement. A second conference met the following year. By that time thirty-four nations had signed the treaty regulating opium. A third conference, proposed for May 1914, was postponed by the United States to pass domestic legislation that would demonstrate its sincerity. On December 14th the Harrison Act was passed by Congress. Three days later it was signed by the president.

Legislation and the Idea of "Danger"

From the social science perspective, the Harrison Act was clearly the result of an elaborate and overlapping web of alliances. The evolution of unions, the genesis of modern medical professions, and the emergence of the United States as a colonial power all contributed to this piece of legislation. In the case of unions, the act symbolized a moral victory over competing Chinese labor. For both medicine and international relations, consensus among publics made the act an example of political authority. Yet, if we reexamined the emic justification for this legislation, we note an ever-present theme: Drugs, in and of themselves, are dangerous and must be controlled. As part of the American worldview drugs were redefined as dangerous substances. What accounted for this redefinition?

Surveys of Western drug users find that they agree with non-users that drugs are "dangerous" or risky. Among crack users in Toronto, Canada (Cheung, Erickson, and Landau 1991), 91 percent responded that regular use of crack involves "great risk." Peyote use among Native Americans and the Huichol is perceived as "tricky." Palm wine is prohibited for Lele females based on the belief that it will harm them. In some respect, the perceptions of danger by users and non-users are similar. Are we therefore to conclude that crack, peyote, and palm wine are dangerous substances? From the social science perspective, the answer to this question is not found in the chemistry of crack, peyote, and palm wine but rather in the process by which anything is defined as dangerous and the function of that definition.

Mary Douglas and Aaron Wildavsky (1982) propose a theory which addresses the question of danger and the definition of danger. They apply this theory to the current environmentalist movement in the United States. Although their historical data on the environmental movement may be flawed (Kaprow 1985), their discussion of the function of danger is applicable to drugs. Using both tribal and industrial societies, they suggest that efforts to mobilize against some dangers are not necessarily proportional to "actual" dangers. The question they pose is, "Why are some threats selected over others?" Not too surprisingly they find that culture, not nature, is the funnel through which all potential threats are filtered. They conclude that the function of danger is to legitimate the cultural order through the adoption of "causes" directed at ameliorating some perceived "problem."

Douglas and Wildavsky found that the organizational character-istics of the environmental movement can best be described as a sectarian sect. Sects are egalitarian groups that require an external threat to maintain or enhance internal order. These external threats are usually global, or at least beyond any immediate risk. For environmentalists, it is the *world's* environment. Both the cause and the alleged victims for these sects are "big." Cause is attributed to "big" business or "big" government. Victims are "our" children, "our" way of life, or some other "our."

Douglas and Wildavsky admit there may be real dangers, but that does not explain why some are selected and others are ignored. It is not until the "cause" of these problems is assigned to some segment of society that they become a meaningful emic explanation for the "problem." For example:

> No doubt the water in fourteenth century Europe was a persistent health hazard, but a cultural theory of perception would point out that it became a public preoccupation only when it seemed plausible to accuse Jews of poisoning the wells. (7)

The attractiveness of their theory is that it redirects our attention away from the thing or things that are the object of emic concern to the organizational principles of society itself. At the emic level, rhetoric, slogans, and membership define the boundaries between developing public sects. The result of this process is a clear distinction between "them" and "us." Thus, the search for a "rational" basis of danger lies not in some mystical, psychological state of awareness but rather in the structures which organize behaviors and beliefs about the world in which we live.

In their wide sample of cultures, Douglas and Wildavsky note that emic definitions of danger and the proposed amelioration of that danger do not rely on the "truth." In cultures with magic or science, evidence to support the claims of sects is carefully selected. Anecdote is chosen over falsifiability; objectivity is rejected and replaced by passion; statistics are tortured to tell the "truth," and everybody is invited in to fight the "war." The reader may conclude from this that I am proposing some knowledge of reality not available to those enmeshed in the activities of the sect. This is not so. From the standpoint of social science, the question of an independent "reality" is not an issue. Rather, we are charged with the responsibility of explaining the antecedent structural conditions that lead to the formation of sect-like organizations, regardless of their specific goals.

If Douglas and Wildavsky are correct, we would predict that concerns about the dangerousness of drugs and the general acceptance of this definition are explained by the characteristics of culture itself. Although not strictly an obligation, being able to demonstrate that "dangerous" substances do not result in bodily injury or harm, including death, would indicate that something other than the substance is the basis for danger.

Drug legislation in the United States has consistently used the "dangerous" substance theme. From the Harrison Act on, control of the opiates, marihuana, cocaine, and the hallucinogens have all been based on "scientific" evidence that they are harmful. Can it be demonstrated that they are dangerous by independent standards?

Heroin: Danger or Culture?

Brecher and his staff (1972) carried out an extensive review of the biomedical literature in search of support for the thesis that opiates are physically harmful. They found no evidence linking even long-term use of opium or heroin and physical debilitation, disease, or organic damage. The one condition often associated with heroin use—infectious diseases such as hepatitis and now AIDS—was the result of sharing needles, not heroin. One classic study (Light and Torrance 1929), using a subsample of 100 from a population of 861 heroin users, challenged conventional wisdom on the general health of addicts. All of those in the sample were addicted for at least five years and had been averaging twenty-one grains of morphine per day, approximately thirty times more than the average street heroin user in New York City in 1971. In their sample, 90 percent were within weight-height standards determined by the insurance industry; 6 percent were overweight, and 4 percent were underweight. The high incidence of pyorrhea and dental caries in this sample was the same as that of non-addicts from the same socio-economic level.

If heroin use is not related to the overall health of addicts, what about the possibility of "overdosing?" In New York City there were less than 100 deaths designated as the result of heroin overdose in 1918. Death due to overdose remained low until the 1950s, whereupon it increased. By 1971 there were over 1,200 reported deaths attributed to heroin "overdose," and it was the leading cause of death for all males in the 15–35 age range. Brecher was puzzled by these reported deaths for two reasons. First, the amount of heroin in a street dose in the 1970s was 30 times lower than in 1918. Based on experimental evidence, the amount necessary to kill someone who is not an addict is approximately 50 New York City bags of heroin taken at one time! Second, fatal poisoning takes from one to twelve hours. This was more than enough time for comatose victims to be given the readily available narcotic antagonistic *nalorphine* which would bring them out of the coma within a few minutes. But in the post-1950s, addicts were dying suddenly. Based on these observations, he concludes that deaths attributed to "overdose" are not from heroin.

What is killing heroin users? Brecher argues that the assignment of "death by overdose" has more to do with the coroner-medical system than with medical proof. Coroners must indicate some cause of death on death certificates. Failure to do so would challenge their expertise. If someone found dead is a known heroin user, or there is other evidence of heroin use before death, the coroner *infers* the cause of death as heroin overdose. In the 1940s, coroners and medical examiners based this cause of death on two findings: "(1) that the victim was a heroin addict who 'shot up' prior to his death; and (2) there was no evidence of suicide, violence, infection, or other natural causes" (Brecher, 106). Brecher concludes that the "cause" of death from "overdose" is in fact a cause of death from Syndrome X, an unknown adulterant or combination of adulterants used to cut street-level heroin. One of these substances is quinine; the other is sugar. Another possible explanation is drug interaction. Users often drink alcohol before, during, or after injection; some combine heroin with barbiturates to make a "speedball." Whatever the combinations in this mixture, there is no evidence that heroin, in and of itself, is the "cause" of death.

Heroin and Clinical Pathology

Attempts to link opiate use with diminished mental capacity have proven fruitless. Opiate users are no more psychotic than non-users. Stanley Einstein's (1983) exhaustive search through the bewildering, often confusing, and contradictory psychological literature from the early 1900s to 1980 finds no support for a connection between "personality" and drug use. It did reveal something about clinicians, however. Drug users were placed into clinical categories for mental illness. Although the psychopathological labels varied over the review period, and although clinicians did not always agree about whether drugs were the "cause" or the "effect" of drug use, the underlying assumption was that drug use, in and of itself, was evidence for mental illness.

Michael Agar (1973) came face-to-face with these *a priori* assumptions of clinicians in his 1960s study of heroin addicts at the NIMH Clinical Research Center in Lexington, Kentucky. He noted that the clinical staff of the hospital defined the addict as a social-psychological failure who lacked "appropriate values, goals and rules of behavior." Agar's field work among addicts in the facility concluded that their *behavior* was an appropriate adaptation to street life. In the street, addicts are constantly threatened. They are "burned" by dealers, ripped off by others, and arrested by the police. In this environment, addicts learned to be skeptical about and suspicious of strangers. Establishing the reliability of others was important for survival and represented a realistic behavioral adaptation to these conditions. When evaluated by middle-class clinicians, their behavior was judged as either "adaptive" or "maladaptive" according to middle-class social experiences. In that world one is not threatened by being burned, ripped off, or arrested. Thus, the clinical diagnosis of street heroin addicts as paranoid (having unrealistic fears) reflects the differences in the social worlds of clinicians and lower-class addicts.

Without demonstrable proof that "drugs" are inherently dangerous, an alternative explanation for drug legislation is the model proposed by social science. This model directs our attention to the structural characteristics of culture and the alliance and descent practices which maintain those structures. Occasionally this model yields explanations which seem to be economic. Certainly the attempts to restrict competition by unions, medicine, and drug manufacturers had positive pecuniary benefits for these public associations. Using just these publics, one might conclude that legislation properly belongs with a discussion of economic systems. Yet not all anti-drug legislation has direct economic consequences for some publics. In the following pages we examine three movements that fall outside the realm of economic motivations—national Prohibition, the anti-peyote movement, and the most recent movement, anti-smoking.

Legislation and Social Class: Alcohol and Prohibition

The relationship between legislation to restrict or prohibit alcohol and social factors has attracted many social scientists. In Melanesia, Mac and Leslie Marshall (1990) examined the linkage between the recent women's movement and Prohibition. Maggie Brady (1990) reviewed changes in Prohibition legislation directed at Australian Aborigines. Joy Leland (1976) carried out an extensive search of the literature to determine the basis of the long history of alcohol prohibition to Native Americans. In spite of their different locations, one notes that any attempt to prohibit alcohol to some segment of a population was accompanied by an emic explanation that alcohol was "dangerous" to the health or well-being of that population. One conclusion from this observation is that prohibition of a substance was one way to symbolically mark the boundaries between some "them" and some "us." How do we interpret an attempt to prohibit the consumption of alcohol to both them and us? One clue is an analysis of Prohibition in the United States.

The United States is one of only a few Western nations that legislated a total prohibition of alcohol.[6] The 18th Amendment and the passage of the Volstead Act effectively banned the sale of alcohol for twenty-one years between 1919 and 1933. The movement associated with passage of this legislation was the Womens' Christian Temperance Union (WCTU). According to Joseph Gusfield (1962), the WCTU was a somewhat unique movement in that it did not seek to gain any power or economic advantage. Rather, its goals were symbolic and moral. Gusfield suggests that the movement reflected changes in the class structure of America. Accompanying these changes, the movement's membership, goals, and tactics also changed.

Gusfield's analysis of the temperance movement focused on the changing composition of the middle class in America. In post-colonial America there was a two-class system. The aristocracy maintained a position of authority based on either commercial capitalism or the feudal capitalistic plantation system of the South. All the rest were simple men who filled the bottom ranks. During this period, drinking followed class boundaries, and there was no drinking "problem" until after the Revolution. Gusfield attributes the emergence of this "problem" to the rise of the small merchant and farmer class who challenged the pre-revolutionary two-class system. The membership of the temperance movement during the middle eighteenth century represented the old aristocracy. Both religiously orthodox and Federalist, they directed their efforts downward to reforming the newly emerging middle classes below them. Dominated by clergy and men of prominence from New England, the prohibitionists eventually became named publics, such as the American Temperance Society in the 1820s. The leadership in these "societies" came from the Presbyterian clergy who were spokesmen for the upper classes. Churches that included temperance as part of church doctrine (such as the Methodists) were not included because their membership was primarily middle and working class.

The decline of the two-tiered class system and a numerical increase in the middle classes changed control of the temperance movement. The Methodists and the revivalists, who had provided religion to the middle and lower classes, were able to wrestle control of the movement from the Presbyterians and the aristocrats. It was not church leaders who controlled the movement; rather, its staff was primarily secular.

Under the Presbyterians there was an emphasis on controlled drinking. With a history of condemning all sales and consumption of liquor, the "new" prohibitionists wanted nothing less than total abolition. This resulted in a changed membership. Wealthy East Coasters withdrew from the movement and were replaced by the new middle class who lived on the western frontier. Along with the change in social class of the membership there was a change in the target population. The new prohibitionists directed their efforts toward their own class. This was a period of self-help. Recruitment efforts emphasized conversion. Members demonstrated their commitment by taking a pledge not to drink, and there were fiery meetings where drunks were dramatically reformed. Abstinence, along with involvement in the church, became the marker for membership in the "new" middle class.

In order for any social movement to survive, it must have adversaries, real or imagined. In other words, there must be danger. In the mid-nineteenth century danger was provided by (1) the large immigration of northern Catholic Europeans who did not bring with them anti-drinking sentiments and who occupied the lower classes, and (2) the increased division of the movement around North-South distinctions. The movement embraced Republicanism, nativism, and anti-slavery. The expanding middle classes (made up of small-town and rural professionals, retailers, and small factory owners who had "made it" on their own and who embraced the ideologies of hard work, self-discipline, and sobriety) took control of the temperance movement.

During the last quarter of the nineteenth century the urban population swelled with migrants to meet the demands for industrial labor. The resultant crowded housing and lower living standards led to an identification of the city as a source of America's "problems." In response to this definition, many reform movements emerged to deal with the problems of the urban proletariat. One of these was the Women's Christian Temperance Union. Founded in 1874, it was a progressive movement. Its middle-class, educated membership believed that the "cure" to the plight of the working classes was abstinence. The movement was labor, child, and prison reform oriented. Unlike the previous phase where recruitment and conversion focused on the middle classes, the progressives directed their missionary zeal on the underclass. Their objective was to convert this underclass into native, rural, non-drinking Protestants.

Paralleling the progressives were the populists. Unconcerned with the urban poor, they focused on the plight of the American farmer.

Faced with a decline in control over markets and reduced income, farmers organized public associations such as the Grange and the People's party. The populist wing of the temperance movement formed alliances with these associations and incorporated many of their goals, such as suffrage, the graduated income tax, government control of the railroads, and abolition of the stock exchange. In exchange, the platforms of these rural associations included abolition. Unlike the progressive wing of the movement that sought to help the poor, the populists worked to influence legislative remedies. Their enemy was big business, which included the liquor industry and the wealthy. It was among the populists in the temperance movement that the ban of liquor was the central issue.

By the late nineteenth century the temperance movement had formed alliances with several different causes. As Gusfield notes:

> Almost every progressive, radical, or conservative movement has some alliance with it. Populists and Progressives, labor and farmer, urban and rural, male and female, Christian and secularist had some reason or opportunity to be an adherent or a sympathizer in the temperance movement. (111)

The alliances that populists and progressives forged with other publics often led to conflict within the movement. In response, the abolitionists abandoned the alliance strategy at the turn of the century. This was replaced by efforts to mobilize the middle-class, church-going members to adopt the goals of the Anti-Saloon League and the Methodist Board of Temperance and Morality—namely, national Prohibition. Protestant churches became actively involved in lobbying local, state, and federal legislators for Prohibition. The social gospel, concern for the poor, and universal suffrage only provided a base for alliances with other groups, but temperance was the central issue. So successful was their lobbying that:

> In the period 1906–17, 26 states passed prohibitionary legislation, although of diverse scope. In 18 of these states, the proposal had been adopted at state elections. In 1914 the House of Representatives had voted in favor of a constitutional amendment. When the Eighteenth Amendment was ratified on January 20, 1919, it was the fruition of a wave of successful Temperance agitation and legislation in the preceding 20 years. (Gusfield 1986, 117)

The passage of the 18th Amendment, and the Volstead Act which provided for enforcement of the amendment, symbolized the success of the middle class. However, changes in the composition of the middle class and difficulties in enforcing the Volstead Act continued the debate. On the rise was a new middle class that was salaried (as opposed to entrepreneurial), corporate (as opposed to small, privately owned businesses), urban (as opposed to rural and small town), and active in the Democratic party. Unlike the pre-Prohibition middle class, where self-control and mastery over things were important values, the new middle class adopted corporate social virtues, such as getting along with other people.

This emerging new middle class formed the corpus of the "Wets," who argued that large-scale violations of Prohibition and the inability of enforcement agencies to control drinking was evidence for violation of an American norm. It was, of course, their own norm. Drinking and the exchange of alcohol symbolized the corporate values of cooperation and sociability and also marked alliances between members of the new middle class. In contrast, the "Drys" intensified their position that they were "true" representatives of the "American way." The swelling ranks of the new corporate middle class did not go unnoticed by political parties. Support for continued Prohibition was absent in the 1932 campaign platforms of both the Democrats and the Republicans. Both unions and manufacturers went on record as supporting an appeal of the amendment. In 1933, the 18th Amendment was repealed and Prohibition officially ended.

The activities of the abolitionists did not stop with repeal of the 18th Amendment, but the class composition of its membership did. The percentage of women from the upper middle class declined and the membership became increasingly lower middle class and lower class (Gusfield 1986, 129). In spite of these changes, the worldview of the old entrepreneurial middle class continued. Present-day prohibitionists are still fundamentalist in church affiliation, nationalistic, and nativistic.

Gusfield's interpretation of the linkage between social factors and the symbolic value of drinking extends beyond the Volstead Act. He suggests that assimilation of the old "dangerous" classes of the early twentieth century—the Germans, the Irish, and the Slavs—reduced their dangerousness (1986, 200). In their place are the new "dangerous" classes—African Americans, Mexicans, American Indians, and youth. Leaving aside the specific historical populations who have been defined as dangerous, his model suggests that when the use of anything is restricted, we should look for changes in the underlying structures of whole societies and cultures.

Changes in Drinking Patterns

We cannot leave our discussion of Prohibition without asking whether legislation changes behavior. More specifically, did this legislation reduce the consumption of alcohol? During Prohibition one does note that rates for pathologies linked to alcohol (cirrhosis of the liver,for example) declined, and there was a decrease in deaths attributed to drunk driving. Another effect was the disappearance of the saloon as a place and "saloon" as a word. Abolitionists, as representatives of the middle class, viewed the saloon as a "dangerous" place which attracted "dangerous" people. With the repeal of Prohibition, drinking places reopened but did not identity themselves as "saloons." Except for its use in Western movies, the word is seldom used to identify public drinking places.[7] Did Prohibition curb or reduce drinking behavior after its repeal? To answer this question, the per capita consumption of pure alcohol from beer, wine, and liquor from 1860 to 1990 was reviewed. This is shown in table 10.4.

Table 10.4.
Per Capita Consumption of Pure Alcohol in the United States by Decade from 1860 to 1990

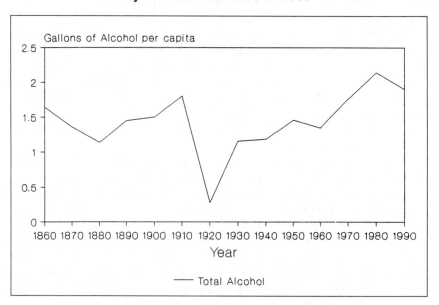

Source: Distilled Spirits Council of the U.S., Inc., September 20, 1991.

Except for the Prohibition years, the consumption figures indicate that the efforts of the abolitionists had no long-lasting effect on the overall consumption of alcohol in the United States. However, a more detailed examination of types of alcoholic beverages shows that while Americans have consistently consumed more beer by volume than either distilled spirits or wine, the percent of alcohol consumed from these three choices has changed. As shown in table 10.5, there was an overall decrease in distilled alcohol consumed from 1860 (where almost 90 percent of total consumption was spirits) to 1990 (where total consumption was less than 40 percent). The only exception to this trend was during Prohibition (1919–1933), where beer consumption declined. Thus, it appears that the enforcement of Prohibition was most effective in reducing the production of beer in barrels, and Americans reverted back to spirit consumption for these two decades.

Table 10.5.
**Comparison of Percent of Total Alcohol Consumption
Spirits, Beer, and Wine: 1860–1990**

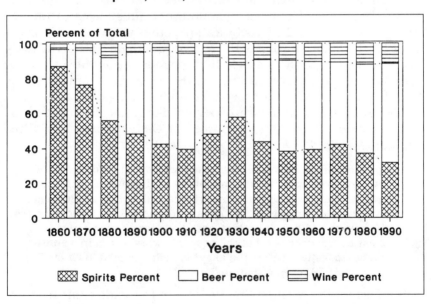

Source of raw data: Distilled Spirits Council of the U.S., Inc., September 20, 1991.

The increase in per capita consumption of alcohol was paralleled by a change in definition of the alcohol "problem." Instead of alcohol being the problem, the individual drinker was the problem. No longer was it an abusive substance but a substance that could *be* abused. This individual "problem" became the property of health professionals who focused on the deviant drinker and the "disease" of alcoholism.

Legislation and Religion

The Native American Church

In chapter 4, we discussed the conditions leading to the emergence of the Native American Church (NAC). Its spread to many American Indian tribes was accompanied by voiced opposition by some Native Americans, Euro-American church leaders, and public officials. The target of this opposition was the use of peyote. Since no legislation prohibiting the use of peyote (or most other drugs for that matter) existed at the turn of the century, attempts were made to include peyote under existing local temperance and prohibition legislation. This effort failed when the courts ruled that existing legislation controlling alcohol did not include other substances (Anderson 1980). The continued efforts by anti-peyotists were, in part, responsible for the incorporation of the Native American Church in 1918. As a church (public association) peyotists sought to escape harassment for peyote use under the First Amendment of the Constitution, which guaranteed freedom of religion.

The crusade to stop the use of peyote, like all moral crusades, did not depend on "facts." For example, the *Denver Post* editorialized on January 12, 1917 that:

> Societies which have interested themselves in the welfare of the Indians have discovered that **peyote is killing** dozens of Indians yearly. The "peyote" eater has dreams and visions as pleasing as those of a "**hophead**." To get a better hold of their **victims**, the peyote peddlers have lent a religious tone to the ceremony of eating the drug, so that the peyote is worshipped in a **semi-barbaric** festival before the **orgy**[8] is held. (Quoted in Omar C. Stewart 1956, emphasis mine)

Support for the prohibition of peyote in Colorado came from the WCTU, the Women's Club, the Ministerial Alliance of Denver, and the Association of Collegiate Alumnae (Anderson, 163). The tactic used by these public associations was to challenge the legitimacy of the Native American *Church* as a religion and therefore the protection of the First Amendment. They argued that the NAC was a pagan religion, filled with superstition, and that the state had an obligation to stop both pagan beliefs and practices "for the good of the Indian." The first victory for the anti-peyotists was in 1926 when a Montana judge upheld that state's statute prohibiting peyote. He ruled that the use of peyote by Indians for religious purposes does not justify its use by everyone. Although the state did protect the free exercise of religion,

> . . . it also provides that the liberty of conscience thereby secured shall not be construed to dispense with the oaths and affirmations, excuse acts of licentiousness or polygamous marriage, or otherwise, or justify practices inconsistent with the good order, peace or safety of the state. (Arthur 1947, 152)

Opposition to peyote was not restricted to Euro-Americans. Opponents included several tribal councils. In 1959, for example, New Mexico passed a bill permitting the use of peyote for bona fide religious use over strong opposition by the Navaho Tribal Council. Whatever the organizational base, the anti-peyote forces were quite successful in convincing states to pass anti-peyote legislation. By 1970, seventeen states ruled peyote to be an illicit substance (LaBarre 1975, 265), and only five exempted members of the NAC. Some of this legislation has been successfully challenged in court cases. A Navaho woman was arrested in 1960 for illegal possession of peyote and pled guilty in an Arizona court. On appeal, the conviction was overturned. Judge Yale McFate ruled that the state statute was unconstitutional as applied to the act of the defendant in the conduct and practice of her religious beliefs. A California case in 1962 involved the arrest of thirty Native Americans who were participating in a peyote ceremony. Under California law, peyote was classified as a narcotic. The defense argued that using peyote was protected under the provisions of both the United States and California Constitutions insuring religious freedom. The defendants were found guilty when the judge ruled that religious freedom did not extend to the use of substances classified as narcotics under California law. This decision was later appealed to the California Supreme Court, which ruled that the use of peyote is protected under the First Amendment *if* those using it can prove that their belief is honest and bona fide.

In all of these cases, the defense was based on freedom of religion (and the antecedent condition that the NAC was a religion), as well as the argument that the use of peyote did not threaten the public welfare. Support for this latter point came from anthropologists and others who had conducted research on Native Americans and the NAC. Much of this testimony addressed the question of whether the use of peyote was harmful to the individual and society. Arguments by proponents included the observation that peyote is not addictive and its effects are not always pleasant. On the behavioral side, there was evidence that peyote use did not take place outside the actual ceremony and that peyotists eschewed alcohol and other drugs. In other words, it is a substance that has a high degree of cultural specificity and is not likely to diffuse outside the membership of the church. On the basis of advocacy by anthropologists and others, the Comprehensive Drug Abuse Prevention and Control Act of 1970 specifically excluded the use of peyote by members of the Native American Church:

> The listing of peyote as a controlled substance in schedule I[9] does not apply to the *nondrug* use of peyote in bona fide religious ceremonies of the Native American Church, and members of the Native American Church so using peyote are exempt from registration. Any person who manufactures peyote for or distributes peyote to the Native American Church, however, is required to obtain registration annually and comply with all other requirements of the law. (7802)

It is customary for states to adopt federal drug regulations. While legislation might exempt members of the NAC from prosecution for the use of peyote as part of religious ritual, that exemption does not necessarily extend outside the boundaries of church. The most recent illustration of this occurred on April 17, 1990 when the United States Supreme Court ruled 6 to 3 that the State of Oregon could deny unemployment benefits to two NAC members fired from their jobs as drug counselors because they used peyote. Writing for the majority Justice Scalia stated:

> We have never held that an individual's religious beliefs excuse him from compliance with an otherwise valid law prohibiting the conduct that the state is free to regulate.

In short, while legislation may protect NAC members from prosecution for the ritual use of peyote (religion institution), this freedom does not apply to securing or maintaining employment (economic institution).

The Ethiopian Zion Coptic Church

The relative success of the NAC in "decriminalizing" peyote use for religious purposes has not extended to other churches and their use of drugs. For example, the Ethiopian Zion Coptic Church (EZCC), a Florida-based church affiliated with the Rastafarian movement, used the First Amendment as a defense against prosecution of five of its members charged with possession of marihuana with intent to distribute. The case was heard in the U.S. District Court of Southern Florida. The ex-attorney general, Ramsey Clark, was the defense attorney. He argued that:

> While there are formal prayer services three times a day, the process of religious inquiry or "reasoning," continues throughout the day, though always in connection with religious observation and never recreationally. (1979)

In a strategy similar to the peyote defenses, Clark collected testimony from health professionals on the harmlessness of marihuana compared to other drugs such as alcohol and tobacco. The court ruled against the defendants saying that the state had shown a compelling interest in prohibiting the use of cannabis by church members.

On the surface, the arguments of these two churches appear quite similar. However, there are some differences. Marihuana, unlike peyote, is defined as a "recreational" substance. It was removed as a Schedule I drug from the 1970 Act, and personal use has been decriminalized in eleven states. In addition, it is estimated that over 35 percent of adult Americans have at least tried it. Conversely, peyote has a very limited distribution and was often accompanied by unpleasant effects such as nausea. One might predict that if a Yanomamö Church were founded in the United States, its use of ebene would be protected by the First Amendment of the Constitution. In contrast, members of an American Batuque Church (chapter 7) could not defend public drunkenness as protected by religious freedom. The difference in acceptability of any substance is a function of cultural definitions. Both marihuana and alcohol, and their behavioral effects, have been ritualized into dominant American institutional arrangements. Accompanying each are definitions of appropriate places and times for their consumption. Peyote and ebene have not been institutionalized. Substantive law reflects these cultural definitions and becomes the basis for legislation and judicial decisions.

Smoking: The New Prohibition

For most readers, Prohibition and peyote are far removed from their experiential worlds, but the most recent prohibition movement in the United States is not. I would predict that most readers have strong sentiments concerning the anti-smoking movement. What does the social science approach tell us of our sentiments and of the movement itself? In a real sense, the analysis of this movement and of our own sentiments from the social science perspective tests our ability to employ the objectivity criteria of social science.

Sects and Cigarettes

In a previous section, the rapid diffusion of tobacco was discussed. Little has been said, however, about the morality of smoking. A review of the history of tobacco illustrates that not all were happy with practices associated with its consumption (Brooks 1952; Corti 1931; Heimann 1960). For example, in 1575 the Catholic Church forbid the smoking of tobacco by both Indians and missionary priests during church services. The high cost of tobacco and of its "addiction" were cause for concern by some authorities in Central Europe in the mid-1600s. Two Popes, Urban VIII and Innocent X, issued formal bulls against tobacco; several German states enacted legislation against it, and smoking was a capital offense in Constantinople. Russian czars and the Japanese government decreed dire penalties for the use of tobacco. In spite of these efforts, smoking, chewing, and snuffing of tobacco continued.

According to Edward Brecher (1972), the modern cigarette did not become popular in the United States until the end of the nineteenth century. In 1903, a new mild tobacco (alternatively called "bright," "flue cured," or "Virginia"), coupled with new paper and the ability to mass produce cigarettes at lower prices, brought "custom-mades" to the smoking public. In 1900, the over-eighteen per capita consumption of cigarettes was 54. By 1929, this had increased to 1,504. The all-time high was 4,345 in 1963. Thereafter it declined and by 1986 it had dropped to 3,275 (Goode 1989, 206). The milder tobacco attracted women and children, and early in the 1900s there arose numerous local and national anti-cigarette leagues. By 1921, fourteen states had passed anti-cigarette ordinances and others were considering similar legislation. By 1927, all this legislation was repealed.

Citing evidence on the linkage between smoking and lung cancer, neonatal weight, and heart disease, the Surgeon General of the United States issued a report in 1964 which urged people to stop the practice. But just as beheading, nose slitting, or prison sentences had failed to halt tobacco consumption in the past, the Surgeon General's report had a short-lived effect on cigarette sales. Within a few months, sales were up to their pre-report level.

Two years after the Surgeon General's report, there was a nationwide survey of cigarette smokers (National Clearinghouse, 1969). It found that 71 percent of these smokers agreed that tobacco was harmful to health; 60 percent hoped their children would never smoke; 55 percent agreed that smoking was a dirty habit, and 45 percent agreed that smoking cigarettes was morally wrong. These negative attitudes among smokers seem, on the surface, to contradict their behavior. It certainly undermines the assumption that what we think determines what we do, or vice versa. Is there a social science explanation for this inconsistency? I think there is, but only if we maintain a distinction between social and cultural phenomena. Smoking *behavior* is social; *attitudes* toward smoking are cultural. Thus, smoking behavior must be explained by social facts while attitudes must be explained by cultural facts. Without assuming any priority, we will examine both a cultural and a social explanation of smoking attitudes.

Purity and Pollution: Cultural Categories

In chapter 7 Mary Douglas' (1966) cultural explanation for definitions of pollution was introduced. She proposed that humans impose order on the world and that any practices or things which fall outside that order are defined as polluted. In addition she suggests several other alternatives for dealing with a practice or a thing which violates cognitive order. These include placing the practice in one or another cultural category, controlling or eliminating the offending item, avoiding the issue/item, attributing danger to it, or simply incorporating it into a ritual. If we examine cigarette smoking cross-culturally we note that it has been categorized in all these different ways. In cultures with a food/non-food distinction, tobacco has been placed in the food category (Carucci 1987). In American culture it is considered a non-food. Where secular/supernatural distinctions are made, smoking may be placed in the supernatural domain (Dole 1984, 1986; chapter 9) or in the secular category. In American culture one notes that smoking is often used to signal the end of one activity and the beginning of another. As part of a larger ritual of work, it signals a "break" in the work cycle; it is often an expressed desire at the end of a meal—and, of course, we should not omit the infamous after-sex cigarette.

If we treat tobacco and smoking as just another cultural trait, we note that it, like every other trait, will be placed into one cognitive category or another. Yet I would suggest that cigarette smoking may, in and of itself, present special dilemmas in its categorization. This ambiguity arises because the cigarette is a "thing" with corporeal reality, yet when smoked it is transformed into a non-thing. When this is coupled with a binary opposition in American culture, the ambiguity of cigarettes and smoking is further strained. In American culture, the body is divided into an inside/outside binary opposition. Things either belong outside or inside the body. Clothes belong on outside; food belongs inside. Thus, it is unclean to eat one's socks, hat, or shorts. Food that gets on clothing pollutes or dirties that clothing. If this is the underlying opposition, then where do cigarettes fit? The cigarette as a thing is outside the body; the smoke goes inside. Following Victor Turner's discussion (chapter 7), cigarette smoking is a liminal activity. It is neither one place nor another; it is betwixt and between. This same liminal position of cigarettes is reflected in the ecological distribution of cigarettes. Readers may have noted that cigarettes are often found at the *end* of aisles in the supermarket rather than *in* a named or lettered aisle. In restaurants, food and drink are taken into the body. Where do we find the cigarette machine? Usually in spaces that are themselves liminal—an entryway between inside and outside of the building, between the eating areas (where things outside are taken *into* the body) and the toilets (where things inside are eliminated *outside* the body). Given its ambiguous location in the inside/outside distinction, it is not surprising that both smokers and non-smokers express negative attitudes toward this practice.

While the cognitive approach may aid in understanding sentiments and their expression as attitudes, it does not appear as fruitful in predicting or explaining behavior. For this, we need to appeal to social variables.

Smoking as Social Behavior

Explanations for why people smoke have been offered at different interpretive levels. Suggestions for why an individual smokes are usually couched in psychological terms. Personality, self esteem, rebellion and other individual-level variables fall short as social science explanations because they cannot explain variations in rates of smoking over time or variations in this behavior by social categories (age, sex, occupation, and so forth). At another level, the explanation is that tobacco, or the nicotine that it contains, is "addicting." This argument rests on the same assumption concerning the consumption of alcohol or any other drug—namely, that the substance has properties that result in a physiological need to continue use. Consistent with our separation of facts, the addicting explanation should be couched in biological or pharmaco-logical facts. Yet in spite of whatever addictive properties cigarettes might have, we note that not all people who have ever tried smoking continue to do so. Even those with long-term smoking histories stop. If smoking is explained pharmacologically in terms of addiction, then we should expect smokers to be distributed equally between social divisions within a society. If, on the other hand, smoking follows existing social distinctions, then a social explanation of smoking and non-smoking is suggested. To test these competing explanations, I have reviewed recent findings from the National Opinion Research Council's (NORC) nation-wide survey of the United States (Davis and Smith 1991). That survey revealed that 32 percent of the American public still smoke cigarettes, a figure that has been declining since the mid-1960s. However, as social scientists, we want to know whether smokers and non-smokers are equally represented in social distinctions characteristic of American society. Since age and sex are universally used as social markers, I compared smokers with non-smokers on these variables. The results are reported in tables 10.6 and 10.7.

Table 10.6.
Comparison of Smokers and Non-Smokers by Age

Response to the Question:
"Do You Smoke?"

	Percent "Yes"	Percent "No"
18–30 years old	37	62
31–41 years old	36	65
42–60 years old	34	66
61 + years old	21	79

Statistically significant difference P < .00000

Table 10.7.
Comparison of Smokers and Non-Smokers by Sex

Response to the Question:
"Do You Smoke?"

	Percent "Yes"	Percent "No"
Male	35	65
Female	30	71

No statistically significant differences

Using the .05 level as a measure of significant differences, we note that self-reported smoking varies by age but not by sex. With age there is an inverse relationship to smoking. The older the respondent, the less likely he or she is to smoke. In contrast, differences in percent of male and female smokers is not statistically significant. Of course, had this been "real" research, I would have attempted to explain this difference in age by controlling for sex or other "suspected" variables. But for our purposes, these data are only being used to identify the smoking and non-smoking populations as a possible clue to broader social distinctions in American society.

One of the characteristics of state-level societies, such as the United States, is that they are hierarchically organized according to power, income, education, influence, or some combination of these attributes. Those that share similar status rankings in this hierarchy can be collectively identified as a **class**. One technique for measuring social class is through self-identification or subjective ranking. Respondents are simply asked to which class they belong. Another distinction in American society is ethnicity or race. As variables, class and race are linked to many other variables, such as marriage patterns, residence, education, consumer patterns, health and life expectancy. Given these correlates of class and race, we can assume that both of these attributes are a condensation of various "life ways" in American society. The relationship between smoking and class and race are reported in tables 10.8 and 10.9.

Table 10.8.
**Comparison of Smokers and Non-Smokers
by Subjective Class Identification**

*Response to the Question:
"Do You Smoke?"*

	Percent "Yes"	Percent "No"
Lower Class	44	56
Working Class	37	63
Middle Class	27	73
Upper Class	24	76

Statistically significant difference P < .00000

Table 10.9.
Comparison of Smokers and Non-Smokers by Race Identification

Response to the Question:
"Do You Smoke?"

	Percent "Yes"	Percent "No"
White	31	69
Black	37	63
Other	30	69

No statistically significant differences

These findings reveal that race distinctions are not marked by differences in smoking behavior. In contrast we found that differences between self-reported classes are related to smoking. Those who identified themselves as lower class were more likely to smoke than those who identified themselves as working, middle and upper class. These social differences cast doubt on any explanation of smoking that rests entirely on physiological variables. At the same time, if the explanation is social, then what social theory might be used to interpret these findings? One possible strategy is offered by Peter Berger (1986) in his analysis of the re-emergence of anti-smoking forces in the United States.

The Anti-smoking Movement

Berger addresses the anti-smoking movement from the sociology of knowledge. Although not a unified field of study (Walter 1967), Berger suggests that it seeks to explain the linkage between social conditions and plausible explanations. For example, what are the social conditions that account for the plausible explanation that witches "caused" illness in seventeenth-century New England but do not in 1995? The sociology-of-knowledge approach suggests that ideas and explanations, both scientific and non-scientific, can only make sense within social contexts.

Berger asserts that the linkage between knowledge and vested interest is fundamental to an understanding of plausibility. Vested interests are amounts of investment people have in some activity. These investments may be either material or ideal. Material interests are generally part of the economic domain in which participants have a pecuniary or career investment. Simply put, there is money or a job at stake. This is the social domain. In contrast, ideal interests are part of an ideological investment. These are rooted in values, beliefs, and worldviews. This is the cultural domain. Berger argues that the anti-smoking movement is part of both social and cultural domains. Further, each domain has a specific organizational manifestation. Social-material interests follow the organizational principles of bureaucracies. Cultural-ideological interests are organized according to the principles found in sects. Sects are single-purpose voluntaristic groupings that rely on the enthusiasm of their membership for survival. Groups such as GASP (Group Against Smoker's Pollution) and ASH (Action on Smoking and Health) have a focused interest, and their membership derives no income from their activities. In contrast, The American Cancer Society, The American Lung Association, the Respiratory Diseases Association, and the office of the Surgeon General have a permanent staff of professionals whose careers and sources of income, in part, come from anti-smoking activities.

Unlike sects, bureaucracies are hierarchical. Leadership is routinized in a ranked set of offices, membership in which is ideally based on experience and competency. Members move through these offices in a pattern which defines a career. In sects, the members donate their time and there is no well-defined leadership. In fact, a concerted effort is made to deny differences among the members. While the anti-smoking sects envision their goal as a crusade which requires aggressive action, including strict enforcement of legislation, bureaucracies place importance on regulation and negotiation. These differences are summarized in table 10.10.

In the presentation of social correlates in table 10.8, we noted that non-smokers come largely from the middle and upper classes. That class differences are marked by differential consumption of tobacco is not new. Sherwin Feinhandler (1986) observed that in seventeenth century England:

> . . . the pleasurable use of tobacco was readily acknowledged in addition to its medical value. Old and young, men and women, and even children smoked—schoolboys being urged to do so as purification of their lungs against disease. . . . But, with restoration of the monarchy in 1660, English culture changed, and smoking practices reflected the changes with powerful symbolism.
>
> The exiled Charles II returned from France to establish a court that had to differentiate itself from a rising merchant class made

Table 10.10.
Organizational Characteristics of Anti-Smoking Interests

Characteristics	Sects	Bureaucracies
Membership	Voluntary	Paid
Leadership	None	Formal
Goals	Focused	Diffuse
Means for Achieving Goals	Abolition	Regulation
Structure	"Democratic"	Hierarchical
View of Tobacco Industry	Evil	Negotiable

newly rich by commerce and a new country gentry who had acquired land under Cornwall. The courtiers distinguished themselves by wearing fancy French dress of brocade and lace, bringing with them also the dainty and ostentatious habit of snuffing: tobacco use in a new and smokeless form. By contrast, the new gentry's pipes were crude and polluting. Eventually the social classes separated and ordered themselves by their tobacco habits and an elaborate social/moral code. Courtiers snuffed in a rarefied atmosphere: ladies kept their parlors pure while their men retired to smoking rooms in special smoking jackets and lavishly embroidered caps. The lower classes and rebellious bohemian youth continued to smoke in the streets and coffee houses. Thus the Victorians established order in their lives. (170–171)

Berger argues that while class in a broad sense distinguishes the membership of the anti-smoking sects, a more accurate name for the specific ranks from which anti-smoking forces are recruited is the "new class" or "knowledge class." Unlike the "bourgeoisie" or old middle class who occupied statuses in the business or industrial sector of the American economy, the new class is composed of those employed in the production and distribution of symbolic knowledge. This would include occupations in "education, the media, the therapeutic and counseling agencies, and the institutions engaged in planning and administering the "quality of life" (Berger, 233).

When viewing the recent changes in attitudes toward smoking in the United States, we must ask the question, "Why have some segments of American society suddenly become interested in other people's health?" Anti-smoking activists and advocates have taken the position that smoking not only directly endangers the health of others but, through passive smoke, endangers their health as well. If the NORC data accurately represent the smoking population in the United States, the efforts of anti-smoking sects are being directed at members of the lower classes. Is smoking therefore a concern for pollution of one class by another? As a social scientist, I would argue that the latter hypothesis cannot be dismissed. However, this is not likely to be acceptable to anti-smoking advocates. The arguments they present are couched in terms of scientific enlightenment, the only acceptable position for a secular sect. The "authority" for their advocacy comes from medical research and findings. Just what do these findings indicate?

Smart versus Proper Ideologies

Behaviors that are socially suspect may become medically suspect. The anti-smoking movement is supported by statements of "facts" that bear a striking similarity to religious sects that appeal to supernatural "truths." The "evil" that they propose to eradicate is based on assumptions about health and cleanliness. Smoking is viewed as the most preventable "cause of death"; the tobacco industry is portrayed as "merchants of death." To support their claims, they appeal to "scientific" evidence which they insist demonstrates an unequivocal link between smoking and unhealthiness.

A systematic review of the medical evidence would not demonstrate a "causal" link, at least not as the term "cause" is used in science. At best we could describe the collective findings of this research, if we do not impose a moral interpretation, as "not proven" (Eysenck 1986). Cancer is not one disease but has many manifestations. No agreed-upon cause of cancer at the molecular level has been demonstrated, and the correlations between smoking and cancer vary widely.

For years in the United States, "evidence" has been presented about the health dangers of smoking cigarettes. The language used to list the ills is scientific, but is that language justified by scientific methods? If one looks closely at the medical evidence, one is surprised by the rather casual use of terms such as "cause," as well as a disregard for methodological attempts to use adequate control variables to disprove relationships. It is conventional in science to assign the term "cause" when the causal agent is both a necessary and a sufficient condition to bring about the appearance of the effect (chapter 2). In contrast to this definition of cause, the 1982 U.S. Surgeon General's report contains the following curious statement, "The causal significance of an association is a *matter of judgement* that goes beyond any statement of statistical probability" (17, emphasis mine). Using this definition as a guideline, the researcher who found an association between country-and-western music in bars and fighting could conclude that country-and-western music "causes" aggressive behavior. A "matter of judgement" may be a reflection of a vested interest, but it is not a scientific proof. Thus *links* between certain kinds of cancer and smoking—the discovery of which may have been prompted by the desire to change socially unacceptable behavior rather than by a dispassionate investigation of a topic—have been translated into *causes*. Medical "evidence" escapes—or obfuscates—charges of special interests. Knowledge about how social science functions allows us to look beneath surface appearances to determine the reliability of sources.

Cross-national data on cigarettes smoked per day and various cancers show wide differences, a finding that should not occur if smoking alone is the cause of cancer. If schoolboys were encouraged to smoke in Elizabethan England to purify their lungs, then the medical data would conclude that one should smoke to avoid colorectal cancer and Parkinson's disease because both of these conditions are negatively related to smoking (Eysenck, 37). The appeal by the anti-smoking forces to medical "truth" cannot be justified on the data itself. However, this is not an issue of "fact." Rather, our interest is in a social science explanation of the anti-smoking movement.

Sects need not rely on empirical findings. The history of all anti-drug movements in the United States rested on "causal" links between opium, marihuana, cocaine, alcohol and negative organic, mental, or social effects. Each of these movements cited scientific "proof" for passage of legislation for the public welfare. The anti-smoking sects have also adopted another characteristic of these movements, namely, the idea of contagion. Contagion is the assumption that even those not taking the drug will "catch" its ill effects. For the anti-smoking forces, the innocent bystanders include co-workers, spouses, children, and the unborn. Passive smoking threatens the non-smoker. Yet Domingo Aviado's (1986) review of the research related to the health consequences of passive smoking concluded there is no scientific evidence to substantiate this claim. The data on passive smoke, like those on cancer, are "not proven."

Regardless of any "real" health claims related to passive smoke, the social scientist's interest would be piqued by the similarity of the anti-smoking claim to contagion and parallel claims of other anti-drug movements. This belief appears to be a necessary ideology for any sect. Danger and pollution must be pervasive, and it must be capable of transmission. No sect, whether religious or secular, can exist very long without an enemy of grand proportions.

Anti-smoking and the Health Movement

In chapter 5, changes in the age and occupational characteristics of the United States were cited as contributing to the proliferation of numerous religious and secular movements during the 1960s. Preceding this tumultuous period were changes in the occupational structure of the United States. Farm and blue-collar occupations continued their decline, and there was a dramatic increase in white-collar and service workers. By the mid-1960s, a younger and more formally educated population was emerging from the universities to take up those occupations which provided the foundation for the new middle class—the knowledge class. Associated with the rise of this new class was a growing ideology which focused on "quality of life"—the health movement. According to Berger:

> . . . health becomes an ultimate, virtually sacral, goal. . . . Western cultures, with America probably in the lead, are replete with health movements which all suggest that, if only one does this and avoids that, one will attain a joyful, wholesome, and (above all) long life. The enormously powerful place attained by the medical establishment is a logical consequence of this cultural theme: doctors are the priesthood of this cult, hospitals are its sanctuaries, and government is urgently expected to support and universalize this new "established religion." (234–235)

Beginning in the 1960s, there was a proliferation of "health" clubs and spas, exercise groups, jogging, as well as "health" and natural food stores.

In her analysis of the health food movement, Jill Dubisch (1981) also found the religious metaphor helpful. Working from the definition offered by Clifford Geertz (1965, 4) that religion is:

> 1) a system of symbols which acts to 2) establish powerful, pervasive, and long-lasting moods and motivations in men by 3) formulating conceptions of a general order of existence and 4) clothing these conceptions with such an aura of factuality that 5) the moods and motivations seem uniquely realistic.

Dubisch reviewed the history of the health food movement in the United States and found that, from its inception, the movement formed alliances with other broader social concerns such as feminism, temperance, and the class struggle. The central focus, however, was on food and the belief that eating "pure" food was a moral virtue. The villain of the early health food movement was medicine, which emphasized curing rather than prevention of disease. The alternative they proposed was wellness and prevention of disease. The resurgence of the health food movement in the late 1960s retained its suspicion of the curative approach in medicine and added a new villain—the food industry. Specific targets were food coloring, preservatives, and sugar. Her analysis of health food publications uncovered several themes, including an emphasis on conversion. Testimonials abound about having suffered from one ailment or another and then suddenly becoming well. The conversion experience was maintained by the continued practice of eating only "pure" foods.

The religion metaphor becomes more appealing when we note a striking parallel in practices of world "religions." Mary Douglas' (1966) discussion of Hebraic food laws and meatless Fridays for the Bog Irish remind us that food is often used to distinguish the chosen from the not-chosen. Foods defined as pure are eaten; those defined as impure are not only avoided but are assumed to be a causal agent for a wide variety of social "problems." Among advocates of the health food movement, sugar was (is) believed to cause a wide range of untoward behaviors, such as wife-beating and delinquency. Salvation, not only of the body but of the psyche and society, could be achieved through eating pure foods. Whether in religions, cults or sects, right practices and right avoidances are rewarded by salvation. The difference between the belief systems we call "religion" and those of the health food movement is that (for health food proponents) salvation will come in this lifetime; also, the health food movement insists that its beliefs can be "factually" proven.

The specific sects of the health movement that emerged in the 1960s were bound together by a view of the world that eschewed "big" anything. Big business and big government were both evils. In their insistence that nature was good and society was bad, each stressed hard work and endurance of pain to achieve the "good" life. Those attracted to this movement—the younger, well-educated "knowledge" class—eschewed the formal church idea of the supernatural but adopted the organizational features of the sect. The secular, but nonetheless sectlike, organizations of the health movement found adversaries or villains among their middle-class colleagues in industry who polluted the big environment and among countless other small polluters in the workplace, the home, and in public places. If visual symbols mark social distinctions, then the new middle class had that symbol in smoking.

One of the characteristics of any sect is a firm conviction that they have discovered the true and only way to live a proper or moral life. Their goal is to convince others that they are right. Conversion is a high priority activity of sects. If efforts to suppress smoking could not be legislated, then the practice could at least be made socially unacceptable. Smokers—like lepers—are to be placed in the back of the bus and plane, outside the house and workplace, or in special facilities. In general, they should be excluded from all public activities. The history of anti-smoking legislation reflects these exclusionary views. In 1966, the Federal Cigarette Labeling and Advertising Act required warning labels on cigarette packs. A year later, the Federal Communication Commission ruled that television and radio must carry anti-smoking messages, and in 1970 all radio and television advertisement for cigarettes were banned. In 1973, the first legislation prohibiting smoking in some public places was passed in Arizona. By 1991, all the states had passed similar legislation.

The ideology of the anti-smoking sects sets forth the utopian goal of making the world "smoke-free." But resting that goal on the assumption that a smoke-free world will result in an end to cancer, heart disease, or any other disease is simply not supported by the medical or any other evidence—quite the opposite. If "healthy" practices result in longer life expectancy, then we would predict that heart disease and cancer deaths will also increase, since both of these causes of death are related to age.

The question of class differences in morbidity and mortality are well established. Where class systems exist (state-level societies), those in the lower classes have higher illness and death rates than those in the upper classes (Syme and Berkman 1976). In the United States, the differences in health between classes has not changed since 1900 in spite of the fact that cigarette consumption was one-fiftieth of the present per capita rate. If current differences in social class continue, we would predict that even if the lower classes stop smoking altogether, their higher rate of death—*from all causes*—will continue. In other words, if you live long enough in a culture which assigns "cause" to death, you will die from either cancer or heart disease!

The "Anti" Movements

"The turn to drugs is more than simple desire for intoxication; the call for abstinence expresses more than concern about the consequences of their use," This statement by David Buchanan (1992) nicely summarizes the social science approach for explaining the emergence of definitions of drugs as "social problems." It should be clear from this discussion that the "discovery" of drugs as problematic is part of a larger political process, an understanding of which is necessary before we can possibly claim any neutral scientific rigor. Yet much of the social science literature from the "problems" approach has been concerned with identifying the social characteristics of people who use drugs and the connection between drug use and other "problematic" behaviors rather than analyzing the characteristics of organizations whose business it is to condemn a practice. Among the most visible adopters of this emic view of "problems" are those who identify themselves as criminologists.

Legislation and Crime

At an elementary level, the passage of formal legislation with formal sanctions defines "crime" and those who violate the formal expectations as "criminals." Leaving aside the issue of whether those who use illicit drugs are "criminals," one question that has attracted large amounts of research funding and publication pages has been the linkage between the use of drugs and criminal behavior. The linkage between drug use and crime highlights an analytical problem in social science, namely, determining whether drugs are the independent or the dependent variable. Do drugs lead to criminal behavior, or is it criminal behavior that precedes the use of drugs? For example, Siamak Movahedi (1978) noted that opium smoking was a traditional practice among the Iranian working class. It was believed to combat fatigue and the discomfort of cold weather. In contrast, smoking for pleasure was less than a century old and was an indulgence of the leisure class and intellectuals. Neither opium nor opium smokers were thought to be a "problem" until the Drug Prohibition Act of 1955, the passing of which was engineered by a few Western-trained Iranian physicians. The consequence of this legislation was the creation of an illicit distribution market supported by corrupt public officials. For users who became "criminals" as a result of this legislation, prosecution resulted in social, psychological, and economic disasters for both the addict and his family (54). The magnitude of the created "problem" helped repeal the Act in 1969. Under new legislation, users could purchase opium if prescribed by a licensed physician.

One of the unanticipated outcomes of the Harrison Act was prosecution of physicians who prescribed opiates for addicts. Musto reports that the Bureau of Internal Revenue did not view maintenance of addiction as medical "treatment" and threatened to arrest physicians if records indicated that they engaged in this practice. Although the courts ruled that physicians could prescribe opiates for their patients, most physicians stopped, fearing that legal action might hurt their practices. In spite of this threat, some physicians continued to "treat" addicts with morphine. The patients of these physicians were part of a larger sample of addicts studied by John O'Donnell (1969). Interested in the crime-addiction relationship, he compared the arrest records of addicts who were supplied with morphine by their personal physicians with addicts who obtained their opiates illegally. He found that only 9 percent of the legal opiate patients had been convicted of any crime. In contrast, 70 percent of the illegal opiate supply sample had been found guilty of some crime, and the majority were multiple offenders. This study certainly questions the drugs ⟶ crime model and suggests that some other variable or variables influence behaviors defined as illegal.

Rodney Stark (1987) quotes a 1934 anecdotal account of a Seattle neighborhood with high delinquency and crime rates. The author of this account attributed this high rate of delinquency to Sicilian Italians, who he described as illiterate, unskilled wine drinkers. Stark noted that this same neighborhood in the 1980s had a high crime rate, yct virtually no Italians lived there. The question he posed is one that we have addressed several times throughout this book. Are the behaviors of people due to some inherent character-istic of the people themselves or of the social settings (in this case, the neighborhood) within which they find themselves? The social science answer is that the "people," no matter how they are classified, are the product of the settings within which they live. This approach to understanding behavior is called **human ecology**.

The beginnings of ecology and the ecological approach are rooted in nineteenth-century naturalism. Naturalists used this approach to map out the interdependencies of life forms in physical environ-ments. Although many nineteenth-century social observers suggested that environmental factors explain behavior, the formalization of a human ecology "school" in sociology is attributed to Robert Park and Ernest Burgess (1925) at the University of Chicago. Like their natural science counterparts, they mapped "natural" areas in cities like Chicago. These mappings included physical characteristics—buildings, quality of housing, transportation, density of population—and behavioral characteristics—marriage patterns, deviance, occupations—of the inhabitants. In keeping with the assumption that cities are "unnatural" places, the focus of much of the Chicago School was on the distribution of "disorganization" as measured by such indices as poverty, crime, divorce, illegitimacy, and so forth. When the distribution of physical characteristics overlapped with behavioral characteristics, the assumption was that the former determined the latter.

According to Jack Roach (1967), the dominance of the ecological approach in sociology gave way to a "voluntaristic" and "mentalistic" approach to human behavior. This perspective, a combination of the theorizing of Talcott Parsons (1949, 1951) and the symbolic interactionist tradition of George Herbert Mead (1934), held that human behavior was a result of how humans perceived and interpreted the environment and each other. Thus, what went on in people's heads determined what they did. Roach insists that this thinly disguised acceptance of the Western assumption of "free will" cannot explain why the behaviors and beliefs of people under conditions of poverty (ecological conditions), regardless of time or place, are strikingly similar (chapter 8).

The use of the ecological model by contemporary sociologists places them in the unenviable position of having to defend their minority position against the more dominant "mentalists." For example, Stark's (1987) "ecological" model of crime contains thirty propositions deduced from five physical conditions of neighborhoods in which crime rates are high. Yet in spite of his attempt to employ an ecological approach, we note that several of his propositions accept the voluntaristic perspective as axiomatic. He suggests that some people are more or less "predisposed to deviance" (895); that "Living in stigmatized neighborhoods (those with poor, dilapidated, and overcrowded housing) causes a reduction in an individual's stake in conformity" (901); that "More successful and conventional people will resist moving into a stigmatized neighborhood" (901); and that "Stigmatized neighborhoods will tend to be overpopulated by the most demoralized kinds of people" (902). In spite of the disclaimer that crime and deviance are the result of where people live, he never abandons the "kinds of people" argument and the dogma of human voluntarism. Stark's model serves to illustrate the difficulties associated with avoiding an individualistic free-will view of social life, even by those who claim that their interpretations are value-free.

Duane McBride and Clyde McCoy's (1981) review of human ecology indicates that the relationship between crime and drug use has been of major interest to criminologists. In spite of research findings that consistently fail to support a causal connection between these two variables, both policy makers and clinicians have accepted a causal link as "fact." It was this assumed linkage that justified the establishment and massive funding of The National Institute on Drug Abuse (NIDA), a federal agency charged with carrying out research and informing policy on drug "abuse."[10]

When human ecologists mapped the distribution of drug users and those who committed property crimes they made two observations. First, the distribution of each was not even—that is, some areas had high concentrations while other areas were very low. Second, both drug use and property crime overlapped with the spatial distribution of other physical and social characteristics such as poor housing, low income, and "disrupted" families. This finding suggests at least two interpretations. One is that drug use and property crime are causally connected; another is that they are independent and are both outcomes of physical and social characteristics.[11]

McBride and McCoy question much recent research that claims to be ecological. Most of this research has tended to be statistical analysis of various rates of different behaviors. For example, if one measured the rate of heroin addicts in treatment in a city and compared these rates with corresponding crime rates over the same period, it is assumed that an ecological analysis has been done. They insist that this is not human ecology, certainly not the ecological approach proposed by Park and his students at the University of Chicago. They are clear when they state:

> Ecological analysis is not the correlation of a few aggregate variables for entire SMSA's (Standard Metropolitan Statistical Areas), but rather, at the very least, is the examination of a complex set of environmental variables, particularly economic and demographic variables, in relation to a specific behavior in a **limited, spatially defined neighborhood**. (286, emphasis mine)

They go on to state:

> The ecological perspective does not suggest that one can apply to the individuals the characteristics of neighborhood; but rather, that those total neighborhood characteristics are

important for permitting certain behaviors such as particular types of drug use and crime, while tending to inhibit the occurrence of other behaviors. (286)

Rather than using the "modern" statistical ecological approach, McBride and McCoy carried out a **pilot study**[12] in the tradition of human ecology. They specifically focused on mapping drug use and property crime by neighborhoods in Dade County, Florida. Data on property crime came from a probability sample of all major misdemeanors and felon arrests from April 1974 through March 1975. Two sources provided data on drug use—drug-related emergency room appearances at the county hospital and drug treatment program admissions. These data revealed three separate populations—non-drug using criminals, non-criminal drug users, and drug-using criminals. The addresses of these three populations were mapped according to census tracks and specific blocks within census tracks as predetermined by the U.S. Census.

In their samples of drug users and criminal arrestees they noted that 90 percent were between the ages of fifteen and forty-five. To control for the possible influence of age they computed a drug user and property crime *rate* based on the total number of people in a tract between those ages. Thus, if they identified 50 drug users in a tract where 100 people were between the ages of fifteen and forty-five, the drug using rate would be .50. When they correlated the different rates for the three populations with census tracts and the characteristics of census tracts, they found that all three were not only from the same types of areas but also from the same neighborhoods within those areas.

Going beyond the specific findings of this study, McBride and McCoy suggest that a direct link between drug using and criminal activity is spurious. They argue that both of these behaviors are the effect of similar ecologies. Thus, any suggestion that stopping drug use will reduce crime is incorrect, and treatment programs based on this claim are bound to fail.

Conclusion

Political systems, in all their varied organizational manifestations, function to facilitate alliances among different publics. One manifestation of this function in urban societies is the passage of legislation. From the social science perspective, the passage of legislation signals the end product of attempts to form alliances between social units when those alliances are not otherwise possible. In a very real sense, legislation is one type of social control. Unlike control that is directed at deviant individuals, legislative control focuses on larger collectivities. Any attempt to understand political systems from a social science perspective must therefore include an analysis of relationships among publics.

In this chapter we have noted that political decision making can be understood from both an emic and etic perspective. Emically, political systems justify their actions based on threat or danger to public order. Whether or not that threat is "real" is not important. Rather, the ability to impose "order" serves to legitimate the function of political systems everywhere. That function is to facilitate alliances between autonomous groupings. Viewed etically, it is not opium and cigarette smoking, alcohol consumption, or heroin injection that is the issue. Each of these cultural practices have alliance and descent functions within social groupings and can be analyzed as such. Rather, analysis of political systems must take into account the broader relationships that make society and culture possible.

With this chapter we close our review of the social science literature on drugs. Our next assignment is to incorporate the previous, focused discussions into a comprehensive social science model. We must finally address the question of the relationship between culture, society, and drugs.

Endnotes

[1] The formula used to determine alliances from a known number of publics is: $[N \times (N-1)]/2$, where N is the number of publics.

[2] These medicines made a variety of claims concerning their curative effects. Widely available in retail outlets, through mail order, and from traveling salesmen, their labels contained no specific information about their contents.

[3] A modern equivalent is the use of cancer as a metaphor to describe a negative social condition.

[4] This does not deny the observation that those who control games of "chance" are economically motivated. For one to be economically successful, however, there must be an audience willing to engage in this activity. The "numbers," lotteries, and games such as *Monopoly* all flourish in periods of economic instability or in populations who face economic uncertainty.

[5] It is this last principle that is the basis of morality. What is emically expressed as right or wrong, correct or incorrect, is a reflection of the autonomy of each commodity in marking the boundaries between institutions. Thus, prostitution is immoral because sex and money belong to two distinct institutions.

[6] Non-western governments, particularly Muslim nations, have passed legislation that carries severe penalties for consumption of alcohol by citizens and visitors alike.

[7] For example, in October 1991 the Alcohol Beverage Board of Virginia rescinded its prohibition of the word "saloon" as a name that could be used to identify a place where alcohol is sold.

[8] The reference to preserving the "virtue" of women has been a constant theme in the anti-drug movement. Attacks on opium and heroin often made reference to either sexually immoral behavior or prostitution as a consequence of drug use. The reference to orgies is another theme. Ethnic minorities are often presumed to be "oversexed" and in constant search for Euro-American females who can be exploited through drugs.

[9] A schedule I drug is defined as any substance that has a high potential for abuse, has no currently acceptable medical use in the United States, and lacks accepted safety standards for use under medical supervision. Included in this category are bufotenine, marihuana, mescaline, peyote, psilocybin, and twelve other substances or chemical compounds.

[10] Officially, NIDA publications do not use the term "drug use" to describe consumption of substances that are legislatively prohibited. It is assumed that the use of these substances always constitutes "abuse."

[11] A third somewhat implausible explanation is that property crime and drug use determine the physical and social characteristics of a neighborhood.

[12] A pilot study is a preliminary analysis of data, usually for the purpose of proposing a larger study.

chapter 11

Drug Use
The Social Science Approach

Descriptive accounts, whether ethnographic or statistical, may provide much insight, but little understanding. The real quest is for right questions, not right answers. Theory can lead to right questions, and through theory we will learn that right questions are both few in number and universally applicable.

—Morris Freilich (1975)

The subtitle to this book is: *The Social Science Approach to Drug Use.* The preceding chapters reviewed and critiqued various perspectives on drug use. Every effort was made to include all the major theoretical orientations used in social science. How, then, can one refer to *the* social science approach? Is there a unifying principle or a limited number of principles that identify a social science approach? If so, what are these principles, and how have they manifested themselves in this review? In this chapter, I address these questions in light of previous discussions. In doing so, I will exercise the "writer's prerogative" to explore the broader implications of what has been written about drug use. But why bother?

It would be much simpler to list several common observations and conclusions revealed through this literature search than to venture onto the uncharted waters of speculation about a grand theory or model for social science. The reason is simple. I entered into this project as a naive observer, without prejudice, predisposition, or career investments in the area of drug research. Using the simple framework proposed in chapter 1, the subsequent chapters focused on specific subjects and topics. In that review, questions were posed and answers suggested that I did not anticipate. There are still some unresolved issues. Perhaps I am still naive, but in the following few pages I will elaborate on those issues and on how they suggested to me an emergent dynamic framework that defines the parameters of the social science approach to drug use.

Normally, one expects theoretical considerations to appear in the early part of a study. The theory serves both as a guide for research and as a template against which findings are compared. In contrast to this ideal, this book was written in real time. That is, chapter 1 was written before chapter 2 and so on until finally this last chapter was written. In reviewing each topic, new questions and issues were revealed. As these accumulated, I began to appreciate the magnitude of the social science venture and the need to construct a comprehensive framework that reflected both what social science does and what it can do. It is now time to take that bold leap which will serve both as a summary of the social science approach to drug use and as a guide for future research.

The Original Model and Sampling Procedures

The model presented in chapter 1 outlined a basic model for social science. The assumption behind that model was that social scientists, knowingly or unknowingly, view and analyze the human condition in a binary fashion. Either they focus on cultural or social phenomena, or they attempt to ascertain the correspondence or priority between the two. Put another way, they either measure behaviors as determinants of worldviews or vice versa. When in doubt about this distinction, some social scientists resort to using the nonspecific concept, **sociocultural**. Its use signals either an overlap of or a disregard for the difference between social and cultural phenomena. One universal empirical observation is clear: one never finds total agreement between measures of worldviews and actual behavior. In part this finding reflects the scientific portion of social science. Without the guidelines of methodology outlined in chapter 2, this incongruence would not be uncovered and social science would be little more than an oratory art, a vast wasteland of debate with no resolution.

In the selection of materials included in this review of drug use, I used the standards of social science research—objectivity, falsifiability, relativity, and so forth— outlined in chapter 2, as well as the social science model presented in chapter 1. These were then ordered into independent chapters which represented major issues—diffusion, change, control, function—or subject areas—religious, economic, and political systems. Since much of the included research defined the concepts of the model differently, it was necessary to translate them into the basic dichotomous distinction between social and cultural phenomena. If my reading of this reformulation is accurate, this task was accomplished without damage to their central arguments.

Within each chapter, specific studies provided a comparative, non-time bound, global perspective on a topic or issue. While any one study might not have contributed solely to this perspective, taken together they provided a mosaic that overcame individual specificity. The process of selection left out more than it included. Several criteria were employed to reject potential materials. One was replication of effort. For example, there were many hundreds of studies of drug use among American students in the 1960s. All of the different samples had the same general conclusion: drug users shared social characteristics (other than drug use) that distinguished them from non-users. Because of this conclusion it was not necessary to include or reference all of these studies. Other studies did not address any theoretical concerns, or the theories they proposed were based on psychopathological-biological models. Another category of rejects were studies that focused on "helping" people who "abused" drugs. Although these studies provided insights into pejorative definitions of drug use and users, they contributed little to our understanding of how drugs fit into a social science framework. The final category of rejects were those studies that employed faulty or misleading samples, inadequate analysis, or premature policy concerns. Frequently all three of these weaknesses were found in the same research.

I am sure that many excellent studies were omitted. In my continuing review of the literature I am still impressed with how much good social science there is. The decision to stop looking is a pragmatic one. At some point it is necessary to draw a line which signals completion; otherwise the search would continue forever.

The Social Science Approach: Units of Analysis

The introductory quote by Morris Freilich (1975) is a comment on the history of science itself. Its beginnings are rooted in a multiplicity of questions which have been whittled down to a manageable few that address central issues and from which specific questions may be asked. As each chapter was written, it became clear that much of the research was directed at answering one or two questions. As Richard Kaplan and Robert Manners (1972) remind us, social science theories are explanations of "how systems work or how systems came to be what they are." In reviewing each of the chapter topics it became clear that drugs and drug use were meaningless outside of this systems framework. For example, when a drug is part of an economic system its meaning is quite different from when it is part of a religious system. It is, in fact, these differences that help us determine the boundaries between systems. Viewed this way, we can conclude that drugs are not a special category of things—simply another category of things. In this sense, there cannot be a general theory of drugs, only a theory or theories directed at understanding how systems work and how they came to be what they are.

The idea that systems are the units of study and analysis in social science was presented in the opening chapter of this book. It was assumed that systems are "normal," self-regulating, and not subject to control by humans. The most inclusive systems are social and cultural systems. Cultural systems are shared references that serve as a guide for "thinking" about the world and also provide a template for conduct. Social systems include both normative behaviors that reflect cultural expectations *and* behaviors that represent elastic adaptive strategies to changing and shifting environments. For each of these systems there are subsystems. Thus, systems of statuses (the least inclusive units within the cultural domain) unified by a common theme identify the boundaries of institutions. Systems of roles (the smallest units of behavior) unified by a common theme form associations. For each of these subsystems, the linkages among units (status systems, role systems, institutional systems, and associational systems) were described as processes. These processes included cooperation, competition, and conflict. Thus, the complete elementary model used six concepts and the three connecting processes within and among them at each level (status-role, institution-association, culture-society). Using this basic dichotomy, as well the connecting processes, we were able to understand "deviant" behaviors of heroin users (chapter 5), inconsistencies between smokers' beliefs and behaviors (chapter 10), kava use as a confirmation of hierarchical structures on Tonga (chapter 6), and egalitarian patterns among hippies (chapter 5).

This exercise in the ability of a systems approach to resolve what, on the surface, appeared to be contradictions between cultural and social systems convinced me that systems operate according to general principles whether drugs were present or not. Drugs do not determine systems. Rather, drugs serve as markers or indicators of how systems work or how they come to be what they are. We would expect, for example, that the bride price system and labor exchange in Ban Lum (chapter 8) would operate according to the same rules with or without opium and that altered states of consciousness found in some religious systems could be achieved with or without the availability of those substances classified as hallucinogens. We would predict that those timetables and schedules that regulate everyday life in America would exist without alcohol or tobacco (chapter 7); that the conflict between Chinese and American labor would have been just as intense without opium (chapter 10); and that age and gender distinctions on Tanna would exist without kava (chapter 6).

Using the systems approach, it is possible to offer several generalizations about drug use. These are:

1. Drugs and drug use are one component of larger systems. Any explanation of drug use must consider the larger system of which it is a part.

2. Drugs and drug use do not constitute a separate system. There is no drug culture or drug society. Consistent with this observation, there are no drug associations or institutions, even though there are associations within which drugs are used and institutions which have rituals and beliefs about drugs.

3. Personality and character do not determine systems. Therefore, differential drug use is not dependent on these characteristics. The determination of who uses drugs, and when and where drugs are used, can only be understood relative to system needs.

4. Systems have extended lifetimes. In contrast, the biophysical effects of drugs, attributed or real, are temporary.

5. Systems regulate time through schedules and calendars. Because the biophysical effects of drugs are of short duration, drugs may serve as temporary markers in those schedules and calendars.

6. Systems are governed by rules and regulations directed at both self-maintenance (descent) and alliances with other systems. Drug use or drug prohibition can identify these two functions.

Throughout this book specific studies of drug use have been presented within a systems framework. In one way or another the two aspects of descent and alliance have been addressed. However, if the goal of science is to reduce the questions down to the smallest number, I think we can go one step further and pose a question which encompasses both of these, a question that was not revealed until writing chapter 10 on political systems. That question is: "How do systems survive?" That is, what factor or factors contribute to the overall survival of those systems which make human life possible? Thus, to speak of *the* social science approach one must eventually address the issue of survival and its companion process, adaptation.

How do Systems Survive?
The Ultimate Social Science Question

As previously discussed, humans are rather frail biological beings. Their success, insofar as being a dominant land species, rests on the ability to organize cooperative activities directed at their environments. Environment, as used here, refers to physical, social, and cultural worlds. The physical world includes factors such as climate, soil conditions, availability of energy sources, and the technological means to exploit that world. Social environments refer to population characteristics such as size, density, age distribution, and so forth, as well as existing behavioral practices. Cultural environments cover values, beliefs, rules regulating labor, and worldviews. The process which describes the strategies of relating to those worlds is adaptation.

Adaptation takes two major forms—social and cultural. Social-behavioral adaptations are the day-to-day adjustments to specific localized environmental demands. We noted this type of adaptation in chapter 8, where the sale of heroin and other drugs were described as one of several adaptive strategies for survival among the urban poor. Such adaptations may be temporary and only practiced by a few, or they may become widespread normative practices. This will depend on the continuation of the environmental conditions which led to these adaptations and the efficacy of the behavioral strategies. When adaptive strategies become widespread and standardized, they are incorporated into existing cultural practices that continue through socialization and enculturation. Viewed in this way, the relationship between social and cultural phenomena is dynamic. Cultural adaptations provide a model for future behaviors but are themselves a reflection of past behavioral adaptive strategies.

Failure to recognize this association between social and cultural adaptations can lead to confusion in social science. For example, much of the underlying theoretical debate within social science has been between those who argue that culture determines behavior versus those who insist that behavior determines culture. Both advocates assume a linear relationship between the two. This debate was critically reviewed by Irwin Deutscher (1973) in his analysis of the social science literature on the connection between sentiments and acts. What he uncovered was that both sides had equal support. How is that possible? It is possible if one adopts the adaptive model which anticipates both of these outcomes, depending on when in the process of adaptation the research is done. If analyzed at one time, a set of behaviors may be a localized adaptation to a set of new environmental conditions and hence inconsistent with past cultural expectations. At a later time, that same practice may be reported as part of "tradition" and hence the basis for future behaviors. The problem that both sides in this debate have is their commitment to a linear model of the world and their failure to recognize the dynamic and changing interplay between social and cultural worlds as systems of adaptations.

The model for this view is borrowed from modern Darwinian theory concerning human evolution—note the word *modern*. Darwin himself did not propose the modern theory. Rather, it developed from his original formulation of natural selection as the process by which organisms evolve characteristics in response to shifting and changing environments. The consequence of this process is that organisms either change (evolve) or become extinct. Modern evolutionary theory adds knowledge derived from population and molecular genetics, neither of which were available to Darwin or others during the nineteenth century. Our understanding of the genetic process of inheritance helps us explain the principles underlying the Darwinian model of continuity and change. The combination of genetic structures during reproduction explains why species reproduce offspring that maintain or perpetrate species characteristics that reflect and acknowledge past successful adaptations to environments. At the same time, it provides us with an understanding of the source of new characteristics, recognizing that the reproductive process does not always follow nice, neat rules. In the process of passing down parental characteristics, "accidents" happen. These accidents produce organisms with different characteristics. Depending on the environment within which the species lives, some of these outcomes are lethal and are not passed on genetically. Others are neutral; that is, they neither contribute to nor impede reproductive success. Lastly, again depending on the environment, the "new" genetic materials may give organisms an advantage which enables them to out-reproduce—and eventually replace—those without it. The importance of this revised Darwinian model is that it recognizes both continuity and potential for chance. Adaptive characteristics continue because they work within an unchanging environment. At the same time, there is a continuous supply of possible adaptive features which appear randomly and provide potentials for survival when environments change. An additional attractive feature of this model is that it does not require us to assume motivation or intention on the part of the biological organisms themselves. In other words, evolution or survival works, in part, because of genetic randomness. This latter observation appealed to me as a way of answering some unresolved issues in social science.

Explaining the Unexplained

Perhaps the best test of this dynamic systems model is whether it can make sense of a question we cannot answer and an observation that challenges the idea that social "science" is possible. The question is one for which there is no direct empirical answer and concerns origins: When did humans first "discover" drugs? The observation is: No matter how hard we try, we never find correlations or linkages that confirm the existence of "laws."

The question of origins fascinated nineteenth-century social scientists. Under the influence of the original Darwinian model and directed by the Western cultural assumption that humans are rational, goal-directed animals, they sought the authorship of a variety of practices. In the absence of physical evidence on where and when these practices originated, the search was abandoned and the question of origins ceased. One clue to this abandonment comes from James Clifton (1976). He suggests that the distinction between **discovery** as accidental invention and invention as a more purposive and rational problem-solving process has become obsolete in anthropology. The key here may be the underlying assumption about humans, namely, that human action is purposive and rational. The denial of "accidental" or random behavior on the part of humans challenges a widespread Western belief about human nature. Yet, regardless of its challenge to Western beliefs, the question still remains: "How were the altering properties of substances such as fly agaric, marihuana, coca leaves, peyote, and kava discovered?" This same question could be asked about other natural substances that were "discovered" to have nutritional value and upon which humans depend. The absence of direct evidence for origins may give license to speculate about some "natural" urge for humans to experience altered states. However, even this "explanation" assumes that humans are goal-directed in their actions but that the goals are hidden at some mysterious molecular genetic level. The acceptance of some randomness as part of the human behavioral repertoire helps answer the questions of origins. If humans ingest everything they encounter in a world of plants, they are bound to "discover" those plants which can alter their senses, as well as those that sustain or extinguish life. That humans construct "history" as what we choose to remember does not negate the fact that much human behavior was and is random and has no direct adaptive consequences. The selectivity of histories gives the appearance of intention but ignores the multitude of unintended outcomes of randomness. This observation further adds to our understanding of why those substances we call drugs get rediscovered and why they may appear in different locations without any apparent connections. The acceptance or rejection of independent discoveries and rediscoveries are, of course, dependent on systemic arrangements, but their genesis lies in repeated random acts that are not goal-directed.

If we accept randomness as part of the human condition, it also helps explain the absence of laws in social science. Although we apply the methodological rules of science we are not able to construct lawlike statements similar to those in the physical sciences. Disregarding the fact that laws in the physical sciences only apply to very specific "unreal" laboratory situations, the acceptance of the scientific method often assumes that adherence to those methods will result in laws. This assumption views science as a set of results rather than a strategy for maximizing our abilities to predict and explain. As illustrated throughout this book, the findings of social science are always probabilistic. There is always unexplained variance. Even with strict adherence to scientific procedures we never uncover statements of relationships that approximate laws in the physical sciences. This inability, I think, illustrates something about social science and its subject matter. We study systems that are real; and the reality of systems is that they change and that change is, in part, rooted in randomness along with the dynamic interplay between social and cultural systems.

Unexplained variation acknowledges what we know about the worlds in which humans live. In fact, without unexplained variation, social and cultural worlds could not exist.

Systems and Social Science Methods

The methods employed in social science do not differ in principle from methods found in other sciences. Scientific methods share the same guidelines. Researchers should demonstrate that they were objective and that they did everything possible to disprove their proposed hypotheses. Failure to do so results in findings that are less credible and more suspect. Science rests as much on what has been rejected as on what it knows, and what it knows is always tentative and subject to change.

One methodological difficulty faced by social science is defining concepts. Many of our concepts are part of a general vocabulary that is laden with ideological and affective meaning. For example, after many years of teaching a basic introduction to Mendelian genetics as part of a general introductory course in anthropology, I still find that students equate the concept of "recessive" genes with any inherited characteristic that is "bad" and "dominant" genes with any characteristic that is "good." Obviously, students internalized this meaning from a history of word use in everyday conversation. Social science is especially beleaguered with this kind of problem. Words such as "culture," "society," "conflict," "status," and "role" are embedded in everyday vocabularies and have shifting meanings. This confusion is even more of a challenge in the area of drugs, where words like "abuse," "pathology," and "abnormal" abound. The word "drug" itself is so frequently bound with the words "problem" and "abuse" that they seem one rather than two words. I would not suggest that the vocabulary of social science concepts be totally revamped—only that we recognize this difficulty as a challenge to social science's ability to insure objectivity.

The question of objectivity has been an issue in social science since its beginnings. Critics of social science, both internal and external, often cite the absence of laws and of an experimental approach as evidence for social science not being "science." The absence of laws has been addressed. The centrality of the experiment in defining "objective" science is another matter. This issue has largely been an expression of comparison to the "sciences," such as physics and chemistry, which have laid claim to objectivity through their use of experimental laboratory methods. Without laboratories, it is assumed, social science cannot be "scientific." Thus, just as the word "drug" is linked to "abuse," critics link "laboratory" with "science." There is little question that the experiment is one of an arsenal of methods by which to do science. It does not follow that it is *the* method. This is especially true when the goal of the scientific enterprise is to study systems—dynamic and changing systems. The fundamental question underlying the selection of any method is its effectiveness in falsifying our hypotheses and hence our theory. Those who criticize social science for its lack of the experiment have forgotten that the object of science is to investigate the world in ways that minimize the influence of the researcher's wishes and desires for a particular result. Objectivity in this pursuit is measured by maximizing falsifiability, however it is done—not by strict adherence to the catechism of the experiment.

The social science approach requires that we follow the principle of falsification. Throughout this book I have been guided by this perspective. We rejected individual psychological explanations for patterns of drug use. We found that chemistry cannot explain the wide varieties of behavioral responses to drugs. We have taken our models and theories into a wide range of times, geographies, and cultural settings to challenge ideas and beliefs about drugs emanating from the contemporary Western world. In short, I have attempted to falsify what we know or think we know about drugs.

Samples and the "People" Question

Underlying much of the history of social science has been a debate on what social science studies. On one side are those who suggest that the object of social science research is people. This is the **humanistic** tradition. Humanism is expressed in two ways—the obvious and the subtle. Obvious humanists contend that the task of social science is to study what they feel are "injustices." These scholars have research agendas driven by a concern for the troubles or problems of some specific population. The primary goal of their work is to identify some other population they assume has "caused" these injustices. Not too surprisingly, their "research" confirms their judgements. It is this tradition that is often the target of those who object to the use of the term "science" as a description of what social science does. While the obvious humanists draw the most attention, subtle humanism is less likely to be recognized. Subtle humanism is the unvoiced assumption that it is people we study. The best example of this is in the selection of samples. By far the most frequent comments made by students who are assigned social science articles to read and critique is that the samples—high school students, college students, factory workers, crack users, heroin addicts in treatment centers, prisoners, and others—are not representative of the total population of high school and college students, factory workers, and so forth. This concern is not limited to students. Within social science, careful attention is paid to sampling techniques and whether they accurately approximate population characteristics. Both students and social scientists agree (subtly of course) that the objects of social science are people.

In contrast to the humanistic tradition are those who insist that our task is to understand how systems work. This is the **scientific tradition**. I would suggest that sampling has another purpose for social science as science. If the object of research is to understand how systems work, then sampling is not of "people" but of attributes which contribute to system functioning. While it is people's behavior and values that we measure directly, it is the attributes of systems that we ultimately wish to understand. Throughout this book, this concern has been illustrated. The study of marihuana street sales (chapter 8) was viewed within the context of how economic systems work. What we want to know is something more about the attribute exchange within the larger systems framework of production, distribution, and consumption of goods and services. The same is true of variations in drug use among high school seniors as an indicator of church participation (chapter 7). The question we ask as social scientists is whether the attributes measured in this study contribute to our understanding of age-grading systems or religious systems, not whether this sample is representative of all high school seniors in the United States. We study bottle gangs in Seattle to understand groups as systems, not to say something about bottle gangs everywhere. Randomizing a sample, from a systems perspective, is done to randomize attributes, not people. Why this emphasis on attributes? The answer is simple. Attributes are units of theory, and theory is the way social science explains how systems work and how they came to be what they are.

Drugs: What Can Be Done About Them?

Robert Michels (1959) observed that:

> It is not the purpose of sociological science to discover, or rediscover solutions, since numerous problems of the individual life and the life of social groups are not capable of "solution"

at all, but must ever remain "open." The sociologist should aim rather at the dispassionate exposition of tendencies and counter-operating forces, of reasons and opposing reasons, at the display, in a word, of the warp and woof of social life. *Precise diagnosis is the logical and indispensable preliminary to any possible prognosis.* (p. viii, emphasis mine)

A recent trend in social science has been toward policy research or applied social science. Fraught by the lack of career opportunities in academe, many credentialed social scientists have taken employment in government and social service agencies. Armed with social science techniques, these social scientists attempt to apply social science knowledge to solving "social problems," including the drug "problem." Two solution models are employed. One suggests that problems are solved by changing systems; the other targets problematic individuals. The changing systems model is reflected in the statement, "Since drug use frequencies are high in low-income populations, drug use will decrease when incomes are increased." The individual model, in contrast, is exemplified by the statement, "Get the drug user into treatment and the drug problem will disappear." Neither of these approaches is social science. The change-the-system model assumes that systems can be changed, and the change-the-individual model assumes that individuals determine systems. Further, both assume that drugs are the only consequence of how systems work. If there is a social science, we must assume that the *units of study—systems—*are not changeable without having consequences for their connection to other parts of larger systems. As noted in chapters 9 and 10, changes in jural and political systems are systemic adjustments to changes in demography, histories, economies, and a host of other antecedent factors, none of which we can change. To assume that changes can target one part of a system without having consequences for other parts is both naive and unscientific. More importantly, it denies the independence of science as a strategy for understanding the world in which we live. When science is used to legitimate moral decisions, it has lost its ability to be objective.

In Search of Social Science: Some Helpful Hints

We began this excursion into the social science literature with a simple model and a set of guidelines for the social science approach to drug use. As readers go beyond my selection of materials, it may be helpful to consider the following questions in their own readings and interpretations of studies and essays on drug use. This list is provided as a generic map for identifying the social science approach to the study of anything. If the answers to the following questions are all "yes," then you have uncovered materials representing a social science approach to some topic.

1. Are systems the units of analysis? Does the author clearly identify which system or systems are analyzed?
2. Are the goals of the analysis to uncover the rules which govern systems? If so, can these rules be applied to understand more than the immediate research problem or question?
3. Are findings interpreted from a relativistic, comparative viewpoint, and are the findings applicable globally and to all time periods?
4. Do the research methods work to maximize falsifiability?

One should not expect that every research endeavor would yield an affirmative answer to every question. The scientific venture is at best an attempt to approximate these goals. Armed with these questions, it will at least be possible to identify those materials that can be rejected as social science.

Epilogue

Someone once said that the best thing about writing is having written. I must admit a certain satisfaction with completion of this manuscript. Through it I have been able to provoke myself to think about this venture called social science, and I hope that it will provoke others to do the same. Science is, or should be, a continuing passionate debate about the adequacy of ideas. I trust that some of the ideas explored here will fuel those fires of debate.

References

Aberle, David F.
1962 A note on relative deprivation theory as applied to millenarian and other cult movements. In Millennial Dreams in Action, Comparative Studies in Society and History, Supplement II. Sylvia L. Thrupp, ed., pp. 209–214. The Hague: Mouton.

Ackerknecht, Erwin H.
1946 Natural diseases and rational treatment in primitive medicine. Bulletin of the History of Medicine 19:467–497.

Adler, Patricia A. and Peter Adler
1980 The irony of secrecy in the drug world. Urban Life 8:447–465.
1982 Criminal commitment among drug dealers. Deviant Behavior 3:117–135.
1983 Relations between dealers: The social organization of illicit drug transactions. Sociology and Social Research 67:260–278.
1989 Shifts and oscillations in deviant careers: The case of upper-level drug dealers and smugglers. In Deviant Behavior: A Text-Reader in the Sociology of Deviance. D. H. Kelly, ed., pp. 601–619. New York: St. Martin's Press.

Agar, Michael H.
1973 Ripping and Running: A Formal Ethnography of Heroin Addicts. New York: Seminar Press.
1984 "Comment" on Robin Room, Alcohol and ethnography: A case of problem deflation? Current Anthropology 25:178–179.

Allen, Catherine J.
1981 To be Quechua: The symbolism of coca chewing in highland Peru. American Ethnologist 8:157–171.

Anderson, Edward F.
1980 Peyote, The Divine Cactus. Tucson: University of Arizona Press.

Applebaum, Richard P.
   1970 Theories of Social Change. Chicago: Markham Publishing.
Archard, Peter
   1979 Vagrancy, Alcoholism and Social Control. London: The Macmillan Press, Ltd.
Arthur, William R.
   1947 Laws of Drugs and Druggists. 3rd ed. St. Paul: West Publishing.
Aviado, Domingo M.
   1986 Health issues relating to "passive" smoking. In Smoking and Society. Robert D. Tollison, ed., pp. 138–165. Lexington, MA: Lexington Books.
Axelrod, Morris
   1956 Urban structure and social participation. American Sociological Review 21:13–18.
Babcock, Barbara A. (ed.)
   1978 The Reversible World: Symbolic Inversion in Art and Society. Ithaca: Cornell University Press.
Bacon, Margaret K., Irvin L. Child, and Herbert Barry III
   1965 A cross-cultural study of drinking: II. Relations to other features of culture. Quarterly Journal of Studies on Alcohol, Supplement 3:29–48.
Bahr, Howard M.
   1973 Skid Row: An Introduction to Disaffiliation. New York: Oxford University Press.
Barber, Bernard
   1967 Drugs and Society. New York: Russell Sage Foundation.
Barnett, H. G.
   1953 Innovation: The Basis of Cultural Change. New York: McGraw-Hill.
Baroja, Julio Caro
   1964 The World of Witches. Trans. by O. N. V. Glendinning. Chicago: University of Chicago Press.
Barrett, Leonard
   1977 The Rastafarians. Boston: Beacon.
Barth, Gunther
   1964 Bitter Strength: A History of the Chinese in the United States, 1850–1870. Cambridge: Harvard University Press.
Beals, Ralph L. and Harry Hoijer
   1971 An Introduction to Anthropology. New York: MacMillian.
Becher, Hans
   1960 Die Surára und Pakidai: Zwei Yanonámi-Stämme in Nordwest-Brasilien, vol. 26. Hamburg: Mitteilungen aus dem Museum für Völkerkunde.
Becker, Howard S.
   1953 Becoming a marijuana user. American Journal of Sociology 59:235–242.
   1967 History, culture and subjective experience: An exploration of the social basis of drug-induced experiences. Journal of Health and Social Behavior 8:166–169.

Ben-Yehuda, Nachman
1986 The sociology of moral panics: Toward a new synthesis. The Sociological Quarterly 27:495–513.

Benabud, A.
1957 Psychopathological aspects of cannabis use in Morocco: Statistics for the year, 1956. Bulletin on Narcotics. 9:1–8.

Benedict, Ruth F.
1959 Psychological types in the cultures of the Southwest. In Anthropologist At Work. Margaret Mead, ed., pp. 248–261. Boston: Houghton Mifflin.

Benítez, Fernando
1975 In the Magic Land of Peyote. Trans. by John Upton. Austin: University of Texas Press.

Berger, Peter L.
1986 A sociological view of the antismoking phenomena. In Smoking and Society. Robert D. Tollison, ed., pp. 225–240. Lanham, MD: The University Press of America.

Berridge, Virginia and Griffith Edwards
1981 Opium and the People: Opiate Use in Nineteenth-Century England. New York: St. Martin's Press.

Bierce, Ambrose
1958 The Devil's Dictionary. New York: Dover. (Orig. 1911.)

Black, Peter Weston
1978 The teachings of Father Marino: Christianity on Tobi atoll. In Mission, Church, and Sect in Oceania. James A. Boutilier, Daniel T. Hughes, and Sharon W. Tiffany, eds., pp. 307–355. Lanham, MD: University Press of America.

1984 The anthropology of tobacco use: Tobian data and theoretical issues. Journal of Anthropological Research 40:475–503.

1985 Ghosts, gossip, and suicide: Meaning and action in Tobian folk psychology. In Person, Self, and Experience. Geoffry M. White and John Kirkpatrick, eds., pp. 245–300. Berkeley: University of California Press.

Bloom, Alan
1987 The Closing of the American Mind. New York: Simon and Schuster.

Blum, Richard A.
1969a A history of tobacco. In Society and Drugs. Richard H. Blum and Associates, eds., pp. 87–97. San Francisco: Jossey-Bass.

1969b A history of alcohol. In Society and Drugs. Richard H. Blum and Associates, eds., pp. 25–44. San Francisco: Jossey-Bass.

Blumer, Herbert
1969 Collective behavior. In Principles of Sociology. Alfred McClung Lee, ed., pp. 65–123. New York: Barnes and Noble.

Bogen, E.
1932 The human toxicology on alcohol tolerance in man. In Alcohol and Man. H. Emerson, ed., pp. 126–152. New York: The Macmillian Co.

Bogue, Donald J.
    1963 Skid Row in American Cities. Chicago: University of Chicago Community and Family Study Center.
    1969 Principles of Demography. New York: John Wiley and Sons.
Bott, Elizabeth
    1987 The kava ceremonial as a dream structure. In Constructive Drinking: Perspectives on Drink from Anthropology. Mary Douglas, ed., pp. 182–204. Cambridge: Cambridge University Press.
Brady, Maggie
    1990 Indigenous and government attempts to control alcohol use among Australian Aborigines. Contemporary Drug Problems 17:195–220.
    1991 Psychoactive substance use among aboriginal Australians. Contemporary Drug Problems 18:273–327.
Brandes, Stanley
    1978 Drinking patterns and alcohol control in a Castilian mountain village. Anthropology 3:1–15.
Bray, Warwick and Colin Dollery
    1983 Coca chewing and high-altitude stress: A spurious correlation. Current Anthropology 24:269–282.
Brecher, Edward M. and the Editors of Consumer Reports
    1972 Licit and Illicit Drugs. Boston: Little, Brown.
Brody, Hugh
    1977 Alcohol, change and the industrial frontier. Inuit Studies 1:31–46.
Brooks, Jerome E.
    1952 The Mighty Leaf: Tobacco Through the Centuries. Boston: Little, Brown & Co.
Buchanan, David R.
    1992 A social history of American drug use. The Journal of Drug Issues 22:31–50.
Buchler, Ira R. and Henry A. Selby
    1968 Kinship and Social Organization: An Introduction to Theory and Method. New York: Macmillian.
Buck, A., T. Sasaki, and R. Anderson
    1968 Health and Disease in Four Peruvian Villages. Baltimore: John Hopkins Press.
Bunker, Stephen G.
    1987 Ritual, respect and refusal: Drinking behavior in an Andean village. Human Organization 46:334–42.
Burchard, Roderick E.
    1992 Coca chewing and diet. Current Anthropology 33:1–24.
Burkett, Steven R. and Melvin White
    1976 School adjustment, drinking, and the impact of alcohol education programs. Urban Education 10:79–94.

Carstairs, G. M.
    1954 Daru and Bhang: Cultural factors in the choice of intoxicants. Quarterly Journal of Studies on Alcohol. 15:220–237.
Carter, William E., Mauricio Mamani, José Moralas, and Phillip Parkerson
    1980 Coca in Bolivia: Report of research performed un National Institute of Drug Abuse grant number ROI DA1774–02, with the University of Florida, Gainesville, FL.
Carter, William (ed.)
    1980 Cannabis in Costa Rica. Philadelphia: ISHI Publications.
Carucci, Laurence Marshall
    1987 Kijen Emaan Ilo Baat: Methods and meaning of smoking in Marshallese society. In Drugs in Western Pacific Societies. Lamont Lindstrom, ed., pp. 51–72. Lanham, MD: University Press of America.
Cashman, John
    1966 The LSD Story. Greenwich, CT: Fawcett Publications.
Cavan, Sherri
    1966 Liquor License: An Ethnography of Bar Behavior. Chicago: Aldine.
Chagnon, Napoleon A.
    1983 Yanomamö: The Fierce People, 3rd ed. New York: Holt, Rinehart and Winston.
Chagnon, Napoleon A., Philip LeQuesme, and James M. Cook
    1971 Yanomamö Hallucinogens: Anthropological, Botanical, and Chemical Findings. Current Anthropology 12:72–74.
Chambliss, William J.
    1977 Markets, profits, labor and smack. Contemporary Crisis 1:53–76.
Chapple, E. D. and C. S. Coon
    1942 Principles of Anthropology. New York: Henry Holt and Co.
Chen, Jack
    1980 The Chinese of America. San Francisco: Harper & Row.
Cheung, Yuet W.
    1993 Beyond liver and culture: A review of theories and research in drinking among Chinese in North America. The International Journal of Addictions 28:1497–1513.
Cheung, Yuet W., Patricia G. Erickson, and Tammy C. Landau
    1991 Experience of crack use: Findings from a community-based sample in Toronto. Journal of Drug Issues 21:121–140.
Childe, V. Gordon
    1948 The Dawn of European Civilization. London: Kegan Paul.
Chin, K. L., T. F. M. Lai, and M. Rouse
    1990–91 Social adjustments and alcoholism among Chinese immigrants in New York City. International Journal of Addictions 25:709–830.
Chopra, I. C. and R. N. Chopra
    1957 The use of cannabis drugs. India Bulletin of Narcotics 9:13.

444　References

Clark, Ramsey
　1979　Memorandum in support of motion to dismiss. Case #79-379-CR-WMH, U.S. v. Morrison, Lawler, Booth, Reilly, Middleton.
Clifton, James
　1976　Discovery and Invention. In Encyclopedia of Anthropology. David E. Hunter and Phillip Whitten, eds., pp. 126–127. New York: Harper & Row.
Cloyd, Jerald W.
　1976　The market-place bar: The interrelation between sex, situation, and strategies in the pairing ritual of Homo ludens. Urban Life 5:293–313.
Cohen, Abner
　1974　Two-Dimensional Man: An Essay on the Anthropology of Power and Symbolism in Complex Societies: London: Routledge & Kegan Paul.
Cohen, Albert K.
　1955　Delinquent Boys. Glencoe: The Free Press.
Cohen, Stanley
　1980　Folk Devils and Moral Panics. New York: St. Martin's Press.
Coleman, James William
　1976　The myth of addiction. Journal of Drug Issues. 6:135–141.
Collmann, Jeff
　1979　Social order and exchange of liquor: A theory of drinking among Australian Aborigines. Journal of Anthropological Research 35:208–224.
Cooper, John M.
　1949　Stimulants and narcotics. Bureau of American Ethnology Bulletin 143:525–58.
Corti, E. C.
　1931　A History of Smoking. London: G.G. Harrap & Co.
Courtney, William J.
　1974　San Francisco Anti-Chinese Ordinances, 1850–1900. San Francisco: R and E Research Associates.
Courtwright, David T.
　1982　Dark Paradise: Opiate Addiction in America before 1940. Cambridge: Harvard University Press.
Crancer, Alfred Jr., James M. Dille, Jack C. Delay, Jean E. Wallace, and Martin D. Haykin
　1969　Comparison of the effects of marihuana and alcohol on simulated driving performance. Science 164:851–854.
Dahrendorf, Ralf
　1964　Homo Sociologicus. Köln: Westdeutscher Verlag.
Dalton, George
　1961　Economic theory and primitive society. American Anthropologist 67:44–65.
　1971　Economic Anthropology and Development: Essays on Tribal and Peasant Economies. New York: Basic Books.

Davis, James A. and Tom Smith
  1991 General Social Survey, 1972–1991; Cumulative Codebook. Chicago: National Opinion Research Center.
Davis, Wade
  1989 Hallucinogenic plants and their use in traditional societies. In Applying Anthropology: An Introductory Reader. Aaron Podolefsky and Peter J. Brown, eds., pp. 243–246. Mountain View, CA: Mayfield Publishing Co.
de Rios, Marlene Dobkin
  1984 Hallucinogens: Cross-Cultural Perspectives. Albuquerque: University of New Mexico Press.
de Rios, Marlene Dobkin and David E. Smith
  1977 Drug use and abuse in cross cultural perspective. Human Organization 36:14–21.
Demerath, N. J. III
  1965 Social Class in American Protestantism. Chicago: Rand McNally.
Deutscher, Irwin
  1973 What We Say/What We Do: Sentiments and Acts. Glenview, IL: Scott, Foresman and Company.
Divale, William T.
  1976 Female status and cultural evolution. A study in ethnographer bias. Behavior Science Research 11:169–212.
Dobrizhoffer, M.
  1822 An Account of the Abipones, An Equestrian People of Paraguay. 3 vols. London: John Murray.
Dole, Gertrude E.
  1964 Shamanism and political control among the Kuikuru. Völkerkundliche Abhandlungen. 7:53–62.
  1986 Anarchy without chaos: Alternatives to political authority among the Kuikuru. In Political Anthropology. M. J. Swartz, V. W. Turner, and A. Tuden, eds., pp. 73–88. Chicago: Aldine.
Dotson, Floyd
  1951 Patterns of voluntary association among urban working class families. American Sociological Review 16:687–693.
Douglas, Mary
  1966 Purity and Danger. London: Routledge & Kegan Paul.
Douglas, Mary and Aaron Wildavsky
  1982 Risk and Culture: An Essay on the Selection of Technological and Environmental Dangers. Berkeley: University of California Press.
Dreher, Melanie C.
  1982 Working Men and Ganja: Marihuana Use in Rural Jamaica. Philadelphia: ISHI.
  1983 Marihuana and work: Cannabis smoking on a Jamaican sugar estate. Human Organization 42:1–8.
Driver, G. R. and John C. Miles
  1968 The Babylonian Laws. London: Oxford University Press.

Driver, Harold E.
   1969 Indians of North America. Chicago: University of Chicago Press.
Driver, Harold E. and William C. Massey
   1957 Comparative studies of North American Indians. Transactions of the American Philosophical Society. XLVII, 165–456.
Dubisch, Jill
   1981 You are what you eat: Religious aspects of the health food movement. In The American Dimension: Cultural Myths and Social Realities. Susan P. Montague and W. Arens, eds., pp. 115–128. Sherman Oaks, CA: Alfred Publishing Co.
Durkheim, Émile
   1938 The Rules of Sociological Method. Trans. by Sarah A. Solovay and John H. Mueller; George E. G. Catlin, ed. New York: The Free Press. (Orig. 1895.)
   1947 The Division of Labor. Trans. by George Simpson. Glencoe: The Free Press. (Orig. 1903.)
   1951 Suicide. Trans. by John A. Spaulding and George Simpson. New York: The Free Press of Glencoe. (Orig. 1896.)
   1965 The Elementary Forms of Religious Life. Trans. by Joseph Ward Swain. New York: Free Press. (Orig. 1912.)
Durrenberger, Paul E.
   1974 The regional context of the economy of a Lisu village in Northern Thailand. Southeast Asia 3:569–575.
   1976 The economy of a Lisu village. American Ethnologist 3:633–644.
DuToit, Brian M.
   1977 Ethnicity and patterning in South African drug use. In Drugs, Rituals, and Altered States of Consciousness. Brian M. DuToit, ed., pp. 74–79. Rotterdam: AA Balkema.
Eames, Edwin and Judith Goode
   1988 Coping with poverty: A cross-cultural view of the behavior of the poor. In Urban Life: Readings in Urban Anthropology, 2nd ed., George Gmelch and Walter P. Zenner, eds., pp. 358–368. Prospect Heights, IL: Waveland Press.
Efron, Vera, Mark Keller, and Carol Guioli (eds.)
   1974 Statistics on Consumption of Alcohol and on Alcoholism. New Brunswick, NJ: Rutgers Center of Alcohol Studies.
Einstein, Stanley
   1983 The Drug User: Personality Issues, Factors, and Theories. New York: Plenum.
Eisenstadt, S. N. F.
   1956 From Generation to Generation. Glencoe: The Free Press.
Eysenck, Hans. J.
   1968 Smoking and health. In Smoking and Society. Robert D. Tollison, ed., pp. 17–88. Lexington, MA: Lexington Books.
Feinhandler, Sherwin J.
   1986 The social role of smoking. In Smoking and Society. Robert D. Tollison, ed., pp. 167–188. Lexington, MA: Lexington Books.

Feldman, Harvey W.
  1973 Street status and drug users. Society 10:32–39.
Feldman, Harvey W., Michael H. Agar, and George M. Beschner
  1979 Angel Dust. Lexington, MA: Lexington Books.
Fenna, D., L. Mix, O. Schaefer, and J. A. L. Gilbert
  1971 Ethanol metabolism in various racial groups. Canadian Medical
        Association Journal 105:472–5.
Fernandez, James W.
  1972 Tabernanthe Iboga: Narcotic ecstasis and the work of ancestor.
        In Flesh of the Gods: The Ritual Use of Hallucinogens. Peter T.
        Furst, ed., pp. 237–260. New York: Praeger. Reprint, Prospect
        Heights, IL: Waveland Press, 1990.
Field, Peter B.
  1962 A new cross-cultural study of drunkenness. In D. J. Pittman and
        C. R. Snyder, eds., Society, Culture, and Drinking Patterns. pp.
        48–74. New York: John Wiley and Sons.
Fields, Allen B.
  1984 "Slinging weed": The social organization of streetcorner
        marijuana sales. Urban Life 13:247–270.
Fischer, C. S.
  1974 Toward a subcultural theory of urbanism. American Journal of
        Sociology 80:1319–1341.
Fisher, A. D.
  1987 Alcoholism and race: The misapplication of both concepts to
        North American Indians. Canadian Review of Sociology and
        Anthropology 24:81–98.
Fort, Joel
  1969 A world view of drugs. In Society and Drugs. Richard H. Blum
        & Associates, eds., pp. 229–243. San Francisco: Jossey-Bass.
Frazer, Sir James
  1928 The Golden Bough, One-Volume Abridged Edition. New York:
        MacMillian.
Freilich, Morris
  1975 Comment on Maria-Barbara Watson-Franke and Lawrence C.
        Watson, Understanding in anthropology: A philosophical
        reminder. Current Anthropology 16:274–262.
Freilich, Morris, Douglas Raybeck, and Joel Savishinsky
  1991 Deviance: Anthropological Perspectives. New York: Bergin &
        Garvey.
Frezza, Mario, Carlo diPadova, Gabriele Pozzato, Maddalena Termpin,
Enrigue Baraona, and Charles Lieber.
  1990 High blood alcohol levels in women. The role of decreased gastric
        alcohol dehydrogenase activity and first-pass metabolism. New
        England Journal of Medicine, Jan. 11 322:95–99.
Friedenberg, Edgar
  1966 Adolescence as a social problem. In Social Problems: A Modern
        Approach. Howard S. Becker, ed., pp. 35–75. New York: John
        Wiley.

Friedl, E.
    1965 Trager medialer begabung im hundukuch and karakorum. Acta Ethnologica et Linguistica. Österreichische Ethnologische Gesellschaft. No. 8. Institut für Völkerkunde der Universität, Vienna.

Frye, Paul A.
    1990 Form and function of North Yemeni qat sessions. The Southern Communication Journal 55: 292–304.

Fuchs, Andrew
    1978 Coca chewing and high-altitude stress: Possible effect of coca alkaloids on erythropoiesis. Current Anthropology 19:277–291.

Fuller, Richard and Richard R. Myers
    1941 The natural history of a social problem. American Sociological Review 6:320.

Furst, Peter T.
    1972. To find our life: Peyote among the Huichol Indians of Mexico. In Flesh of the Gods: The Ritual Use of Hallucinogens. Peter T. Furst, ed., pp. 136–184. New York: Praeger. Reprint, Prospect Heights, IL: Waveland Press, 1990.

    1978 The art of "being Huichol."In Art of the Huichol Indians. Kathleen Berrin, ed., pp. 18–34. New York: Harry N. Abrams.

Gajdusek, D. C.
    1979 Recent observations on the use of kava in the New Hebrides. In Ethnopharmocologic Search for Psychoactive Drugs. D. H. Efron, ed., pp. 119–125. New York: Raven Press.

Galton, Francis
    1989 Note on the Australian marriage systems. Journal of the Royal Anthropological Institute 18:70–72.

Geertz, Clifford
    1965 Religion as a cultural system. In Anthropological Approaches to the Study of Religion. ASA Monograph #3. Michael Banton, ed., New York: Frederick A. Praeger.

Gibson, James A. and Daniella Weinberg
    1980 In vivo communitas: Wine and identity in a Swiss Alpine village. Anthropological Quarterly 53:111–121.

Glock, Charles and Rodney Stark
    1965 Religion and Society in Tension. Chicago: Rand McNally.

Gluckman, Max
    1963 Gossip and Scandal. Current Anthropology 4:307–316.

Goode, Erich
    1972 Drugs in American Society. New York: Alfred A. Knopf.

    1989 Drugs in American Society, 3rd ed. New York: Alfred A. Knopf.

Goodman, Jordan
    1993 Tobacco in History: The Culture of Dependence. New York: Routledge.

Gottlieb, David
    1957 The neighborhood tavern and the cocktail-lounge: A study of class differences. American Journal of Sociology 62:559–562.

Grinspoon, Lester
  1971 Marihuana Reconsidered. Cambridge: Harvard University Press.
Gusfield, Joseph R.
  1962 Status conflicts and the changing ideologies of the American
        temperance movement. In Society, Culture, and Drinking
        Patterns. David J. Pittman and Charles R. Snyder, eds., pp.
        101–120. New York: John Wiley & Sons.
  1963 Symbolic Crusade. Urbana: University of Illinois Press.
  1986 Symbolic Crusade, 2nd ed. Urbana: University of Illinois Press.
  1987 Passage to play: Rituals of drinking time in American society. In
        Constructive Drinking: Perspectives on Drink from Anthropology.
        Mary Douglas, ed., pp. 73–90. New York: Cambridge University
        Press.
Hagaman, Barbara L.
  1980 Food for thought: Beer as a social and ritual context in a West
        African society. Journal of Drug Issues 10:203–214.
Hagen, John
  1989 The addictive sanction. In Structural Criminology. John Hagen,
        ed., pp. 70–100. New Brunswick, NJ: Rutgers University Press.
Hall, Edward T.
  1966 The Hidden Dimension. New York: Anchor.
  1973 The Silent Language. New York: Anchor.
Hamid, Ansley
  1980 A Pre-Capitalistic Mode of Production: Ganja and the Rastafarians
        in San Fernando, Trinidad. Doctoral Dissertation, Columbia
        University.
Harner, Michael J.
  1974 The role of hallucinogenic plants in European witchcraft. In
        Hallucinogens and Shamanism. Michael J. Harner, ed., pp.
        125–150. New York: Oxford University Press.
Harris, Marvin
  1966 The cultural ecology of India's sacred cattle. Current
        Anthropology 7:51–66.
  1968 The Rise of Anthropological Theory. New York: Harper & Row.
  1979 Cultural Materialism: The Struggle for a Science of Culture. New
        York: Vintage.
  1981 Why Nothing Works: The Anthropology of Daily Life. New York:
        Touchstone.
Haviland, William A.
  1993 Cultural Anthropology. New York: Harcourt Brace Jovanovich.
Heath, Dwight B.
  1962 Drinking patterns of the Bolivian Camba. In Society, Culture, and
        Drinking Patterns. D. J. Pittman and C. R. Snyder, eds., pp.
        22–36. New York: John Wiley and Sons.
  1984 "Comment" in Robin Room, Alcohol and ethnography: A case
        of problem deflation? Current Anthropology 25:180–181.
  1987 A decade of development in the anthropological study of alcohol
        use, 1970–1980. In Constructive Drinking: Perspectives on Drink

from Anthropology. Mary Douglas, ed., pp. 16–69. Cambridge: Cambridge University Press.

1990–91 Uses and misuses of the concept of ethnicity in alcohol studies: An essay in deconstruction. The International Journal of Addictions 25:607–628.

Heimann, R. K.
1960 Tobacco and Americans. New York: McGraw-Hill.

Helmer, John
1974 Drugs and Minority Oppression. New York: The Seabury Press.

Herrmann, Gretchen M. and Stephen M. Soiffer
1984 For fun and profit: An analysis of the American garage sale. Urban Life 12:397–421.

Higgins, Benjamin
1963 Foreword. In Clifford Geertz, Agricultural Involution, pp. vi–xv. Berkeley: University of California Press.

Hinton, Peter
1983 Why the Karen do not grow opium: Competition and contradiction in the highlands of North Thailand. Ethnology 22:1–16.

Hirshi, Travis and Rodney Stark
1969 Hellfire and delinquency. Social Problems 17:202–213.

Hollister, Leo E.
1971 Marihuana in man: Three years later. Science 172:21–28.

Horton, Donald
1943 The function of alcohol in primitive societies: A cross-cultural study. Quarterly Journal of Studies on Alcohol 4:199–320.

Hovland, Carl Iver and Robert R. Sears
1940 Minor studies of Aggression, VI: Correlation of lynchings with economic indices. Journal of Psychology 9:301–310.

Hughes, Charles C.
1968 Medical Care: Ethnomedicine. In International Encyclopedia of the Social Sciences. David Sills, ed., Vol. 10: pp. 87–92. New York: Crowell Collier and Macmillian.

Huizinga, J.
1950 Homo ludens. Boston: Beacon Press.

Hunt, Leon Gibson and Carl D. Chambers
1976 The Heroin Epidemics. A Study of Heroin Use in the United States, 1965–75. New York: Spectrum Publications.

Inciardi, James A.
1986 The War on Drugs: Heroin, Cocaine, Crime, and Public Policy. Palo Alto, CA: Mayfield.

Jackson, Joan K. and Ralph Connor
1953 The skid row alcoholic. Quarterly Journal of Studies on Alcohol 14:468–486.

Jocelson, W.
1905 The Koryak: Part I: Religion and Myth. Memoirs of the American Museum of Natural History 6:148–205.

Johnson, Bruce D.
1973 Marihuana Users and Drug Subcultures. New York: Wiley.

Johnson, Bruce D., Paul J. Goldstein, Edward Preble, James Schmeidler, Douglas S. Lipton, Barry Spunt, and Thomas Miller
1985 Taking Care of Business: The Economics of Crime and Heroin Abusers. Lexington, MA: Lexington Books.
Johnson, R. C., C. T. Nagoshi, S. Y. Schwitters, F. M. Ahern, J. R. Wilson, and S. H. L. Yuen.
1987 Cultural factors as explanations for ethnic group differences in alcohol use in Hawaii. Journal of Psychoactive Drugs 19:67–75.
Johnston, Lloyd D., Patrick M. O'Malley, and Jerald Bachman
1986 Drug Use Among American High School Students, College Students, and Other Young Adults: National Trends Through 1985. Rockville, MD: National Institute on Drug Abuse.
1987 National Trends in Drug Use and Related Factors Among American High School Students and Young Adults, 1975–1986. Rockville, MD: National Institute on Drug Abuse.
Kandel, D. B.
1980 Drug and drinking behavior among youth. Annual Review of Sociology 6:235–285.
Kaplan, Abraham
1964 The Conduct of Inquiry. San Francisco: Chandler.
Kaplan, David and Robert A. Manners
1972 Culture Theory. Englewood Cliffs, NJ: Prentice-Hall. Reprint, Prospect Heights, IL: Waveland Press, 1986.
Kaprow, Miriam Lee
1985 Manufacturing danger: Fear and pollution in industrial society. A Review of Mary Douglas and Aaron Wildavsky, Risk and Culture. American Anthropologist 87:342–356.
Katz, Elihu, Martin L. Levin and Herbert Hamilton
1963 Traditions of research on the diffusion of innovation. American Sociological Review. 28:240–252.
Kennedy, J. G., J. Teague, and L. Fairbanks
1980 Qat use in North Yemen and the problem of addiction. A study in medical anthropology. Social Science and Medicine 17:783–94.
Kennedy, John G.
1987 The Flower of Paradise: The Institutionalized Use of the Drug Qat in North Yemen. Dordrecht, Holland: D Reidel.
Kimball, Solon T., and James E. McClellan Jr.
1966 Education and the New America. New York: Random House.
Kitzinger, Sheila
1969 Protest and mysticism: The Rastafari cult of Jamaica. Journal for the Scientific Study of Religion. 8:240–262.
Klineberg, Otto
1934 Notes on the Huichol. American Anthropologist 36:446–460.
Knipe, Ed
1984 Gamrie: An Exploration in Cultural Ecology. Lanham, MD: University Press of America.

Kung, S. W.
1962 Chinese in American Life: Some Aspects of their History, Status, Problems, and Contributions. Westport, CT: Greenwood Press.

LaBarre, Weston
1938 Native American beers. American Anthropologist 40:224–234.
1948 The Aymara Indians of the Lake Titicaca altiplano, Bolivia. American Anthropological Association Memoir 68.

LaBarre, Weston
1970 The Ghost Dance: Origins of Religion. New York: Doubleday. Reprint, Prospect Heights, IL: Waveland Press, 1990.
1972 Hallucinogens and shamanic origins of religion. In Flesh of the Gods: The Ritual Uses of Hallucinogens. Peter T. Furst, ed., pp. 261–292. New York: Praeger. Reprint, Prospect Heights, IL: Waveland Press, 1990.
1975 The Peyote Cult. New York: Schocken Bofirewaters.

Lavengood, R., P. Lowinger, and K. Schoof
1973 Heroin Addiction in the Suburbs—An Epidemiological Study. American Journal of Public Health. 63:209–214.

Leach, E. R.
1966 Ritualization in man: Ritualization in man in relation to conceptual and social development. Philosophical Transactions of the Royal Society of London, Series B, Biological Sciences, Sir Julian Huxley, ed., 251:403–408.

Leacock, Seth
1964 Ceremonial drinking in an Afro-Brazilian cult. American Anthropologist 66:334–354.

Lebot, Vincent, Mark Merlin, and Lamont Lindstrom
1992 Kava: The Pacific Drug. New Haven: Yale University Press.

Leland, Joy
1976 Firewater Myths: North American Indians Drinking and Alcohol Addiction. Rutgers Center of Alcohol Studies Monograph 11.

LeMasters, E. E.
1975 Blue-Collar Aristocrats: Life-Styles at a Working-Class Tavern. Madison: University of Wisconsin Press.

Levinson, David and Martin J. Malone
1980 Toward Explaining Human Culture: A Critical Review of the Findings of Worldwide Cross-Cultural Research. New Haven: HRAF Press.

Levy, Jerrold E. and Stephen J. Kunitz
1973 Indian drinking: Problems of data collection and interpretation. In Proceedings of the First Annual Conference of the National Institute of Alcohol Abuse and Alcoholism, pp. 217–236. Rockville, MD.

Lewis, Oscar
1966 The Culture of Poverty. Scientific American 215:19–25.

Lewis, William F.
1986 The Rastafari: Millennial cultists or unregenerate peasants? Peasant Studies 14:5–26.

Light, Arthur B. and Edward G. Torrance
1929 Opium Addiction. Chicago: American Medical Association.
Lindesmith, Alfred R.
1947 Addiction and Opiates. Chicago: Aldine. (Revised, 1968)
1963 Basic problems in the Social Psychology of addiction and a theory. Paper read before the Chatham Conference, Perspectives on Narcotic Addiction, Chatham, Cape Cod, MA. September.
1968 A sociological theory of addiction. American Journal of Sociology 43:593–613.
Lindstrom, Monty
1982 Grog Blong Yumi: Alcohol and Kava on Tanna, Vanuatu. In Through a Glass Darkly: Beer, and Modernization in Papua New Guinea. Mac Marshall, ed., pp. 421–432. Institute of Applied Social and Economic Research Monograph 18.
Llewellyn, Karl N. and E. Adamson Hoebel
1941 The Cheyenne Way. Norman: University of Oklahoma Press.
Lyman, Stanford M.
1977 Chinese secret societies in the Occident: Notes and suggestions for research in the sociology of secrecy. In The Asian in North America. Stanford M. Lyman, ed., pp. 77–94. Santa Barbara, CA: ABC-Clio.
Ma, L. Eve Armentrout
1991 Chinatown organizations and the anti-Chinese movement, 1882–1914. In Entry Denied: Exclusion and the Chinese Community in America, 1882–1943. Sucheng Chan, ed., pp. 147–169. Philadelphia: Temple University Press.
MacAndrew, Craig and Robert B. Edgerton
1969 Drunken Comportment: A Social Explanation. Chicago: Aldine Publishing.
Madge, John
1965 The Tools of Social Science. New York: Anchor Books.
Maine, Henry Sumner
1906 Ancient Society. New York: Henry Holt. (Orig. 1861.)
Mandelbaum, David C.
1965 Alcohol and culture. Current Anthropology 6:281–294.
Manqin, W.
1957 Drinking among Andean Indians, Quarterlly Journal of Studies on Alcohol 18:55–66.
Marett, R. R.
1914 The Threshold of Religion, 2nd Edition. London: Methuen and Company.
Marshall, Mac and Leslie B. Marshall
1990 Silent Voices Speak: Women and Prohibition in Trek. Bailment, CA: Wadsworth.
Martin, M. Marlene
1978 Women in the HRAF files: A consideration of Ethnographic Bias. Behavior Science Research 13:303–314.

Martin, Richard
   1970 The role of coca in the history, religion, and medicine of South
         American Indians. Economic Botany 24:422–37.
Marx, Karl
   1909 Das Kapital. Trans. by E. Unterman. Chicago: W. Reeves. (Orig.
         1867.)
Mauss, Marcel
   1954 The Gift. Trans. by I. Cunnison. Glencoe: The Free Press. (Orig.
         1925.)
McAllester, David P.
   1949 Peyote Music. Viking Fund Publications in Anthropology No. 13.
McBride, Duane C. and Clyde B. McCoy
   1981 Crime and drug-using behavior: An areal analysis. Criminology
         19:281–302.
McClelland, David C.
   1961 The Achieving Society. Princeton: D. Van Nostrand.
McGlothlin, William and Louis J. West
   1968 The marijuana problem: An overview. American Journal of
         Psychiatry 125:372.
McNett, Charles W. Jr.
   1970 A cross-cultural method for predicting nonmaterial traits in
         archeology. Behavioral Science Notes 5:195–212.
Mead, George Herbert
   1934 Mind, Self and Society. Charles W. Morris, ed. Chicago: University
         of Chicago Press.
Merlin, Mark David
   1984 On the Trail of the Ancient Opium Poppy. London: Associated
         University Presses.
Merton, Robert K.
   1959 Notes on Problem-Finding in Sociology. In Sociology Today:
         Problems and Perspective. Robert K. Merton, Leonard Broom, and
         Leonard S. Cottrell, Jr., eds., pp. ix–xxxiv. New York: Basic Books.
Messick, Brinkley Morris
   1978 Transactions in Ibb: Economy and Society in a Yemeni Highland
         Town, unpublished PhD thesis, Princeton University.
Michels, Robert
   1959 Political Parties. Trans. by Eden and Ceder Paul. New York:
         Dover.
Miller, Stuart Creighton
   1969 The Unwelcome Immigrant: The American Image of the Chinese,
         1785–1882. Berkeley: University of California Press.
Mieczkowski, Thomas
   1986 Geeking up and throwing down: Heroin street life in Detroit.
         Criminology 24:645–666.
Miller, Walter
   1958 Lower class culture as a generating milieu of gang delinquency.
         The Journal of Social Issues 14:5–19.
Miranne, Alfred C.
   1979 Marihuana use and achievement orientations of college students.
         Journal of Health and Social Behavior 29:194–199.

Moore, Harvey C.
1956 Review of: Enemy way music: A study of social and aesthetic value as seen in Navaho music, by David P. McAllester [Reports of the Rimrock Project, Values Series No. 3, Papers of the Peabody Museum Archaeology and Ethnology (1954)]. American Anthropologist 58:220.

Moreno, J. L.
1934 Who Shall Survive? Washington, DC: Nervous and Mental Disease Publishing.

Moskalewicz, Jacek
1984 "Comment" on Robin Room, Alcohol and ethnography: A case of problem deflation? Current Anthropology 25:184.

Movahedi, Siamak
1978 The drug addict and addiction: Cultural stereotypes and clinical theories. Urban Life 7:45–66.

Murdock, George Peter
1949 Social Structure. New York: Macmillan.

Murphy, H. B. M.
1963 Le cannabisme, revue de la litterature psychiatrique recente. Bulletin on Narcotics. 15:15–23.

Musto, David F.
1987 The American Disease: Origins of Narcotic Control. New York: Oxford University Press.

Myerhoff, Barbara G.
1974 Peyote Hunt: The Religious Pilgrimage of the Huichol Indians. Ithaca, NY: Cornell University Press.
1978 Peyote and the mystic vision. In Kathleen Berrin, ed., Art of the Huichol Indians. pp. 56–81. New York: Harry N. Abrams.

Nail, Richard, Eric Gunderson, and Douglas Kolb
1974 Motives for drug use among light and heavy users. Journal of Nervous and Mental Disease 159:131–136.

Naroll, Frada, Raoul Naroll and Forrest H. Howard
1961 Position of women in childbirth: A study in data quality control. American Journal of Obstetrics and Gynecology 82:943–954.

Naroll, Raoul
1961 Two solutions to Galton's problem. Philosophy of Science 28:15–39.
1964 A fifth solution to Galton's problem. American Anthropologist 66:863–67.

Naroll, Raoul and R. G. D'Andrade
1963 Two further solutions to Galton's problem. American Anthropologist 65:1053–67.

Nash, George
1964 Bowery bars. Bowery Project, Bureau of Applied Social Research, Columbia University. Unpublished Project Memorandum, pp. 20–21.

National Clearinghouse for Smoking and Health
  1969 Use of Tobacco. Washington, DC: U.S. Department of Health, Education, and Welfare.
Nelson, Hart M. and James F. Rooney
  1982 Fire and brimstone, lager and pot: Religious involvement and substance use. Sociological Analysis 43:247–256.
Netting, Robert Mac
  1962 A West African beer complex. Current Anthropology 6:281–293.
  1964 Beer as a locus of value among the West African Kofyar. American Anthropologist 66:375–384.
Ngokweay, Ndolamb
  1987 Varieties of palm wine among the Lele of the Kasai. In Constructive Drinking: Perspectives on Drink from Anthropology. Mary Douglas, ed., pp. 113–121. Cambridge: Cambridge University Press.
Nimuendaju, C.
  1963 Tribes of the lower and middle Xingu River. In Handbook of South American Indians. Vol. 3. The Tropical Forest Tribes. J. H. Steward, ed., pp. 213–243. New York: Cooper Square Publishers.
Mangin, W.
  1957 Drinking among Andean Indians. Quarterly Journal of Studies on Alcohol 18:55–66.
O'Donnell, J. A., H. L. Voss, R. R. Clayton, G. T. Slatin, and R. G. W. Room.
  1976 Young Men and Drugs—A Nationwide Survey. Rockville, MD: National Institute on Drug Abuse.
O'Donnell, John A.
  1969 Narcotic Addicts in Kentucky. U.S. Public Health Service Publication No. 1881. Chevy Chase, MD: National Institute of Mental Health.
Obayemi, Ade M. U.
  1976 Alcohol usage in an African society. In Cross-cultural Approach to the Study of Alcohol: An Interdisciplinary Perspective. Michael W. Everett, Jack O. Waddell, and Dwight B. Heath, eds., pp. 198–208. The Hague: Mouton.
Oldenberg, Ray
  1989 The Great Good Place. New York: Paragon House.
Opler, Morris E.
  1938 The use of peyote by the Carrizo and Lipan Apache tribes. American Anthropologist 40:271–285.
Otterbein, Keith F.
  1972 Comparative Cultural Analysis. An Introduction to Anthropology. New York: Holt, Rinehart and Winston.
Ottinger, Cecilia A.
  1984 1984–85 Fact Book on Higher Education. New York: American Council on Education/Macmillan Publishing Company.

Pandian, Jacob
1991 Culture, Religion, and the Sacred Self: A Critical Introduction to the Anthropological Study of Religion. Englewood Cliffs, NJ: Prentice-Hall.
Park, R. E. and E. W. Burgess
1925 The City. Chicago: University of Chicago Press.
Parson, Elsie Clews
1939 Pueblo Indian Religion. Chicago: University of Chicago Press.
Parsons, Talcott
1949 The Structure of Social Action: New York: The Free Press.
1951 The Social System. New York: The Free Press
Partridge, William L.
1977 Transformation and redundancy in ritual: A case from Columbia. In Drugs, Rituals and Altered States of Consciousness. Brian M. DuToit, ed., pp. 59–73. Rotterdam: A.A. Balkema.
1973 The Hippie Ghetto: The Natural History of a Subculture. New York: Holt, Rinehart and Winston. Reprint, Prospect Heights, IL: Waveland Press, 1985.
Peterson, Jack W. and Milton A. Maxwell
1958 The skid row "Wino": Social Problems 5:308–316.
Pinson, Ann
1985 The institution of friendship and drinking patterns in Iceland. Anthropological Quarterly 58:75–82.
Polanyi, Karl
1944 The Great Transformation. New York: Holt, Rinehart.
1947 Our obsolete market mentality. Commentary 3:109–117.
Polanyi, Karl, C. M. Arensberg, and H. W. Pearson (eds.)
1957 Trade and Market in Early Empires. Glencoe: The Free Press.
Pope, H.
1969 Tabernanthe iboga: An African narcotic plant of social importance. Economic Botany 23:174–184.
1981 Drug use and life-style among college undergraduates. Archives of General Psychiatry, 38:588.
Pospisil, Leonard
1968 Law and order. In Introduction to Cultural Anthropology. James A. Clifton, ed., pp. 201–222. New York: Houghton Mifflin.
Preble, E. and J. Casey
1969 Taking care of business: The heroin user's life on the streets. International Journal of the Addictions 4:1–24. Quotations in chapter 8 are reprinted by permission of Marcel Dekker, Inc.
Proctor, Charles H. and Charles P. Loomis
1951 Analysis of Sociometric Data. In Research Methods in Social Relations, Part II: Selected Techniques. Marie Johoda, Morton Deutsch, and Stuart W. Cook, eds., pp. 562–585. New York: Dryden Press.

Pryor, Frederic L.
   1976 The diffusion possibility method: A more general and simpler solution to Galton's Problem. American Ethnologist 3:731–749.
Quinney, Richard
   1974 Class, State and Crime: On the Theory and Practice of Criminal Justice. New York: McKay.
Ray, Oakley
   1972 Drugs, Society, and Human Behavior. St. Louis: The C.V. Mosby Company.
   1983 Drugs, Society, and Human Behavior, 2nd ed. St. Louis: The C.V. Mosby Company.
Redfield, Robert
   1943 Rural sociology and the folk society. Rural Sociology 8:68–71.
Reid, Sue Titus
   1988 Crime and Criminology. New York: Holt, Rinehart and Winston.
Richards, Cara E.
   1963 City taverns. Human Organization 22:260–268.
Riesman, David, Robert J. Potter, and Jeanne Watson
   1960 The vanishing host. Human Organization 19:17–27.
Roach, Jack L.
   1967 A theory of lower-class behavior. In Sociological Theory: Inquiries and Paradigms. Llewellyn Gross, ed., pp. 294–314. New York: Harper & Row.
Roach, Jack L. and Orville R. Gursslin
   1967 An evaluation of the concept "Culture of Poverty." Social Forces 45:383–392.
Roberts, John M., Malcolm J. Arth, and Robert R. Bush
   1959 Games in culture. American Anthropologist 61:597–605.
Rodriguez, Argos
   1965 Possibilities of crop substitution for the coca leaf of Bolivia. Bulletin on Narcotics 17:13–20.
Roebuck, Julian B. and Wolfgang Frese
   1976 The after-hours club: An illegal social organization and its client system. Urban Life 5:131–164.
Rogers, Everett M.
   1962 Diffusion of Innovation. New York: The Free Press of Glencoe.
Rogers, Spencer L.
   1982 The Shaman. Springfield, Illinois: Charles C. Thomas.
Rollwagen, Jack
   1988 New directions in urban anthropology: Building an ethnography and an ethnology of the world system. In Urban Life: Readings in Urban Anthropology, 2nd ed. George Gmelch and Walter P. Zenner, eds., pp. 149–160. Prospect Heights, IL: Waveland Press.
Room, Robin
   1984 Alcohol and ethnography: A case of problem deflation? Current Anthropology 25:169–191.

Rooney, James F.
1961 Group processes among skid row winos: A reevaluation of the undersocialization hypothesis. Quarterly Journal of Studies on Alcohol 22:444–460.

Rosenhan, David L.
1973 On being sane in insane places. Science 179:250–258.

Rothstein, William G.
1972 American Physicians in the Nineteenth Century: From Sects to Science. Baltimore: Johns Hopkins University Press.

Roueché, Berton
1963 Alcohol in human culture. In Alcohol and Civilization. Salvatore P. Lucia, ed., pp.167–182. New York: McGraw-Hill.

Rubin, Vera and Lambros Comitas
1975 Ganja in Jamaica. The Hague: Mouton.

Rubington, Earl
1968 The bottle gang. Quarterly Journal of Studies on Alcohol 29:943–955.

Sandmeyer, Elmer Clarence
1973 The Anti-Chinese Movement in California. Urbana: University of Illinois Press.

Schafer, James M. (ed.)
1974 Studies in Cultural Diffusion: Galton's Problem. New Haven: HRAF Press.
1976 Theory in alcohol studies. In Cross-Cultural Approaches to the Study of Alcohol: An Interdisciplinary Perspective. M. Everett, J. Waddell, and D. Heath, eds., pp. 341–52. The Hague: Mouton.

Schlegel, Alice
1972 Male Dominance and Female Autonomy: Domestic Authority in Matrilineal Societies. New Haven: HRAF Press.

Schopen, Armin
1978 Das Qat: Geschichte and Gebrauch des Genusmittels Catha edulis Forsk. in der Arabischen Republik Jemen. Wiesbaden: Franz Steiner.

Schultes, Richard E.
1938 The appeal of peyote (Lophophora williamsii) as a medicine. American Anthropologist 40:698–715.
1967 The botanical origins of South American snuff. In Ethnopharmacologic search for psychoactive drugs. Daniel H. Efron, ed., pp. 291–306. Washington, DC: U.S. Public Health Service Publication no. 1645.
1969 Hallucinogens of plant origin. Science 163:245–254.
1972 An overview of Hallucinogens in the Western Hemisphere. In Flesh of the Gods. Peter T. Furst, ed., pp. 3–54. New York: Praeger Publishers. Reprint, Prospect Heights, IL: Waveland Press, 1990.

Schultes, Richard E. and Albert Hofmann
1979 Plants of the Gods. New York: McGraw-Hill.

Schultes, Richard E. and Bo Holmstedt
  1968 The vegetal ingredients of the myristacaceous snuffs of the northwest Amazon. Rhodora 70:113–160.
Schwartz, Michael and George Henderson
  1964 The culture of unemployment: Some notes on Negro children. In Blue Collar World. Arthur B. Shostak and William Gombert, eds., pp. 459–469. Englewood Cliffs, NJ: Prentice-Hall.
Scott, James M.
  1969 The White Poppy: A History of Opium. New York: Funk and Wagnalls.
Siegel, Ronald
  1989 Intoxication: Life in the Pursuit of Artificial Paradise. New York: E. P. Dutton.
Simmel, Georg
  1969 The metropolis and mental life. In Classic Essays on the Culture of Cities. R. Sennet, ed., pp. 47–60. New York: Appleton-Century-Crofts. (Orig. 1905.)
Simpson, George E.
  1956 Jamaican revivalist cults. Social and Economic Studies. 5:322–442.
Siu, Paul C. P.
  1952 The sojourner. American Journal of Sociology 58:34–44.
Smelser, Neil J.
  1962 A Theory of Collective Behavior. New York: Free Press.
Smith, M. G.
  1963 A structural approach to comparative politics. Paper delivered at the 1963 Annual Meeting of the American Political Science Association, New York City. September.
Smith, M. G., R. Augier, and R. Nettleford
  1960 The Ras Tafari Movement in Kingston, Jamaica. Kingston: Institute of Social and Economic Research, Mona, Jamaica.
Spencer, B. and F. J. Gillen
  1968 The Native Tribes of Central Australia. New York: Dover. (Orig. 1899.)
Spradley, James P.
  1970 You Owe Yourself a Drunk: An Ethnography of Urban Nomads. Boston: Little, Brown and Company.
  1974 Beating the drunk charge. In Conformity and Conflict. James P. Spradley and David W. McCurdy, eds., pp. 377–384. Boston: Little, Brown and Company.
Spradley, James P. and Brenda J. Mann
  1975 The Cocktail Waitress: Woman's Work in a Man's World. New York: John Wiley & Sons.
Spradley, James P. and David W. McCurdy
  1975 Anthropology: The Cultural Perspective. New York: John Wiley (1980). Reprint, Prospect Heights, IL: Waveland Press, 1989.
  1989 Anthropology: The Cultural Perspective, 2nd ed. Prospect Heights, IL: Waveland Press.

Stark, Rodney
  1972 The economics of piety: Religious commitment and social class. In Issues in Social Inequity. Gerald W. Thiebar and Saul D. Feldman, eds., pp. 483–503. Boston: Little, Brown.
  1987 Deviant places: A theory of the ecology of crime. Criminology 25:893–909.
Steinmetz, E. F.
  1960 Kava Kava (Piper methysticum): Famous Drug Plant of the South Sea Islands. San Francisco: Level Press.
Steward, Julian H.
  1955 Theory of Cultural Change: The Methodology of Multi-lineal Evolution. Urbana: University of Illinois Press.
Stewart, Omar C.
  1956 Peyote and Colorado's Inquisition Law. Colorado Quarterly 5:79–80.
Storer, Norman W.
  1966 The Social System of Science. New York: Holt, Rinehart and Winston.
Sue, S., N. Zane, and J. Ito
  1979 Alcohol drinking patterns among Asian and Caucasian Americans. Journal of Cross-Cultural Psychology 10:41–56.
Sumner, William Graham
  1906 Folkways. Reprinted in 1960. New York: New American Library.
Suwanwela, Charas, Vichai Poshyachinda, Prida Tasanapradit, and Ayut Dharmkrong-At
  1980 Opium use among the hill tribes of Thailand. Journal of Drug Issues 10:215–220.
Syme, Leonard and Lisa F. Berkman
  1976 Social class, susceptibility, and sickness. The American Journal of Epidemiology. 104:1–8.
Szwed, John F.
  1966 Gossip, drinking, and social control: Consensus and communication in a Newfoundland parish. Ethnology 5:434–441.
Tapp, Nicholas
  1986 The Hmong of Thailand: Opium People of the Golden Triangle. Cambridge, MA: Anti-Slavery Society.
Tarde, Gabriel
  1903 The Laws of Imitation. Trans. by Elsie Clews Parsons. New York: Holt, Rinehart and Winston.
Taswell, Ruth
  1985 Marihuana/Hashish. Cultural Survival Quarterly 9: 7–9.
Taylor, Rex
  1978 Marilyn's friends and Rita's customers: A study of party selling as play and work. Sociological Review 13:293–296.
Teske, Raymond H. C. Jr. and Bardin H. Nelson
  1974 Acculturation and assimilation: A clarification. American Ethnologist 1:351–367.

Thrasher, Frederick M.
1937 The Gang. Chicago: University of Chicago Press.
Timasheff, Nicholas Sergeyevitch
1976 An Introduction to the Sociology of Law. Westport, CT: Greenwood Press.
Turner, James W.
1986 "The water of life": Kava ritual and the logic of sacrifice. Ethnology 25:203–214.
Turner, Victor W.
1969 The Ritual Process: Structure and Anti-Structure. Chicago: Aldine.
Tylor, Edward B.
1871 Primitive Culture. London: J. Murray.
U.S. Surgeon-General
1982 The Health Consequences of Smoking—Cancer. Washington: U.S. Department of Health and Human Services.
Ukers, William
1935 All About Coffee. New York: The Tea and Coffee Trade Journal
United Nations
1950 Report on the Commission of Enquiry on the Coca Leaf. Economic and Social Council Special Supplement 1.
Valentine, Charles
1968 Culture and Poverty: Critique and Counter-Proposals. Chicago: University of Chicago Press.
van Gennep, Arnold
1961 The Rite of Passage. Chicago: University of Chicago Press.
Waddell, Jack O.
1975 For individual power and social credit: The use of alcohol among Tucson Papagos. Human Organization 34:9–15.
Wagner, Roy
1975 The Invention of Culture. Englewood Cliffs, New Jersey: Prentice-Hall.
Wallace, Anthony F. C.
1966 Religion: An Anthropological View. New York: Random House.
Walter, Benjamin
1967 The sociology of knowledge and the problem of objectivity. In Sociological Theory: Inquiries and Paradigms. Llewellyn Gross, ed., pp. 335–357. New York: Harper & Row.
Wasson, R. G.
1979 Fly agaric and man. In Ethnopharmocologic Search for Psychoactive Drugs. D. H. Efron, ed., pp. 405–414. New York: Raven Press.
Wasson, R. G., and V. P. Wasson
1957 Russia, Mushrooms and History, 2 vols. New York: Pantheon.
Weakland, John H.
1969 Hippies: What the scene means. In Society and Drugs. Richard H. Blum and Associates, eds., pp. 343–372. San Francisco: Jossey-Bass.

Weber, Max
  1958 The Protestant Ethic and the Spirit of Capitalism. Trans. by Talcott Parsons. New York: Free Press. (Orig. 1904–1905.)
  1960 Bureaucracy. In Images of Man: The Classic Tradition in Sociological Thinking. C. Wright Mills, ed., pp. 149–191. New York: G. Braziller.
  1963 The Sociology of Religion. Trans. by Ephraim Fishoff. Boston: Beacon Press. (Orig. 1922.)
Weigand, Phil C.
  1978 Contemporary social and economic structure. In Art of the Huichol Indians. Kathleen Berrin, ed., pp. 101–116. New York: Harry N. Abrams.
Weil, Andrew
  1973 The Natural Mind: Another Way of Looking at Drugs and the Higher Consciousness. Boston: Houghton-Mifflin.
Weir, Shelagh
  1985 Qat in Yemen: Consumption and Social Change. London: British Museums Publications.
Weppner, Robert S. (ed.)
  1977 Street Ethnography: Selected Studies of Crime and Drug Use in Natural Settings. Beverly Hills: Sage Publications.
Westermeyer, Joseph
  1974 Opium dens: A social resource for addicts in Laos. Archives of General Psychiatry. 31:237–240.
  1982 Poppies, Pipes, and People: Opium and its Use in Laos. Berkeley: University of California Press.
White, Helene Raskin, Angela Aidala, and Benjamin Zablocki
  1988 A longitudinal investigation of drug use and work patterns among middle-class, white adults. The Journal of Applied Behavioral Science 24:455–469.
White, Leslie A.
  1949 Ethnological theory. In Philosophy for the Future: The Quest of Modern Materialism. R. W. Sellers, V. J. McGill, and M. Faber, eds., pp. 357–384. New York: Macmillian.
Whiting, John W. M., Irvin L. Child, William W. Lambert
  1966 Field Guide for a Study of Socialization. New York: John Wiley and Sons.
Whyte, Martin K.
  1978 Cross-cultural studies of women and male bias problem. Behavior Science Research 13:65–80.
Whyte, William Foote
  1943 Street Corner Society: The Social Structure of an Italian Slum. Chicago: University of Chicago Press.
Williams, Eric
  1966 Capitalism and Slavery. New York: Capricorn.
Wilson, Bryan
  1973 Magic and the Millennium. New York: Harper and Row.

Wissler, Clark
    1923 Man and Culture. New York: Thomas Y. Crowell.
Witt, Shirley Hill
    1965 Nationalistic trends among American Indians. Midcontinent
          American Studies Journal 6:51–74.
Wolcott, Harry F.
    1974 The African Beer Gardens of Bulawayo. New Brunswick, NJ:
          Rutgers Center of Alcohol Studies.
Wolf, Eric R.
    1982 Europe and the People Without History. Berkeley: University of
          California Press.
Wong, Bernard P.
    1988 Patronage, Brokerage, Entrepreneurship, and the Chinese
          Community of New York: New York: AMS Press.
Yinger, Milton J.
    1960 Contraculture and subculture. American Sociological Review
          25:625–635.
Young, Michael and Peter Willmott
    1957 Family and Kinship in East London. London: Routledge and
          Kegan Paul.

Name Index

Subject Index

471